French Feminists on Religion

French Feminists on Religion: A Reader offers the first representative selection of important writings by French feminist thinkers on the topic of religion, including the most influential and provocative texts on the subject from Luce Irigaray, Julia Kristeva, Hélène Cixous, Monique Wittig and Catherine Clément. Each thinker is introduced by a bibliographical preface, while individual essays are preceded by an editorial commentary explaining the context and significance of each piece for the study of religion.

The collected texts cover a broad range of religious practices and discourses focusing primarily on Jewish and Christian concerns, but including elements of ancient goddess traditions, witchcraft, Hinduism and Buddhism. Critically examined themes include:

- Jewish and Christian notions of sin, defilement, purity and redemption;
- the relationship between subjectivity and divinity, as conceived in the feminine;
- the feminist re-imagining of the Virgin Mary, and of Catholic theologies of love;
- the repression of the maternal in Judeo-Christian culture.

Brought together for the first time in *French Feminists on Religion: A Reader*, these essays demonstrate the central importance of French feminism for the study of religion, and at the same time make evident the significance of religious themes, figures and concepts to the work of French feminists.

Morny Joy is Professor of Religious Studies at the University of Calgary. She has edited numerous collections on women and religion and is currently completing a book on Luce Irigaray, women and religion. **Kathleen O'Grady** is the Bank of Montreal Visiting Scholar at the Institute of Women's Studies, University of Ottawa. She has authored several articles on feminist philosophy and religious studies and is co-editor of *Bodies, Lives, Voices: Gender in Theology*. **Judith L. Poxon** is Lecturer in the Department of Humanities and Religious Studies at California State University, Sacramento, and moderates the electronic discussion list french-feminism@lists.village.virginia.edu on French feminist thought.

French Feminists

on Religion

A Reader

Edited by

Morny Joy, Kathleen O'Grady
and Judith L. Poxon
with a foreword
by Catherine Clément

London and New York

First published 2002
by Routledge
11 New Fetter Lane, London EC4P 4EE

Simultaneously published in the USA and Canada
by Routledge
29 West 35th Street, New York, NY 10001

Routledge is an imprint of the Taylor & Francis Group

Typeset in Perpetua and Bell Gothic by Graphicraft Limited, Hong Kong
Printed and bound in Great Britain by Biddles Ltd, Guildford and King's Lynn

British Library Cataloguing in Publication Data
A catalogue record for this book is available from the British Library

Library of Congress Cataloging in Publication Data
French feminists on religion : a reader / edited by Morny Joy, Kathleen O'Grady, and
    Judith L. Poxon ; with a foreword by Catherine Clément.
        p. cm.
    Includes bibliographical references.
    1. Feminism—Religious aspects.   2. Feminism—France.   I. Joy, Morny.
II. O'Grady, Kathleen, 1967–   III. Poxon, Judith L., 1952–

BL458.F74 2001
200'.82—dc21   2001041995

ISBN 0–415–21537–4 (hbk)
ISBN 0–415–21538–2 (pbk)

It seems we are unable to eliminate or suppress the phenomenon of religion. It reemerges in different forms, some of them perverse: sectarianism, theoretical or political dogmatism, religiosity . . . Therefore, it is crucial that we rethink religion, and especially religious structures, categories, initiations, rules and utopias, all of which have been masculine for centuries.

Luce Irigaray, *Sexes and Genealogies*

It is because I am separate, forsaken, alone vis-à-vis the other that I can psychologically cross the divide that is the condition of my existence and achieve not only ecstasy in completion (complétude: reunion with the father, himself a symbolic substitute for the mother) but also eternal life (resurrection) in the imagination.

Julia Kristeva, *In the Beginning*

When I have finished writing, when I am a hundred and ten, all I will have done will have been to attempt a portrait of God. Of the God. Of what escapes us and makes us wonder. Of what we do not know but feel. Of what makes us live. I mean our own divinity, awkward, twisted, throbbing, our own mystery . . .

Hélène Cixous, *Coming to Writing*

There was a time when you were not a slave, remember that. You walked alone, full of laughter, you bathed bare-bellied. You say you have lost all recollection of it, remember . . . You say there are no words to describe this time, you say it does not exist. But remember. Make an effort to remember. Or, failing that, invent.

Monique Wittig, *Les Guérillères*

I will tell you what the sacred is for me. The memory of my family lineage, the head of my children (on which I swear an oath), relationships of love and friendship, homage to the dead, the Jewish lamp in front of the photo of my mother taken in the last year of her life, the ancestral rituals. Am I a Confucian? No. I am definitely Jewish. The rabbi who buried my mother said that for the Jews the only belief in an 'after-life' has to do with the survival of Israel from generation to generation: the hereafter is nothing else than memory. Here is my sacred; it is, by definition, unwavering in its commitment.

Catherine Clément, *Le Féminin et le sacré*

Contents

Foreword
by Catherine Clément
Translation by Sharon Hackett and
Morny Joy

A T FIRST GLANCE, it might seem that there is nothing to indicate that French feminists are favourably disposed towards religions. French, Belgian or Bulgarian, born before or during the Second World War, we were all engaged in the reconstruction of Europe after its devastation. We were not directly involved in this task, but it was the background of our adolescence and formative for our adulthood in the 1960s. We were serious students, busy finding our place in the intellectual world during a period of growth where there was no unemployment. When May 1968 arrived, our lives were already formed. It is doubtless that this formation, clearly more precocious then than today, was well planned, but difficult, painful and flawed. This gave rise to our feminist revolt. Nothing religious there? Indeed.

The constitution of family life cannot exempt itself from the religious in France, where the majority is Catholic. The Jewish religion as well is founded first and foremost on the family. Religious taboos are a heavy weight to carry, and it was the energy of feminism that first began to lift this burden of tradition in our countries. To break this hold, we sought other paths. Whether it is called writing, psychoanalysis, fiction, philosophy, semiotics or theatre – these were the escape routes from the domain of the family. These paths that we forged were all connected with the sacred. This term 'sacred' does not refer to religions, but their reverse. *Le sacré*. Sorceresses, mystics, writers or psychoanalysts all had direct access to the sacred. Off the beaten path, far from the masculine hierarchy of clergy – be they priests, rabbis, psychoanalytic pontiffs or popes – the field was open. It's only logical. Each one made of it what she would in her own way.

Once we were connected to the sacred, however, we were also faced with religions. Of course, some feminists reject religions. Aside from a few rare

African cases where women are priestesses, all religions are meant to keep women in control. In the field of religion, the feminine cannot rise up except by escaping, like steam that has been compressed for too long.

Having travelled to distant places and having lived in India and Africa, I have been amazed to see countless women break free of the confinement of religion and escape, by trance, dance, ecstasy and rapture. Men sometimes join them, when they can no longer suffer from repressed drives, similar to ours. And what is the result of this? An atheism that is easy to understand. This does not involve an activist conflict with the diverse religions, but a free and unimpeded way to experience oneself that can be called, if you will, sacred, divine, writing, source or impetus. The masculine clergy doesn't like this, and they are right to be concerned. It is their power that is at stake.

In France, women's participation in political life does not exceed 10 per cent – it is a backward country in this respect. We fought a hard battle for political equality between men and women. It has only recently been won. Its application to the real world is yet to be demonstrated. Yet the struggle that feminists face with male clergy has yet to be accomplished, and this is not unique to France. In India, in all Muslim countries, in Israel and the diaspora, in the United States of America, in all of Latin America and in Japan, religions are still a site of struggle for many women. In Africa, the vast number of animist religions operate in the same way. Must we become involved with this situation? Indeed yes, and with the utmost urgency.

There are many of us who are very fortunate: those of us whose sexual organs are not excised, who are free to choose our partners, who are not traded for a dowry and on whom no-one imposes a co-wife. As always, it is economic independence that marks the beginnings of liberty, for example in Bangladesh with the Grameen Bank, and in West Africa with its lending circles. After all, it is because we were engaged in the working world that we became feminists.

On further reflection, the confrontation of women with the religions has only just begun.

Preface

SELECTING THE FINAL MATERIAL for inclusion in this volume was exceedingly difficult, since it required leaving valuable texts by the wayside.

Our first painful editorial decision involved selecting who was to be included in our list of French feminist thinkers. Since this book is a reflection (albeit a critical one) of the so-called 'French feminist movement' and its impact on the fields of Theology and Religious Studies, we knew an inclusion of the 'big three' – Kristeva, Irigaray and Cixous – was without doubt. We were able to add Catherine Clément and Monique Wittig to this list when a cursory glance at the secondary source material from these disciplines revealed that their work has also carried influence. There remain many important thinkers whose writings we could not include in this volume – Nicole Brossard, Chantal Chawaf, Jovette Marchessault, Christine Delphy, to name just a few – since space did not permit us this luxury.

It was evident from the outset that there was more than enough material from these five thinkers alone to have comprised several books under the rubrics 'French Feminisms' and 'Religion'. In order to narrow our selections further, we chose to include only one or two essays from each of their major publications. We also included only those writings that speak specifically and intentionally about religious themes. We were careful to include essays from each period of their work and writings that reflect on a variety of religious traditions. We also chose to present many texts that have not been anthologised elsewhere. It is our hope that the final selections are representative of the complete body of work for each of the French feminists.

Further editorial encroachments made our task a difficult one. Restrictions from word count limits and copyright laws did not always allow us to include everything we wished. Some important texts originally written in French, and sometimes Bulgarian or Italian, were not included due to issues of translation. Our selections are comprised of previously translated material only.

One of the drawbacks of writing about living authors is that it is difficult to keep up with them. As we go to print there are already new books of relevance that have just been or are in the process of being published or translated and could not be incorporated in this book. Kristeva and Clément have co-authored a book specifically on the topic of the divine (*Le Féminin et le sacré*, soon to be translated); Clément has authored a novel that details the importance of the world's religions, *Theo's Odyssey*, as well as *Jésus au Bûcher*; and Kristeva, Wittig and Cixous are in the process of releasing new books; in addition, new translations of older texts are appearing rapidly. While this means that a reader of this sort can never be exhaustive, it also bodes well for the continued health of French feminist writing and its impact on the fields of Theology and Religious Studies.

Organisation of the reader

This text has been organised into five parts with each comprised of the writings of a specific French feminist. The order of inclusion is based on their influence on Religious Studies. For this reason, Irigaray and Kristeva appear first, followed by Clément, Cixous and Wittig. Each part contains a brief introductory essay outlining the major religious or theological themes of the specific French feminist. Each chapter is further introduced with a few paragraphs providing publication details, context, and comments on the relevance of the passage for the field of Religious Studies.

It was generally not possible to include the full text of the selected essays. Abridgements of the original are indicated on the Contents page; in the body of the essay, the marking '[. . .]' designates that text has been omitted.

Notes from the original writings have been maintained and placed at the end of each chapter, though the numbers differ from the original since the excerpts typically appear in abridged form (with consecutively numbered notes). Our own (few) comments on the primary texts are also contained in these notes and marked '[eds]'. Square brackets in the body of the essays indicate translators' comments contained in the original, except where '[sic]' indicates an error in the original.

Acknowledgements

THE COLLABORATIVE EFFORTS OF many people not only made this book possible, but also made it a pleasure to undertake.

We would like to thank our Research Assistants – Carole Noël, Sharon Hackett, John Abraham, Lynn Nugent and Sheila Ward – for their hard work and unfailing dedication in typescript preparation, translation and bibliographic research.

Colleagues, staff and students have contributed in many important ways to this work, from providing engaging discourse on French feminism and related philosophical topics to proofing the typescript and covering our course work when necessary. Diane Jonte-Pace, Janet Martin Soskice, Anne Moore, Philo Hove and Ann White all deserve our gratitude. Ellen Armour, Amy Hollywood, Susan St. Ville and Susan Simonaitis also merit a warm thanks for their encouragement during the earliest stages of this project.

Family and friends always hear more than they need to about any book in progress and we have had many attentive and considerate listeners.

Morny would like to thank John King for his constant encouragement and advice, as well as the Department of Religious Studies, University of Calgary, for providing a very supportive environment for her work.

Kathleen would like to thank Lee Tunstall, Mebs Rehemtulla, Cathy Brehaut, Viveka von Rosen, Carolyn Saunders, Meena Nallainathan, Joe Artinger, Rubina Ramji, Harold Remus and Amardeep Johar for contributing to this project through home-cooked meals and generous encouragement when it was most needed. She is further indebted to her family, Mark Logan, Marlene O'Grady, Ron O'Grady, Christine O'Grady and Cindy Livesey for their gracious love and devotion.

Judith would like to thank Nancy Jim Poxon, Terry Poxon, Rachel Poxon and Mark David Wood for their unfailing support of all of her endeavours, academic and otherwise.

We would like to thank several institutions for their monetary support of this project. The Institute of Women's Studies and Gender Studies, University of Toronto, provided office space for Kathleen during her stay in Toronto and were unstinting in their camaraderie and support of this project. The Social Sciences and Humanities Research Council of Canada assisted Morny in her research with a generous grant.

We would also like to thank several individuals at Routledge for their continued interest and assistance in this project. Anna Gerber, Roger Thorp, Hywel Evans, Elisa Tack and Clare Johnson offered editorial comments at every stage of typescript preparation. We would especially like to thank Adrian Driscoll for supporting this project from its earliest stages.

The 'French Feminists' themselves offered encouraging advice through regular correspondence and we would like to thank Catherine Clément and Luce Irigaray in particular for their willingness to participate in this project (and its forthcoming companion anthology).

Finally, we would like to offer the greatest of thanks to each other for engaging in what has been a truly feminist, collaborative project.

Permissions

by Kathleen O'Grady. Reprinted with permission of the author and Philosophy Documentation Center.

Excerpts from 'Approaching Abjection' and 'Semiotics of Biblical Abomination', from *Powers of Horror: An Essay on Abjection*, by Julia Kristeva. Copyright © 1982 by Columbia University Press. Reprinted with permission of the publisher.

'Credence-Credit' and excerpts from 'Credo', from *In the Beginning Was Love: Psychoanalysis and Faith*, by Julia Kristeva. Copyright © 1987 by Columbia University Press. Reprinted with permission of the publisher.

'Stabat Mater', from *Tales of Love*, by Julia Kristeva. Copyright © 1987 by Columbia University Press. Reprinted with permission of the publisher.

Excerpts from 'Psychoanalysis – A Counterdepressant' and 'Holbein's Dead Christ', from *Black Sun: Depression and Melancholia*, by Julia Kristeva. Copyright © 1989 by Columbia University Press. Reprinted with permission of the publisher.

'The Chosen People and the Choice of Foreignness', from *Strangers to Ourselves*, by Julia Kristeva. Copyright © 1991 by Columbia University Press. Reprinted with permission of the publisher. Reprinted in the UK and Europe by permission of Pearson Education Limited.

'Reading the Bible', from *New Maladies of the Soul*, by Julia Kristeva. Copyright © 1995 by Columbia University Press. Reprinted with permission of the publisher.

Excerpts from 'Sorceress and Hysteric' and 'The Child, the Savage', from *The Newly Born Woman*, by Hélène Cixous and Catherine Clément. English translation and Introduction copyright © 1986 by the Regents of the University of Minnesota. Used by permission of the publisher. Used in the British Commonwealth, Europe, Australia and the Middle East by permission of I. B. Tauris & Co. Ltd.

Excerpts from 'Introduction: Where am I?' and 'Jouissances: Between the Angel and the Placenta', from *Syncope: The Philosophy of Rapture*, by Catherine Clément. Copyright © 1994 by the Regents of the University of Minnesota. Used by permission of the publisher.

Excerpts from 'Sorties', from *The Newly Born Woman*, by Hélène Cixous and Catherine Clément. English translation and Introduction copyright © 1986 by the Regents of the University of Minnesota. Used by permission of the publisher. Used in the British Commonwealth, Europe, Australia and the Middle East by permission of I. B. Tauris & Co. Ltd.

Excerpts from 'Coming to Writing' and 'The Author in Truth', reprinted by permission of the publisher from *'Coming to Writing' and Other Essays* by Hélène Cixous, Cambridge, Mass.: Harvard University Press, Copyright © 1991 by the President and Fellows of Harvard College.

Excerpts from 'Grace and Innocence', from *Readings: The Poetics of Blanchot, Joyce, Kafka, Kleist, Lispector, and Tsvetayeva*, by Hélène Cixous. Edited, translated and introduced by Verena Andermatt Conley. *Theory and History of Literature*, Volume 77. Copyright © 1991 by the Regents of the University of Minnesota. Used by permission of the publisher.

Excerpts from 'The School of Dreams', from *Three Steps on the Ladder of Writing*, by Hélène Cixous. Copyright © 1993 Columbia University Press. Reprinted with permission of the publisher.

Excerpts from 'Writing Blind', from *Stigmata*, by Hélène Cixous. Copyright © Hélène Cixous. Reprinted by permission from the author and M. Diocaretz, Worldwide Rights & Publishing Consultants. A first version of this translation of 'Écrire aveugle' was published in: *Triquarterly*, 97 (1996): 7–20. The present excerpt was published in 'Writing Blind: Conversation with the Donkey', trans. Eric Prenowitz, *Stigmata: Escaping Texts*, Routledge, London, 1998.

Excerpts from *The Lesbian Body*, by Monique Wittig. Originally published in French as *Le Corps lesbien*. Copyright © 1973 by Les Éditions de Minuit. Reprinted by permission of Georges Borchardt, Inc.

Introduction: French Feminisms and Religion

The construction of 'French feminism'

I T HAS ALREADY BEEN twenty years since the publication of a special issue of the journal *Signs* dedicated to 'French Feminist Theory', featuring primary source works from Julia Kristeva, Hélène Cixous and Luce Irigaray (Gelpi *et al.* 1981). In the same year *Yale French Studies* devoted a volume to the impact of 'French feminism' on American critical theory, 'French Texts/American Contexts', with Kristeva, Cixous and Irigaray receiving the principal focus (Gaudin *et al.* 1981).[1] The year 1981 also marked the publication by *Feminist Studies* of a series of essays dedicated to uncovering the complexities of *écriture féminine*, a theoretical construct believed to be the defining characteristic of French feminist writing, featuring commentary on the writings of Irigaray, Cixous and Kristeva.[2]

While it might first appear that these texts crowned and canonised a fledgeling movement, bestowing on it a proper designation and ascribing to it a defined agenda and scope, 'French feminism' had long had popular currency in Anglo-academic circles. The previous year, Elaine Marks and Isabelle de Courtivron anthologised writings by 'the big three' – Cixous, Irigaray and Kristeva – among others, in a volume entitled *New French Feminisms* (Marks and de Courtivron 1980). Indeed, critics have often credited (or accused) the editors of this text with coining the label 'French feminism', but their introductory remarks make it clear that neither the term nor its accompanying suppositions was their invention; 'French feminism' was already a well-worn appellation in the proliferation of English-language papers on the topic in the years preceding their edited volume (Marks and de Courtivron 1980: 1).[3]

More than ten years later, Nancy Fraser and Sandra Lee Bartky published *Revaluing French Feminism* (1992), further solidifying the term and the notion that this 'movement', as it is so often described, was here to stay (Fraser and Bartky 1992). As the editors noted at the time, French feminism is 'a distinctive cultural object for English-speaking readers' and 'for many English-speaking readers today "French feminism" simply *is* Irigaray, Kristeva and Cixous' (1992: 1). Their text did little to change this focus. In slightly over a decade, the Anglo-academy had reduced the variegated social, political and theoretical strands of French feminisms to three thinkers; the 'holy trinity' was firmly in place.

What has been common among these edited book and journal collections from the beginning has been a reluctance – or, at best, a resigned and apologetic acceptance – by the editors to employ the term 'French feminism' itself. Similarly evident from a review of the hundreds of journal articles on this topic over the last two decades is that while the term 'French feminism' is widely used in Anglo-academic circles and appears to bear specific meaning for a large group of people who claim to be reading, writing or teaching 'French feminism', the term itself is rarely defined. As a construct, 'French feminism' seems to have sprung fully formed from an anonymous source and, despite protestations, qualifications, and a general hesitation and wringing of hands before each usage, the phrase seems to have stuck.

When pressed, Anglo-academics typically define French feminism in terms of its main thinkers (Cixous, Kristeva and Irigaray) rather than by reference to a core set of concepts. However, this does not answer the riddle of 'French feminism', since of these three theorists, two – Cixous and Kristeva – are hostile to the term 'feminism', with its links to American second-wave (liberal) feminist activism, and none of the three identifies as explicitly 'French' – Kristeva is Bulgarian, Irigaray is Belgian and Cixous is of Algerian origin.[4] Similarly, to promote *écriture féminine* – understood as a particularly valued feminine use of language – as the defining topos of the trio is also misleading, since Kristeva has never employed this term in her work and is dismissive of Cixous's theoretical work in this area; Irigaray and Cixous also have different, and some may argue, dissonant understandings of *écriture féminine*. Publicly, the three have never come together to promote their work collectively and have never quoted or referenced each other's work at any length.

What becomes clear is that a historical sketch of the term 'French feminism' amounts to little – there is no one source from which it originates, and so no one person to blame – and a semantic investigation of the term is even less satisfying, since it cannot be said that the key writers of this movement are 'feminists' or 'French' – thus certainly, together, not 'French feminists' – since they view themselves as distinct and even divergent thinkers. Critics have suggested from the outset that 'French feminism' does not demarcate a 'move-ment' from France that travelled to the Anglo-American scene, book by book across cold Atlantic waters, but rather is emblematic of the way in which particular French writers were taken up, rather selectively, and used within Anglo-feminist circles. While it might be overly coy to say it, they seem to suggest: 'There is no such thing as French feminism'.

Christine Delphy is one of the more vocal antagonists of the anglophone field of 'French feminism', labelling it an 'imperialist invention' by American academics (Delphy 1996, 1995: 192). Delphy's primary concern is the feminist movement as it actually exists – in all of its complexity and diversity, whether it be its social, political or theoretical strands – in contemporary France. For Delphy, the use of the term 'French feminism' to encompass the writings of only a handful of thinkers is grossly misleading since it suggests that they are representative – and deemed as such by French women – of the grassroots feminist movement in France (and in other Francophone regions). There is very little connection, Delphy notes, between feminism as it is known within France, and 'French feminism' as it is defined by those from outside the culture. '"French feminism" is not feminism in France,' she firmly states from her materialist perspective (Delphy 1995: 190). Her summation is damning: the invention of 'French feminism' comes from *without* and not *within* the culture it claims to represent.

In spite of Delphy's critique, however, the most recent writings on French feminism have strayed little from the 'holy trinity'. A new anthology edited by Kelly Oliver, *French Feminism Reader* (2000), includes writings by Michèle Le Dœuff, Christine Delphy and Colette Guillaumin, among others, in an attempt to demonstrate that 'feminism in France is as varied as it is any place else in the world'; however, writings by Cixous, Kristeva and Irigaray continue to dominate the book's content. Interestingly, Oliver justifies her selections by defining 'French feminists' as those figures 'that have been the most influential to feminist theory *in the English speaking world*'; thus, she presents her Reader as a 'representative sample of French feminism *in an Anglo-American context*' (Oliver 2000: vii, our emphasis). Critics such as Claire Moses and Bronwyn Winter have gone a step further in their work, with Moses referring to French feminism as a movement 'made-in-America', and Winter labelling French feminism a 'misnomer', an 'intellectual fiction' and a 'massive con' (Moses 1996: 26; Winter 1997: 213, 214, 221). As Delphy has argued and Oliver and others concede, French feminism is 'an Anglo-American strand of intellectual production within an Anglo-American context' (Delphy 1996: 384).[5]

With such strong arguments denouncing the artificial construction of 'French feminism' the obvious question arises: Why do academics continue to use this term? (And why do we use it ourselves in bold letters on the cover?) Surely not just to sell books, though, it is true, editors are fond of the catchy phrase and it has a certain street value in publishing houses. But there are also sound ideological reasons for maintaining the terminology, albeit with trepidation. 'French feminism' firmly displays its own internal coherence in philosophical terms. A more accurate phrase for this occurrence of philosophical consonance might be the less streamlined, even ungraceful appellation, 'the feminism of sexual difference'. This focus, which one can find consistently expressed in the works of Cixous, Kristeva and Irigaray – and one could add here, the abundant writings of Catherine Clément – did not emerge haphazardly from these particular writers, as critics would have it, nor is it the invention of American academics; rather, it is the product of a larger cultural strand of feminism in France that emerged during the events of May 1968.

'MLF' Inc.™, or the Mouvement de libération des femmes

According to Julia Kristeva, in her much-quoted essay 'Women's Time', the beginnings of the modern women's movement in France were characterised by the struggles of suffragists and existential feminists (among whose number, certainly, would be included Simone de Beauvoir) who travailed in the arena of egalitarian discourse typical of classical liberalism, with ambitions to achieve the legislative changes necessary for women to be defined as rational citizens entitled to an equal place in the social order.[6] This emphasis on the level of equality, law and social activism has been continued by a strong contingent of what some historians have called an 'egalitarian' strand of feminism, which includes those feminists aligned with traditional left-leaning political parties and unions. Of these, the most visible and coherently organised groups include feminists within the French Communist Party (PCF) and the Socialist Party (PS) who, over the last three decades, have largely been involved with including feminist priorities in the traditional platforms of class struggle, as well as establishing a focus on abortion rights, the availability of child-care and equal wages for female workers. This left-leaning and often markedly Marxist feminism asserts itself in a loosely organised materialist and explicitly anti-psychoanalytic agenda that finds expression in the journals *Questions féministes* (now defunct) and (the rejuvenated) *Nouvelles questions féministes*, and most notably today in the writings of Christine Delphy. Much of the important work accomplished by contemporary feminism in France has been because of this 'egalitarian feminism' that has fought its battles in the arena of politics and political action encased in the rhetoric of rights.

However, as noted historians of the modern French feminist movement have remarked, feminism in France consists of more than this single (activist) expression (see Claire Duchen 1986, 1987; Caryl L. Lloyd 1992; Nicole Ward Jouve 1990; Jane Jenson 1990). A second important group of 'French feminists' emerged as a result of the events in Paris in May 1968, when a wide-ranging series of protests – aligned with leftist politics and marked by participation from students, workers and professionals – called into question conventional strategies of working for change within the system. Methods of spontaneous, non-hierarchical, often disorderly political practice were employed, aimed at disrupting the very structures of the social order in which earlier feminists had fought to participate.

The events of May 1968 gave birth to a new feminist movement in France that was marked by a rejection of the liberal ideal of full participation by women in existing socio-economic structures and institutions and an assertion of the necessity of a kind of sexual(ised) politics that would allow for a radical transformation of those very structures and institutions. This new strand of feminism, which came to be known as Psych et Po (Psychanalyse et Politique) advocated an unveiling of the psychosexual dynamic central to women's oppression that the liberal rhetoric of egalitarian feminism was not able to encompass. As Nicole Ward Jouve has recognised, the group's name comes from their primary tenet that 'psychoanalysis [was] the single existing discourse that had grappled with the question of sexuality' (1990: 130). 'Psychoanalysis' was thus seen as the missing 'political' link of the feminist movement as this group brought the two terms together. Psych et Po sought to 'psychoanalyse' the 'political' and to make 'political' the 'psychoanalytic' distinction of the sexes.

Members of the group focused on articulating the sexual difference that was implicit in the very structuration of cultural productions and set out to highlight the previously silenced libidinal economy of the feminine. As Duchen has accurately summarised:

> The work of, for instance, Hélène Cixous, Luce Irigaray and Julia Kristeva reminds us that our entire cultural framework is predicated on the differentiation of gender, on the repression/suppression of the feminine. *Psych et Po*'s project has been specifically named the 'Revolution of the Symbolic' (so named by themselves), a revolution to bring about the existence of the feminine, while the three theorists named above have concentrated in their different ways on women's relation to language, theory and sexuality, and from these connections, have made tentative speculations about the feminine.
>
> (Duchen 1986: 85)

Psych et Po argued that women's experiences in all of their specific corporeality cannot be articulated in a language and within a cultural landscape that does not make a place for their differences but effaces them to masculine advantage. Members of the group were concerned with giving voice to an irreducible feminine identity and discourse, which would be, by virtue of its fluidity and polyvocality, constituted on its own terms and not in relation to masculine identity.

Social and egalitarian feminists had little time for the theoretical articulation of 'feminine difference' which was at the heart of the Psych et Po movement.

However, for a short while, both strands of French feminism, egalitarian feminists and the feminists of sexual difference (Psych et Po), along with other important branches of modern feminism – including lesbian separatism, represented by the writings of Monique Wittig – were loosely associated under the collective banner Mouvement de libération des femmes (MLF). But not long after May 1968, the divisions between various member groups became irreconcilable and they experienced widely public vocal rifts and schisms. The final blow to any possibility of collective organisation between the different factions came when members of Psych et Po, under the direction of Antoinette Fouque, registered the name, Mouvement de libération des femmes (MLF), its initials and its logo as if it were a commercial trademark, and thus prevented other women's groups from using it for their activist ends. This particularly troubled egalitarian feminist organisations since Psych et Po publicly declared itself 'antifeminist', in so far as they eschewed identity politics and any association with the (androcentric) rhetoric of liberal feminism. However, from the perspective of Psych et Po the registration of MLF for their organisation was successful since it established them in the public eye as the central and the representative force of the feminist movement in France.

Psych et Po capitalised further on their visible dominance (of all the strands of the French feminist movements) at this time by establishing a successful publishing house, Éditions des femmes, and subsequently opening a number of feminist bookshops in Paris to highlight writings aligned with their psychoanalytically informed theoretical focus on sexual difference. Éditions des femmes published writings by variously allied Psych et Po thinkers, including Cixous and Kristeva, and promoted their writings, along with other psychoanalytically informed feminists such as Luce Irigaray and Catherine Clément, through a growing consortium of Psych et Po magazines and journals.

It is thus that 'French feminism', as we now employ the term, came to Anglo-academic circles in the late 1970s and the 1980s, not as part of the reality of the broad-based and varied feminist movement in France, but as a specific and concentrated brand of theoretical feminism that was disseminated by a powerful collective that controlled publishing houses, magazines, journals and book-shops, as well as the trademarked Mouvement de libération des femmes (MLF). With the export of their ideas outside of the francophone world, and particularly to the United States, where the head of the Psych et Po movement, Antoinette Fouque, immigrated, one could say that Psych et Po trademarked not only the 'MLF' label, but the English equivalent – 'French feminism' – as well.

That the anglophone expression 'French feminism' does not represent the actual diversity of feminists in France goes without question; however, to attribute completely this monopoly of thought by title to American academics, as Delphy does, or only to the selective attentions of the anglophone academy, as

do other critics, is too vast a condemnation and does not adequately accommodate the troubled history of modern feminism in France.

It is not our intention to sweep over the problematics of the term 'French
feminism' with a historic footnote. But what becomes clear from this brief
sketch of the beginnings of the modern feminist movement in France is that
there is a cogent link between the thinkers of the 'holy trinity' after all, and a few
others, including Clément, that involves their flirtations with the Psych et Po
group in its heyday. Each of them was affiliated with the movement to varying
degrees, and regardless of the level of their individual investment in the group
itself, their writings were regularly promoted by loyal Pysch et Po strong
guards; while each thinker has since had distinct concerns with the group and its
leadership, they nevertheless continue to share a bedrock of theoretical object-
ives that have characterised the Psych et Po group from its inception. The
commonalities of concern that unite these thinkers do not necessarily make their
work *compatible*, as even a cursory reading of the texts in this reader will
demonstrate, but they are certainly of the same philosophical moment and spirit
and linked by a cluster of theoretical approaches and aims. In this sense, 'French
feminism' as it is called in the anglophone academy, denotes and represents
accurately an important and undeniable current of post-'68 feminism in France.

The central uniting feature of French feminist thought is a passionate
engagement with the psychoanalysis of Jacques Lacan. While all of the French
feminists are, to varying degrees, critical of the Lacanian project, they are
nevertheless indebted to him for his theories of subject formation and gender
construction, in particular his demonstration of the ways in which the unconscious
functions to radically de-centre subjectivity, thus destabilising the mastery of
consciousness and challenging the metaphysical presuppositions of the Cartesian
cogito and post-Cartesian philosophies of subjectivity. Equally vital are Lacan's
notions that the subject is socially constructed in language – that in the entrance
into language the subject is inscribed within the Oedipal, paternal social order
(governed by what Lacan calls the Law of the Father, and claiming the phallus
as its privileged signifier) – and that neither gender nor sexuality is biologically
given but rather conferred as one of the effects of the socio-linguistic construction of subjectivity. Thus, as Duchen notes, 'Lacan's model provides Psych
et Po with a conceptual framework from which they elaborate a theory of the
feminine. [But] unlike Lacan, they believe that the feminine can be defined and
brought into an existence that defies the Symbolic Order' (1986: 79).

Another figure whose influence on the development of French feminist theory
can hardly be exaggerated is deconstructionist literary critic and philosopher
Jacques Derrida. His method of reading texts 'against the grain', revealing
that unacknowledged meanings both supplement and call into question the
explicit signification of any text, influenced much French feminist writing.
Moreover, Derrida's project articulates several notions that carry special weight

for a feminism of sexual difference. First is his claim that the Western onto-theological tradition embodies a 'metaphysics of presence' that organises reality into hierarchically arranged binary oppositions (of which the pair man/woman is the paradigmatic example, with others including presence/absence, speech/writing, culture/nature, good/evil, etc.), in which one term is privileged, or presenced, at the expense of the other. Derrida further argues that a movement of what he calls *différance* – an endless play of differing and deferring that underwrites signification itself – functions to disrupt this 'logocentric' meta-physical order, and (more significantly for French feminism) that 'woman' is a privileged site of *différance*, and as such, of the possibility for the disruption of the totalising logic of logocentrism. Clearly this argument opens the way for the claims made by many of the French feminists that 'the feminine' lies outside of the Western logic of representation, whence it insists on the equivocality of all meaning, and indeed of all identity.[7]

In this anthology of primary texts, we present writings by four of the most notable thinkers to have participated, in varying degrees, with the feminist philosophical currents in and around the Psych et Po movement. Irigaray, Kristeva, Cixous and Clément have each contributed significantly to this psycho-analytically informed literature of 'sexual difference' as it has been produced in France, post-May '68. We have further added the passionate writings of Monique Wittig, lesbian separatist and vocal critic of the Psych et Po movement, to our compilation, since she steps beyond the masculine–feminine dichotomy so crucial to the other thinkers of sexual difference, and targets this bi-polarity *itself*, and the resulting heterosexism implicit in social and cultural structures, as the defining feature of women's oppression. Her work functions as counter-balance to the other four, since, while she vehemently rejects psychoanalytic discourse and Lacanian theory specifically, and the biologism implicit in several theories of sexual difference, she nevertheless responds to this discourse in an informed way and it provides a springboard from which she produces many of her writings; and unlike many of her materialist counterparts (of which she is also critical), Wittig believes that the arena of symbolic discourse is the central site of feminist struggle, and that there is a need for a theoretical framework to challenge and revolutionise this order. Thus, Wittig is more at home in this volume with her antagonists, than with her anti-theoretical material compatriots. Each of these five theorists represents in her own manner the vitality and creativity of 'sexual difference feminism' as it continues to emerge from France.

'Let the priests tremble, we're going to show them our sexts'

With their focus on the symbolic structurations of cultural productions, it was not long before the French feminists passed through literature, art and poetic representations of sexual difference, to come at long last to the hallowed halls of religion. While their secular counterparts continued with important social and legislative change, the 'French feminists' were able to provide a vocabulary and direction for a detailed and complex analysis of religious institutions, informed by psychoanalysis and deconstruction, in ways that French egalitarian feminism, with its emphasis on equality rhetoric, could not.

Within the sphere of religious or theological studies, French feminist thought offers an important critique of religion, understood primarily, though not exclusively, as the Judeo-Christian tradition. Informed by the problematics outlined above, religious engagement in the symbolic arena represents, to many French feminists, the supreme instance of the 'phallogocentrism' of Western metaphysics, with its privileging of the (masculine) God as the centre and source of all truth, the transcendent signified of which all thought is a more-or-less successful signifier.

French feminist writing, through varying strategies, strongly indicts the hegemonic power of Judeo-Christian monotheism, seeing in this tradition an authority equal to if not greater than that of the state to promulgate a model of subjectivity as subjection to the Law of the Father, and argues that a Trinitarian God conceived on the model of father–son–spirit is the necessary product of and foundation for the 'logic of the same' that orders metaphysical thinking. This critique draws on the claim that the fundamental discursive structuring of Western subjectivity operates on a paternal/patriarchal model that, as such, is incapable of representing the feminine as anything other than the negative counterpart of the masculine.

Since the 1980s, texts by Julia Kristeva have included critical reflection and revisioning of such Judeo-Christian concepts as love, sin, forgiveness and transubstantiation, as well as on the works of such theologians as Augustine, Thomas Aquinas, Duns Scotus and Bernard of Clairvaux, and on texts and artwork inspired by such religious figures as the Virgin Mary, St Anne, Ruth, Jesus, and St Paul. During the same period, Luce Irigaray has written extensively on the need for a feminine conception of divinity that would help to restore what she sees as the repressed genealogy of mothers and daughters, and has explored the potential significance of the figure of the angel for feminist theorisations of love. Hélène Cixous, Catherine Clément and Monique Wittig have offered detailed critical commentaries on the major religious traditions of Western culture, and have re-examined the relationship between women and divinity, particularly in the context of historical goddess mythologies.

Each thinker, to varying degrees, re-envisions religious structures in a process that is simultaneously *critical* (of that which has gone before) and *creative* (of what could be). This may mean a revolutionary reassessment of traditional religious figures and a thoughtful re-appraisal of standard philosophies of religion, or a more radical process of re-imaging and re-visioning religious discourse or, even, of inventing divinity anew.

It is no surprise, then, that with each passing year, French feminist thought has emerged as an increasingly significant interpretive tool in Anglo-American theological and religious studies.[8] It is important to note that by no means has the reception of French feminist writing on religion been understood uniformly. Scholars have varied in the ways in which they adopt French feminist writing on religion, using French feminist theory as a means to defend traditional religious views, to rewrite or reform standard theologies, to re-imagine the divine in radical new ways, or to reject religion outright. What *is* clear, however, is that French feminist thinkers themselves have undertaken the tasks both of *critiquing* traditional religious structures and discourses and *constructing* radical new modes of thinking about divinity and of the divine.

These important writings on religion by some of the most significant French feminist thinkers of the last few decades are collected together in this volume for the first time. The essays are organised into five main parts, by author, with an introduction that details the significance of the work of the respective French feminist thinker within the study of feminism and religious studies. Each essay (or chapter) is further introduced to highlight the significant issues and concerns of the text within the larger body of the writer's work. What we hope to make clear from this collection of primary texts is that the religious themes that dominate the work of the French feminists are not occasional and haphazard, incidental to their œuvre, but inform much of their creative and theoretical work, and at the same time, that their theoretical writings constitute critical commentaries on and radical revisionings of those same religious themes.

Cixous calls her writings, inscribed as they are by the feminine body, 'sexts', thus at once collapsing 'sex'(-ed) and 'text' in the same semantic container and charging the pages of a dusty tome with the sensual contours of the physical body. When this 'sexual/textual' writing, as Toril Moi calls it, focuses on the topic of religion, as it is in this volume, the 'sexed' 'text' further 'sects' itself from the ordinary throes of institutionalised religion, and offers up a challenge to its orthodox traditions with a body language that seduces with a fecund and fleshy semiotics. Included in this volume are the 'sexts' of Irigaray, Kristeva, Cixous, Clément and Wittig. And we can think of no better way to introduce the important and radical revisioning of religion found herein than with Cixous's prophetic pronouncement (or is it a dare?): 'Let the priests tremble, we're going to show them our sexts' (Cixous 1976).

Notes

1   This volume contains the oft-cited and reprinted essays by Gayatri Chakravorty Spivak (1981), 'French Feminism in an International Frame' and Alice Jardine (1981), 'Pre-Texts for the Transatlantic Feminist'.

2   DuPlessis, Rachel Blau *et al.* (eds) (1981) *Feminist Studies* 7, 2 (Summer).

3   As Moses has noted, *Signs* was first to publish English translations of Kristeva and Cixous as early as 1975–6, and the first English commentaries on the feminist movement in France in 1978, while *Sub-Stance*, *Diacritics* and *Yale French Studies* had occasional commentaries on these French writers in the same period (Moses 1996: 17).

4   They all write regularly in the French language; however, Kristeva occasionally writes in Bulgarian and Irigaray in Italian, while many of Cixous's published works appear as English translations only without publication of the French original.

5   Delphy overstates the American influence on the perpetuation of 'French feminism'. While it is true that Americans have widely engaged with the writings associated with French feminism, it is more accurate to depict the movement as originating in primarily 'Anglo-academic' circles, since Moi, one of Delphy's major targets, is Norwegian and was educated in the United Kingdom, and other early popularisers of the work of Irigaray, Cixous and Kristeva, such as Elizabeth Grosz, Margaret Whitford, Teresa Brennan, John Lechte, and many others, come from a wide variety of English-speaking countries, with a strong contingent from the United Kingdom and Australia.

6   Kristeva, Julia (1979), 'Le Temps des femmes', 34/44: Cahiers de recherche de sciences des textes et documents, Université Paris VII, 5: 5–19; in English as (1981), 'Women's Time', *Signs, Journal of Women in Culture and Society* 7(1): 13–35. Alice Jardine and Harry Blake, trans.

7   Other influences would include such figures as Louis Althusser, who articulated a neo-Marxist critique of ideology as a discursive structure whose function it is to 'interpellate' the subject into the dominant social order; Roland Barthes, who developed a theory of mythology to account for the ways that myths 'naturalise' existing social practices, making them seem inevitable and thus masking their specific historical location; and Michel Foucault, who argued for the interpenetration of knowledge and power, asserting the impossibility of any knowledge not structured by and implicated in the perpetuation of dominant discursive practices. Also influential, for feminism as well as for the French intellectual community in general, were such figures as Jean-Paul Sartre, Merleau-Ponty, Claude Lévi-Strauss (whose work is vital to the Lacanian project), and Emmanuel Levinas – thinkers who, in various ways, gave voice to the concern for 'the Other' that motivates so much contemporary Continental thought. Vitally important as well, of course, is Hegel – whose work figures in France as a paradigm of the totalising/totalitarian force of Western metaphysics, and

against whom, for that reason, much of French critical thinking, both feminist and non-feminist, is directed.

8   Please see our forthcoming anthology of critical essays for more information: Morny Joy, Kathleen O'Grady and Judith L. Poxon (eds), *French Feminisms and Religion: Critical Perspectives* (Routledge, 2002).

PART ONE

Luce Irigaray

L UCE IRIGARAY IS ONE of the most widely read French theorists of sexual difference. Born in Belgium, she moved to Paris in 1960 and has lived there since, with the exception of several extended stays abroad. She has written or edited over fifteen books, which have been translated into various languages; her writing career spans several decades, and covers a diversity of subjects, among them philosophy, psychoanalysis, linguistics, social theory, literature and religion. This richness of interests and methodologies combines to make her work difficult to read, since she presumes a familiarity on the part of her readers with the various fields in which she works. Nevertheless, it is clear that the problem of sexual difference lies at the heart of all of her work; she argues, in *An Ethics of Sexual Difference* (1993a [1984]), that this is the central problem of the current age. Because of this emphasis, it has been suggested that of the three theorists (Irigaray, Cixous and Kristeva) most often associated in the anglophone world with the French feminist movement, it is Irigaray who has manifested the most enduring commitment to feminist theory and politics.[1] However, for many critics Irigaray's emphasis on sexual difference at the expense of other crucial differences (of race, class, sexual orientation, etc.) continues to be extremely problematic.

The breadth of Irigaray's interests is evident in the many courses of study she has pursued. She holds master's degrees in literature, philosophy, psychology and psychopathology, and doctorates in linguistics and philosophy. She is trained as a Lacanian analyst, and continues to practise psychoanalysis in spite of her expulsion from Lacan's École Freudienne following the publication in 1974 of her second doctoral dissertation as *Speculum of the Other Woman*. She has taught and lectured extensively throughout France and Europe, and has worked since the early 1960s at the Centre Nationale de la Recherche Scientifique, in Paris, where she is currently Director of Research.

In spite of her reservations about the term 'feminist' — reservations that stem from the association of that term with a particular kind of struggle for political equality — Irigaray has been active in feminist politics in France for several decades. Although she has refused to identify with any one group in the highly factionalised French women's movement, she has lobbied publicly for women's right to abortion and contraception, and has lectured widely on feminist issues. Since the 1980s, she has openly supported the Italian Communist Party, and has published original texts in Italian.

In her early work, Irigaray follows both Lacan and Derrida in claiming that within Western metaphysics, the feminine as such is repressed due to its being essentially unrepresentable. This results historically in femininity's being understood according to masculine models, that is, as deficient masculinity, or as masculinity's (inferior) opposite or complement. To demonstrate this, Irigaray considers some of the key texts of the Western tradition, employing a method of 'mimesis' — a technique of reading that ironically mimics that which is read — in order both to expose the fallacies and omissions that mark those texts and to suggest a new, specifically feminine, mode of philosophising. In contrast to what she claims is the (masculine) drive for identity, unity and sameness that characterises the tradition — a drive that she identifies as 'phallogocentric' — Irigaray posits the feminine as irreducibly 'not one' (1985b), always at least two by virtue of the structure of her sexual organs. However, this argument is not biologistic in any simple way, although early reception of Irigaray's work in the anglophone world often dismissed her as an 'essentialist' because of this claim. Rather, the appeal to the link between women's anatomy and feminine multiplicity is based on a 'morphological' understanding of the relationship between bodies and discourses. In other words, the body is never simply 'natural', for Irigaray; rather, it enacts and is acted upon by a range of both biological and socio-linguistic forces. Thus, for Irigaray, there is an isomorphism between masculine anatomy and patriarchal discourse, and the non-patriarchal discourse that might allow women to give voice to a specifically feminine subjectivity must be based on a corresponding isomorphism with feminine anatomy. The motivation for the stylistic experimentation that characterises her early work, then, can be seen to lie in her sense that women must transform language if they are to be successful in liberating themselves from the constrictions of patriarchal (non)identity.

Two of these early books, *Speculum of the Other Woman* (1985a [1974]) and *This Sex Which Is Not One* (1985b [1977]), are by far the best-known of Irigaray's works, among English-speaking readers. While neither book contains a sustained critique of the religious traditions of the West or elaborates a vision of what post-patriarchal religion might be, portions of *Speculum* are of particular interest to students and scholars of religious studies. One such is the short essay called 'La Mystérique' (the title is left untranslated in the English edition), in which Irigaray explores female mysticism and mystical discourse. Here she argues that mysticism is the proper domain of the feminine because of its overturning of reason in favour of other, more embodied, ways of knowing. She also offers an affirming vision of Christ, in which he is linked to women's suffering by virtue of his wounds. The second portion of particular interest appears as part of Irigaray's lengthy reading of Plato's myth of the cave. Here she offers a brief critique of the Western notion of God as the image of a perfection that can only be available to men — albeit hypothetically, as idealised limit. For Irigaray, the cave stands as emblem of a mode of knowing that is essentially false, in that it is based on a willed forgetting of the importance of the primal 'cave': the womb. As a result of this repression of the maternal in the religious and philosophical traditions of the West, she argues, women have been denied their voice, their identity.

This theme of the forgetting or repression of the maternal/feminine continues to appear throughout Irigaray's work of the 1980s, and it is increasingly developed in a religious or ethical context. In *Marine Lover of Friedrich Nietzsche* (1991e [1980]), for example, Irigaray suggests that Nietzsche appropriates the maternal/feminine position for himself and for the masculine gods of ancient Greece, and simultaneously erases the importance of actual women, associated here with the element of water, in the production and reproduction of culture. The closing section of the book, 'When the Gods Are Born', is an extended prose-poem that plays upon Nietzsche's reading of Dionysus and Christ. In Irigaray's view, both gods (or god-men) emerge as offspring of motherless births, products of all-male genealogies constructed to honour the Law of the Father at the expense of the maternal/feminine.

The collected essays of *An Ethics of Sexual Difference* (1993a [1984]) present readings of some of the major figures of Irigaray's philosophical heritage, among them Plato, Aristotle, Descartes, Spinoza, Levinas and Merleau-Ponty. Here again we find Irigaray's claim that the Western philosophical and theological tradition has wilfully forgotten the feminine. For example, Irigaray observes that both time and space are conceived as belonging to the Father God who created them, and thus gendered masculine; for this reason, space and time need to be reconceptualised, in order to free them of their masculine bias, before an ethics of sexual difference can emerge. Irigaray further argues for a rethinking of divinity, illustrating her vision with images of the angel — understood as intermediary between body and spirit — and of mucosity — seen as the mutual inter-permeability of inside and outside. Taking seriously the interval, the place between man and woman where genuine exchange may occur, leads inevitably for Irigaray to a new understanding of God, and in turn to new possibilities of human relationships that would not be based on suppression of the feminine gender in favour of the masculine. Irigaray also traces some of the ways that the women have been limited by the Western tradition in their ability to speak, to find their own identity, to love themselves, and to mother. She suggests that an ethics of sexual difference would require the (re)discovery of wonder between women and men, so that it could become possible for women and men to meet each other as if for the first time, without the constrictions of preconceived ideas about gender. This would lead, for Irigaray, to the freeing of women from the necessity of propping up masculine identity by reflecting men's vision of reality back to them.

In several of the essays collected in *Sexes and Genealogies* (1993c [1987]), Irigaray's concern with religious themes becomes explicit. In 'Divine Women', for example, she argues that women must begin to envision a feminine divine — not a goddess on the models of ancient Western cultures — if a specifically feminine subjectivity is ever to emerge. In 'Belief Itself', she begins by taking up Freud's famous story of the *fort/da* game, demonstrating once again how the maternal body is elided in the Western tradition, especially in the religious traditions centred around the Father-God. She also further elaborates on the angel as a figuration of the divinised interval, the mediation between flesh and spirit. Finally, in 'Women, the Sacred, and Money', Irigaray considers the importance of sacrifice in Western culture, showing that sacrifice is primarily the sacrifice of women and women's work, and arguing that women need to develop their own religion, language and monetary system if a new social order, not built on sacrifice, is to be accomplished.

The vision of such a social order animates *I Love to You: Sketch of a Possible Felicity in History* (1996a [1992]). Here Irigaray meditates on what relations between women and men might be like in a world where sexual difference is recognised and respected, rather than repressed. In 'A Breath that Touches in Words', she begins to develop the link between breath and divinity that becomes more prominent in her subsequent work; she notes that an emphasis on speech (which occurs with ex-spiration, death/breathing out) too often accompanies a devaluing of silent reflection (in-spiration, life/breathing in), and suggests that a religion that figures God as the Word might indicate a lack of respect for life. In 'Practical Teachings: Between Passion and Civility', she extols 'love in sexual difference' as a form of both spiritual and carnal transformation, a relation in which divinity might be manifested.

In three of her most recent works, *Le Souffle des femmes: Présente des credos au féminin* (1996b), *Entre Orient et Occident: De la singularité à la communauté* (1999b), and *The Age of the Breath* (1999a [2000]) Irigaray continues to explore the connection between divinity and breath, and asserts the importance, for women especially, of taking responsibility for one's breathing as a spiritual exercise. She suggests that breathing for oneself, which she sees as the autonomous gesture *par excellence*, is necessary to the cultivation of a divinity that would sanctify the body and all of physical reality. Arguing that Western culture has overvalued language and art at the expense of the body, she recommends yoga and other practices drawn from Asian traditions — a move that some critics see as an idealised appropriation of Hindu and Buddhist practices which is problematic in a time of postcolonial criticism. Finally, in her essay in *Le Souffle des femmes*, she returns to a theme of *Marine Lover*: that is, the need for re-imagining the traditional Christian theology of incarnation, based not on Jesus but on Mary, who emerges for Irigaray as a privileged mediatrix of the divine and the material.

Thus, Irigaray's work can be seen to trace a distinctive path from the silenced women of *Speculum* to the infinite (feminine) becomings sketched out in her later books. Irigaray sees this development as leading to a new era in which women and men can enter into a genuine relationship with each other for the first time, and where together they can both realise the divine.

Note

1   Naomi Schor (1994), 'Previous Engagements: The Receptions of Irigaray', in *Engaging with Irigaray*, ed. Carolyn Burke *et al.* (New York: Columbia University Press), 4.

Chapter 1

Plato's *Hystera*[1]

■ [Abridged] This extract is from a much longer chapter entitled 'L'ὑστέρα de Platon', which first appeared in *Speculum de l'autre femme* (Minuit, 1974). The English translation, 'Plato's *Hystera*', appears in *Speculum of the Other Woman*, translated by Gillian C. Gill (Cornell University Press, 1985).[2]

Editors' introduction

FOR IRIGARAY, WESTERN METAPHYSICS is constructed on a deception; its delusive structures are organised so as to confirm men in their own image. Women, excluded from this homogenous system, are neither acknowledged in their crucial material/maternal role of reproduction, nor are they permitted access to language, the basis of knowledge and the means of self-representation.

In the chapter from which this extract is drawn, Irigaray explores Plato's myth of the cave as a symbol of this foundation of Western metaphysics. In this myth, which is found in *The Republic*, Plato compares ignorance to imprisonment in a dark cave where individuals are condemned to watch shadows moving on the wall and mistake them for the whole of reality. Freedom from ignorance, then, consists in escaping the cave to enter the 'enlightened' world of the Platonic Forms, those ideals of which the moving shadows are merely pale projections. For Irigaray, Plato's path to knowledge, exemplified by the passage from the darkness of the cave to the light, is unconscious of its debt to the maternal, and, by extension, to all things female. This is because in Platonic philosophy/theology there is no acknowledgement of the meaning of the cave itself – the womb from which all things are born. The primacy of the female aspect, as the very foundation of all life, is thus erased from consciousness. This is the primal act of forgetfulness.

In Irigaray's understanding, men remain condemned to a life of repetition because they constantly look to women to mirror back to them their own illusions of identity. There is no openness to the other, to any form of difference whereby the fictive structures of male self-representation could be challenged.

It is the resultant masculine conception of reality, of self-reproduction, that Irigaray characterises as the world of 'sameness' or repetition.

Irigaray also observes this form of sameness operating in the ideals of Truth, Goodness and Beauty that are aligned with the notion of God (the Father). Here she moves beyond Plato to describe the soul, that divine spark in men, as founded on the selfsame principle of identity. Thus God functions as the paradigm of male perfection which men mirror back to God. For Irigaray, this God figure, abstracted from the world of flesh and desire, remains ultimately unknowable. Nonetheless, men constantly affirm God's identity in their mimicry of this idealised other. They also appeal to laws and other social constructs allegedly sanctioned by this divinity.

In such constructions, women play no part. Nor does the philosophical or theological system allow women to have knowledge of themselves or gain access to the mechanisms that control this process of their exclusion. As Irigaray notes: 'They have no proper form' (1985a: 342). Women's only hope in this scheme of things, if they seek autonomy, would seem to be imitation of men. Given the limitations of this male model, however, Irigaray does not endorse such a project.

Women are thus condemned to silence, to darkness. There exists no structure that allows their voices to be heard. According to Irigaray, for women's presence to be acknowledged, the binary and abstract structure of knowledge would have to be replaced, as would all social structures. This is because Irigaray does not believe that the seeming immutability of this world of knowledge, as it has been constructed from Plato onwards, can be amended. This is due to its dualist, oppositional framework, with its separation of body and soul, woman and man. For Irigaray, this framework does not allow a way back to the cave, to the body of the mother. Yet this is the only route which would allow the repressed female realm to be remembered and to be given its due place at the beginning/centre of creation. The hope of such a return, however, will provide the basis for Irigaray's quest for new modes of knowing and ethics.

Life in Philosophy

[. . .]

A *korē* dilated to the whole field of the gaze and mirroring herself [3]

The only men who love each other are, in truth, those who are impatient to find the same over and over again. And, in order to do this, they must not turn or direct their quest toward some other part of man or any object whatsoever, but only toward that very thing in which they see themselves: that *mirror of vision* in which they can look at themselves in the very gaze of the other, perceiving, in one and the same glance, their view and themselves.[4] But this image (of oneself) in a pupil is always dependent upon a *korē*. That is to say upon a *young girl*, a young *virgin*, or even on a *doll*. A reduced image, then, which cannot satisfy someone who wishes to have knowledge of the All. But he must not linger too long over the double of man that the *korē* represents (for him). The specula(riza)tion is too limited, involving only one organ which, though exemplary, nonetheless remains too matrical when envisaged in this way. The reflection (of self) that would rely entirely on a support like this would risk forgetting the most important thing: the gaze of the soul. Veiled in/by this mirage, upon which one must learn to close one's eyes, so as not to succumb to the exclusive attraction of appearances. Even if the gaze is that of a young boy. Abusing what attracts one most in his eyes sometimes leads to drowning clear reason in mirrors that are not faithful enough, not *frozen* enough. It is rather the soul which has been educated and strengthened in good sense – the philosopher's soul, for example – that one should ask for the guarantee of self-knowledge. More specifically one must turn to that point in the soul which is the seat of the thought of Sameness itself and of the most satisfactory knowledge. In a like manner, is the pupil that point in the gaze by which one regulates oneself in order to catch sight of sameness, and to see oneself? Going beyond this discernment, which remains rooted in the senses, one seeks what one needs in that part of the soul that is most identical to the self, the part that reflects best – the most divine part. For this self-identity is most certainly to be found by conforming to the divine principle, sharing in the attributes of him who, from all eternity, in(de)finitely knows himself, in a total self-transparence. A mirror clearer, purer, more resplendent with light than all those which, already, have been made in his image.[5] A mirror untouched by any reflection, *like a pupil – a korē –* dilated to encompass the whole field of vision, and *mirroring itself*. Reflecting nothing (but) its own void, that *hole* through which one looks. Which, of course, is not one (hole) anymore, as then it would risk being sometimes bigger and sometimes smaller. This could never happen to the gaze of God which, ever on high, sees everything at one and the same time, looming over the whole universe from his high place. From that perspective one cannot glimpse, calculate, or even imagine what the vanishing point might be. A summit infinitely receding from the convergence of all verticals. Supreme erection that exceeds every horizon; even the sharpest, the most piercing gaze will be incapable of calculating its angles of incidence, for the eye remains captive in the world of the visible and does not embrace the totality of viewpoints and their harmonious organization.

Only the divine vision is without liabilities, encompassing the All, with no trace of opaqueness left. Light that nothing resists, going through *any paraphragm*, reaching everywhere, without deviation of any sort. Ever identical to itself in its rectitude. Not allowing itself to be bent by any mirror since it knows itself throughout time (as) the one who has the most power of all. Gazing upon itself (as) that which in reality is brightest.[6] Good, alien to all shadow, outshining the Sun itself: its clear-sightedness will never be dazzled by any stars, for it overflows the sphere of their orbit, encircling the All which turns around in the space of its field. Gaze that no bodily organ, nor even any essence, can limit. Without any blind spot, even one that might represent something forgotten. For God is *in the instant* all that (he) has been and will be. Such tenses of becoming are inadequate to analyze his present, which has neither before nor after, earlier nor later. Being has nothing that predates it, nor anything ahead that it should aim for. Everything is already (in) Him. *Arkhē* and *telos*. And if he sows forth seeds of light and truth, it is from excess of goodness. He has no need to pour forth in this way. Or else the need is only to supplement Good and is born of a desire for everything to be like Him. Flooding the universe with the seeds he scatters everywhere. Ever equal to himself. Lofty and all-powerful. Absolute model of sovereignty who must be imitated if one is not to fall back into lower states.

Thus, every 'being' (étant) in his 'being' (être) can only try to mimic God, copy him more or less well, for there is no other perfection to rely on. The whole Universe, in its essence, conforms to his divine projections. There is nothing outside, or even behind, that is not subject to his designs. *Everything is enclosed in a super-celestial gaze*, moving in a circle, after confused with before, future with past, earlier with later, in harmonious circumvolutions. And the autarchy of this motion is always the sign that some divine principle is involved. Auto-nomous, auto-mobile tropism, index of omnipotence that would resorb *into the en soi of its circle* anything that might still be withholding itself on the other side, any remaining cause, outside the self, capable of disrupting the sovereign economy. Gravitating endlessly around its axis, describing a circle while the things on the other side, whether future or past, are always constituted *from the inside* of the circle. As for the something that had not been envisaged, represented, or representable, it is *expelled outside* this sphere. It constitutes *the back of the set*, available to the divine rays only, penetrating man, the paraphragm-envelope (of the) All, in some way rectally. And man himself is no more aware of his own back than he is able to bear the vision of the Good face to face.

Divine knowledge

The back reserved for God

The mime becomes loftier and more sublime, but remains necessarily within the scenography of sameness. Thus the magicians, the tutors and philosophers, the Demiurge, or God-the-Father always have a fall-back position. They alone have some point of view on the backside of things. But this is denied *in the facts* which they claim are their exclusive interest. Facts projected upon the back side of the cave, of the picture, of the soul, all screens of representation that must never, under any circumstances, be turned around. The retroversion is forbidden to public scrutiny, masked in the circularity of the process which gives the impression of turning the inside out and *thereby showing it right side up*. A kaleidoscopic optical illusion out of which, eternally invisible, steals God. Hidden *behind* what each being can look at during his life. God is the foundation hidden from sight but offering himself to intuition, placed infinitely far away, above and in front, in his teleological Beauty and Goodness. How desperately hard it is for mortals to understand and, more especially, to demonstrate God's reality and truth; yet these have the force of law. They regulate the orderliness of the universe that has been formed in God's image. All that *really* exists is like Him. Anything divergent will be abandoned – at least for a while – to the depths of the earth, or of the sea. Thus he finds himself in the presence of his Ideas alone, though this is not to say that he recognizes himself equally in each, male and female. The fact that each is in some measure his reflection still allows for a hierarchy in the degrees of self-realization, the degrees of affiliation, of ancestry. A complex network of relationships is set up in which the generations interweave in order to define the exact form of each, male and female. To ensure a good game, each piece on the backgammon board is placed by the 'King' in the proper position, determined once and for all, since God will never leave the place from which He watches.[7] Eminence that nothing can move ever again, and that embraces the All of all eternity. [. . .]

The father knows the front side and back side of everything, at least in theory

[. . .] How, then, does God know the *sensible* face of things, given that his relationship with them must be wholly theoretical? Only in Principle does he have correspondance [sic] with existence, for his word sustains the logical and geometrical order of the life of this Universe without his ever participating in it. (The) All resembles him, but there is no reciprocity. ❨Everything mimics him, but he *imitates nothing*, or so the story goes❩ Pure Truth, defined once and for all in its fixed Ideas that nothing and nobody will ever succeed in moving, or even modifying or swaying. In the Immutability of his reflection, God would have resolved in advance all the ob-jections placed in his way, and would never need to ask anything of anyone. He is, for all eternity, right about everything. And this cannot be shared, or even duplicated (except in Himself) for fear of no longer knowing infallibly where science is, or fiction, or ignorance.[8] Or wisdom, or craziness, or stupidity. And a decision has to be made. The Father alone, therefore, would know absolutely everything. But this knowing would result from the fact that everything is made in his image. Ultimately he only recognizes himself; that is to say, once again, *the organization of his field of projection*. And the 'others' would have to internalize the 'proper' characters and identify themselves therein so that the 'world' can go on turning in the right direction. This makes them the same, by cutting them off from themselves, or at least from the irascible and passionate parts of their 'souls' that must bend little by little before (good) mimicry. They do not abreact mimicry, bring it into consciousness, since it is still correlated to their material, matrical, and thus hysterical heritage, but they bend and twist so as to offer their newly polished surfaces to the Father's desire. In order to assimilate and incorporate it. Guarantee of immortality. Forgetful (of self) in order to remember what had been before they were conceived. And that, of course, never falls simply under the senses. Absence of 'representation'/presence of being (être). A *blindness* bars the way that would lead from the beginning to the end. Faint, that line would begin to curve back upon itself; the before, the after, would begin to be confused with the behind, the anterior, as if nothing had ever happened apart from the insistence of these/ its circumvolutions – and not the detour, but also the experience of being thrown out of true, of ecstasy in the point of view of God. Center projected in unnoticeable ways, inserted into the soul and around which one must now turn. But the places where these two trajectories might possibly intersect are the object of a radical blindness. Even the hypothesis is lacking here.

The meaning of death for a philosopher

Thus the father's 'face' is never made known to the son, the excellence of his Good can never be fully demonstrated. He is not in fact in any *spot*, or at least any that can be represented, nor on any *plane* that can be conceived by man. Man always remains *beneath* the project God has for him. At least in this lower life, separated from the 'other' by that *impenetrable paraphragm*, death. Obviously, no mortal will gaze upon death as he experiences it at the very moment of dying. He will still not know whether or not 'the entrance to another existence' corresponds to the desire to appropriate the 'other side' of representation which constitutes his 'interiority' but remains outside the field of his perspective. Break-through into what *remains* God's secret; which ensures the repetition of the same (history). No upheavals, no revolutions in which what had always *been* would appear as the *flip side* of what might be, the *shadow*, masked as such, of what would be, or else a possible perspective on things, a potential interpreta-tion of reality which, because withheld from evidence and always positioned *behind*, defies all comparison. By excluding the gaze of the other, or others, this extrapolated point of view organizes and projects the world into a paralyzed empire. Formalizations of laws laid down in perpetuity, logos of the Father. And

He never questions that (Id) which causes (him) but lays univocal claim to all that is, in his absolute science.[9] Which would give account of everything without any change, for all eternity. Embracing from the outset all enumerations of 'beings,' their proportions and relationships, all the abstract operations that can occur betwen [sic] them and the very development of those relationships. Which are essentially copulative. Their causes, ends, and results. And perhaps their modes as well? [. . .]

A one-way passage

[. . .] As for women, unless raised to the dignity of the male essence, they would have no access to the sublimer circles of sameness, to the heights of the intelligible. It is true that in their highest moments – *when they are most like the male sex, naturally* – women aspire to that sublimity. They rarely, however, rise above the level of exchanged sensations, of communal daydreams; at best they express opinions on events in the city, or merely pass on the opinions that are making the rounds. Therefore women are incapable of realizing whether some idea – Idea – in fact corresponds to themselves, or whether it is only a more or less passable imitation of men's ideas. Unaware of the value of the names given them by the logos – assuming that some really specific names exist – women would, it seems, not know their definition, their representation, or the relationships with others, and with the All, that are maintained in this way. Women would thus be *without measure*, as a result of being without limits, without proportions that have been established once and for all and that can be referred back to the whole. *They have no proper form.* Given that this is so, how could they devote themselves to loving those like them in soul, the guarantee in another way of the permanence of their relationship to the origin? This process, this progress, toward representing the identical and the eternal return of sameness would not be woman's lot. Unless, let it be noted again, women renounce their inferior condition and choose to be men in order to have a better life – which may take ten thousand years. [. . .]

A misprized incest and an unrealizable incest

[. . .] She herself knows nothing (of herself). And remembers nothing. Providing the basis for the wise man's auto-logical speculations, she lives in darkness. At/as back of the scene of representation which she props up by not/without knowing it. She makes no show or display. For if she were to shine, then the light would no longer, simply, belong to sameness. The whole of the current economic system would have to be re-calculated. And if she is granted the life of appearance, it will be a darkling affair. Underground shadow theater, lunar reflection of the star that makes everything light and fertile. A lack-luster double of the self-duplication that man carries within him, his 'soul', when 'she' doesn't stand in the way with her 'body.' With that still amorphous extension. Virginity that continues to resist the philosopher's speculative solicitations, and that is indeed mandatory for the purity of conception. Polished surface that will not be scratched or pierced, lest the reflection be *exaggerated* or *blurred*.

Thus, ideal command forbids the 'path' between outside and inside. That path is doubtless doubled in different ways on each side, but it no longer provides a transition between the two. How, then, can one return into the cave, the den, the earth? Rediscover the darkness of all that has been left behind? Remember the forgotten mother?

Notes

1   Plato himself does not use the word 'hystera' for the cave. Irigaray discusses the reason for her change of words in *Speculum* (p. 243), where she states that Plato's description of 'living underground in a dwelling formed like a cave' is the equivalent of 'hystera' [eds].

2   In *Speculum*, the second extract, '*La Mystérique*', appears before 'Plato's *Hystera*'. We have decided to change the order because 'Plato's *Hystera*' sets the stage for the Western philosophical/theological tradition against which all of Irigaray's work is directed. '*La Mystérique*' is one instance of the way women have tried to speak out against their silencing by the Western tradition [eds].

3   In the English translation of this section, the term korē is used rather than χόρη, which is used in the French version. The same term reappears in a later extract from Irigaray, 'The Forgotten Mystery of Female Ancestry', in *Thinking the Difference* (1994). The word here is translated as Kōrē, who is the daughter of Persephone. There would not appear to be any consistency in the use of this term either in the French or English [eds].

4   *Alcibiades*, 132d–e, 133a. ('*Socrates.* Can we think of any objects, in looking at which we see not only them but ourselves at the same time? *Alcibiades.* Clearly, Socrates, mirrors and the like. *Soc.* Very true. Now is there not something of a mirror in the eye with which we see? *Alcib.* Certainly. *Soc.* Did you ever observe that the face of a person looking into the eye of another is reflected as in a mirror; and in the visual organ which is over against him, and which is called the pupil [*korē*] there is a sort of image of the person looking? *Alcib.* That is quite true. *Soc.* Then the eye, looking at another eye, and at that eye which is most perfect and which is the instrument of vision, will there see itself? But looking at anything else either in man or in the world except at what this resembles, it will not see itself. *Alcib.* Very true. *Soc.* Then if the eye is to see itself, it must look into

the eye, and at that part of the eye where sight which is the virtue of the eye resides? . . . May we say, then, that as mirrors are truer and clearer and brighter than the mirror within the eye, so also is God by His nature a clearer and brighter mirror than the most excellent part of our own soul?') –Tr.

5   *Alcibiades*, 133b–c.

6   *Republic*, VII, 518c.

7   *Laws*, X, 903d–e.

8   *Parmenides*, 133 and following.

9   This reading of 'ça' ('that') as 'Id' is an interpretation of Irigaray's intent by the translator, and is not, in the view of the editors of this reader, supported by the context [eds].

Chapter 2

La Mystérique

■   This essay first appeared in *Speculum de l'autre femme* (Minuit, 1974). It was published in English as part of *Speculum of the Other Woman*, translated by Gillian C. Gill (Cornell University Press, 1985).

Editors' introduction

THE TITLE OF THIS essay, 'La Mystérique', appears untranslated in the English edition of *Speculum* because the French conveys so many meanings that would otherwise be lost, suggesting as it does mysticism (*mysticisme*), hysteria (*hystérie*), and mystery (*mystère*), all conceived in the feminine gender (*la*). Indeed, the whole essay is dense with meaning. Although Irigaray, in the French style, does not cite her references, this text alludes to, among other things, the mystical experience of Teresa of Avila; Simone de Beauvoir's treatment of female mysticism in *The Second Sex*; Bernini's famous statue of Teresa; and Lacan's well-known discussion of women's desire, which uses Teresa's mystical experience as an emblem of feminine eroticism. Moreover, in this essay, which occupies the central position in *Speculum*, Irigaray plays again with the image of the mirror (*speculum*), an image that is significant both to Christian mystical discourse and to Irigaray's own theorisations of women's place in patriarchy. She notes that the mystic's desire to erase her own personal identity in order to mirror God affirms the difference between Creator and creature; according to Irigaray, the mystic sees her identity as so inherently imperfect that she must obliterate it if she is to reflect divine perfection. Irigaray points out, however, that in the process of mirroring the divinity, the mystic is able to participate in the divine identity, so that this mirroring also collapses the experienced distinction between them. This logic, whereby mirroring at once effaces and reaffirms the identity of the mystic, is much the same as that at work in Irigaray's notion that women under patriarchy affirm male identity by serving as mirrors that reflect masculine self-sameness. At the same time, however, the illusion of masculine self-sufficiency is undermined by this same mirroring (with its reliance on being mirrored in the other – woman). In her use of this image in this context, then, Irigaray condenses many of the arguments that she elsewhere elaborates at much greater length.

Irigaray is particularly interested in female mysticism because it represents, for her, the possibility of woman occupying the place of a speaking subject. Within the limits of mystical discourse, says Irigaray, women find one of the only places in Western history where they may speak and act publicly. In fact, mysticism *per se* is the domain of the feminine; here the unconscious speaks, and the categories of subject/other and inner/outer, so necessary for the constitution of Western (masculine) identity, understood as self-sameness, break down altogether. Moreover, Irigaray is drawn to female mysticism because she sees the transcendence achieved by mystics like Teresa as an embodied transcendence, a transcendence that operates through immanence. This essay, then, anticipates Irigaray's later desire to conceive of a 'sensible transcendental' that would overturn the opposition between transcendence and immanence.

In this excerpt, Irigaray also proposes a favourable reading of Christ. He emerges as 'that most female of men, the Son' — the one man who, through his suffering, was able to understand what it means to be woman. In Teresa's mystical vision of the symmetry between the wound in Christ's side and the 'wound' of the female genitals, Irigaray finds the basis for a notion of Christ as fully incarnated divinity, embodying both maleness and femaleness in his flesh and thereby able to redeem both women and men. This reading stands in stark contrast with the critical view in *Marine Lover of Friedrich Nietzsche* (1991e), in which Irigaray positions Christ in a trajectory of male gods who have appropriated maternity and feminine eros, thus rendering women superfluous.

Finally, however, Irigaray is not satisfied with the transcendence that she attributes to female mystics, whether that transcendence be embodied or not. This is so because the relative autonomy attained by female mystics fails to challenge the patriarchal hierarchy of the Church. Observing that the (male) priests who hear the mystics' confessions 'will not always lend an approving ear' — that is, that the structure of the Church need not accommodate itself to the egalitarian visions of feminine mysticism — Irigaray suggests that the women who enjoy such visions are complicit in their own subordination because they continue to accept priestly mediation. This critical view of the Church lays the groundwork for Irigaray's turn, in later work, to the project of envisioning a feminine divine that could serve as a foundation for the emergence of a community of fully autonomous female subjects, independent of the limitations of masculine conceptions of identity.

La Mystérique*

*Take a concave mirror and put it next to a dry and inflammable material; then expose
the mirror to the rays of the sun; the dry material will catch fire and burn because
of the heat of the sun and the concavity of the mirror.*

Ruysbroeck the Admirable

Woman is the most noble way to address the soul, and it is far nobler than virgin.

Meister Eckhart

The Word was made flesh in order to make me God.

Angela of Foligno

La mystérique: this is how one might refer to what, within a still theological
onto-logical perspective is called mystic language or discourse. Consciousness
still imposes such names to signify that other scene, offstage, that it finds *cryptic*.
This is the place where consciousness is no longer master, where, to its extreme
confusion, it sinks into a dark night that is also fire and flames. This is the place
where 'she' — and in some cases he, if he follows 'her' lead — speaks about the
dazzling glare which comes from the source of light that has been logically
repressed, about 'subject' and 'Other' flowing out into an embrace of fire that
mingles one term into another, about contempt for form as such, about mistrust
for understanding as an obstacle along the path of jouissance and mistrust for the
dry desolation of reason. Also about a 'burning glass.' This is the only place in
the history of the West in which woman speaks and acts so publicly. What is
more, it is for/by woman that man dares to enter the place, to descend into it,
condescend to it, even if he gets burned in the attempt. It is in order to speak
woman, write to women, act as preacher and confessor to women, that man
usually has gone to such excesses. That he has accepted the need to take the
detour through metaphors that can scarcely be called figures. That he has given
up his knowledge in order to attend to woman's madnesses. Falling — as Plato
would say, no doubt, — into the trap of mimicking them, of claiming to find
jouissance as 'she' does. To the point when he can no longer find himself as
'subject' anymore and goes where he had no wish to follow: to his loss in that
a-typical, a-topical mysteria. Where it will already have been noted — to the
amazement of all — that the poorest in science and the most ignorant were the
most eloquent, the richest in revelations. Historically, that is, women. Or at
least the 'female.'

But how is this done? Given that the horizon line is already drawn, and drawn,
in fact, by the 'subject' who defines himself at the same time, in a circularity that
knows no end except the return, over and over again, upon itself/himself. The
problem is to break down the walls around the (male) one who speaks, sees,

thinks, and thereby now confers being upon himself, in a prison of self-sufficiency and a clarity made of the shadows of denial. The task is to go back through the house of confinement and the darkness of the night until once again he feels the light that forms and other speculative veils had shrouded from his gaze in an effort to weaken its white heat. All this left man hungry and thirsty. At least sometimes, at least in some places. Even now.

But as the eye is already guardian to the reason, the first necessity is to slip away unseen. And in fact without seeing much either. In a blind breaching of the philosopher's closed chamber, from the matrix of speculation in which he had cloistered himself in order to consider everything clearly. The 'soul'[1] escapes outside herself, opening up a crack in the cave (une antr'ouverture) so that she may penetrate herself once more. The walls of her prison are broken, the distinction between inside/outside transgressed. In such ex-stasies, she risks losing herself or at least seeing the assurance of her self-identity-as-same fade away. This will probably not happen all at once, since she is already caught, enveloped in various representations, in different configurations and chains that lead her, bit by bit, back to her unity. To resembling what she would ideally be in her own form, or substance. And the road she will have to take in order to flee the logic that has framed her thus is not nothing. Moreover, she doesn't know where she is going, and will have to wander randomly and in darkness. And her eye has become accustomed to obvious 'truths' that actually hide what she is seeking. It is *the very shadow of her gaze* that must be explored. Night for all sensible, all solar vision, a blaze of light that would make the sun itself repent its self-conceit. Night, above all, beyond the mind's speculation, beyond theoretical contemplation, even that centered upon Being itself. And if man once thought that straight vision could allow him to escape the opaque barrier that every body presents to the light, now, in his impetuous desire, he is plunged into the darkness that a supposedly enlightened gaze had projected in its very rings and reversals.

Yet, in this nocturnal wandering, where is the gaze to be fixed? The only possibility is to push onward into the night until it finally becomes a transverberating beam of light, a luminous shadow. ⟨Onward into a *touch* that opens the 'soul' again to contact with divine force, to the impact of searing light⟩ She is cut to the quick within this shimmering underground fabric that she had always been herself, though she did not know it. And she will never know it or herself *clearly* as she takes fire, in a sweet confusion whose source cannot at first be apprehended. She is torn apart in pain, fear, cries, tears, and blood that go beyond any other feeling. The wound must come before the flame. But already there is delight and longing in this torment, if she has entrusted herself to a skill subtle enough in its strength. Though the path she is cutting is a difficult one, she is impatient to set everything else aside and pleads to go on. But she cannot specify exactly what she wants. Words begin to fail her. She senses something *remains to be said* that resists all speech, that can at best be stammered out. All the words are weak, worn out, unfit to translate anything sensibly. For it is no longer a matter of longing for some determinable attribute, some mode of essence, some face of presence. What is expected is neither a *this* nor a *that*, not a *here* any more than a *there*. No being, no places are designated. So the best plan is to abstain from all discourse, to keep quiet, or else utter only a sound so inarticulate that it barely forms a *song*. While all the while keeping an attentive ear open for any hint or tremor coming back.

For how does one chart a course in this ignorance that can gain enlightenment only from the embrace of fire? No doubt we must edge our way through narrow doorways and along knife-edge paths, dark and terrible, squeeze painfully between two walls, wedge our bodies through slits in order to move into the full light of the caves to be explored. Endless open space, hung emptily between here and there, dizzying height, steep ascent, even retreat – all these lie ahead perhaps. But how does one tackle these things, even if one felt passionately about them, if there is no sense of *vocation*? No directing goal is in sight, no cause can be taken for a point of reference. No 'natural light' is available to help us along this path that has already been erased and eroded in the confusion with those reflecting walls of the 'soul' which she had made her own in the cold reasonableness of optics. The light is out in this night, a strange awakening is vaguely expected while everyone sleeps; and the higher mental faculties are in a deep slumber, the understanding in a virtual stupor. What is beginning to happen takes place in such secrecy and deep oblivion that no intelligence, no common sense, can have precise knowledge of it. A faraway solitude reigns in this silent touching, which yet is moved to its very depths. And which can so easily be distracted, disturbed in its still uneasy suspense. No decision can break in. All is passive waiting, unpremeditated abandon. Refusal of any willed, concerted activity that could stand in the path of 'grace.' Expectant expectancy, absence of project and projections. Unbearable sweetness and bitterness, aridity, dizzy horror before the boundless void. Just an elusive memory that flees representation, re-presentation, repetition. Even in dream.

A gulf that opens up ahead, moves away, strains, never knowing or imagining (itself) in its unfathomable nakedness. An abyss that swallows up all persons, all names, even proper names. For in fact all properties (and proprieties) will have to be shed to continue this penetration. Love, wish, affection, delight, interest, profit must all go as they are still related to a self-as-same, clothing it in a surplus value whose deceptive and treacherous charms are felt only by one who has yet to experience union in its most outrageous nakedness. Its lack of any marketable asset except this desperate immodesty. This 'simplicity' stripped of all attributes that will soon sink to the bottom of the bottomless, engulfing the last dwellings of the soul to/in infinity. Turning the soul's chambers, her den, upside down so as to lead her to that abyssal source that she could never have found otherwise.

For the soul was closed up over the possesion [sic] of a knowledge which made her quite obtuse, particularly in her claims to the immaculate state that no creature had yet been able to pierce or undo. And which is mixed in a jouissance so extreme, a love so incomprehensible, an illumination so unbounded that unknowledge thereby becomes desire. Nothing has a price in this divine consumation [sic] and consumption. Nothing has value, not even the soul herself, set apart from standardization, outside the *labor* market. The soul spends and is spent in the margins of capital. In a strictly non-negotiable currency, an expenditure without accountability, in the resources of its loss. At least so far. Or perhaps for ever. Even simple counting hinders her fall into the abyss of her prodigality, her madness, expansion and dissipation of self. At the final reckoning, the richest person will certainly be the one who has most depleted the stores. But even saying that is being too calculating, too logical even in this reversal of all known economics. No more measure(s) should be taken. We must reach the final dispossession of the last imaginary retreat into pure objectivity: the 'I' calculated and therefore still knew *where* it stood. Reference points, drafting plans to survey this extension, this mother-matter – all these are henceforward taken from mastery. All surfaces and spatial constructions also collapse in a conflagration that pushes further and further back the depths of a gulf where now everything is burning. Fire flares up in the inexhaustible abundance of her underground source and is matched with an opposing but congruent flood that sweeps over the 'I' in an excess of excess. Yet, burning, flowing along in a wild spate of waters, yearning for even greater abandon, the 'I' is *empty* still, ever more empty, opening wide in rapture of soul.

But alone and without help, alas! the soul cannot prevent herself from being buried and sealed off in her crypt. Hidden away, she waits for the rapture to return, the ecstasy, the lightning flash, the penetration of the divine touch. These come intermittently, briefly, rarely, hastily, and the soul is left in great sorrow. She is all comprehension and consent, but her two lips, parted to receive other embraces, soon become dry and retracted over their mourning, if the wait is too long. No voice is hers to call, no hands can fill the open hungry mouth with the food that both nourishes and devours. Abandoned, the soul can barely keep faith. No image, no figure alleviates such mortal absence. No picture, no portrait, no face could serve to ease the waiting, even if they were available in this lack of all defined form. Finding the self imposes a *proximity* that knows no aspect, mode, or figure. No metaphors can designate the radiant splendor of that touch. Any intermediary would risk deferring the fleeting *moment* of its coming. Not even a supportive, evocative *milieu* can sustain, prepare, or recall its intuition. Any addition or adornment might cosset the touch into a complacency incompatible with the difficult trail it must blaze. Like a bolt from the blue.

But can life go on in such violence, however sweet it may be? Does one not die from dying, or die from not dying? How to decide at a time of earthshattering jouissance and pain? Swooning, fainting, bones and flesh torn apart with a crack that covers up the sound of all words of remission. Fire and ice freeze and singe without respite, and nothing lies between their endless, alternating intemperance. Without spring or autumn, morning or evening. The implacable harshness of midday in summer, midnight in winter, mingling their extremes with no lull, no neutral interval in the switch from one to another. *Everything is relentlessly immediate* in this marriage of the unknowable, which can never be evaded once it has been experienced. In a deeper unity than the still, already, speculative unity that underlies the sense of these wrenching contradictions. The bottom, the center, the most hidden, inner place, the heart of the crypt to which 'God' alone descends when he has renounced modes and attributes. For this most secret virginity of the 'soul' surrenders only to one who also freely offers the self in all its nakedness. This most private chamber opens only to one who is indebted to no possession for potency. It is wedded only in the abolition of all power, all having, all being, that is founded elsewhere and otherwise than in this embrace of fire whose end is past conception.

Each becomes the other in consumption, the nothing of the other in consummation. Each will not in fact have known the identity of the other, has thus lost self-identity except for a hint of an imprint that each keeps in order the better to intertwine in a union already, finally, at hand. Thus I am to you as you are to me, mine is yours and yours mine, I know you as you know me, you take pleasure with me as with you I take pleasure in the rejoicing of this reciprocal living – and identifying – together. In this cauldron of identification will melt, mingle, and melt again these reversing matrices of our last embraces.

But how to remember all this if the fire was so fierce, the current so strong as to remove all traces? If everything has become fire and water and nothing remains but a burning shimmer and flowing stream? If the brazier was so deep as to erase all memory of the path of touch that still guides us in our ecstatic transports? If nothing remains but/of an incandescent hearth that none can reach?

Unless this 'center' has also always been of glass/ice too. Mirror made of matter so fluid, so ethereal that it had already entered and mingled everywhere? What if matter had always, already, had a part but was yet invisible, beyond the senses, moving in ways alien to any fixed reflection. What if everything were already so intimately specularized that even in the depths of the abyss of the 'soul' a mirror awaited her reflection and her light. Thus I have become your image in this nothingness that I am, and you gaze upon mine in your absence of being. This silvering at the back of the mirror might, at least, retain *the being* (l'être) – which we have been perhaps and which perhaps we will be again – though our mirage has failed at present or has been covered over by alien speculations. A living mirror, thus, am I (to) your resemblance as you are mine. We are both singular and plural, one and ones, provided that nothing tarnishes the mirrors that fuse in the purity of their exchange. Provided that one, further-more, does not exceed the other in size and quality. For then the other would be absorbed in the One (as) to infinity.

When I look upon you in the secret of my 'soul', I seek (again) the loss of specularization, and try to bring my 'nature' back to its mirroring wholeness. And if 'God' had already appeared to me with face unveiled, so my body shines with a light of glory that radiates it. And my eyes have proved sharp enough to look upon that glory without blinking. They would have been seared had they not been that simple eye of the 'soul' that sets fire to what it ad-mires out of its hollow socket. A burning glass is the soul who in her cave joins with the source of light to set everything ablaze that approaches her hearth. Leaving only ashes there, only a hole: fathomless in her incendiary blaze.

Thus 'God' has created the soul to flare and flame in her desire. And if beyond this consummation He/she endures, it is because He/she is nothing but adoration of that warmth, passion for the hearth that none can appropriate, light suited to that lone mirror, *and* its virtual reduplication. *Or* again because this has been explained – by the theological, teleological imagination – as the mutual attrac-tion of the father and the son felt in a loving breast – thereby rescuing the 'soul' of man from being completely lost to that attraction. Man's identity in the hommologous, his reason in hommosexuality was preserved by the interpreta-tion. But such conceptions of the mind do not lead to 'God's' finest excesses. For 'God' goes beyond all representation, however schematic in its approximation. ⟨And perhaps He has chosen *her* body to inscribe His will, even if she is less able to read the inscription, poorer in language, 'crazier' in her speech, burdened with matter(s) that history has laid on her, shackled in/by speculative plans that paralyze her desire. Sometimes even the 'soul,' in a kind of sensuality of reason, deprives her of tremendous good fortune by leaving her in ignorance of the extremes of jouissance. Her 'soul' is at fault vis-à-vis the body because, in its elevation and revelation of her, it seems not to have understood that physical ills are always an obstacle to the highest good. That the delicacy and sensitivity of the 'body' have great importance, that the division of the 'heart' of man is the fault, the crack, in which love is lost in controversies that merely scratch the surface of the problem.⟩

But the path she follows to bring together and revive this wide, wild, unwary space that she is (on) earth will be more savage and cruel than if she could simply fall back right now upon a 'soul' that was a kind of cocoon, swathing the most secret self and folded over the specula(riza)tion of its source. But she is still darkness to herself through and through, nor does she understand the world surrounding her. In this undifferentiated blindness she will be able to achieve distinctness only by a certain number of cuts, severings. She gives herself up to 'others' only after she has effected this separation from everyone and from her habits, in which pain enables her to feel herself again and to gather her strength. This strength soon becomes exalted in such a flood of potency that she is taken to be possessed. Therefore she is condemned by confessors or inexperienced voyeurs who are horrified to see or hear her fall stricken to the ground, toss and turn, shriek, grunt, groan convulsively, stiffen, and then fall into a strange sleep. They are scandalized or anxious at the idea of her striking herself so terribly, thrusting sharp points into her stomach, burning her body to put out the fire of lust, searing her whole frame, using these extreme actions both to calm and to arouse her sleeping passions. The explosion of these passions strikes whoever witnesses them dumb. In their apollonian wisdom, witnesses are persuaded to try any devilry that will drive back these furies, which now she can no longer contain. Hiding them one moment, flaunting them the next. Intending to keep them secret, not able to do so always, or anymore, when these violent attacks go through her, though alien to her. Sometimes they shake her, at other times they leave her prostrate, pale, like a dead woman. Stretched out, once again, (on) the ground. In the dark. Always without consciousness.

But a 'God' already draws near in these/her fainting states. What does it matter that all judge her mad if the 'prince of the world' has noticed her and if henceforward he will be her companion in solitude. She awakes full of joy, only to fall back into new torments. For how, in one's unworthiness, can one keep doubt at bay? How could 'God' reveal himself in all his magnificence and waste his substance on/in so weak and vile a creature as woman? She has so often been humiliated, and every particle in her being seems but decay and infection. *Waste, refuse, matter.* Thus she will abase herself over and again in order to experience this love that claimed to be hers, and pass again through those imaginings that forbid her to respond. She takes on the most slavish tasks, affects the most shameful and degrading behavior so as to force the disdain that is felt toward her, that she feels toward herself. And perhaps, at the bottom of the pit, she finds her purity again. In this way, the blood, the sores, the pus that others clean away and she absorbs will wash her clean of all stain. She is pure at last because she has pushed to extremes the repetition of this abjection, this revulsion, this horror to which she has been condemned, to which, mimetically, she had condemned herself. She is chaste because she has faced the worse perversions, has prostituted herself to the most disgusting acts, the most filthy and excessive whims. She has been redeemed in all her purity within this absence of all representations of her that now obtains, in this void, empty even of repulsion, this nothingness of soul that she knows herself to be. And she has left the others behind, disconcerted, unable to follow her that far. Unable to go and see.

And if 'God,' who has thus re-proved the fact of her non-value, still loves her, this means that she exists all the same, beyond what anyone may think of her. It means that love conquers everything that has already been said. And that one man, at least, has understood her so well that he died in the most awful suffering. That most female of men, the Son.

And she never ceases to look upon his nakedness, open for all to see, upon the gashes in his virgin flesh, at the wounds from the nails that pierce his body as he hangs there, in his passion and abandonment. And she is overwhelmed with love of him/herself. In his crucifixion he opens up a path of redemption to her in her fallen state.

Could it be true that not every wound need remain secret, that not every laceration was shameful? Could a sore be *holy*? Ecstasy is there in that glorious slit where she curls up as if in her nest, where she rests as if she had found her home – and He is also in her. She bathes in a blood that flows over her, hot and purifying. And what she discovers in this divine passion, she neither can nor will translate. At last, she has been authorized to remain silent, hidden from prying eyes in the intimacy of this exchange where she *sees* (herself as) what she will be unable to express. Where she sees nothing and where she sees everything. She is closed over this mystery where the love placed within her is hidden, revealing itself in this secret of desire. In this way, you see me and I see you, finally I see myself seeing you in this fathomless wound which is the source of our wondering comprehension and exhilaration. And to know myself I scarcely need a 'soul,' I have only to gaze upon the gaping space in your loving body. Any other instrument, any hint, even, of theory, pulls me away from myself by pulling open – and sewing up – unnaturally the lips of that slit where I recognize myself, by touching myself there (almost) directly.

And in the rapturous vision of the place of your joyous expansion and mortal ecstasy, *a lightning flash has lit up the sleeping understanding within me.* Resisting all knowledge that would not find its/my sense in this abyss. Now I know it/myself and by knowing, I love it/myself and by loving, I desire it/myself. And if in the sight of the nails and the spear piercing the body of the Son I drink in a joy that no word can ever express, let no one conclude hastily that I take pleasure in his sufferings. But if the Word was made flesh in this way, and to this extent, it can only have been to make me (become) God in my jouissance, which can at last be recognized. Now the abyss opens down into my own self, and I am no longer cut in two opposing directions of sheer elevation to the sky and sheer fall into the depths. I know, now, that both height and depth spawn – and slit – each other in(de)finitely. And that the one is in the other, and the other in me, matters little since it is in me that they are created in rapture. *Outside of all self-as-same.* Never the same, always new. Never repeated or repeatable in their transports of joy which can never be counted or determined by measurement. Indeed they are (or it is) eternal because immense. Mystery, me-hysteria, without determinable end or beginning. More intimate than the 'soul' even. Crypt for the reciprocal sharing of the abyss between 'her' and God. Into which she will have to (re)descend in order to find, at last, the quietude and rest in herself-God. She is transformed into Him in her love: this is the secret of their exchange. In her and/ or outside her, as, in her jouissance, she loses all sense of corporeal boundary. Her distance from herself is all the greater because the fire was more deeply 'inward.' Because the deepest summit of her cave has been touched. Her remoteness in ecstasy, the flights of her soul, are all the greater because they reach further into that absence of soul that she is.

How strange is the economy of this specula(riza)tion of woman, who in her mirror seems ever to refer back to a transcendence. Who moves away (for) who comes near, who groans to be separated from the one who holds her closest in his embrace. But who also calls for the dart which, while piercing through her body, will with the same stroke tear out her entails [sic].[2] Thus 'God' will prove to have been her best lover since he separates her from herself only by that space of her jouissance where she finds Him/herself. To infinity perhaps, but in the serenity of the spacing that is thus projected by/in her pleasure. At present that pleasure is still hemmed in by representations – however metaphysical – and by prescriptions – still ethically onto-theological – which determined it (and her) and thus limit their extension. And if she does not feel raped by God, even in her fantasies of rape, this is because He never restricts her orgasm, even [if] it is hysterical. Since He understands all its violence.

Thus (re)assured of the complicity of this all-powerful partner, they/she play(s) at courtship, kneeling in self-abasement at one moment, adorning themselves with gold and diamonds the next, touching, smelling, listening, seeing, embrac(s)ing each other, devouring, penetrating, entering, consuming, melting each other. She is trusting as a dove, arrogant as a queen, proud in her nakedness, bursting with the joy of such exchanges. Her divine companion never tires of praising her and encouraging her (auto)eroticism that has so miraculously been rediscovered. Her confessor will not always lend an approving ear to this, especially if he lacks experience in such things. But what does that matter, she knows that she can no longer be mistaken. It is enough to know that 'God' loves for her to live, and die.

And if someone were to object that, with the Good thus within her, she no longer needs to receive it, she would reply in her ateleological way, that, for her, the one doesn't rule out the other.

Notes

*   (The French title's economy and richness cannot be matched in English. Four elements are fused in LI's neologism: mysticism, hysteria, mystery, and the femaleness ['*la* mystérique'] fundamental to the previous three. – Tr.)

1   (For almost the next page the pronoun 'elle' is repeated, at increasing distance from its apparent antecedent 'l'âme.' Rather than adopting the conventional strategy of repeating the word 'soul' at judicious intervals and otherwise using 'it' and related forms, I have hypothesized that LI is not *naming* a specific entity but evolving something unnamed but essentially female, and I have therefore adopted the pronoun 'she' without further nouns. – Tr.)

2   (In her famous vision of the Flaming Heart, Saint Teresa of Avila wrote: 'I saw an angel close by me, on my left side, in bodily form. He was not large, but small of stature and most beautiful – his face burning, as if he were one of the highest angels, who seem to be all of fire. I saw in his hand a long spear of gold, and at the iron's point there seemed to be a little fire. He appeared to me to be thrusting it at times into my heart and to pierce my very entrails; when he drew it out, he seemed to draw them out also, and to leave me all on fire with a great love of God. The pain was so great that it made me moan, and yet so surpassing was the sweetness of this excessive pain that I could not wish to be rid of it. The soul is satisfied now with nothing less than God.' Quoted by Victoria Sackville-West in *The Eagle and the Dove* [London: Doubleday, 1944], p. 94. – Tr.)

Chapter 3

Divine Women

■   [Abridged] This extract from 'Divine Women' appears in French as 'Femmes divines' in *Sexes et parentés* (Minuit, 1987). The English translation was published in *Sexes and Genealogies*, translated by Gillian C. Gill (Columbia University Press, 1993).

Editors' introduction

ACCORDING TO IRIGARAY'S INDICTMENT of the history of Christianity, which constitutes the focus of this essay, the fundamental problem has been that God has always been conceived in accordance with the ideals of the masculine gender. Women, not having recourse to a divinised feminine, have had their identities dictated to them by the rule of man/God as other/Other. As virgin mother, or as property of the male, women have played a part in the proceedings, but have not been able to claim a fully autonomous identity or subjectivity.

In this essay, Irigaray argues that if women are ever to be accorded their due, they must first be able to conceive of God in their own image – according to the dimensions of their own gender. But what is needed is not a reinstallation of Goddess figures, archaic or newly imagined, nor a promulgation of new laws and demands. Instead, for Irigaray, the emphasis is on 'becoming divine'. This process, open to the infinite, would be a constant and creative endeavour. Though it entails a movement towards self-fulfilment, it is, nevertheless, an endless task, unlimited by the necessity of conforming to pre-ordained ideals.

Irigaray has been influenced by the work of Feuerbach, in particular *The Essence of Christianity*; however, where Feuerbach regards God as the expression of man's idealised projections, thus rendering his view vulnerable to atheistic appropriations, Irigaray moves in another direction.[1] Although fully sympathetic to the antipathy felt by many women towards this God in man's image, she believes that rather than banishing God altogether, it is necessary to re-envision God in a feminine mode.

For Irigaray, the process of constructing a feminine figure of God will be a deliberately conscious one – not simply an unconscious projection of unsatisfied feminine desires. She believes that women need to conceive of this God in the context of 'becoming', not 'being', with its fixed ontological properties. This emphasis on becoming opens up a space of intersubjective play, a place that allows for inner as well as external explorations, and a 'unity of instinct, heart and knowledge' (Irigaray 1993b: 67).

For Irigaray, an important part of the procedure will be a reclamation of the mother figure, so that woman is not simply identified with maternal qualities – specifically those aligned with the virgin-mother of Christianity. Women must also claim an affirmative genealogy – one that acknowledges the mother–daughter bond in a way that does not set daughter against mother in conflict, as in the oedipal script. For Irigaray, an immanent God can be present in this potentially divine relationship between mothers and daughters.

Thus, Irigaray does not ascribe any specific 'feminine' qualities to her divine. Instead, she focuses on a new mode of relationship – to oneself and to other women. This provides the opportunity for women to appreciate that their route to autonomy, their becoming divine, is not subject to transcendental norms, but is rather an incarnate process that affirms their experiences as women.

[. . .] Man is able to exist because God helps him to define his gender (*genre*), helps him orient his finiteness by reference to infinity. The revival of religious feeling can in fact be interpreted as the rampart man raises in defense of his very maleness.

To posit a gender, a God is necessary: *guaranteeing the infinite.*[2] Science does not have the capacity to be constantly positing the infinite of the finite. In fact it is little concerned with positing the finite of the infinite. Science makes limits by closing things off. Thereby banning becoming? Willfully? Or does science have no will? A science that has no subject assumes a theory or a vision of the world that has *no will*.

Are we able to go on living if we have no will? This seems impossible. We have to will. It is necessary, not for our morality, but for our life. It is the condition of our becoming. In order to will, we have to have a goal. The goal that is most valuable is to go on *becoming*, infinitely.

In order to become, it is essential to have a gender or an essence (consequently a sexuate essence) as horizon. Otherwise, becoming remains partial and subject to the subject. When we become parts or multiples without a future of our own this means simply that we are leaving it up to the other, or the Other of the other, to put us together.

To become means fulfilling the wholeness of what we are capable of being. Obviously, this road never ends. Are we more perfect than in the past? This is not certain. Could this be because woman has no gender through which she can become? And man, clearly, is able to complete his essence only if he claims to be separate as a *gender*. If he has no existence in his gender, he lacks his relation to the infinite and, in fact, to finiteness.

To avoid that finiteness, man has sought out a unique *male* God. God has been created out of man's gender. He scarcely sets limits within Himself and between Himself: He is father, son, spirit. Man has not allowed himself to be defined by another gender: the female. His unique God is assumed to correspond to the human race (*genre humain*), which we know is not neuter or neutral from the point of view of the difference of the sexes.

It is true that Christianity tells us that God is in three persons, three manifestations, and that the third stage of the manifestation occurs as *a wedding between the spirit and the bride*. Is this supposed to inaugurate the divine for, in, with women? The female?

Divinity is what we need to become free, autonomous, sovereign. No human subjectivity, no human society has ever been established without the help of the divine. There comes a time for destruction. But, before destruction is possible, God or the gods must exist.

If women have no God, they are unable either to communicate or commune with one another. They need, we need, an infinite if they are to share *a little*. Otherwise sharing implies fusion-confusion, division, and dislocation within themselves, among themselves. If I am unable to form a relationship with some horizon of accomplishment for my gender, I am unable to share while protecting my becoming.

Our theological tradition presents some difficulty as far as God in the feminine gender is concerned. There is no *woman* God, no female trinity: mother, daughter, spirit. This paralyzes the infinite of becoming a woman since she is fixed in the role of mother through whom the *son* of God is made flesh. The most influential representation of God in our culture over the last two thousand years has been a male trinitary God and a virgin mother: a mother of the son of God whose alliance with the father is given little consideration. Is she the wife? By what mediation? The spirit? Who is represented as an angel, a young man, or a bird? The virgin's relations with the Father always remain in the shadow. Just as the Father himself? Her relations with the spirit are presented a number of times: the annunciation and the Pentecost, at the very least. The angel (plus bird in the habitual iconography) and the fire would seemingly be the representatives or vehicles of the spirit.

Is the angel of the Annunciation an appearance of the Father (as well as of the spirit)? Coming to visit and announce the virgin's fertile condition. But the Father is not single. He is three. The virgin is alone of her sex. Without a daughter or love between them, without a way of becoming divine except through her son: God-man, without a divine bridegroom. Unless we have known only two stages in Western culture and the third, the stage of the spirit and the wedding with the bride, has yet to come.

Would this correspond to what the astrologers announce as the stage of science? Which stage? And this era is prefigured or prophesied in the Old and the New Testament.

If this were the case, women would have some reason to be interested in religion, in science, in the relations between them, since women are represented as receivers of the spirit and not just as rather malformed monsters: manifestations of the eras of transition, between this incarnation and some other.

The love of God has often been a haven for women. They are the guardians of the religious tradition. Certain women mystics have been among those rare women to achieve real social influence, notably in politics.

Religion marks the place of the absolute *for us*, its path, the hope of its fulfillment. All too often that fulfillment has been postponed or transferred to some transcendental time and place. It has not been interpreted as the infinite that resides within us and among us, the god in us, the Other for us, becoming with and in us – as yet manifest only through his creation (the Father), present in his form (the son), mediator between the two (spirit). Here the capital letter designates the horizon of fulfillment of a gender, not a transcendent entity that exists outside becoming.

This God, are we capable of imagining it as a woman? Can we dimly see it as the perfection of our subjectivity? Which assumes respect for these two dimensions: the nocturnal-internal dimension of motherhood, whose threshold is closed during gestation and opened (too wide?) for and after birthing; the dimension between darkness and light occupied by the female, whose threshold is always half open, in-finite. The becoming of women is never over and done with, is always in gestation. A woman's subjectivity must accommodate the dimensions of mother and lover as well as the union between the two.

Our tradition presents and represents the radiant glory of the mother, but rarely shows us a fulfilled woman. And it forces us to make murderous choices: either mother (given that a *boy* child is what makes us truly mothers) or woman (prostitute and property of the male). We have no female trinity. But, as long as woman lacks a divine made in her image she cannot establish her subjectivity or achieve a goal of her own. She lacks an ideal that would be her goal or path in becoming. Woman scatters and becomes an agent of destruction and annihilation because she has no other of her own that she can become.

The (male) ideal other has been imposed upon women by men. Man is supposedly woman's more perfect other, her model, her essence. The most human and the most divine goal woman can conceive is to become *man*. If she is to become woman, if she is to accomplish her female subjectivity, woman needs a god who is a figure for the perfection of *her* subjectivity.

The impotence, the formlessness, the deformity associated with women, the way they are equated with something other than the human and split between the human and the inhuman (half-woman, half-animal), their duty to be adorned, masked, and made up, etc., rather than being allowed *their own* physical, bodily beauty, their own skin, their own form(s), all this is symptomatic of the fact that women lack a female god who can open up the perspective in which *their* flesh can be transfigured.

The only diabolical thing about women is their lack of a God and the fact that, deprived of God, they are forced to comply with models that do not match them, that exile, double, mask them, cut them off from themselves and from one another, stripping away their ability to move forward into love, art, thought, toward their ideal and divine fulfillment. [. . .]

'God is the mirror of man' (Feuerbach, p. 63). Woman has no mirror wherewith to become woman. Having a God and becoming one's gender go hand in hand. God is the other that we absolutely cannot be without. In order to *become*, we need some shadowy perception of achievement; not a fixed objective, not a One postulated to be immutable but rather a cohesion and a horizon that assures us the passage between past and future, the bridge of a present *that remembers*, that is not sheer oblivion and loss, not a crumbling away of existence, a failure, simply, to take note.

A *female* god is still to come. We are not purely redeeming spirits, not pure flesh, not a veil for the wisdom of the world, not mere mothers, not mere devils . . . All these predicates speak to something of us, often of us as we are seen by men and as men need us to be.

How is our God to be imagined? Or is it our god? Do we possess a quality that can reverse the predicate to the subject, as Feuerbach does for *God* and *man* in the analysis of *The Essence of Christianity*? If there is no one quality, which of the many would we choose to conceive our becoming perfect women? This is not a luxury but a *necessity*, the need for a finalized, theoretical, and practical activity that would be both speculative and moral. Every man (according to Feuerbach) and every woman who is not fated to remain a slave to the logic of the essence of man, must imagine a God, an objective–subjective place or path whereby the self could be coalesced in space and time: unity of instinct, heart, and knowledge, unity of nature and spirit, condition for the abode and for saintliness. God alone can save us, keep us safe. The feeling or experience of a positive, objective, glorious existence, the feeling of subjectivity, is essential for us. Just like a God who helps us and leads us in the path of becoming, who keeps track of our limits and our infinite possibilities – as women – who inspires our projects. These might include not just *opposition to, criticism of* but also *positing new values* that would essentially be divine. To have a goal is essentially a religious move (according to Feuerbach's analysis). Only the religious, within and without us, is fundamental enough to allow us to discover, affirm, achieve certain *ends* (without being locked up in the prison of effect – or effects). Our goal has always come to us women from outside: from man, child, city. We have failed to place our goal *inside as well as outside ourselves*, failed to love, failed to *will* ourselves and one another. Because this can only be a divine project. God conceives and loves himself. That part of God has always been denied us. Thus we women have become weak, formless, insecure, aggressive, devoted to the other because unaware of ourselves, submissive to the other because we were unable to establish our own order. If we are not to obey the other, we have to set a goal of our own, make our own law or laws. If we are to escape slavery it is not enough to destroy the master. Only the divine offers us freedom – enjoins it upon us. Only a God constitutes a rallying point for us that can let us free – nothing else. These words are but a statement of *reason*. So far it requires no faith other than the faith in the possibility of our autonomy, our salvation, of a love that would not just redeem but glorify us in full self-awareness: thought directed at the self and for the self that is free to love but not obliged.

To be capable of autonomy, to be capable of our God (still in the darkness, already made flesh, mediation between), is this not the test women must undergo if we are to become what we are and realize in a different mode our individual and collective task? Community means only dependence as long as each man, each woman, is not free and sovereign. Love of other without love of self, without love of God, implies the submission of the female one, the other, and of the whole of the social body.

No one has truly taught us love of God. Only love of neighbor. But how can one love one's neighbor without loving God? This is no more than a moralism of guilt, impossible to sustain, a kind of egotism or even death. Certain social doctrines, certain political regimes have already shown us how difficult it is to 'love one's neighbor' without loving God. The obstacle is also an economic one. Men seem to lack the generosity to care for the good of others before caring for their own. God is man's good and his goods. Love of neighbor is an ethical consequence of becoming divine. To claim that man is capable of caring about his neighbor's good, careless of his own, seems an idealist and utopic hypothesis that brings in its wake physical and psychic misery, the decline of the mother-earth culture, and of the values of speech and spiritual autonomy.

Love of God has nothing moral in and of itself. It merely shows the way. It is the incentive for a more perfect becoming. It marks the horizon between the more past and the more future, the more passive and the more active – permanent and always in tension. God forces us to do nothing except *become*. The only task, the only obligation laid upon us is: to become divine men and women, to become perfectly, to refuse to allow parts of ourselves to shrivel and die that have the potential for growth and fulfillment.

And in this we still resemble plants. We climb toward God and remain in Him, without killing the mother earth where our roots lie, without denying the sky either. Rooted in the earth, fed by rain and spring waters, we grow and flourish in the air, thanks to the light from the sky, the warmth of the sun.

There is no *individual law* that concerns divine becoming, no *collective law* passed down to the race of woman. . . . But, if we do not have that – divine – perspective we – as divine – cannot incarnate our gender or make a race.

Can the word *woman* be subject? predicate? If it can be neither one nor the other, what status does the word have in discourse? The status of 'women' as indeterminate plural, as obscure part of the human race. Must we assume that man is 'women' (one + one + one . . .) *plus* a penis? or that God is 'women' (all women), *plus* something that fences in the infinite: a difficult figuration of a relation men have to their penis or their gender? Since only man and God are subjects.

This 'women' would amount to a kind of chaotic, amorphous, archaic multiple which, if it is ever to achieve a form, needs some representation of unity to be imposed upon it. 'Women' would be like the soup, the clay, the earth and blood, the water, the ocean, out of which man emerges as man, and God as God. Woman, the one, single, *unique*, would at best be viewed as a place of procreation or of partition into objects of seduction.

If there is ever to be a consciousness of self in the female camp, each woman will have to situate herself freely in relation to herself, not just in relation to the community, the couple, the family. Feuerbach writes that without the woman-mother (but he seems to take little account of the difference between woman and mother, hence there is no correspondence with a possible state of identity for the woman as woman) there is no God. The mother of God is the keystone of theology, of the Father–son–spirit relationship. Without the mother of God, there can be no God. And Feuerbach adds that Protestants, who have done away with the mother of God – she who gives birth to the Lord as flesh – should logically have renounced God purely and simply: 'Where faith in the Mother of God sinks, there also sinks faith in the Son of God, and in God as the Father. The Father is a truth only where the Mother is a truth. Love is in and by itself essentially feminine in its nature. The belief in the love of God is the belief in the feminine principle as divine. Love apart from living nature is an anomaly, a phantom. Behold in love the holy necessity and depth of Nature' (*The Essence of Christianity*, p. 72). [. . .]

We women, sexed according to our gender, lack a God to share, a word to share and to become. Defined as the often dark, even occult mother-substance of the word of men, we are in need of our *subject*, our *substantive*, our *word*, our *predicates*: our elementary sentence, our basic rhythm, our morphological identity, our generic incarnation, our genealogy.

To be the term of the other is nothing enviable. It paralyzes us in our becoming. As divinity or goddess of and for man, we are deprived of our own ends and means. It is essential that we be God *for ourselves* so that we can be divine for the other, not idols, fetishes, symbols that have already been outlined or determined (see *The Essence of Christianity*, p. 182). It is equally essential that we should be daughter-gods in the relationship with our mothers, and that we cease to hate our mothers in order to enter into submissiveness to the father-husband. We cannot love if we have no memory of a native passiveness in our relation to our mothers, of our primitive attachment to her, and hers to us.

Current theory, even theological theory, makes women out to be monsters of hatred and thus makes us submit to an existing order. Does respect for God made flesh not imply that we should incarnate God within us and in our sex: daughter–woman–mother? Yet this duty is never imposed upon us – quite the contrary. What a strange error in human ethics! By our culture, our religion.

This error is protracted and encouraged by the spiritual technicians: the psychologists, psychoanalysts, etc. And yet, without the possibility that God might be made flesh as a woman, through the mother and the daughter, and in their relationships, no real constructive help can be offered to a woman. If the divine is absent in woman, and among women, there can be no possibility of changing, converting her primary affects.

The God we know, the gods we have known for centuries, are men; they show and hide the different aspects of man. He (they) do(es) not represent the qualities or predicates of the *female* made God. Which explains, perhaps, why *women who have grown used to the God/s of men will have no more to do with Him/them* (as men do?) and are ready to give up their own divinity. They renounce the path of becoming or being women. For how can that goal, that project, be sustained without a divine that marks or establishes its realization, that figures its incarnation, its mediations?

When women get bogged down in their search for freedom, for liberation, there seem to be many themes: the absence of a God of their own and inadequate management of the symbolic. The two things are linked and necessary to the constitution of an identity and a community. Many women have made or are making great efforts to fall back under the thrall of the phallocratic and patriarchal monopoly on values. They lack, we still lack, the affirmation and definition of values *of our own*, values often condemned by women themselves, even in dealings with other women. This leaves us in our infancy, in our bondage, slaves to male paradigms and to the archaic powers and fears of elementary struggles for life that are divided between submission to a technical imperialism alien to us and regression to *magical* thinking.

According to this world, these worlds, female identity always comes down to empirical parameters that prevent a woman, and the world of women, from getting them*selves* together as a unit. The sexual–familial dimension remains one of these parameters. 'Are you a virgin?' 'Are you married?' 'Who is your husband?' 'Do you have any children?' these are the questions always asked, which allow us to place a woman. She is constituted from outside in relation to a social *function*, instead of to a female identity and autonomy. Fenced in by these functions, how can a woman maintain a margin of singleness for herself, a non-determinism that would allow her to become and remain herself? This margin of freedom and potency (*puissance*) that gives us the authority yet to grow, to affirm and fulfill ourselves as individuals and members of a community, can be ours only if a God in the feminine gender can define it and keep it for us. As an other that we have yet to make actual, as a region of life, strength, imagination, creation, which exists for us both within and beyond, as our possibility of a present and a future.

Is not God the name and the place that holds the promise of a new chapter in history and that also denies this can happen? Still invisible? Still to be discovered? To be incarnated? Archi-ancient and forever future.

Notes

1   Feuerbach references from *The Essence of Christianity*, Ludwig Feuerbach, transl. George Eliot (New York: Harper Torchbooks, 1957) [eds].

2   This interpretation of the 'essence of man' and of the difference between man and animal is developed by Feuerbach in *The Essence of Christianity*, especially in the introduction. Readers interested in an exact understanding of 'Divine Women' should refer to this essay.

Chapter 4

When the Gods Are Born

■ [Abridged] This extract from 'When the Gods Are Born' originally appeared as part of the third section of *Amante marine de Friedrich Nietzsche* (Minuit, 1980). The English version was published as *Marine Lover of Friedrich Nietzsche*, translated by Gillian C. Gill (Columbia University Press, 1991).

Editors' introduction

IN THE BOOK FROM which these extracts are taken, Irigaray engages in an extended poetic conversation with Nietzsche. She takes the role of lover (*amante*, a feminine subject who is contrasted with *aimée*, the passive object of desire) in order both to appreciate and to go beyond some major themes in Nietzsche's work. She argues, in the first two sections of the book, that water is the element most foreign to Nietzsche's thought, and that in his preference for lofty mountain air over oceanic depths he reveals an unwillingness to engage with or be affected by the otherness of feminine difference. In so doing – and in spite of his powerful critique of the foundations of Western metaphysics – Nietzsche remains, for Irigaray, trapped within the economy of sameness that has marked Western thought since Plato.

In passages included here, Irigaray turns her attention specifically to Nietzsche's well-known criticisms of Christianity, in order to question his view that Christianity represents a slave morality. While Irigaray herself is critical of traditional Christian thought, and especially of its tendency, both before and after Kant, to be reduced to legalistic moralising, she nevertheless asserts the possibility of a Christianity that would be otherwise, that would affirm the multiple becomings inherent in a true theology of incarnation. Towards this end, her reading of Nietzsche emphasises the place of the body in his thought, and, as in all of Irigaray's projects, the body is first and foremost a sexed body.

In the opening sections of 'When the Gods Are Born' (not excerpted here), Irigaray re-examines the birth of male gods and sons in Greek mythology – specifically the figures of Dionysus and Apollo, with whom Nietzsche was so fascinated – in order to show how the emerging male gods of patriarchy took upon themselves the maternal function in order to erase the role of woman as mother, as the source of all embodied life. In the following passages, she argues that the place of Christ in Christian doctrine also supports this usurping of maternal–feminine difference. In spite of the importance accorded to the notion of incarnation in Christian thought, Irigaray suggests, the exclusive emphasis on the Father–Son relationship pre-empts female maternity, effectively denying the value of embodied life and placing it in the service of a transcendent Father-God who demands that flesh be sacrificed to spirit.

In place of this tragic sacrifice, Irigaray offers the possibility of another doctrine of incarnation, one that recognises and affirms the significance of female maternity. In place of a Christ envisioned as the legislating and judging ambassador of the God of ontotheology, she presents the reader with the figure of Mary, understood here as the power of divinity to truly inhabit flesh. The divinised flesh of Mary represents a god who approaches humanity not with the violent eroticism of Dionysus, nor with the Christian denial of the erotic, but with a reciprocal love that leaves both partners free and separate – autonomous.

Irigaray closes this text with the claim that Nietzsche recapitulates the Christian sacrifice of the body, his forceful critique of Christianity notwithstanding. In his drive to overcome everything, she suggests, he destroys genuine difference, reducing any possible otherness to a mirroring of his sameness. For Irigaray, finally, the Nietzschean tragedy – like the tragedy of traditional Christian thought – lies in its preference for a transcendent idea(l) instead of an embodied, and therefore sexed, life.

The crucified one

Epistle to the last Christians

The son of Man is born in Bethlehem of Judaea, in a poor stable. He is brought into the world by a teenage virgin pregnant by the Holy Spirit. Begotten not made. In Mary, the word was made flesh. And God came among us.

This mysterious conception leads, first of all, to the repudiation of the woman in which it takes place. And then, as soon as the child of this miraculous event is born, he will risk being massacred by the king. Were it not for the intervention of the angels and of dreams, he would not have received life, or would not long have survived. And this son of the Word will enter into his glory only when he has suffered crucifixion and death.

How is this story to be interpreted? This testamentary narrative? This new pattern of relations between God and men? This Christic symbol that dominates the Christian era?

'The Word was made flesh and dwelt among us, and we beheld his glory, the glory as of the only begotten son of the father, full of grace and truth.' (The Gospel of St. John, 1:14, in the King James Bible).

Word made flesh – does this mean it has come into a body that is forever separate from others, and from the whole of the universe? And that it will find communion with the whole and within the unique only through the sacrifice of his person to the Father? Must the individual be immolated if unity with God is to be achieved once more?

The coming of Christ, following on the time of Apollo, would seem to destroy the illusion of a life without horror. Open up the wound at man's heart. Claiming, as potential redemption, that passion and death can lead to the Kingdom.

The Christ thus makes manifest a new way to overcome the pain of living. Instead of the rapture of cosmic fusion invoked by Dionysos, he asks man to look to the resurrection through participation in the glory of the Father. Dionysos, that slightly recalcitrant son of Zeus, sings, dances, draws every thing, every man, every woman into the orgy of a return to a primitive mother-nature. Apollo casts a spell over men through the oracle of the God of gods, leading them away from the original intoxication, toward another illumination, another cadence, another rhythm, a tempo that checks excessive outbursts, hinders regression into the infinite of the relationship to nature, masking his approach with dreams that simulate nature, thus maintaining a distance from the whole and between all men, wrapping each man in the beauty of his pose, the appearance of a proper skin.

The Christ would open up the walls of this tomb. Not toward the depths of the earth but toward the abysses of Heaven, not through or for the mother's passion, but by identification with the Father's Word. He would go from the Father to the Father, without a backward look at his birth into the body. Bridge between Life and Life, tying the end to itself, without beginning. Coming from On High, and returning there. Ring or wedding band that seems a new link to the earth, here below, but no longer marries/makes merry (ne fait plus la noce) with simple living beings – the dead. He comes from the Father. To the Father he aspires. Toward the Father he walks and never falters. By the Father alone he fears to be forsaken. Showing the path to be followed if one is to obtain transfiguration, resurrection, ascension – become the Father's Word, and accept agony and crucifixion as passages from incarnation into eternal life.

This is the most common interpretation, and in general the values of sin and redemption it espouses have formed the basis of Christian ethics. This Christic model consecrates an historic stage where man stands between nature and God, flesh and Word, body and speech. Moment in which man constitutes himself in boundless allegiance to the Father's will, and in which the attraction of the original mother, wife, sister, mistress disappears, even as enchanting reflections.

Not that women are absent from the evangelists' path. But they appear there as virgins or repentant sinners. Softer, more submissive than the mother of Apollo, they listen to the Lord's word, and it is enough to fill their cup with joy. Are they nothing but ears? With just a bit of mouth, eyes, and as much hand and leg as is needed to reach out and follow after Him. They seek Him, not He them. If He does occasionally take notice of them, it is out of his infinite benevolence, neither needed nor earned. Sex is virtually absent from their meetings, except for a few confessions or avowals of morbid symptoms. He listens, but does not marry/make merry with women, for already he is bound to his heavenly Father. At best, he takes part in some symbolic union that ignores, or defers to a time after death, the fulfillment of carnal exchange. [. . .]

Et incarnatus est. Must this coming be univocally understood as a redemptory submission of the flesh to the Word? Or else: as the Word's faithfulness to the flesh? With the penetration of the word into a body still recalling and summoning the entry of that body into a word. Exit from the tombs. Access to a beyond here now. Passage from body-corpses to a saying that transfigures them – pulls them out of the walls of their death. Crossing their own frontiers in a meeting with the flesh of the other. Living, if she speaks. She too incarnating the divine.

Et incarnatus est manifesting a different relationship between flesh and word. Approach into a touch that no longer drains bodies of their animation by the saying of them – either in acts or in words. Bonds in which human and divine are wedded.

And not just people gathering around some 'Good News' which they expect will be repeated in the Parousia. Can the people hear its prophet or prophets? Heeding only the signs handed down in a testamentary Scripture. That proclaims or attests the Truth of the letter. Accomplishing the rites prescribed by the text. Mimicking the gestures the Lord is reported to have made. Each man striving to be like Him, in order to be pleasing to the Father. To become Him, in order to live again in God. Each man like Him and like his fellow – all united in one mystic body? Excess or dearth to the communion of the flesh? Effusion into something that, here, cannot be shared? Or offering 'in God' of a bonus born of the exchange that has been made? Action of assistance to a people in exile? Or place for the projection of the supplement of power for something that cannot be realized at the time? Both? In that case, what is referred to as 'God' has nothing to forbid. The more his people live, the more 'He' exists. And his glory would demand merely that life increase. [. . .]

When are we to have an 'Annunciation,' an 'Advent,' a 'Christmas' in which 'Mary' is conceived and anticipated as a divine manifestation? Meaningless phrases? In part. But . . . According to Christianity, God is found only in Distance, the relationship to the Father only takes place at a remove and in the respect for separation. God – the Different, who is encountered only through death and resurrection.

And what if, for Mary, the divine occurred only near at hand? So near that it thereby becomes unnameable. Which is not to say that it is nothing. But rather the coming of a reality that is alien to any already-existing identity. Relationship within a more mysterical place than any proximity that can be localized. An effusion that goes beyond and stops short of any skin that has been closed back on itself. The deepest depths of the flesh, touched, birthed, and without a wound.

This divine is still to be revealed. Which doesn't mean it can never be expressed. But it is always aborted as soon as announced. Never expected or recognized in its coming into the world. Its incarnation. Which surpasses the limits of individuation – and without a wound or an abyss. Except in the idea that man creates of it for himself and imposes. When he imagines a virgin-mother conceiving by the Holy Spirit so that in her neither the uniqueness of a living cosmic dwelling nor the infiniteness of woman's jouissance should deprive the Father of his Will and of his Heaven.

But what is meant by the spirit? What is Mary listening to in the message of the angel? Only the Word of the Father? Or is she heedful of the universe that bears her, of a heaven and an earth that have always been and are still virgin of culture? And that, going beyond and falling short of the word, make its engendering possible. Woman–mother consubstantial with a nature by which the word is nourished and fostered. Since her sexuate body never separates from the place where it has place. Never is she folded back upon herself, except when the figures and names that encrypt her are laid down. Always in communion with the *cosmos* which she lives in and which lives in her, and shelters in her. Cradle of infancy in which what remains to be revealed can be sown, can germinate and come into the world. Some word still to be incarnated, perhaps?

Hers is a divine that does not need to erect any capital letter. Hers an omni-presence that pertains to no Person. Creeping through the mesh of any code of law, the nets of institutions, the organization of Churches. That uproot her from her most living source of inspiration. By assigning her a place in the religious scenario. As a receptive-passive female extra, not as a divine source. Flesh that has already become word beyond any locatable figure. The holy spirit? [. . .]

Whether on the far side or the near side of any Christian tradition, does not the Christ – second son of Adam, innocent son of the Father – manifest the tragic destiny of love and desire imprisoned in a single body? Seeking to express themselves through all the senses, and in the end being crucified – on the level of touch. That mediatory sense par excellence. The sense that, most darkly, overcomes the distances between, the enclosure within distinct forms, the borders dividing up territories and private estates. Sense that gets through the walls of the tomb where the flesh lies captive. Sepulcher of stone, ice, dream or letter – an impermeable skin that shuts each man up within the boundaries of his death. A necessary perspective, no doubt, but one which, again and again, could open up to permit an ever renewed becoming. In which the limit of each man was respected but which allowed access to something more than individuation, to an exchange with the other in his/her difference.

'The very word Christianity rests upon a misunderstanding; basically there has only been one Christian, and he died on the cross. The "Gospel" died on the cross.' (Antichrist, sec. 39). The 'Good News' was crucified as it was heralded. In order to fulfill the will of the Father? or because it could not be received. Do these two interpretations still and forever amount to the same thing?

What is the meaning of the event of the incarnation which follows upon the metamorphoses of God's presence recorded in the Jewish tradition, and the decadent triumph of measured restraint in Greek culture? What does it mean that the word is made flesh? Why does its prophecy have such a wide influence? And, despite all the well-known horrors and repressions, how do we account for all the works of art which that prophecy gave rise to? What energy let them root and flourish, through the centuries, as places where the divine lives and breathes? Can the legalism, the sentence, even the ressentiment of Christianity claim and take credit for the enthusiasm and exuberance of that creation? Or does the inspiration blossom despite and in opposition to all moralizing? And can that creative strength be reduced to the power of the love between son and father, that matrix for idealism, with the virgin-mother as its sensory-substrate? Are the desire and the sharing of the flesh not at work here? Don't they sing here? Don't they paint? Sculpt? Speak? In a language that of course goes beyond and stops short of any grammar of reason. Cryptic, or mystic, in its language. In accordance with sketches, shapes, a graphic system, a symbolism that has no preestablished framework. Something always, and at each opportunity, heretical in the eyes of orthodoxy. Which condemns anything that does not obey the norm.

And therefore condemns Christ? Figure of love transgressing the limits of written history, law, letter. Reopening and circulating the flow of life despite all that captures, encloses, restrains life – tomb, mask, signs. But must he who breaks the seal of the letter suffer the penalty in return? Crucified for a word? Like a word? Or a symbol? Whereas – or just because – the use he made of it was intended as a parabolic approach. Never definitive, never completed. Never definitively plumbed in its meaning, perhaps, never wholly decoded? Revelation of something still to come that is looking for its figure? Its covenant?

Is this store any more understood or accepted, in its openness, than nature or women might have been for Dionysos? Wasn't it necessary to strike to find life there and make it spring forth? To kill, so that the women might rise from the dead? As if that movement of bloom and decay, of flowering and dying back, of death and resurrection were not already natural? And as if a recreation of a divine nature were necessary. A doubling of a movement already in place. A kind of recapitulation, of mimicry occurring in Heaven, that supposedly gives rise to everything. Or gives rise to everything again?

For example the child-god. Who is not even procreated in the womb of a mortal woman. Son of the Father conceived by the Word in a virgin. Immaculate in his conception, as she in hers. [. . .]

The word made flesh in Mary might mean – might it not? – the advent of a divine one who does not burst in violently, like the god of Greek desire, does not simply rule the world from a heaven of dreams, and does not remain closed in a text of law either. Neither bursts on the scene nor slips suddenly away, does not act to defer the possibility that the presence will occur. The god does not brutally enter a body, only to throw it off at once, leaving it to madness and the death of a boundless passion. He does not hide behind an unending series of appearances that ease the pain of living by giving mortals a chance to gaze upon an alien perfection. He is not made known only through writing.

He is made flesh. Continues on in the flesh. Closes with and is close to himself, from within a living body. That can be affected by *pathos* – his own and that of others.

This aspect of Christ is still to be discovered. After the unveiling of the figures who made him into the God of ontotheology: master of truth or of morality. Masks that are still made to the pattern of an idolatrous fiction. God constituted by the standard of men's desires at compromising periods of history. Man is called to yield, to grovel, to give the self up so as to find it again within an All-Powerfulness that has been forged according to an overabundance of passions paralyzed by fear, obedience, and ressentiment. Father created by man in his idea or his image. According to a model that today is doomed to decline.

But perhaps a certain kind of divine has never taken place, even though it has been heralded. One that has never been mummified in a single name, face, or figure. A single letter or law that has already been fetishized. One that is coming. That comes near in the flesh with a certain restraint. Not eternally deferring its coming, but expecting the expectation of the other before it presents itself, offers itself. Penetrates the other lovingly. Dwells in the other, without taking over. And receives, in return. [. . .]

Nietzsche – perhaps – has experienced and shown what is the result of infinite distance reabsorbed into the (male) same, shown the difference that remains without a face or countenance. By wishing to overcome everything, he plunges into the shadows – lit up and with no perspective. As he becomes the whole of the world's time, he has no point of view left that would allow him to see. Ariadne, or Diotima, or . . . no longer even return his mask or his gaze. He is mask and blinded eye. Once his creation is realized, he lives it. And nothing else. There is no other that might allow him to continue to make himself flesh. No other to set the limits of his corporeal identity with and for him, putting his latest thought into the background so a new one can be born.

The sacrifice he makes to the Idea is inscribed in this – that he preferred the Idea to an ever provisional openness to a female other. That he refused to break the mirror of the (male) same, and over and over again demanded that the other be his double. To the point of willing to become that female other. Despite all physiology, all incarnation. Hermit, tightrope walker or bird, forgetful of her who gave him birth and company and norishment [sic], he soars up, leaving everything below him or inside him, and the chasm becomes bottomless.

And what would Ariadne's or Diotima's or anyone else's 'yes' have changed? Nothing in his thinking. Unless a woman refuses to be a woman, at least according to his definition. Asserts her difference. Therefore not Ariadne, that abyss for his passion. An Apollonian partner? Setting him up once and for all as a work of art? Paralyzing him in his Dionysian becoming. Insoluble fate. Sensing the impotence to come, Nietzsche declares he is the crucified one. And is crucified. But by himself.

Either Christ overwhelms that tragedy, or Nietzsche overcomes Christ. By repeating-parodying the Christian advent, what does he unmask in his gesture? That Christ is nothing that still deserves to live, or that his age is yet to come?

This reevaluation is possible only if he goes beyond the Father–Son relationship. If he announces – beyond Christianity? – that only through difference can the incarnation unfold without murderous or suicidal passion. Rhythm and measure of a female other that, endlessly, undoes the autological circle of discourse, thwarts the eternal return of the same, opens up every horizon through the affirmation of another point of view whose fulfillment can never be predicted. That is always dangerous? A gay science of the incarnation?

To which the female side would, up to now, have served only as a protective shadow. Setting up perspective, through a kind of resistance to the already-existing light. Never desired or loved for herself, but forming a screen for the dazzling and blinding collusion of Father-son. A reminder that man comes from the earth-mother, that he returns to her, and that at each step a shadow walks by his side.

The will to leap over that shadow or to lend her light that does not suit her, amounts once again to belittling her as other. To entering into autistic madness. Making oneself the only God. If that Idol means the whole of love, then love always amounts to a murder – the murder of the other. Which remains a crime whether or not it is sublimated under a capital letter as Difference or Distance. Which consecrates crime. Glorifying it despite, or within, the sacrifice once more subsumed into the same. Thanks to the passion of the 'son' perhaps?

But doesn't his cross mark the impossibility of any relationship to the other? The love that ebbs backward into sameness, unable to either give or receive. To exchange or pattern oneself among different bodies, words, flesh? The lonely fading away of a gesture that was motivated also by the other? And plunges down into the abyss, rather than surrender.

Is the Crucified One the sign of such an economy of love and desire? To interpret him therefore means 'go beyond' if possible without return. Not be satisfied with such a love. Leave it to the men of ressentiment, and try to create another world.

And if it is another love that he heralds, then deliver him from his masks of death, and set him once more in his flesh. While trying not to kill him, one more time, with hatred, albeit veiled, of the law. A law that congeals an ideal figure of love. Sending that figure back to some hideaway in the Infinite does not wipe out its unique qualities. The idol keeps from falling. Never allows itself to be perceived as such. Remains, nonetheless, the only place of cathexis. Of aspiration that exhausts the whole of the breath. All the more alluring because eternally deferring the encounter. Promise of a something beyond death, in which life would leave the tombs behind at last, and enter into its glory.

Men – perhaps? – know no other way to the divine, even if some sense it nostalgically. The immediate coming of the god brings them nothing but madness or paralysis. And as they constantly back away from such a sudden experience of the divine, they measure up only to themselves, even in regard to their God. Measuring out the path that marks the boundary of their world. From hell to Heaven.

But this way they always stay within their limits. Anything set on either side of those limits is defined by them. Whether they know it or not, wish it or not.

They include in this circle the other of nature, by mimicking her, perfecting her artistically, that is certain. They operate by taking things over. God, the name given to the abyss in which nature is established and prevented from revealing herself. Only the world they create exists. Visible and invisible offered or withheld according to their will alone, their gaze alone. In which any nativity would germinate, to which it would return. In nativity man would still and always see only himself. Giving pictures and names only to his creatures.

A love that knows no other. Except as a foundation or shadow for an idea of self that never puts itself on display in a simple way. The other would be merely one of the masks of the same. One figure, one face, one sort of presence accompanying man's becoming. Sometimes tragic, sometimes serenely contemplative. Now dark with shadows, now beaming forth an excess of light as it waits to be disposed in new landscapes. In hollow, in lack or in excess, man would perceive and receive nothing except from his own eye.

The other has yet to enlighten him. To tell him something. Even to appear to him in her irreducibility. The impossibility of overcoming her. And if, to the whole of himself, he says 'yes' and also asks her to say 'yes' again, did it ever occur to him to say 'yes' to her? Did he ever open himself to that other world? For him it doesn't even exist. So who speaks of love, to the other, without having even begun to say 'yes'?

To 'go beyond.' Or decode the Christic symbol beyond any traditional morality. To read, in it, the fruit of the covenant between word and nature, between *logos* and *cosmos*. A marriage that has never been consummated and that the spirit, in Mary, would renew?

The spirit? Not, this time, the product of the love between Father and son, but the universe already made flesh or capable of becoming flesh, and remaining in excess to the existing world.

Grace that speaks silently through and beyond the word?

Chapter 5

Sexual Difference

■ [Abridged] This chapter first appeared in French as 'La Différence sexuelle' in *Éthique de la différence sexuelle* (Minuit, 1984). The English edition appears in *An Ethics of Sexual Difference*, translated by Carolyn Burke and Gillian C. Gill (Cornell University Press, 1993).

Editors' introduction

FOR IRIGARAY, SEXUAL DIFFERENCE is the most important problem of our age. It is an issue that needs to be revised and acted upon if women are to be accorded full recognition and respect in their own right, and regarded as having a distinct identity. This development has significant implications for any notion of the divine and particularly its realisation in human relationships.

According to Irigaray, the acknowledgement of sexual difference will entail a recasting of both philosophy and ethics – traditionally conceived of and applied according to the designs of men. Difference, historically understood as an oppositional or complementary characteristic, must be reconceived in order to affirm a generative exchange between two discrete entities. What is needed is a healing of the epistemological split between subject and object to be replaced by a new mode of relationship. This has significance not just for the mode of interaction between women and men, but also for that between human beings and the world or cosmos, between body and spirit, between space and time. Towards this end a place of mediation must be created, an interval that would allow for a free circulation between the two entities involved so that neither partner controls the other by imposing its own particular frame of reference. In this new correlation, another's difference is thus not thought of as a threat, but as providing a possibility for creative interaction. This mediatory space also enhances a mode of 'becoming', rather than the static notion of being – an emphasis which is central to Irigaray's thought.

One of the figures that Irigaray uses to represent this new mediatory mode of thinking and acting is the angel. For Irigaray, angels are in constant motion. They never allow the containers or envelopes of separate identities to remain closed in on themselves. The angel represents a constant passage from one to the other – a form of communication, of circulation, that focuses on the present and never anticipates an outcome. The angel also does not allow personal manipulations which promote self-sufficiency or finality. There always exists a remainder, rather than a neat closure, but, for Irigaray, this remainder is not to be assigned to a god-figure conceived of as an unknown or absolute being. 'God' should not be thought of as belonging to another order of reality, but needs to be appreciated as incarnate, as immanent in the new forms of relationship forged by an acknowledgement of difference. This difference, in turn, continually puts into question received assumptions regarding both god and relationships. Knowledge is no longer a product of epistemological structures, but inherent in a poetics of knowing.

Intrinsic to this new mode of relation, with its lack of preconceptions, is the primordial passion of wonder, which Irigaray adapts from Descartes. Wonder allows that each encounter be 'as if for the first time'. This openness leads to fecundity – the dynamic and creative aspect of a relationship. Irigaray also re-examines the symbolic significance of the progeny of relationships, suggesting that the child should no longer be seen as a symbol of the outcome of sexual union that justifies and completes the relationship. Rather, the relationship itself takes precedence as a vital source of life for each participant. When this occurs, desire is no longer a yearning for the unattainable, or the need to fulfil conventional romantic scripts. Aligned with wonder, desire, operating in a mediatory mode, permits the inception of a love that is divine. However, the divine here is no longer a male who presides over a dichotomous universe, but imbues all existence and is realised (or incarnated) in the love relationship of a man and a woman. Thus transcendence and immanence are no longer mutually exclusive, but are interactive aspects of a new ethics. This ethics of sexual difference recognises a new way of being, or rather, 'becoming', that is revolutionary in its appreciation of love and relationships – particularly as they support the integral and distinct role of women.

Sexual difference is one of the major philosophical issues, if not the issue, of our age. According to Heidegger, each age has one issue to think through, and one only. Sexual difference is probably the issue in our time which could be our 'salvation' if we thought it through.

But, whether I turn to philosophy, to science, or to religion, I find this underlying issue still cries out in vain for our attention. Think of it as an approach that would allow us to check the many forms that destruction takes in our world, to counteract a nihilism that merely affirms the reversal or the repetitive proliferation of status quo values – whether you call them the consumer society, the circularity of discourse, the more or less cancerous diseases of our age, the unreliability of words, the end of philosophy, religious despair or regression to religiosity, scientistic or technical imperialism that fails to consider the living subject.

Sexual difference would constitute the horizon of worlds more fecund than any known to date – at least in the West – and without reducing fecundity to the reproduction of bodies and flesh. For loving partners this would be a fecundity of birth and regeneration, but also the production of a new age of thought, art, poetry, and language: the creation of a new *poetics*.

Both in theory and in practice, everything resists the discovery and affirmation of such an advent or event. In theory, philosophy wants to be literature or rhetoric, wishing either to break with ontology or to regress to the ontological. Using the same ground and the same framework as 'first philosophy,' working toward its disintegration but without proposing any other goals that might assure new foundations and new works.

In politics, some overtures have been made to the world of women. But these overtures remain partial and local: some concessions have been made by those in power, but no new values have been established. Rarely have these measures been thought through and affirmed by women themselves, who consequently remain at the level of critical demands. Has a worldwide erosion of the gains won in women's struggles occurred because of the failure to lay foundations different from those on which the world of men is constructed? Psychoanalytic theory and therapy, the scenes of sexuality as such, are a long way from having effected their revolution. And with a few exceptions, sexual practice today is often divided between two parallel worlds: the world of men and the world of women. A nontraditional, fecund encounter between the sexes barely exists. It does not voice its demands publicly, except through certain kinds of silence and polemics.

A revolution in thought and ethics is needed if the work of sexual difference is to take place. We need to reinterpret everything concerning the relations between the subject and discourse, the subject and the world, the subject and the cosmic, the microcosmic and the macrocosmic. Everything, beginning with the way in which the subject has always been written in the masculine form, as *man*, even when it claimed to be universal or neutral. Despite the fact that *man* – at least in French – rather than being neutral, is sexed.

Man has been the subject of discourse, whether in theory, morality, or politics. And the gender of God, the guardian of every subject and every discourse, is always *masculine and paternal*, in the West. To women are left the so-called minor arts: cooking, knitting, embroidery, and sewing; and, in exceptional cases, poetry, painting, and music. Whatever their importance, these arts do not currently make the rules, at least not overtly.

Of course, we are witnessing a certain reversal of values: manual labor and art are being revalued. But the relation of these arts to sexual difference is never really thought through and properly apportioned. At best, it is related to the class struggle.

In order to make it possible to think through, and live, this difference, we must reconsider the whole problematic of *space* and *time*.

In the beginning there was space and the creation of space, as is said in all theogonies. The gods, God, first create *space*. And time is there, more or less in the service of space. On the first day, the first days, the gods, God, make a world by separating the elements. This world is then peopled, and a rhythm is established among its inhabitants. God would be time itself, lavishing or exteriorizing itself in its action in space, in places.

Philosophy then confirms the genealogy of the task of the gods or God. Time becomes the *interiority* of the subject itself, and space, its *exteriority* (this problematic is developed by Kant in the *Critique of Pure Reason*). The subject, the master of time, becomes the axis of the world's ordering, with its something beyond the moment and eternity: God. He effects the passage between time and space.

Which would be inverted in sexual difference? Where the feminine is experienced as space, but often with connotations of the abyss and night (God being space and light?), while the masculine is experienced as time.

The transition to a new age requires a change in our perception and conception of *space-time*, the *inhabiting of places*, and of *containers*, or *envelopes of identity*. It assumes and entails an evolution or a transformation of forms, of the relations of *matter* and *form* and of the interval *between*: the trilogy of the constitution of place. Each age inscribes a limit to this trinitary configuration: *matter*, *form*, *interval*, or *power* [*puissance*], *act*, *intermediary-interval*.

Desire occupies or designates the place of the *interval*. Giving it a permanent definition would amount to suppressing it as desire. Desire demands a sense of attraction: a change in the interval, the displacement of the subject or of the object in their relations of nearness or distance.

The transition to a new age comes at the same time as a change in the economy of desire. A new age signifies a different relation between:

- man and god(s),
- man and man,
- man and world,
- man and woman.

Our age, which is often thought to be one in which the problematic of desire has been brought forward, frequently theorizes this desire on the basis of observations of a moment of tension, or a moment in history, whereas desire ought to be thought of as a changing dynamic whose outlines can be described in the past, sometimes in the present, but never definitively predicted. [. . .]

To arrive at the constitution of an ethics of sexual difference, we must at least return to what is for Descartes the first passion: *wonder*. This passion has no opposite or contradiction and exists always as though for the first time. Thus man and woman, woman and man are always meeting as though for the first time because they cannot be substituted one for the other. I will never be in a man's place, never will a man be in mine. Whatever identifications are possible, one will never exactly occupy the place of the other – they are irreducible one to the other.

> *When the first encounter with some object surprises us, and we judge it to be new, or very different from what we formerly knew, or from what we supposed that it ought to be, that causes us to wonder and be surprised; and because that may happen before we in any way know whether this object is agreeable to us or is not so, it appears to me that wonder is the first of all the passions; and it has no opposite, because if the object which presents itself has nothing in it that surprises us, we are in nowise moved regarding it, and we consider it without passion.*
>
> (René Descartes, *The Passions of the Soul*, article 53)[1]

Who or what the other is, I never know. But the other who is forever unknowable is the one who differs from me sexually. This feeling of surprise, astonishment, and wonder in the face of the unknowable ought to be returned to its locus: that of sexual difference. The passions have either been repressed, stifled, or reduced, or reserved for God. Sometimes a space for wonder is left to works of art. But it is never found to reside in this locus: *between man and woman*. Into this place came attraction, greed, possession, consummation, disgust, and so on. But not that wonder which beholds what it sees always as if for the first time, never taking hold of the other as its object. It does not try to seize, possess, or reduce this object, but leaves it subjective, still free.

This has never existed between the sexes since wonder maintains their autonomy within their statutory difference, keeping a space of freedom and attraction between them, a possibility of separation and alliance.

This might take place at the time of the first meeting, even prior to the betrothal, and remain as a permanent proof of difference. The *interval* would never be *crossed*. Consummation would never take place, the idea itself being a delusion. One sex is not entirely consumable by the other. There is always a *remainder*.

Up until now this remainder has been entrusted to or reserved for *God*. Sometimes a portion was incarnated in the *child*. Or was thought of as being *neuter*. This neuter (in a different way, like the child or God?) suggests the possibility of an encounter but puts it off, deferring it until later, even when it is a question of a secondary revision [*après-coup*]. It always stays at an insurmountable distance, a respectful or deadly sort of no-man's-land:[2] no alliance is forged; nothing is celebrated. The immediacy of the encounter is annihilated or deferred to a future that never comes.

Of course, the neuter might signify an alchemical site of the sublimation of 'genitality', and the possibility of generation, of the creation of and between different genders and genres. But it would still have to be receptive to the advent of difference, and be understood as an anticipation from this side and not as a beyond, especially an ethical one. Generally the phrase *there is* upholds the present but defers celebration. There is not, there will not be the moment of wonder of the *wedding*, an ecstasy that remains *in-stant*.[3] The *there is* remains a present that may be subject to pressure by the god, but it does not form a foundation for the triumph of sexual fecundity. Only certain oriental traditions speak of the energizing, aesthetic, and religious fecundity of the sexual act: the two sexes give each other the seed of life and eternity, the growing generation of and between them both.

We must reexamine our own history thoroughly to understand why this sexual difference has not had its chance to develop, either empirically or transcendentally. Why it has failed to have its own ethics, aesthetic, logic, religion, or the micro- and macrocosmic realization of its coming into being or its destiny.

It is surely a question of the dissociation of body and soul, of sexuality and spirituality, of the lack of a passage for the spirit, for the god, between the inside and the outside, the outside and the inside, and of their distribution between the sexes in the sexual act. Everything is constructed in such a way that these realities remain separate, even opposed to one another. So that they neither mix, marry, nor form an alliance. Their wedding is always being put off to a beyond, a future life, or else devalued, felt and thought to be less worthy in comparison to the marriage between the mind and God in a transcendental realm where all ties to the world of sensation have been severed.

The consequences of the nonfulfillment of the sexual act remain, and there are many. To take up only the most beautiful, as yet to be made manifest in the realm of time and space, there are *angels*. These messengers who never remain enclosed in a place, who are also never immobile. Between God, as the perfectly immobile act, man, who is surrounded and enclosed by the world of his work, and woman, whose task would be to take care of nature and procreation, *angels* would circulate as mediators of that which has not yet happened, of what is still going to happen, of what is on the horizon. Endlessly reopening the enclosure of the universe, of universes, identities, the unfolding of actions, of history.

The angel is that which unceasingly *passes through the envelope(s)* or *container(s)*, goes from one side to the other, reworking every deadline, changing every decision, thwarting all repetition. Angels destroy the monstrous, that which hampers the possibility of a new age; they come to herald the arrival of a new birth, a new morning.

They are not unrelated to sex. There is of course Gabriel, the angel of the annunciation. But other angels announce the consummation of marriage, notably all the angels in the Apocalypse and many in the Old Testament. As if the angel were a representation of a sexuality that has never been incarnated. A light, divine gesture (or tale) of flesh that has not yet acted or flourished. Always fallen or still awaiting parousia. The fate of a love still torn between here and elsewhere. The work of a love that is the original sinner, since the first garden, the lost earthly paradise? The fate of all flesh which is, moreover, attributable to God![4]

These swift angelic messengers, who transgress all enclosures in their speed, tell of the passage between the envelope of God and that of the world as micro- or macrocosm. They proclaim that such a journey can be made by the body of man, and above all the body of woman. They represent and tell of another incarnation, another parousia of the body. Irreducible to philosophy, theology, morality, angels appear as the messengers of ethics evoked by art – sculpture, painting, or music – without its being possible to say anything more than the gesture that represents them.

They speak like messengers, but gesture seems to be their 'nature.' Movement, posture, the coming-and-going between the two. They move – or stir up? – the paralysis or *apatheia* of the body, or the soul, or the world. They set trances or convulsions to music, or give them harmony.

Their touch – when they touch – resembles that of gods. They are imperious in their grace even as they remain imperceptible.

One of the questions which arises about them is whether they can be found together in the same place. The traditional answer is no. This question, which is similar to and different from that of the co-location of bodies, comes back to the question of sexual ethics. The mucous should no doubt be pictured as related to the angel, whereas the inertia of the body deprived of its relation to the mucous and its gesture is linked to the fallen body or the corpse.

A sexual or carnal ethics would require that both angel and body be found together. This is a world that must be constructed or reconstructed. A genesis of love between the sexes has yet to come about in all dimensions, from the smallest to the greatest, from the most intimate to the most political. A world that must be created or re-created so that man and woman may once again or at last live together, meet, and sometimes inhabit the same place.

The link uniting or reuniting masculine and feminine must be horizontal and vertical, terrestrial and heavenly. As Heidegger, among others, has written, it must forge an alliance between the divine and the mortal, such that the sexual encounter would be a festive celebration and not a disguised or polemical form of the master–slave relationship. Nor a meeting in the shadow or orbit of a Father-God who alone lays down the law, who is the immutable spokesman of a single sex.

Of course, the most extreme progression and regression goes under the name of God. I can only strive toward the absolute or regress to infinity under the guarantee of God's existence. This is what tradition has taught us, and its imperatives have not yet been overcome, since their destruction brings about terrible abandonments and pathological states, unless one has exceptional love partners. And even then . . . Unhappiness is sometimes all the more inescapable when it lacks the horizon of the divine, of the gods, of an opening onto a beyond, but also a *limit* that the other may or may not penetrate.

How can we mark this limit of a place, of place in general, if not through sexual difference? But, in order for an ethics of sexual difference to come into being, we must constitute a possible place for each sex, body, and flesh to inhabit. Which presupposes a memory of the past, a hope for the future, memory bridging the present and disconcerting the mirror symmetry that annihilates the difference of identity.

To do this requires time, both space and time. Perhaps we are passing through an era when *time must redeploy space*? A new morning of and for the world? A remaking of immanence and transcendence, notably through this *threshold* which has never been examined as such: the female sex. The threshold that gives access to the *mucous*. Beyond classical oppositions of love and hate, liquid and ice – a threshold that is always *half-open*. The threshold of the *lips*, which are strangers to dichotomy and oppositions. Gathered one against the other but without any possible suture, at least of a real kind. They do not absorb the world into or through themselves, provided they are not misused and reduced to a means of consumption or consummation. They offer a shape of welcome but do not assimilate, reduce, or swallow up. A sort of doorway to voluptuousness? They are not useful, except as that which designates a *place*, the very place of useless-ness, at least as it is habitually understood. Strictly speaking, they serve neither conception nor jouissance. Is this the mystery of feminine identity? Of its self-contemplation, of this very strange word of silence? Both the threshold and reception of exchange, the sealed-up secret of wisdom, belief, and faith in all truths?

(Two sets of lips that, moreover, cross over each other like the arms of the cross, the prototype of the crossroads *between*. The mouth lips and the genital lips do not point in the same direction. In some way they point in the direction opposite from the one you would expect, with the 'lower' ones forming the vertical.)

In this approach, where the borders of the body are wed in an embrace that transcends all limits – without, however, risking engulfment, thanks to the fecundity of the porous – in the most extreme experience of sensation, which is also always in the future, each one discovers the self in that experience which is inexpressible yet forms the supple grounding of life and language.

For this, 'God' is necessary, or a love so attentive that it is divine. Which has never taken place? Love always postpones its transcendence beyond the here and now, except in certain experiences of God. And desire fails to act sufficiently on the porous nature of the body, omitting the communion that takes place through the most intimate mucous membranes. In this exchange, what is communicated is so subtle that one needs great perseverance to keep it from falling into oblivion, intermittency, deterioration, illness, or death.

This communion is often left to the child, as the symbol of the union. But there are other signs of union which precede the child – the space where the lovers give each other life or death? Regeneration or degeneration: both are possible. The intensity of desire and the filiation of both lovers are engaged.

And if the divine is present as the mystery that animates the copula, the *is* and the *being* in sexual difference, can the force of desire overcome the avatars of genealogical destiny? How does it manage this? With what power [*puissance*] does it reckon, while remaining nevertheless incarnate? Between the idealistic fluidity of an unborn body that is untrue to its birth and genetic determinism, how do we take the measure of a love that changes our condition from mortal to immortal? Certain figures of gods become men, of God become man, and of twice-born beings indicate the path of love.

Has something of the achievement of sexual difference still not been said or transmitted? Has something been held in reserve within the silence of a history in the feminine: an energy, a morphology, a growth and flourishing still to come from the female realm? An overture to a future that is still and always open? Given that the world has remained aporetic about this strange advent.

Notes

1   *The Philosophical Works of Descartes*, trans. E. S. Haldane and G. R. T. Ross (Cambridge: Cambridge University Press, 1931; reprinted Dover, 1955), I: 358.
2   (In English in the original text. –Tr.)
3   (*Instance* is rendered here as 'in-stant' to underscore Irigaray's emphasis on the term's root meaning, standing within the self, as opposed to 'ecstasy,' standing outside the self. –Tr.)
4   See Luce Irigaray, 'Epistle to the Last Christians,' in *Marine Lover of Friedrich Nietzsche*, trans. Gillian C. Gill (New York: Columbia University Press, 1991).

Chapter 6

The Forgotten Mystery of Female Ancestry

■ [Abridged] This excerpt was originally published in Italian, as part of *Tempo della differenza: Diritti e doveri per i sessi. Per una rivoluzione pacifica* (Editori Riuniti, 1989). It appeared in French in *Le Temps de la différence: Pour une révolution pacifique* (Librairie Générale Française, 1989), and was translated into English in *Thinking the Difference: For a Peaceful Revolution*, translated by Karin Montin (Routledge, 1994).

Editors' introduction

THE FOLLOWING PASSAGE WAS presented as part of a lecture given in Italy in 1989, at the invitation of the Italian Communist Party. The essay as a whole, along with the others that are collected in *Thinking the Difference*, reflects Irigaray's growing concern with issues of social justice and civil rights for women. This activist emphasis does not preclude Irigaray's continuing investigation of the dominant structures of the Western symbolic order; indeed, her focus in this excerpt is on the ways in which mythological themes function to support the legal and social institutions and practices of Western culture. She takes up Freud's view that the ancient Greek myths that have survived to the present day hold clues to understanding the ways men and women relate to each other. To illustrate this, she turns to the well-known myth of Demeter and Korē/Persephone, which she claims has much to say about the ways in which the mother–daughter relationship – seen as paradigmatic of and foundational to relationships among women – has been sacrificed to the needs of patriarchy.

Irigaray introduces her reading of this myth by touching on themes that are familiar from elsewhere in her work, including the absence of any spiritual (or divine) element in the love relationship between women and men; the importance of Aphrodite as a model for autonomous female sexuality; and the need for a specifically feminine form of identity within Western culture. She retells the myth of Demeter and Persephone (included here in condensed form) in order to illustrate how the bond between mothers and daughters has been subverted by masculine desire. This desire, according to Irigaray, tricks daughters into betraying their love for their mothers and thus reduces daughters – and, by extension, all women – to mere trophies of patriarchal power. She goes on to argue that the Freudian theorisation of the Oedipal triangle perpetuates this seduction by mandating that daughters cease their identification with their mothers and, in its place, experience desire for their fathers, in order to attain full psycho-sexual development as women. Thus Freud, for Irigaray, takes the place of Hades in the Persephone myth, seducing daughters away from mothers by trickery and relegating them to the status of masculine possessions.

This essay concludes by reasserting Irigaray's view that patriarchy is founded upon the commodification of the daughter's virginity and the subversion of maternal love for daughters. According to Irigaray, what is necessary to institute basic social justice and rescue the natural world from the destruction represented by rapacious masculine desire is the resurrection of the mother–daughter bond in all its mythic fullness. For Irigaray, this change can only come about through continued questioning of the primary symbol systems of our culture, including religion and the law.

In some ancient yet very advanced traditions, it is the woman who initiates the man into love. This initiation does not mean making use of a whole set of tricks to awaken some basic sexual pleasure [jouissance] in the man; neither is it the same as female seduction in accordance with the most rudimentary of male instincts. These patterns of behaviour are the mere relics of woman's role in love. Today's pornography trade would have us believe that eroticism boils down to that, that we humans are capable of nothing else. Eroticism is supposedly a drug for us, a means of forgetting ourselves, the prostitution of women to male drives, the 'little death' for men, a fall, annihilation, etc. [. . .]

Today it is accepted that it is the man who must initiate the woman into love, and that he may do it with neither education nor experience, as if, by virtue of being a man, he is knowledgeable in love. Most often, the man does not initiate the woman into anything much, except perhaps a pleasure that society does its utmost to forbid her to enjoy except with the man, in order to induce her to worship him. This pleasure revealed by the male lover is the outcome of instincts and male drives whose residual human aspects are often singularly difficult to define (unless it is perhaps the man's obscure need to return to the mother's womb, if this much can be said to be human). The man/lover thus induces the woman to forget herself, to fall from herself, although the fall may procure her pleasure. By this I mean that (with rare exceptions) there is no longer anything very subtle or spiritual about the initiation into love, and that this initiation does not take into consideration the different qualities of men and women so as to embody them fully. It is accepted that eros destroys identity, not that it fulfils it. Which always amounts to reverting to an economy of desire preceding Aphrodite's birth, to the desire separate from love that psychoanalysts talk about, for example.

The path to reciprocal love between individuals has been lost, especially with respect to eroticism. And instead of contributing to individuation, or to the creation or re-creation of human forms, eroticism contributes to the destruction or loss of identity through fusion, and to a return to a level of tension that is always identical, always the lowest, with neither development nor growth. Eros could only return to a sort of zero point, a sort of state of equilibrium for man – and so is not likely to have a positive future here on earth.

This notion of love has led women to forget themselves, to submit childishly or slavishly to male sexuality, and to console themselves, through motherhood, for their fall and exile from themselves. Motherhood – promoted by spiritual leaders as the only worthwhile destiny for women – most often means perpetuating a patriarchal line of descent by bearing children for one's husband, the state, male cultural powers, thereby helping men escape from an immediate incestuous desire. To women, more secretly, motherhood represents the only remedy for the abandonment or for the fall inflicted in love by male instincts, as well as a way for them to renew their ties to their mothers and other women.

How have we come to this – all of us, and especially we women? One of the lost crossroads of our becoming women lies in the blurring and erasure of our relationships to our mothers and in our obligation to submit to the laws of the world of men-amongst-themselves.

The destruction of female ancestry, especially its divine aspect, is recounted in a variety of ways in the Greek myths and tragedies. Aphrodite's mother is no longer mentioned; she is supplanted by Hera, and Zeus remains the God who has many lovers, but no female equivalent. The goddess Aphrodite can thus be said to have lost her mother. Iphigeneia is separated from her mother to be offered as a sacrifice in the Trojan War. And though oracular speech was originally passed on from mother to daughter, beginning with Apollo it is often assimilated to the oracle at Delphi, which still has a place for Pythia, but not for mother–daughter relationships. Antigone's uncle, the tyrant Creon, punishes by death her faith, her loyalty to her maternal ancestry and its laws, in order to safeguard his power in the polis. The Old Testament does not tell us of a single happy mother–daughter couple, and Eve comes into the world motherless. Although Mary's mother, Anne, is known, the New Testament never mentions them together, not even at the moment of the conception of Jesus. Mary goes to greet Elizabeth, not Anne, unless Elizabeth is Anne, as in Leonardo da Vinci's interpretation. Mary's leaving her mother for a marriage with the Lord is more in keeping with the tradition that was already several centuries old.

Perhaps the best illustration of the fate of the mother–daughter relationship is to be found in the myths and rites surrounding Demeter and Kōrē. You are probably fairly familiar with these myths. You live in a place that still bears traces of them, memories of them. As is almost always the case, there are several versions of the myths. This means that they appeared at different times and in different places.

Most ancient Greek myths are of Asian or unknown origin. This is true of those concerning Aphrodite, Demeter and Kōrē/Persephone. Their evolution should be understood as the result of migrations to different places where they were adapted to varying degrees, and the effect of historical developments. (For myth is not a story independent of History, but rather expresses History in colourful accounts that illustrate the major trends of an era.) The temporality of History is expressed in this form because in those days, speech and art were not separate. As a result, they retained a special relationship to space, time and the manifestation of the forms of incarnation. History as expressed in myth is more closely related to female, matrilineal traditions.

In myths concerning mother–daughter relationships and myths about the goddess/lover and god couples, the story, setting and interpretation were masked, disguised to varying degrees by the patriarchal culture that was growing up. This culture erased – perhaps out of ignorance, perhaps unwittingly – the traces of an earlier or contemporaneous culture. Thus many sculptures were destroyed or buried in the ground, rites were eliminated from traditions or transformed into patriarchal rituals, myths and mysteries were interpreted from the patriarchal perspective, or simply as representing the Prehistory of the patriarchal era.

The same applies to the myths of Demeter Kōrē/Persephone. It seems to me that there are at least two different versions. In one, Demeter's daughter is abducted by the god of shadows, fog and the Underworld, and then seduced by him despite herself, so that she cannot return to her mother for good. When she is first carried off by Hades – also called Erebus or Aidoneus by Homer – she is looking at spring flowers with other maidens, and just as she is about to pick a narcissus, the earth opens up, and the prince of the Underworld takes her away with him. He has not yet made her his wife when Hermes, Zeus' messenger, comes to fetch her at the request of Demeter, her mother, who in her grief has made the earth barren. The god of the Underworld has no choice but to obey, but he gives Persephone a poisoned gift behind Hermes' back: he gives her pomegranate seeds to eat, and anyone who accepts a gift from Hades becomes his captive.

This is the version of the Homeric hymn. In later versions or interpretations, Kōrē/Persephone has become more or less responsible for her own fate, and is thus more like Eve the seductress, who leads man to his fall. It was nothing like that in the initial versions. But the story of Demeter and Kōrē/Persephone is so terrible and so exemplary that it is understandable that the patriarchal era wished to make the seductive woman bear the responsibility for its crimes.

It seems that Kōrē/Persephone's only sin was to reach out to pluck a narcissus. Of course it is preferable to leave flowers rooted in the earth rather than pick them, especially in spring, but should the girl be punished for picking a flower, even a marvellous narcissus, by being carried off to the Underworld? [. . .]

The story of Kōrē/Persephone shows that the daughter is not responsible. The mother is a little more responsible, for she begins to console herself for the disappearance of her daughter by nursing a boy-child. But her acceptance of this substitute is also a form of revenge. A god has stolen her daughter, so she renounces life among the immortals and tries to force a mortal upon them as a god. When this solution fails, she refuses any proposition from the God of gods, unless he gives her back her daughter. Zeus understands that there is no other way to save the mortals and the immortals. He sends Hermes to Erebus [Hades] to fetch Persephone. Hades must obey, but he is still plotting to keep his mastery: he induces Persephone to eat a pomegranate seed, which, unknown to her, makes her a hostage of the Underworld.

Mother and daughter are happily reunited. Demeter asks Persephone to tell her everything that has happened to her. She does so, beginning at the end. In a way, she goes back in time, as must any woman today who is trying to find the traces of her estrangement from her mother. That is what the psychoanalytical process should do: find the thread of her entry into the Underworld, and, if possible, of her way out.

But let us return to the reunion of Demeter and Persephone. They spend all day pouring their hearts out to each other, comforting each other, expressing their joy to each other. Hecate joins them and, ever since, she has held an important place in the mysteries surrounding Kōrē/Persephone. In particular, she follows her when she descends to the Underworld and precedes her on her return to earth.

Indeed, the poisoned gift that Persephone accepted from Hades is apparently enough to make her his captive at least a third of the year, the cold season. Similarly, yet differently, eating an apple is all it later took to be excluded from earthly paradise. Then, it is true, the prohibition was clearly stated before the sin was committed, which was not the case for Kōrē/Persephone. But both are stories of fairly similar traps or taboos involving flowers or fruits; in one, the prince of darkness is clearly responsible, and in the other, a woman is blamed. It is true that Eve is no longer a woman, since she is made from Adam's rib. Eve is only part of Adam, created without a mother; this is not the case of Kōrē/Persephone, who is a goddess, a daughter of a goddess, of a god couple. The bond between humanity and divinity is thus unbroken. Sometimes it is woven in one direction, sometimes in the other, with curious tests or tricks, strange prohibitions imposed upon women to establish a patriarchally transmitted ancestry and theology.

All these codes are beyond the little girl. She may make a mistake, but she does not decide to do so. She is caught up in the dealings, contractual or otherwise, between men, between men and male gods. According to their agreements, she should refuse everything from men and gods so that she will not be seduced through a mistake on her part. She should keep well away from mankind, men's contracts, men's relationships, until her virginity is no longer a subject of negotiations between men. She should remember that virginity signifies her relationship to her physical and moral integrity, and not the price of a deal between men. She should learn to keep herself for herself, for her gods and her love, for the love of which she is capable if she is not taken outside herself, abducted, raped and deprived of freedom of action, speech, thought. Obviously this freedom must be real and not controlled; the freedom to seduce in accordance with male instincts or to gain equality of rights within a unisex male order is only a superficial freedom that has already exiled woman from herself, already deprived her of any specific identity. She thus becomes a sort of puppet, or movable object, reduced to being subjected to basic drives with passive goals. She thinks she needs to be 'screwed' by a man, she suffers from a basic oral need (partially an inverted projection stemming from male desire), Freud writes learnedly, without considering that this need might be symptomatic of woman's submission to male instincts. According to Freud, this need is a sort of relic of the initial chaos that male desire opened up in the earth's womb.

Indeed, this chaos still exists. It is manifested in the libido's economy of drives without genitality, the economy in which woman is imprisoned. One of the two – he – is stuck in incestuous regression and anal possession, while the other – she – is reduced to oral mendicancy. Woman supposedly always hungers for him without any return to herself. She thus eventually becomes hungry from the abyss that he has opened up in her; she becomes ill with a bottomless hunger, because it is not her hunger, but the abyss inside her of the natural and cultural hunger of the other.

None of this could happen if she had not been separated from her mother, from the earth, from her gods and her order. This is the original sin that makes woman a seductress against a backdrop of nothingness. But why abduct her from her mother? Why destroy female ancestries? To establish an order man needed, but which is not yet an order of respect for and fertility of sexual difference.

To make an ethics of sexual difference possible once again, the bond of female ancestries must be renewed. Many people think or believe that we know nothing about mother–daughter relationships. That is Freud's position. He asserts that on this point, we must look beyond Greek civilization to examine another erased civilization. Historically, this is true, but this truth does not prevent Freud from theorizing on and imposing, in psychoanalytical practice, the need for the daughter to turn away from the mother, the need for hatred between them, without sublimation of female identity being an issue, so that the daughter can enter into the realm of desire and law of the father. This is unacceptable. Here Freud is acting like a prince of darkness with respect to all women, leading them into the shadows and separating them from their mothers and from themselves in order to found a culture of men-amongst-themselves: law, religion, language, truth and wisdom. In order to become a woman, the virgin girl must submit to a culture, particularly a culture of love, that to her represents Hades. She must forget her childhood, her mother; she must forget herself as she was in her relationship to Aphrodite's *philotes*.

If the rationale of History is ultimately to remind us of everything that has happened and to take it into account, we must make the interpretation of the forgetting of female ancestries part of History and re-establish its economy.

The justifications given for breaking up mother–daughter love are that this relationship is too conducive to fusion. Psychoanalysis teaches us that it is essential to substitute the father for the mother to allow a distance to grow between daughter and mother. Nothing could be further from the truth. The mother–son relationship is what causes fusion, for the son does not know how to situate himself in regard to the person who bore him with no possible reciprocity. He cannot conceive within himself. He can only artificially identify with the person who conceived him. To separate himself from his mother, man must therefore invent all sorts of objects for himself, even transcendental ones – gods, Truth – in order to resolve this insoluble relationship between the person who carried him inside her and himself.

The situation is different for the daughter, who is potentially a mother and can live with her mother without destroying either one of them even prior to the mediation of specific objects. To them, nature is a preferred environment; the ever-fertile earth is their place, and mother and daughter coexist happily there. They, like nature, are fertile and nurturing, but this does not prevent them from having a human relationship between them. This relationship depends upon the establishment of female lines of descent, but not solely. Therefore the daughter's words to the mother may represent the most highly evolved and most ethical models of language, in the sense that they respect the intersubjective relationship between the two women, express reality, make correct use of linguistic codes and are qualitatively rich. For little girls, education, the social world of men-amongst-themselves and the patriarchal culture function as Hades did for Kōrē/Persephone. The justifications offered to explain this state of affairs are inaccurate. The traces of the story of the relationship between Demeter and Kōrē/Persephone tell us more. The little girl is taken away from her mother as part of a contract between men-gods. The abduction of the daughter of the great Goddess serves to establish the power of male gods and the structure of patriarchal society. But this abduction is a rape, a marriage with the consent of neither the daughter nor the mother, an appropriation of the daughter's virginity by the god of the Underworld, a ban on speech imposed on the girl/daughter and the woman/wife, a descent for her (them) into the invisible, oblivion, loss of identity and spiritual barrenness.

Patriarchy is founded upon the theft and violation of the daughter's virginity and the use of her virginity for commerce between men, including religious commerce. Carrying on this commerce involves money changing hands, but also exchanging real property; at stake are either symbolic or narcissistic powers. Patriarchy has constructed its heaven and hell upon this original sin. It has imposed silence upon the daughter. It has dissociated her body from her speech, and her pleasure from her language. It has dragged her down into the world of male drives, a world where she has become invisible and blind to herself, her mother, other women and even men, who perhaps want her that way. Patriarchy has thus destroyed the most precious site of love and its fertility: the relationship between mother and daughter, the mystery of which is guarded by the virgin daughter. This relationship does not separate love from desire, or heaven from earth, and it knows nothing of hell. Hell appears to be a result of a culture that has annihilated happiness on earth by sending love, including divine love, into a time and place beyond our relationships here and now.

To re-establish elementary social justice, to save the earth from total sub-jugation to male values (which often give priority to violence, power, money), we must restore this missing pillar of our culture: the mother–daughter rela-tionship and respect for female speech and virginity. This will require changes to symbolic codes, especially language, law and religion.

Chapter 7

Practical Teachings: Love – Between Passion and Civility

■   [Abridged] This extract originally appeared as part of a chapter entitled 'Enseignements practiques: L'amour – entre passion et civilité', in *J'aime à toi* (Grasset, 1992). This was published in English as *I Love to You: Sketch of a Possible Felicity in History*, translated by Alison Martin (Routledge, 1996).

Editors' introduction

I N THIS EXCERPT, Irigaray appreciates the notion of love as a form of both spiritual and carnal transformation, a divine relation that potentially exists between men and women, but that has rarely, if ever, been manifested in reality. One example of the possibility for divinised love relations, according to Irigaray, is represented by the Greek goddess Aphrodite, who offered her partners a fully differentiated love. For Irigaray, this means Aphrodite was neither a mere object of man's undifferentiated needs, which are simply instinctual, nor was she only seeking to gratify her own needs. In Aphrodite's orientation towards a partner, desire is transformed into a mode of living relations where unmediated drives are not allowed to dominate. Thus, there is intersubjective communication and an acknowledgement of the other's identity as distinct, never to be negated or absorbed by either partner's uncontrolled passions.

Irigaray's position is that the unconscious internalisation of the incest taboo has prevented men from becoming aware of their finite human condition, as they seek, through reproduction, to avoid the terrors of death and prenatal undifferentiated fusion with the mother. This lack of a reflective acknowledgement of the place and integrity of women leads to men's proprietary actions regarding women – mainly by confining them to specified roles of wives, mothers and daughters. This denies women a recognition of their integrity, and of the state of 'virginity', defined by Irigaray as female self-sufficiency, even in marriage. As a result, Irigaray laments, there has never been a true meeting of the sexes.

In a significant move, Irigaray suggests here that the practice of yoga is conducive to the mastery and differentiation of drives which is requisite for this new form of relationship. The various physical and mental exercises of yoga, including conscious control of the breath and cultivation of energy centres known as *chakras*, help to differentiate and refine the various charges and flows of bodily energies. The inherent association of divinities with these practices is also acknowledged, so that nature becomes spiritualised and vice versa. In addition, for Irigaray, the gods and goddesses do not need to remain disembodied and merely objects of meditation; they prefigure the possibility of differentiated and loving relationships between men and women.

Another possible model for this regenerative and transformative bond between men and women proposed by Irigaray depends on a reinterpretation of the Annunciation story. Instead of seeing Mary as simply a handmaiden who does the Lord's bidding, Irigaray proposes a different version of the roles of both Mary and God. God's speech respects Mary as a woman in her own right, and her considered response is dramatised as alone recognising the momentous importance of that respect, both for the birth of a child, and for the fate of the world. It is a world that is in need of carnal and spiritual redemption. The union of God and Mary comes about not simply as an inevitable capitulation to God's potency, but as a differentiated relation which fosters both intersubjectivity and respect for the integrity of each of the persons participating. Mary's 'virginity' is thus assured.

For Irigaray, these figures of divine and differentiated love provide the basis of a renewal of sexual relationships, so that not only can the couple be transformed, but both the earth and the cosmos can be redeemed, signalling the birth of a new era.

A return to the origins of our culture shows [. . .] that there was an era in which it was the woman who initiated love. At that time, woman was goddess and not servant, and she watched over the carnal and spiritual dimension of love. In her, love and desire were indivisible. The goddess's principal attribute was tenderness, not a quality denoting a universal goodness directed towards all beings but rather a differentiated sentiment vis-à-vis the other gender, being brought to bear in the carnal act itself. According to our mythology, it is Aphrodite who represents the first figure of love incarnated in a human body, love that is not chaotic, without measure, without rhythm or temporality, a simply cosmic, pure and incestuous love. Consequently, attaining a sexed identity does not derive from the paternal prohibition of incest but from the realization of the desire between woman and man with each being respected, and from their membership of the human species.

According to our Western tradition, sexual chaos reigned both prior to and after Aphrodite, and one of the reasons for the regression appears to be the man-father's seizure of power which is linked to the man-lover's incapacity to differentiate himself from the mother, who is once again assimilated to a nature without consciousness. The incest taboo decreed by the father has not stopped man from returning to chaotic drives, whereby the energy accumulated in being estranged from the woman-mother is then expended without measure and without sharing. The obligation to reproduce figures as the remedy for death and for the return to indifferentiation, imagined as a prenatal situation in which there is a state of fusion with the mother. The only realities likely to help man not to sacrifice himself entirely to eros seem to be procreation and forming a family, aside from labor and the acquisition of family capital, which in our culture appear as forms of punishment or redemption with regard to the vicissitudes of the flesh or the possibility of a for-itself corresponding to the marriage contract between the married couple.

In this perspective, the relation between the genders is determined by man's needs with no consideration for woman's identity, which consists more of the desire for and with another – woman or man. Woman, who is born of the same as herself, is far less familiar with this nostalgia for regression into the mother; for her it is artificial.

The girl feels desire for relations with her mother, a desire then transferred almost exclusively to the man for both good and bad reasons, as our tradition lacks the mediations enabling her to keep her identity as a woman. As I have already suggested, it is moving to observe that the most intersubjective language is produced by the little girl in her relation with her mother, the reverse not being true. It is from a desire for exchange that women's melancholy ensues rather than from nostalgia for return, particularly for a regression to undifferentiated nature.

However, given the prevalence of *one* genealogy, a patriarchal one, female filiation is erased, and while the wife (of a son) becomes mother (of a son), the father's virgin daughter, by virtue of her status as such, becomes a currency among men. Justice would mean woman's being virgin and mother for herself, these properties of her nature founding her spiritual becoming, her rights and duties, instead of her being reduced to an elementary naturalism in which virginity is equated with the presence of the hymen, and maternity with the fact of having actually given birth. Is it not true that even today religious and State institutions still actually consider woman to be the natural body of which man remains the spiritual head, whether he is head of the church, head of state, or head of a family?

In such an economy, intersubjective relations between the genders are lacking in maturity, particularly sexual maturity. Man and woman do not consider themselves as two people with a different identity. And they marry or come together on the basis of contracts concerned with having: food, shelter, goods, children, etc. Restricting ourselves to civil undertakings of this kind exposes, among other things, existing prohibitions and prudishness regarding the sexual domain. But legal formulations such as these do not encourage the realization of subjective interiority. The demand for equal rights, particularly legal rights, might itself be a regressive step in the definition of an identity proper to each gender.

In fact, there is still an absence of a culture of sexuality, of flesh, of generic identity.

We are between: love (it goes without saying, the less we talk about it, the better it is), and a system of taboos weighing heavily upon the relations between the sexes. Which love are we talking about, then?

The approach of Far-Eastern traditions, especially the practice of yoga, coupled with the philosophical meditation inseparable from it, has taught me another way, a way leading not to a discharge but to an energetic recharge, to a regeneration and a culture of energy. In concrete terms that means, as I suggested in the *Introduction*, that in our bodies, there are energetic centers, *chakras*, situated at the crossroads of various physiological and spiritual functions. Traditionally, the arousal and the circulation of energy through these conduits are linked to the elemental states of matter — earth, water, fire, air, ether — to which there are corresponding densities, forms, colors, syllables, divinities, and specific cardinal points.

And so, 'in the body of the believer, that part of the body between the feet and the knees is related to the Earth element; Earth is square and yellow in color; it is symbolized by the syllable Lam; the circulation of breath in this area of the body is accompanied by meditation upon Brahma, the golden-colored god . . .'[2]

The person following these techniques will endeavor to bring the different *chakras* of his/her body and the dimensions of the universe into relation with one another by appropriate postures and gestures, by mastering breathing, visualizing forms and colors, and emitting sounds. Such a knowledge of energy is gained thanks to the preferably oral teaching of an experienced practitioner. The spiritualization of nature, be it micro- or macrocosmic, is associated with the worship of divinities, guardians of certain parts of the body and the world; divinities themselves always subordinate to becoming and to the incarnation of energy. It may be realized by the renunciation of carnal desire between the sexes, an option quite similar to Western monasticism except that the place for retreat is the forest or mountain rather than a cloister; hermitism is preferred over community life and chastity is chosen after a fulfilled erotic life.

Indeed, this is often expressed in those texts which disclose the worship of a Goddess (worship of her body and her sex) by man. But there is nothing to stop knowledge of energy from becoming the vehicle for a carnal and spiritual relation between man and woman, a dual and reciprocal relation, in which the genders are united as micro- and macrocosmic humanity.

Love between man and woman thus becomes the mastery and culture of energy rather than its instinctual expenditure, to be redeemed by procreation here on earth and faith in asexual happiness in the beyond — the path to this being the acquisition of an insensible *logos*. The carnal act ceases to be a regression to degree zero for pleasure or words; rather it is the locus for the lovers' revival and becoming. Love is accomplished by two, without dividing roles between the beloved and the lover, between objectival or animal passivity on the one hand, and generally conscious and valorous activity on the other. Woman and man remain two in love. Watching over and creating the universe is their primary task, and it remains so. [. . .]

Love, even carnal love, is therefore cultivated and made divine. The act of love becomes the transubstantiation of the self and his or her lover into a spiritual body. It is a feast, celebration, and a renaissance, not a decline, a fall to be redeemed by procreation. Love is redemption of the flesh through the trans-figuration of desire *for* the other (as an object?) into desire *with* the other. [. . .]

We may be given a further lesson in love through a non-patriarchal interpretation of the Annunciation, taken as a symbol of the relations between the sexes.

The Annunciation is given the following rather univocal interpretation nowadays: Mary, you who are young and still a virgin, thus beautiful and desirable, the Lord, who has power over you, is informing you through his messenger that he wishes to be the father of a son to whom you will give birth. Mary can only say 'yes' to this announcement because she is the Lord's posses-sion or his property. The mystery of the angel remains.

There is another possible interpretation: Mary, you who, from adolescence, are divine, because you were born of a woman faithful to herself – Anne, the one said to have conceived without sin – you who are thus capable of intersubjectivity, the expression of love between humans, do you want to be my lover and for us to have a child together, since I find you worthy of this even though you are young, inexperienced and without any possessions. It is only thanks to your *yes* that my love and my son may be redemptive. Without your word, we may not be carnally redeemed or saved.

Such an interpretation of the Annunciation, which is how I now view it, is supported by the tradition of the physical and spiritual centers of the body, the *chakras*.

And so, in the iconography:

> words coming from the sky,
> the ray of sunlight,
> the song of the bird,
> the hands of Mary (and sometimes those of the Angel)

touch and designate the body between heart, breath and word, instead of announcing a spiritual conception.

In other words, the Lord does not take Mary without having exchanged with her in the place where word and flesh fecundate one another intentionally.

<Words and listening shared voluntarily between the lovers enable a divine child to be conceived> This conception is preceded by the transition from an almost undifferentiated corporeal matter, and from a separation between the genders, to an alliance in the word between man and woman. The announcement of the child's coming or incarnation is represented by angels in our tradition, angels who are messengers from the Lord and the cosmic realm.

In the Indian tradition, the bird is often the one to assist in the birth of life or in its safeguarding, and then in the acquisition of wisdom. It is a bird that helps Vishnu, the creator, as well as Brahmin [sic], and every postulant of spiritual becoming. The bird accompanies the god with his body as a support for his movement in space, and then with his questions. The assistance of the bird comes closer and closer to speech. In interpersonal relations, the divine messenger is an angel, able to walk while keeping his wings, symbols of a harmonious relation with the air, with breath, whether it is a question of movement, of breathing, or of speaking.

The announcement to Mary can thus be interpreted as questions addressed to her in the form of speech, a question asking if she agrees to become the lover of the Lord and mother of his son. That question (which is incomplete, of course, since it principally concerns conception – the conception of a son moreover; it is also elliptical in that it situates Mary's speech as what separates Father and Son without stating this explicitly) is to be understood as the announcement of the spiritual assumption of Mary thanks to a Lord capable of knowing his own desire, of interiorizing it and sharing it in word and flesh.

This Lord would then be a figure surpassing or accomplishing Buddha: the awakened one who is compassionate, agrees to speak, love, and engender in order to redeem, as a couple, the whole of the macro- and microcosmic universe. With this gesture the Lord actually renounces having, the object, power, in order to accede to being-man and to the realization of intersubjectivity with the being of woman, who is able to conquer or retain her virginity. And that alliance, a dual then communal alliance, could incarnate the finality of History, or at least lead the way to another era.

Notes

1   See 'Le mystère oublié des généalogies féminines,' in Le temps de la différence: pour une revolution pacifique (Paris: Librairie générale français, 1989) and Le rôle d'Éros et d'Aphrodite dans les cosmogonies grecques, Jean Rudhart, PUF, Collège de France, Essais et conférences, 1986.

2   Extract from the Yogatattva Upanishad, reprinted in Upanishads du Yoga (trans. Jean Varenne), Gallimard, Coll. Tel Unesco. See also Kundalini, l'énergie des profondeurs, Lilian Silburn, Les Deux Océans, Paris, 1983. My translation. (Tr.)

PART TWO

Julia Kristeva

JULIA KRISTEVA IS CONSIDERED one of the most influential and prolific writers of the contemporary French thinkers. Her theoretical writings bridge the disciplines and are studied equally in departments of women's studies, literature, philosophy, psychology and religious studies. Her work has been characterised from its inception by an interest in the relation between subjectivity (the subject) and the production of meaning (language), as well as by an investigation of those cultural representations – dynamic signs, symbols, rituals and texts – which are semantically charged and overloaded, and marked by an ambivalent signification.

At the age of twenty-five (1965), Julia Kristeva left her home in Communist Bulgaria to take up a doctoral research fellowship in the study of semiology in Paris, at L'École Pratique des Hautes-Études (EPHE). Here, over the course of several years, she was supervised by many of the top French intellectuals of the day – Lucien Goldman, Roland Barthes and Emile Benveniste, among others – while attending lectures given by Jacques Lacan and working as a laboratory assistant for Claude Lévi-Strauss. Her Eastern European background, which included experience working as a journalist for a Communist newspaper in Sophia, Bulgaria, combined with Kristeva's academic interest in linguistics, aligned her early on with the prominent Parisian group Tel quel. This body of scholars, which included such important thinkers as Jacques Derrida, Michel Foucault, Philippe Sollers (who later became her husband), Marcelin Pleynet and Jacques Henric, together produced the *Tel quel* journal. *Tel quel* regularly published controversial poetry, prose and critical theory, to much media acclaim, and became the home for many of Kristeva's early semiotic articles; this journal was later transformed into *L'Infini*, which today continues to publish Kristeva's essays.

Kristeva radically transformed the field of linguistics almost immediately after her arrival in Paris. As early as 1967, with her essay 'Word, Dialogue and Novel', and 1968, with 'Problèmes de la structuration du texte', she provided detailed readings of the work of Mikhail Bakhtin, a theorist well known in the Communist bloc but unknown to French intellectuals of the time, as well as the school of Russian formalism.[1] In these essays, Kristeva explores Bakhtin's concepts of the 'carnivalesque', which details the ambivalent relation between bi-polar oppositions, and of the 'dialogic novel', which sketches the interdependence of texts. From this Bakhtinian base, Kristeva began her work on alterity in signification (the way in which a sign is always both 'one' and 'other', and so marked by an ambiguous denotation). She further coined her own term, 'intertextuality', to account for the influence of other 'texts' on textual production itself (writing) and on the act of reading and the construction of meaning. 'Intertextuality' remains a widely used and recognised concept in Western theories of linguistics, even when its origins are forgotten (writers often neglect to credit Kristeva for this neologism).

Language the Unknown: An Initiation into Linguistics (1989b [1969]), *Sèméiotikè* (1980 [1969]), *Le Texte du roman* (1970) and *Polylogue* (1980 [1977]) are all early samples of Kristeva's linguistic and semiotic writings, culminating in her monumental doctoral thesis, *La Révolution du langage poétique* (1984 [1974]). It is in these early works (1969–79) that Kristeva expounds her now famous theory of *poetic language*, her understanding of the *semiotic* and *symbolic* components of language, her introduction of the *chora*, and the base for much of her later theoretical work: the *subject-in-process*.

The literary texts of Mallarmé, Lautréamont and other modernists are the focus for Kristeva's work in this early period. *Revolution in Poetic Language* highlights that aspect of literary language that exceeds linear structures of meaning, and that cannot be accounted for by other standard theories of linguistics. Here, Kristeva examines the material component of language – its rhythms, acoustic patterns and phonetic qualities. This 'other side' of language conveys meaning, but without providing a specific denotative reference, thus opening the text up to multiple and contradictory meanings, and calling into question the belief, presumed and implicit in linguistics as well as in all other social scientific disciplines, that a sign can ever convey a single, contained and absolute meaning. *Revolution in Poetic Language* begins as a standard text of literary analysis, but ends with a condemnation of the univocal façade of language.

Kristeva further unfolds her own theoretical paradigm – which she calls *semanalysis* – of language operation. She identifies two components that together constitute all linguistic operation: the *semiotic* and the *symbolic*. The *semiotic*, which for Kristeva is gendered feminine (though not necessarily 'female'), is the rhythmic and tonal part of any language usage that provides its measure and cadence, and can be marked by whimsy and incongruity in so far as its use is not dictated by a linear logic. She names the *symbolic*, which she genders masculine, that part of language which expresses simple, univocal and direct meaning without inconsistency. The language of science and law would be its kingly representatives, and absolute logic (grammar and syntax) would mark its sequencing.

Kristeva calls 'poetic language' the operation of the *semiotic* aspect of language in dialogue with the *symbolic* component. She theorises that every language use — not just poetry and prose, where it is more easily tracked — involves an expression of these two forces intermingling, transforming and renewing one another, while providing multiple and varied meanings to any given utterance. Alterity (difference) is thus part of the signification process, as meaning is always heterogeneous, dynamic and processual.

Kristeva's *semanalysis* theorises that the *semiotic* is the material representation in language of our bodily origins and unconscious drives and desires that the *symbolic* attempts to mask or efface with the illusion of mastery and univocal semantics. The *chora*, a term Kristeva borrows from Plato and reworks significantly, represents our maternal and nourishing origins, our bodily affects and drives, and is what provides the *semiotic* aspect of language with its rhythm and lyrical movement. The chora is biological (undeniably maternal and dictated by unconscious bodily drives), but always already shaped by social and cultural forces; it is the place from which the *semiotic* receives its motivation to rupture the sequential logic of the *symbolic*. Kristeva thus inscribes the body within the signification process.

Further, both the reader and the writer are implicated in the *semiotic-symbolic* dialogue as a *subject-in-process*. There is no judging, unified subject (cogito) that exists outside of language, Kristeva insists, but a split-subject that results from the confrontation between the two forces active in language. The subject of language is created and destroyed and constructed again (forever in process), by and through the rhythms of the *semiotic* in dialogue with the *symbolic*. The subject is not stagnant, but dynamic and open to the process within language itself.

Kristeva's reformulation of structural linguistics brought her wide regard in the humanities and social scientific circles, and she was offered the position of Professor of Linguistics at the University of Paris VII (1973), as well as a Permanent Visiting Professorship in the Department of French Literature at Columbia University, New York (1974); she has since been named a Permanent Visiting Professor at the Department of Comparative Literature, University of Toronto (1992). Kristeva currently maintains her academic positions at each of these three universities.

Many feminist thinkers welcomed Kristeva's theory of poetic language as a means to trace the hitherto unexamined semiotic (feminine) component of signification, as well as the inscription of the body (and its maternal origins) in all language use. Her subject-in-process further highlighted the illusion of mastery implicit in the normative (masculine) subject of texts and other cultural productions, and displaced this patriarchal illusion with a decentred subject of (the unconscious and bodily traces in) language. Feminist critics of Kristeva, however, were quick to note that her examples of poetic language came almost entirely from male writers, and that when she spoke of the subject-in-process she used exclusively the masculine pronoun. Some, too, accused Kristeva of consigning 'feminine' speech to the realm of babble and illogicality, thus simply reifying, though in positive terms, what patriarchal discourse had already firmly established. While many feminists find Kristeva's theory of language and subjectivity useful for feminist analysis, the controversy continues over how it should be characterised, with critics labelling it everything from anti-feminist propaganda to radical feminist theory.

Kristeva confounds easy classification by resisting the label of feminist, and consistently taking an ambiguous position on the merits of feminist theory. *About Chinese Women* (1977 [1974]) constitutes Kristeva's first overt foray into what some would call 'feminist analysis'. This text is the result of Kristeva's trip to China, with other members of the Tel quel group, to witness the impact of Maoism on Chinese society. The book is an uncritical and romantic celebration of the freedoms experienced by Chinese women throughout their 'matriarchal' history to the Cultural Revolution and the Maoist regime. *About Chinese Women* created conflict between Kristeva and the feminist publishing collective, Éditions des femmes of the Psych et Po movement, that produced it – the collective was unhappy with it and requested several alterations that Kristeva refused to make – and was to be her only publication with this influential feminist publishing house.

Not long after the appearance of *About Chinese Women*, Kristeva published the essay 'Women's Time' (1981 [1979]) which is a careful philosophic examination of the history of the modern women's movement.[2] She critically views the suffragist and liberal-socialist feminist agenda to achieve equality within traditional institutional power, as well as the radical feminist glorification of the feminine in biological terms, as grossly universal and global in their approach, ignoring different social, cultural and individual heritages. In her view, both approaches forcibly constrain a variety of women under a single unified identity – Woman – and dangerously espouse a group polity that cannot accommodate such difference.

It is no coincidence that Kristeva spurns the group identification necessary in both social and radical feminisms. After living through Communism (in her native Bulgaria), and experiencing a personal disillusionment with Marxism

(Paris 1968) and Maoism (her trip to China), it is not surprising to find that Kristeva indicates here a firm refusal to adopt any meta-narrative – even feminism – as the necessary response to the conditions of oppressed groups in society. Instead, Kristeva offers a highly individualised, subjectivist ethics, influenced heavily by psychoanalysis.

A growing interest in Freudian and Lacanian theory, as well as object relations theory (Klein, Winnicot, Green), soon led Kristeva to pursue seriously the study of psychoanalysis. She became qualified to practise analysis in 1978, and today continues her work as an analyst in addition to her many academic posts. There is a discernible shift in Kristeva's work during this period (1979–present), from a distant, academic prose style to a more personal, introspective and literary writing voice. Kristeva remains absorbed with linguistic concerns, but now weaves together semiotics with psychoanalysis to augment her early theoretical constructs, with an increasing focus on early subject formation and its traces in cultural artefacts.

While Kristeva's linguistic work demonstrates a marked interest in modern literature, the texts from this later period exhibit a preoccupation with religious texts and writers, as well as a detailed investigation of Jewish and Christian (primarily Catholic and Orthodox) concepts and religious figures. This makes one wonder if the shift from linguistics to psychoanalysis generated this new interest in religious discourse, with one religious studies scholar arguing that Kristeva's aim is to rewrite each of Freud's classic books on religion (Jonte-Pace 1997: 241).

Many secular feminist scholars in the West, however, have been troubled by Kristeva's focus on religion, dismissing it as a faith-inspired nostalgia or even a Christian orthodoxy, and as such, necessarily regressive and sentimental (O'Grady 2002). But it must be said that just as Kristeva's relationship to feminism is marked by ambivalence, so her attitude towards religion is difficult to catego-rise. Kristeva was educated from an early age by French Dominican nuns in a Catholic school in her native Bulgaria. She has stated that she came from a family of believers, and has referred to her father as a 'would-be priest' who found regular solace as a member of the choir for the Orthodox Cathedral in Sophia (*In the Beginning Was Love*, 1987a [1985]).[3] Kristeva's childhood was steeped in Christian images and constructs, but she has often stated that she does not believe in God, or have a personal investment in the Catholic or Orthodox traditions generally;[4] rather, she seems to echo Freud in calling religion an 'illusion', albeit 'a glorious one' (1987a [1985]: 11).

For many Western feminists, religious discourse in any form has come to signify the narrow-minded intolerance that comes from a dogmatic system of beliefs. For Kristeva, however, who was not raised in the West, but in Com-munist Bulgaria, religious discourse demonstrates a rebellious vivacity and richness that could survive like very little else the strictures, rigid regulations and homogenising rigour of a Communist regime. So, though religions have failed many feminists in the West, Kristeva has witnessed the ability of religious discourse and rituals to support the individual in times of great personal and cultural distress. Thus, Kristeva is not a Christian apologist, as many have accused her of being, but rather a psychoanalyst who examines the many-faceted face of religious discourse with theories that attempt to unravel the imaginary constructs that have made religions both a vehicle of oppression and infantilisation, as well as an individual and cultural opportunity for liberation and subjective renewal for so many people throughout history.

Three texts from this second period in Kristeva's writing are often taken together and read as a trilogy on the history of human subjectivity: *Powers of Horror* (1982 [1980]), *Tales of Love* (1987b [1983]) (and one could add here, the related text, *In the Beginning Was Love* (1987a [1985])), and *Black Sun* (1989 [1987]). Together, these volumes mark Kristeva's reworking of Freudian theory, and her intention to uncover the operations of a pre-Oedipal stage of a subject's development. During this time period, Kristeva gave birth to a son (1976), and consequently, the theme of maternity, including her own experiences of motherhood, finds expression in many of these writings. Each of these three texts highlights in some manner the role of the mother in language acquisition and subject formation; Kristeva thus makes visible the maternal debt that founds the production of meaning itself, and hence, of all cultural constructs, with a primary focus on the origins of religion.

In *Powers of Horror*, Kristeva accounts for the way a child must push aside the maternal (semiotic) embrace and venture to the (symbolic) world of language. This 'abjection' of the mother by the child is echoed in religious structures that provide social rules and regulations to control and dominate phenomena (particularly those which are related to the feminine body) that evoke this earliest moment of subject formation, and thus prevent the subject from slipping back under the sway of the mother; these prohibitions also work to erase any trace of the semiotic (maternal) in the symbolic realm of religious institutions.

But in *Tales of Love* and *In the Beginning Was Love*, Kristeva notes that maternal abjection is not the only means by which a speaking subject comes into existence; rather, this move to autonomy by the child is made possible through a love identification with an Other beyond the mother–child union (establishing a bridge from the semiotic towards the symbolic). Kristeva calls the identification with this loving Other 'agape', and thus gives it an instant theological resonance. She further hypothesises that this loving identification with an Other is the necessary substratum for imaginary processes, such as art, religion and psychoanalysis (which she regularly, now, in these later writings, places on equal footing). *Black Sun* examines what happens when a subject refuses identification with this loving (symbolic) Other, and thus the subject is stripped of all possibility for meaning, imagination and faith. Kristeva describes this complete refusal of the Other as melancholia, felt as separation, abandonment and division (from the maternal origin), and details it in atheistic terms (which is always, for Kristeva, a dangerous form of repression).

Most recently, Kristeva continues to assess religious language and structures as significant sites of study. *New Maladies of the Soul* (1995 [1993]) is a loose assemblage of previously published journal essays that mark Kristeva's continued psychoanalytic investigation of religious productions. Along with *Le Féminin et le sacré* (1998a), a series of letters exchanged with Catherine Clément on the significance of 'the sacred' in an age inundated by banal spectacle and lacking moral and ethical volition, Kristeva has created a lengthy corpus of theoretical work that heralds the efficacy of religion, its cathartic and aesthetic capacity to infuse the individual subject with a meaning, and thus a healthy stability. She is careful, however, to reaffirm her commitment to psychoanalysis as a more favourable arena than religion since the latter does not make manifest, but actively conceals, the means through which it operates.

In the late 1980s and early 1990s, Kristeva also produced a number of texts concerning early subjective processes that take as their focus themes of estrangement, foreignness and exile. This concentration is not only personal (Kristeva's position as an immigrant in France), nor solely concerned with political issues (nationalism, racism, immigration), but highlights the internal crisis that founds every individual subject. In *Strangers to Ourselves* (1991 [1988]), *Nations without Nationalism* (1993), and *Crisis of the ~~European~~ Subject* (2000a), Kristeva advocates a recognition of alterity – an understanding of the stranger within (unconscious bodily drives, charges and desires that mark the subject as divided and not homologous) – to better understand our response to the external stranger. This is not just a theoretical move for Kristeva; rather, she views this as an ethical project that is imperative for our cohesion as a polynational society. Here, again, Kristeva takes religion as a privileged site of praxis wherein the stranger has been variously accommodated, subsumed or marginalised from different faith organisations, and where the internal alterity of the individual subject has long been the focus of sacred texts and theologies.

Her examination of alterity in subject formation, as it is realised in politics, religion and artistic representation, has also found expression in Kristeva's fictional work. *The Samurai* (1992 [1990]) is Kristeva's first novel, and has been widely recognised as a nod and a wink to Simone de Beauvoir's *The Mandarins.*[5] Like de Beauvoir, Kristeva's text is more *roman-à-clef* than fiction, recounting the activities of many major Parisian intellectuals during the events prior to and immediately after May 1968. In this text Kristeva assesses her position as a foreigner and a stranger (and as the only woman) in the Tel quel group, and considers the way in which this outsider-position has marked her theoretical writing. Kristeva's second novel, *The Old Man and the Wolves* (1994

[1991]) examines the real human costs of political suppression and the marginalisation of difference as it is realised in a Communist state. This is a work of fiction written in the style of a classic detective story, yet Kristeva also recounts the death of her father within the narrative. The varied aesthetic and cathartic capacity of her father's Orthodox religious faith is contrasted here with the homogenising and totalising force of Communism. *Possessions* (1998b [1996]), also a murder mystery, tells the story of a female detective (not without resemblance to Kristeva) who explores the vagaries of murder through a psychoanalytic lens, with an emphasis on mother–child relations.

More recently Kristeva has returned to classical literary and philosophical analysis, with *Time and Sense: Proust and the Experience of Literature* (1996b [1994]) and *Le Génie féminin: la vie, la folie, les mots: Hannah Arendt* (1999), the first volume in a series of three, to include Melanie Klein and Colette. Each of these works is as much a celebration of the representative thinkers as it is a continuation of Kristeva's theoretical work on the subjects of alterity and identity formation. With the publication of two books of her seminars, *The Sense and Non-Sense of Revolt* (2000b [1996]) and *La Révolte intime* (1997b), Kristeva revisits the themes of transgression, excess and revolution in subjectivity, through a detailed reading of Aragon, Sartre and Barthes. Here she explores the possibility of imaginary identification and experience of the sacred in an age bombarded by media images and consumer goods.

Linguist, semiotician, psychoanalyst, writer and critic, Julia Kristeva continues to blur disciplinary boundaries and genre categories. In itself, this mixing and melding of intellectual place and identity is a tangible representation of the dynamic subjectivity that Kristeva wishes to celebrate. Her work has been met by some with hostility, and by others with confusion and anxiety, since it demands a careful and dedicated reader, one who is willing to risk everything – even her position *outside* of the text – and relax into the vertiginous lure of the writing itself. Intrepid and tenacious readers have found this risk worth taking.

Notes

1   Kristeva, Julia (1967), 'Bakhtine, le mot, le dialogue et le roman', *Critique* 13: 438–65; in English as 'Word, Dialogue and Novel', pp. 34–61 in *The Kristeva Reader*, 1986; and Kristeva, Julia (1968) 'Problèmes de la structuration du texte; la sémiotique: science critique et/ou critique de la science', pp. 298–317 in Roland Barthes *et al.* (eds), *Théorie d'ensemble*, Paris: Seuil; excerpt in English as 'Semiotics: A Critical Science and/or a Critique of Science', pp. 74–88 in *The Kristeva Reader*, 1986.

2   Kristeva, Julia (1981), 'Women's Time', *Signs: Journal of Women in Culture and Society* 7(1): 13–35, Alice Jardine and Harry Blake, trans. French edition (1979), 'Le Temps des femmes', 34/44: Cahiers de recherche de sciences des textes et documents, Université Paris VII, 5: 5–19.

3   Hughes-Hallet, Lucy (1992), 'Egghead out of Her Shell', *The Independent on Sunday*, 9 February 1992, Review Page, 26.

4   Hughes-Hallet, p. 26.

5   De Beauvoir, Simone (1986) *The Mandarins*, trans. L. Friedman, London: Fontana. French edition (1954) *Les Mandarins*, Paris: Gallimard.

Chapter 8

Approaching Abjection *and* Semiotics of Biblical Abomination

■ [Abridged] The following excerpts first appeared in *Pouvoirs de l'horreur: Essai sur l'abjection* (Seuil, 1980). This was translated into English by Leon S. Roudiez as 'Approaching Abjection' and 'Semiotics of Biblical Abomination', in *Powers of Horror: An Essay on Abjection* (Columbia University Press, 1982).

Editors' introduction

ABJECTION IS ONE OF the more widely cited of Kristeva's theoretical concepts, equally disputed and hailed by a wide range of scholars in the humanities and social sciences. Like René Girard and Mary Douglas, two theorists who have greatly influenced her work in this text, Kristeva attempts the monumental task of unveiling the foundational constructs that make up our social order, while also laying bare the dynamics at work in the social construction of the human body. As with most of her work, Kristeva's emphasis is on the psychological make-up of the individual subject: the way in which the child removes itself from a dependence on the mother's body towards the social and symbolic world of language and representation. The relation of the child to the maternal body is the primary focus of this text, which demonstrates, through an examination of such diverse cultural sites as the Hebrew scriptures, Christian theology and the anti-Semitic literature of Céline, the ways in which society continues to play out on a grand scale each subject's earliest crises of separation and individuation from the body of the mother.

The excerpts in the first section of this essay come from the introductory chapter of *Powers of Horror*, which provides, in poetically and personally charged prose, a lengthy description of the process Kristeva labels 'abjection' and the products commonly categorised as 'abject'. She speaks of the visceral horror, dread or anguish that an individual experiences when confronted by specific substances. Common materials that evoke this bodily repulsion ('abjection') are products of the body's orifices: faeces, urine, vomit, saliva, pus, semen, blood, all commonly thought of as waste products that will defile those who come into direct physical contact with them. These 'abject' substances are felt to be intrinsically abhorrent; the disgust experienced by their proximity is felt so strongly that the individual believes her response to be natural, universal and absolute.

From the Latin root 'abjectus' ('cast away'), 'abjection' is characterised by that which is cast out, rejected and expelled from the social order; this is not a simple logic of rejection but a violent and visceral repulsion (that may involve gagging, choking, nausea, convulsions, paroxysms and other bodily signs of disgust). But, Kristeva notes, there is always a certain beguiling enchantment to those things which are abject, which need not be only substances, but can include states (disease, decay, rotting), persons (criminals, the insane, the stranger) and actions (murder, incest). For what is expelled in abjection is not the abject substance itself, but its ambivalence, its transitional identity, that both repels and enthrals.

For Kristeva, abjection is both 'somatic and symbolic': '[abjection] is above all a revolt against an external menace from which one wants to distance oneself, but of which one has the impression that it may menace us from the inside' (1982: 118). For the 'abject' does not encompass a substance which is abhorrent in and of itself (along with Douglas, Kristeva makes the claim that 'there is no such thing as absolute dirt'). Rather, abject substances are those things (states and individuals) which confuse boundaries and borders, disturb divisions, and upset the margins of identity. The abject is an ambiguous non-thing (neither this nor that, both inside–outside, such as bodily fluids) which by its transitional or liminary position on the threshold calls into question the clean and clear divisions necessary for the functionality of the symbolic order.

For Kristeva, 'abjection' stirs the ghost of the maternal body. 'Abject' elements are not abject in themselves, but abject because by their very ambiguity they endanger what Kristeva believes to be the weak boundaries of the symbolic subject. In order for a subject to become a speaking subject, differentiated from the maternal, there is an inevitable pushing away of the mother, as she must be expelled in order for the child to come into her own within a social network of symbolic systems that will provide her with individual meaning. But, for Kristeva, this thrusting aside of the maternal body is never completed and never wholly satisfactory. There is always the threat of, and with it, the desire for, a re-unification with the site of origins (the maternal body). In its very ambiguity, the abject represents the previously undifferentiated state (mother–child) that was the origin of each person. The abject thus both threatens and promises a collapse of those symbolic structures which enabled a subject's first step away from the mother towards individual identity.

All 'abjection' then becomes a perpetual (and Kristeva posits, a necessarily enduring) rejection of the maternal hold in favour of the symbolic system that attempts to replace (and overwrite) our indebtedness (as subjects) to the mother. As she lucidly summarises in an interview on *Powers of Horror*, 'This relation to abjection is finally rooted in the combat which every human being carries on with one's mother'.[1]

The ensuing portions of the book apply this concept of abjection to specific cultural constructs in order to demonstrate the ways in which all societies (and their religions) are structured by what has been abjected – and continues to be cast out – from the social order. Kristeva mitigates such a wide-sweeping and universal claim with culturally specific analyses to uncover the distinct methods – be they ritual proscriptions, taboos or prohibitions – that societies employ to protect themselves from the maternal threat present in the abject. In her reading of Leviticus, for example, Kristeva reveals the ways in which the ancient Hebraic tradition abjected the fecund properties of the female body, and any trace of maternal origins ('the body must bear no trace of its debt to nature'), and instilled a rigid (sexual) division at the heart of the sacred.

Approaching abjection

Neither subject nor object

There looms, within abjection, one of those violent, dark revolts of being, directed against a threat that seems to emanate from an exorbitant outside or inside, ejected beyond the scope of the possible, the tolerable, the thinkable. It lies there, quite close, but it cannot be assimilated. It beseeches, worries, and fascinates desire, which, nevertheless, does not let itself be seduced. Apprehensive, desire turns aside; sickened, it rejects. A certainty protects it from the shameful – a certainty of which it is proud holds on to it. But simultaneously, just the same, that impetus, that spasm, that leap is drawn toward an elsewhere as tempting as it is condemned. Unflaggingly, like an inescapable boomerang, a vortex of summons and repulsion places the one haunted by it literally beside himself.

When I am beset by abjection, the twisted braid of affects and thoughts I call by such a name does not have, properly speaking, a definable *object*. The abject is not an ob-ject facing me, which I name or imagine. Nor is it an ob-jest, an otherness ceaselessly fleeing in a systematic quest of desire. What is abject is not my correlative, which, providing me with someone or something else as support, would allow me to be more or less detached and autonomous. The abject has only one quality of the object – that of being opposed to *I*. If the object, however, through its opposition, settles me within the fragile texture of a desire for meaning, which, as a matter of fact, makes me ceaselessly and infinitely homologous to it, what is *abject*, on the contrary, the jettisoned object, is radically excluded and draws me toward the place where meaning collapses. A certain 'ego' that merged with its master, a superego, has flatly driven it away. It lies outside, beyond the set, and does not seem to agree to the latter's rules of the game. And yet, from its place of banishment, the abject does not cease challenging its master. Without a sign (for him), it beseeches a discharge, a convulsion, a crying out. To each ego its object, to each superego its abject. It is not the white expanse or slack boredom of repression, not the translations and transformations of desire that wrench bodies, nights, and discourse; rather it is a brutish suffering that 'I' puts up with, sublime and devastated, for 'I' deposits it to the father's account [*verse au père* – *père-version*]: I endure it, for I imagine that such is the desire of the other. A massive and sudden emergence of uncanniness, which, familiar as it might have been in an opaque and forgotten life, now harries me as radically separate, loathsome. Not me. Not that. But not nothing, either. A 'something' that I do not recognize as a thing. A weight of meaninglessness, about which there is nothing insignificant, and which crushes me. On the edge of non-existence and hallucination, of a reality that, if I acknowledge it, annihilates me. There, abject and abjection are my safeguards. The primers of my culture.

The improper/unclean

Loathing an item of food, a piece of filth, waste, or dung. The spasms and vomiting that protect me. The repugnance, the retching that thrusts me to the side and turns me away from defilement, sewage, and muck. The shame of compromise, of being in the middle of treachery. The fascinated start that leads me toward and separates me from them.

Food loathing is perhaps the most elementary and most archaic form of abjection. When the eyes see or the lips touch that skin on the surface of milk – harmless, thin as a sheet of cigarette paper, pitiful as a nail paring – I experience a gagging sensation and, still farther down, spasms in the stomach, the belly; and all the organs shrivel up the body, provoke tears and bile, increase heartbeat, cause forehead and hands to perspire. Along with sight-clouding dizziness, *nausea* makes me balk at that milk cream, separates me from the mother and father who proffer it. 'I' want none of that element, sign of their desire; 'I' do not want to listen, 'I' do not assimilate it, 'I' expel it. But since the food is not an 'other' for 'me', who am only in their desire, I expel *myself*, I spit *myself* out, I abject *myself* within the same motion through which 'I' claim to establish *myself*. That detail, perhaps an insignificant one, but one that they ferret out, emphasize, evaluate, that trifle turns me inside out, guts sprawling; it is thus that *they* see that 'I' am in the process of becoming an other at the expense of my own death. During that course in which 'I' become, I give birth to myself amid the violence of sobs, of vomit. Mute protest of the symptom, shattering violence of a convulsion that, to be sure, is inscribed in a symbolic system, but in which, without either wanting or being able to become integrated in order to answer to it, it reacts, it abreacts. It abjects. [. . .]

The abjection of self

If it be true that the abject simultaneously beseeches and pulverizes the subject, one can understand that it is experienced at the peak of its strength when that subject, weary of fruitless attempts to identify with something on the outside, finds the impossible within; when it finds that the impossible constitutes its very *being*, that it *is* none other than abject. The abjection of self would be the culminating form of that experience of the subject to which it is revealed that all its objects are based merely on the inaugural *loss* that laid the foundations of its own being. There is nothing like the abjection of self to show that all abjection is in fact recognition of the *want* on which any being, meaning, language, or desire is founded. One always passes too quickly over this word, 'want,' and today psychoanalysts are finally taking into account only its more or less fetishized product, the 'object of want.' But if one imagines (and imagine one must, for it is the working of imagination whose foundations are being laid here) the experience of *want* itself as logically preliminary to being and object – to the being of the object – then one understands that abjection, and even more so abjection of self, is its only signified. [. . .]

Before the beginning: separation

The abject might then appear as the most *fragile* (from a synchronic point of view), the most *archaic* (from a diachronic one) sublimation of an 'object' still inseparable from drives. The abject is that pseudo-object that is made up *before* but appears only *within* the gaps of secondary repression. *The abject would thus be the 'object' of primal repression.*

But what is primal repression? Let us call it the ability of the speaking being, always already haunted by the Other, to divide, reject, repeat. Without *one* division, *one* separation, *one* subject/object having been constituted (not yet, or no longer yet). Why? Perhaps because of maternal anguish, unable to be satiated within the encompassing symbolic.

The abject confronts us, on the one hand, with those fragile states where man strays on the territories of *animal*. Thus, by way of abjection, primitive societies have marked out a precise area of their culture in order to remove it from the threatening world of animals or animalism, which were imagined as representatives of sex and murder.

The abject confronts us, on the other hand, and this time within our personal archeology, with our earliest attempts to release the hold of *maternal* entity even before ex-isting outside of her, thanks to the autonomy of language. It is a violent, clumsy breaking away, with the constant risk of falling back under the sway of a power as securing as it is stifling. The difficulty a mother has in acknowledging (or being acknowledged by) the symbolic realm – in other words, the problem she has with the phallus that her father or her husband stands for – is not such as to help the future subject leave the natural mansion. The child can serve its mother as token of her own authentication; there is, however, hardly any reason for her to serve as go-between for it to become autonomous and authentic in its turn. In such close combat, the symbolic light that a third party, eventually the father, can contribute helps the future subject, the more so if it happens to be endowed with a robust supply of drive energy, in pursuing a reluctant struggle against what, having been the mother, will turn into an abject. Repelling, rejecting; repelling itself, rejecting itself. Ab-jecting.

In this struggle, which fashions the human being, the *mimesis*, by means of which he becomes homologous to another in order to become himself, is in short logically and chronologically secondary. Even before being *like*, 'I' am not but do *separate, reject, ab-ject*. Abjection, with a meaning broadened to take in subjective diachrony, *is a precondition of narcissism*. It is coexistent with it and causes it to be permanently brittle. The more or less beautiful image in which I behold or recognize myself rests upon an abjection that sunders it as soon as repression, the constant watchman, is relaxed. [. . .]

As abjection – so the sacred

Abjection accompanies all religious structurings and reappears, to be worked out in a new guise, at the time of their collapse. Several structurations of abjection should be distinguished, each one determining a specific form of the sacred.

Abjection appears as a rite of defilement and pollution in the paganism that accompanies societies with a dominant or surviving matrilinear character. It takes on the form of the *exclusion* of a substance (nutritive or linked to sexuality), the execution of which coincides with the sacred since it sets it up.

Abjection persists as *exclusion*, or taboo (dietary or other) in monotheistic religions, Judaism in particular, but drifts over to more 'secondary' forms such as *transgression* (of the Law) within the same monotheistic economy. It finally encounters, with Christian sin, a dialectic elaboration, as it becomes integrated in the Christian Word as a threatening otherness – but always nameable, always totalizeable.

The various means of *purifying*, the abject – the various catharses – make up the history of religions, and end up with that catharsis par excellence called art, both on the far and near side of religion. Seen from that standpoint, the artistic experience, which is rooted in the abject it utters and by the same token purifies, appears as the essential component of religiosity. That is perhaps why it is destined to survive the collapse of the historical forms of religions. [. . .]

Semiotics of biblical abomination

Leviticus: a purity of place, a purity of speech

Dietary instructions crop up after the burnt offering presented by Moses and Aaron to the Lord Yahweh (as they do after Noah's burnt offering to the Lord Elohim). Two officiants at the sacrifice, having 'offered strange fire' to the Lord Yahweh, become 'devoured' by the sacred fire (Leviticus, 10:1–2). At that moment, a communication from the Lord seems to indicate that the sacrifice 'in itself' cannot assume the status of a divine covenant, unless that sacrifice is *already* inscribed in a logic of the pure/impure distinction, which it would consolidate and enable one to hand down.

> Do not drink wine nor strong drink, thou, nor thy sons with thee, when ye go into the tabernacle of the congregation, lest ye die: it shall be a statute for ever throughout your generations:
>   And that ye may put difference between holy and unholy, and between unclean and clean;
>   And that ye may teach the children of Israel all the statutes which the Lord hath spoken into them by the hand of Moses.
>
> (Leviticus 10:9–11)

The sacrifice has efficacy then only when manifesting a logic of separation, distinction, and difference that is governed by admissibility to the holy place, that is, the appointed place for encountering the sacred fire of the Lord Yahweh.

A *spatial* reference is thus called forth, in a first stage, as criterion of purity, provided that the *blood* of the expiational goat not be brought in (Leviticus 10:18). But such prerequisites for purity (holy space, no blood) seem to have been deemed insufficient, for the following chapter modifies them. The pure will no longer be what is restricted to a *place* but what accords with a *speech*; the

impure will not only be a fascinating *element* (connoting murder and life: blood)
but any infraction to a *logical conformity*. Thus,

> And the Lord spake unto Moses and to Aaron, saying unto them,
>> Speak unto the children of Israel, saying, These are the beasts
> which ye shall eat among all the beasts that are on the earth.
>> Whatsoever parteth the hoof, and is clovenfooted, and cheweth
> the cud, among the beasts, that ye shall eat.
>> Nevertheless these shall ye not eat of them that chew the cud, or
> of them that divide the hoof: as the camel, because he cheweth the
> cud, but divided not the hoof; he is unclean unto you.
>
> (Leviticus 11:1–4)

And so forth.

The list of the occasionally specious prohibitions that make up this chapter
becomes clear when it is understood that there is a strict intent of establishing conformity with the logic of the divine word. Now such a logic is founded
on the initial biblical postulate of the man/God difference, which is coextensive
with the prohibition of murder. As J. Soler has shown,[2] what is involved, as
in Deuteronomy 14, is the establishment of a *logical field* preventing man from
eating carnivorous animals. One needs to preserve oneself from murder, not incorporate carnivorous or rapacious animals, and there is only one prescription for
that: eating herbivorous, cud-chewing animals. There are ruminants that do not
follow the general rule as to hoofs, and they will be thrust aside. The pure will
be that which conforms to an established taxonomy; the impure, that which
unsettles it, establishes intermixture and disorder. The example of fish, birds,
and insects, normally linked to one of three elements (sea, heaven, earth), is very
significant from that point of view; the impure will be those that do not confine
themselves to one element but point to admixture and confusion.

Thus, what initially appeared to us as a basic opposition between man and
God (vegetable/animal, flesh/blood), following upon the initial contract, 'Thou
shalt not kill,' becomes a complete system of logical oppositions. Differing from
burnt offerings, this system of abomination presupposes it and guarantees its
efficacy. Semantically controlled, initially at least, by the life/death dichotomy,
it becomes in course of time a code of differences and observance of it. It goes
without saying that the pragmatic value of those differences (the function of this
or that animal in everyday life possibly affecting the pure/impure designation),
like their sexual connotations (I shall return to this point), does not detract from
the remarkable fact of having a system of taboos constituted like a true formal
system – a taxonomy. Mary Douglas brilliantly emphasized the logical conformity of Levitical abominations, which, without a design of 'separation' and
'individual integrity,' would be incomprehensible.

Food and the feminine

A brief and very important chapter of Leviticus, chapter 12, is inserted between those dietary prohibitions and the expansion of their logic to other domains of existence. Between the theme of food and that of the sick body (Leviticus 13–14), the text will deal with the woman in childbed. Because of her parturition and the blood that goes with it, *she* will be 'impure': 'according to the days of the separation for her infirmity shall she be unclean' (Leviticus 12:2). If she gives birth to a daughter, the girl 'shall be unclean two weeks, as in her separation' (Leviticus 12:5). To purify herself, the mother must provide a burnt offering and a sin offering. Thus, on *her* part, there is impurity, defilement, blood, and purifying sacrifice. On the other hand, if she gives birth to a male, 'the flesh of his foreskin shall be circumcised' (Leviticus 12:3). Circumcision would thus separate one from maternal, feminine impurity and defilement; it stands instead of sacrifice, meaning not only that it replaces it but is its equivalent – a sign of the alliance with God. Circumcision can be said to find its place in the same series as food taboos; it indicates a separation and at the same time does away with the need for sacrifice, of which it nevertheless bears the trace. Such a comment on circumcision within a text on feminine and particularly maternal impurity, illuminates the rite in fundamental fashion. I agree that it concerns an alliance with the God of the chosen people; but what the male is separated from, the other that circumcision carves out on his very sex, is the other sex, impure, defiled. By repeating the natural scar of the umbilical cord at the location of sex, by duplicating and thus displacing through ritual the preeminent separation, which is that from the mother, Judaism seems to insist in symbolic fashion – the very opposite of what is 'natural' – that the identity of the speaking being (with his God) is based on the separation of the son from the mother. Symbolic identity presupposes the violent difference of the sexes.

Let me take a further step. The terms, impurity and defilement, that Leviticus heretofore had tied to food that did not conform to the taxonomy of sacred Law, are now attributed to the mother and to women in general. Dietary abomination has thus a parallel – unless it be a foundation – in the abomination provoked by the fertilizable or fertile feminine body (menses, childbirth). Might it be that dietary prohibitions are a screen in a still more radical separating process? Would the dispositions *place-body* and the more elaborate one *speech-logic of differences* be an attempt to keep a being who speaks to his God separated from the fecund mother? In that case, it would be a matter of separating oneself from the phantasmatic power of the mother, that archaic Mother Goddess who actually haunted the imagination of a nation at war with the surrounding polytheism. A phantasmatic mother who also constitutes, in the specific history of each person, the abyss that must be established as an autonomous (and not encroaching) *place* and *distinct* object, meaning a *signifiable* one, so that such a person might learn to speak. At any rate, that evocation of defiled maternality, in Leviticus 12, inscribes the logic of dietary abominations within that of a limit, a boundary, a border between the sexes, a separation between feminine and masculine as foundation for the organization that is 'clean and proper,' 'individual,' and, one thing leading to another, signifiable, legislatable, subject to law and morality.

After that confrontation with the boundary between the sexes, the biblical text continues its journey fully within the image of the body and its limits.

Boundaries of the self's clean and proper body

Chapters 13 and 14 of Leviticus locate impurity in leprosy: skin tumor, impairment of the cover that guarantees corporeal integrity, sore on the visible, presentable surface. To be sure, leprosy does objectively cause serious damages in a people with a strong community life and, moreover, an often nomadic one. But one may note furthermore that the disease visibly affects the skin, the essential if not initial boundary of biological and psychic individuation. From that point of view, the abomination of leprosy becomes inscribed within the logical conception of impurity to which I have already called attention: intermixture, erasing of differences, threat to identity.

The shift taking place between chapters 12 and 13 seems significant to me; it goes from within the maternal body (childbirth, menses) to the decaying body. By means of what turnabout is the mother's interior associated with decay? I have already noted that turning among split subjects (see pp. 53–55).[3] It is reasonable to assume that the biblical text, in its own way, accurately follows the path of an analogous fantasy. Evocation of the maternal body and childbirth induces the image of birth as a violent act of expulsion through which the nascent body tears itself away from the matter of maternal insides. Now, the skin apparently never ceases to bear the traces of such matter. These are persecuting and threatening traces, by means of which the fantasy of the born body, tightly held in a placenta that is no longer nourishing but devastating, converges with the reality of leprosy. One additional step, and one refuses even more drastically a mother with whom pre-Oedipal identification is intolerable. The subject then gives birth to himself by fantasizing his own bowels as the precious fetus of which he is to be delivered; and yet it is an abject fetus, for even if he calls them his own he has no other idea of the bowels than one of abomination, which links him to the ab-ject, to that non-introjected mother who is incorporated as devouring, and intolerable. The obsession of the leprous and decaying body would thus be the fantasy of a self-rebirth on the part of a subject who has not introjected his mother but has incorporated a devouring mother. Phantasmatically, he is the solidary obverse of a cult of the Great Mother: a negative and demanding identification with her imaginary power. Aside from sanitary effectiveness, that is the fantasy that Levitical abominations aim at cutting back or resorbing. Possibly, one could link to the same rejection of nonconformity with corporeal identity the abjection brought about by physical defect:

> For whatsoever man he be that hath a blemish, he shall not approach;
> a blind man, or a lame, or he that hath a flat nose, or any thing
> superflous,
>   Or a man that is brokenfooted, or brokenhanded, ...
> .... he shall not come nigh to offer the bread
> of his God.
>
> (Leviticus 21:18–21)

The body must bear no trace of its debt to nature: it must be clean and proper in order to be fully symbolic. In order to confirm that, it should endure no gash other than that of circumcision, equivalent to sexual separation and/or separation from the mother. Any other mark would be the sign of belonging to the impure, the non-separate, the non-symbolic, the non-holy:

> Ye shall not round the corners of your heads, neither shalt thou mar
> the corners of thy beard.
>   Ye shall not make any cuttings in your flesh for the dead, nor print
> any marks upon you . . .
>
> (Leviticus 19:27–28)

Chapter 15 confirms that view: this time it is flow that is impure. Any secretion or discharge, anything that leaks out of the feminine or masculine body defiles. After a reference to sacrifice (chapter 16), we again have a designation of the impurity of blood:

> For it is the life of all flesh; the blood of it is for the life thereof:
> therefore I said unto the children of Israel, Ye shall eat the blood
> of no manner of flesh: for the life of all flesh is the blood thereof:
> whosoever eateth it shall be cut off.
>
> (Leviticus 17:14)

After the path we have followed, it is easier to understand the various connotations of blood impurity. It takes in the following: prohibition of meat diet (following upon the prohibition against killing), the postdiluvian classification of meat as in conformity or nonconformity with the divine word, the principle of identity without admixture, the exclusion of anything that breaks boundaries (flow, drain, discharge). From food to blood, the loop of prohibitions has no need of being looped, for we are still and from the beginning within the same logic of separation. But we are again led back to the fundamental semanticism of that logic, which persists in positing an agency that is *other* than that of the nutritious, the sanguine, in short, the 'natural' maternal.

Notes

1   Baruch, Elaine Hoffman (1988), 'Julia Kristeva' in *Women Analyze Women: In France, England, and the United States*, New York: New York University Press, p. 136.
2   J. Soler, 'Sémiotique de la nourriture dans la Bible,' *Annales*, July–August 1973, pp. 93ff.
3   Of original text.

Chapter 9

Credence-Credit *and* Credo

■ [Abridged] These excerpts first appeared in a series of short lectures published as *Au commencement était l'amour: psychanalyse et foi* (Hachette, 1985). The English translation by Arthur Goldhammer appeared as *In the Beginning Was Love: Psychoanalysis and Faith* (Columbia UP, 1987).

Editors' introduction

IN THIS TINY BOOK that numbers fewer than a hundred pages, Kristeva presents for the first time, in a clear and concentrated series of small essays, her psychoanalytic understanding of religious faith, as well as her 'religious' understanding of psychoanalysis. That is, at the same time that Kristeva employs psychoanalytic theory to understand religious conviction, she also uses religious language, images and theology, to unfold and develop her theory of psychoanalysis. As the individual chapter titles indicate, with names such as 'Credence-Credit', 'Credo' and 'Credo in Unum Deum', her focus is almost entirely Christian; specifically, Kristeva details Catholic theological traditions. But this text is equally about the mode of psychoanalysis that Kristeva espouses, which is the result of an almost devout, albeit critical, alliance with Freud, coupled with substantial influence by André Green, the French object relations psychoanalyst famous for emphasising the importance of the maternal, and Jacques Lacan, with his emphasis on the linguistic contract.

Kristeva weaves together reflections on her religious upbringing – in an Orthodox family in her native Bulgaria, and as a student in a French Catholic school – with her psychoanalytic training and personal analysis, along with psychoanalytic and philosophical theory. *In the Beginning* thus reads more like an exploratory essay than a formulaic theoretical work on religious faith. Kristeva unites her disparate themes with a focus on the importance of love in the theological and psychoanalytic traditions that concern her. And while, in the end, Kristeva supplants Christianity with psychoanalysis (in her view, a demystified understanding of the fantasies that sustain the self and the community), she nevertheless finds value in Christian practice, causing many of her secular critics to accuse her of a heady nostalgia for Christianity.

For Kristeva, both analysis and Christian theology employ a discourse of love towards an 'impossible Other' (in Christian terms, none other than divine love). It is the affect of this language, its power, efficacy and capacity to renew the subject (with visceral effect), that concerns Kristeva, and she turns to the process of language acquisition in order to uncover the transformative powers of language. Ensconced deeply in psychoanalytic rhetoric, Kristeva augments the Oedipal structure of Freud and Lacan by locating the acquisition, and the subsequent power and affect of language, in the realm of the pre-Oedipal, the *maternal* realm.

What Kristeva wishes to uncover is the movement of each subject from the mother–child entity (non-differentiation) towards the speaking subject (Oedipalization and individuation). Kristeva finds in Freud's essay 'The Ego and the Id' an undeveloped reference to a third party, an 'archaic father', which Freud names 'the father in individual prehistory'. Critics have accused Kristeva of a misguided loyalty to Freud in the preservation of this dubious, masculinist term. For Kristeva, however, this so-called 'pre-Oedipal father' is not an anthropomorphic, sexed figure. In fact, the term is misleading since the 'archaic father' does not denote an 'entity' outside of the mother at all. What Kristeva develops, in fact, is the desire that the mother has for someone outside of the mother–child dyad. This desire becomes the third term, the 'archaic father', and provides a tertiary logic to the hitherto dyadic formation of the pre-Oedipal realm.

In other words, for Kristeva, while the child understands itself only in its relation to the mother (since it is not yet distinct, as a subject, from the mother) the mother does not define herself *only* in relation to the child. The mother has desires that extend beyond the child, to someone other than the child itself. The desire experienced by the mother for someone other is expressed in and through language, and it is this discourse that opens up a space for difference or alterity within the previously undifferentiated mother–child entity. The mother's desire is itself what motivates the child towards the 'speaking other', the object of the mother's desire, and thus the beginnings of individual subjectivity for the child is born out of this indirect gift of love (which Kristeva labels with the Christian term denoting God's unmerited love, *agape*).

In Kristeva's configuration the child is neither the object nor the recipient of the desire, yet remains its indirect beneficiary. The mother's desire provides mobility for the child, from homogeneity (sameness), towards heterogeneity (difference) through language. The child's movement towards this Other is what, for Kristeva, characterises 'primary identification' (preceding Oedipalization) – an immediate and affective identification with a loving agency that propels the subject towards the paternal, symbolic world of signs, yet motivated by the semiotic (maternal) relation. Kristeva thus grounds the imaginary realm of language, art and religion firmly to the maternal arena.

For Kristeva, religious faith, artistic practice and psychoanalysis are marked by the separation and suffering of an individual who is alone, separated from her (maternal) origins; however, Kristeva maintains, this crisis of the subject can be alleviated through a renewal of the pre-Oedipal process of primary identification. For Kristeva, this process is none other than an openness to the Other found in the discourse of love.

Credence-credit

As *you know*, the history of patristics consists in large part of controversies over the definition of faith. There is discussion of the relative importance of rational certainty versus grace and of the relation among the Father, the Son, and the Holy Spirit. Heresy and dogma derive from these controversies, which I shall not explore here. For the sake of simplicity I shall consider the Credo, the basis of Catholic faith and cornerstone of the Church. But before reading this text, let us attempt a direct, naive phenomenology of faith.

I am not a believer, but I recall having been born into a family of believers who tried, without excessive enthusiasm perhaps, to transmit their faith to me. My unbelief was not, however, a matter of oedipal rebellion and signal of a rejection of family values. In adolescence, when Dostoevsky's characters first began to impress me with the violence of their tragic mysticism, I knelt before the icon of the Virgin that sat enthroned above my bed and attempted to gain access to a faith that my secular education did not so much combat as treat ironically or simply ignore. I tried to imagine myself in that enigmatic other world, full of gentle suffering and mysterious grace, revealed to me by Byzantine iconography. When nothing happened, I told myself that faith could not come until I had endured difficult trials. The road to belief was blocked, perhaps, by the lack of hardship in my life. But the vitality, not to say excitability, of my adolescent body came between mournful images of death and everyday reality, and my macabre thoughts soon gave way to erotic daydreams.

Later, in reading about famous mystical experiences, I felt that faith could be described, perhaps rather simplistically, as what can only be called a primary identification with a loving and protective agency. Overcoming the notion of irremediable separation, Western man, using 'semiotic' rather than 'symbolic' means, reestablishes a continuity or fusion with an Other that is no longer substantial and maternal but symbolic and paternal. Saint Augustine goes so far as to compare the Christian's faith in God with the infant's relation to its mother's breast. 'What am I even at the best but an infant sucking the milk Thou givest, and feeding upon Thee, the food that perisheth not?'[1] What we have here is fusion with a breast that is, to be sure, succoring, nourishing, loving, and protective, but transposed from the mother's body to an invisible agency located in another world. This is quite a wrench from the dependency of early childhood, and it must be said that it is a compromise solution, since the benefits of the new relationship of dependency are entirely of an imaginary order, in the realm of signs. However intelligible or reasonable this dynamic may be (and theology excels at describing it), it appears to be driven, in essence, by infra- or trans-linguistic psychic processes which behave like primary processes and gratify the individual in his or her narcissistic core. At the dawn of psychic experience Freud saw a primary identification, a 'direct and immediate transference' of the nascent ego to the 'father of individual prehistory,' who, according to Freud, possessed the sexual characteristics and functions of both parents.[2]

This 'direct and immediate transference' to a form, a structure, or an agency (rather than a person) helps to bring about primary stabilization of the subject through its enduring character; because it is a gift of the self, it both encourages and hinders the disintegrative and aggressive agitation of the instincts. This is perhaps what Christianity celebrates in divine love. God was the first to love you, God is love: these apothegms reassure the believer of God's permanent generosity and grace. He is given a gift of love without any immediate requirement of merit, although the question of just deserts does eventually arise in the form of a demand for asceticism and self-perfection. This fusion with God, which, to repeat myself, is more semiotic than symbolic, repairs the wounds of Narcissus, which are scarcely hidden by the triumphs and failures of our desires and enmities. Once our narcissistic needs are met, we can find images of our desires in stories recounting the experience of faith: the story of the virgin birth, for instance – that secret dream of every childhood; or that of the torment of the flesh on Golgotha, which mirrors in glory the essential melancholy of the man who aspires to rejoin the body and name of a father from whom he has been irrevocably severed.

In order for faith to be possible, this 'semiotic' leap toward the other, this primary identfication [sic] with the primitive parental poles close to the maternal container, must not be either repressed or displaced in the construction of a knowledge which, by understanding the mechanism of faith, would bury it. Repression can be atheist; atheism is repressive, whereas the experience of psychoanalysis can lead to renunciation of faith with clear understanding. The subsequent loss of a certain kind of pleasure brings the pleasure of another kind of understanding to the subject who has made such a decision; this other kind of understanding is not positive knowledge but strictly private, involving the fundamental dynamics of the psyche.

My adolescent rejection of faith probably had more to do with repression or with my overcoming auto-erotic guilt than with analytic detachment. By contrast, the ordeal of analysis requires, at a minimum, that I (analyst or analysand) accept the existence of an other. As Lacan rightly said, 'There is an Other.' The treatment of psychosis may suggest to the optimistic analyst that meaning – as well as the subject – is always already there, simply waiting to be established through his interpretation. A certain fideism, or even degraded forms of spiritualism, thereby find their way into psychoanalytic ideology. I hope, however, that through vigilant listening and strict adherence to interpretive logic we can be sure of continuing to see man as divided (both biological organism and talking subject, both unconscious and conscious), and to understand that man is (tenuously and intermittently) a subject only of the language enunciated by the other – the object, for each member of the group of his or her desires and hatreds. Other in language, otherness in speech, here and now rather than in some 'other' world, the analyst listens and speaks, and by so doing makes the other less hellish ('Hell,' said Sartre, 'is other people'). The result is not to prepare that other for some sort of transcendental existence but rather to open up as yet undefined possibilities in this world. [. . .]

Credo

'I *believe in* one God the Father Almighty . . .'

Credo: one of the most charged and enigmatic words in the European lexicon. Ernout and Meillet suggest the etymon **kred-oh* (see the Vedic *srad-dhati*, 'he believes'), but the derivation leading to the Latin form *cred-* is not clear: the same with **dhe*, 'to set down,' which gives several Latin forms ending in *-do* (*condo*, 'to set down together,' *abdo*, 'to locate far from,' and *sacer dos*, **sakro-dho-ts*, 'priest'). The composite **kred-dh* is formally impossible in Indoeuropean, where **kret-* and **dhe* were independent. The real problems have to do with **kret-*.

Darmesteter was the first to interpret *credo*, *srad-dhati*, **kre-dh-* as 'to put one's heart into something.' Ernout and Meillet feel that this 'relation [with the heart] is a hypothesis for which there is no basis,' and Benveniste makes a similar point when he remarks that in Indoeuropean 'heart' can no more be a metaphor for life or spirit than 'lung' or 'kidney.'[3] Mayrhofer, however, feels that the hypothesis is justified: *kred-*, he says, is the composite form of **kerd-*, whereas Ernout and Meillet assume an alternating root, *k'erd-/krd*. Dumézil, who was at one time critical of Darmesteter's interpretation, has withdrawn his objections. According to the dictionary of Monier Williams, the corresponding Vedic word *srat-*, attested only in the composites *srad-dha-*, 'to believe,' and *srat-kar-*, 'to vouch for, give assurance of,' is considered in traditional Indian etymology a synonym of *satya-*, 'truth.' He sees a parallel between *srat-* and the Latin *cor*, *cordis*, as well as the Greek χαρδια.

Benveniste's comments on the question are important. After reviewing the various etymological interpretations, he argues that from the beginning *credo/ sraddha* had both a *religious* meaning and an *economic* meaning: the word denotes an 'act of confidence implying restitution,' and 'to pledge something on faith in the certainty that it will be returned,' religiously and economically. Thus the correspondence between *credence* and *credit* is one of 'the oldest in the Indoeuropean vocabulary.' Vedic man deposits his *desire*, his 'token,' his 'magical strength' (more than his heart) with the gods, trusting them and counting on their reward: *Indra* is the god of assistance, *Sraddha* the goddess of offerings. The Vedic religion, it has been said, can be summed up in the three terms faith, gift, and pleasure in giving. Having received the *srad*, god returns it to the believer in the form of his protection; trust in god is based on return, and 'faith' implies certainty of remuneration. It is easy to see how the notion could have been secularized to mean 'credit' in the financial sense. As for the heart, Christianity would later glorify it as the seat of faith. Saint Augustine was among the first to use this metaphor, for example, in his exhortation to 'read the Holy Scripture with your eyes fixed firmly on your heart.'[4]

In its two-thousand-year history Christianity has known a variety of mystical experiences unique for their psychological subtlety: in extreme cases mystics have gone so far as to reject not only credit-recompense but even the very act of prayer, which they viewed as a selfish request. Nevertheless, in its general tenor and institutional embodiment the Christian faith appears not to be inconsistent with the Indoeuropean model of belief.

Do the Indoeuropean languages reflect a type of culture in which the individual suffers dramatically because of his separation from the cosmos and the other? Presumably implicit in such a separation and its attendant suffering is the act of offering – a bridge across the gap – together with the expectation of reward. The human, however, is immersed in the rhythms of the cosmos, which in the Indoeuropean world dominate the separation that underlies faith.

In reality, it is the biblical God who inaugurates separation at the beginning of creation. He creates a division which is also the mark of His presence: 'In the beginning God created the heaven and the earth.' *Bereschit*. The source and meaning of Christianity lie in Judaism, which Christians today seem to be rediscovering after years of separation. Psychologically, however, it is Christ's Passion, the 'folly on the cross,' as Saint Paul and Pascal called it, that reveals the somber division that is perhaps the paradoxical condition of faith: 'Father, Father, why hast thou forsaken me?'

It is because I am separate, forsaken, alone vis-à-vis the other that I can psychologically cross the divide that is the condition of my existence and achieve not only ecstasy in completion (*complétude*: reunion with the father, himself a symbolic substitute for the mother) but also eternal life (resurrection) in the imagination. For the Christian believer the completion of faith is real completion, and Christ, with whom the believer is exhorted to identify, expiates in human form the sin of all mankind before achieving glory in resurrection. [. . .]

Notes

1   Saint Augustine, *Confessions*, E. B. Pusey, tr. (New York: Dutton, 1951), IV, 1, 1.

2   Sigmund Freud, *The Ego and the Id* (New York: Norton, 1963).

3   Emile Benveniste, *Vocabulaire des institutions indo-européennes* (Paris: Éditions de Minuit, 1969), 1: 175.

4   Saint Augustine, *De doctrina Christiana* IV, 5, 7.

Chapter 10

Stabat Mater

■   This essay, reprinted here in full, first appeared as 'Hérétique
de l'amour' in *Tel quel* 74 (1977) and was reprinted as 'Stabat Mater'
in *Histoires d'amour* (Denoël, 1983). It first appeared in English as
'Stabat Mater', translated by Arthur Goldhammer, in *Poetics Today* 6,
1–2 (1985). It was then translated into English by Leon S. Roudiez as
'Stabat Mater' in *The Kristeva Reader*, edited by Toril Moi (Columbia
University Press, 1986), and reprinted in Kristeva's *Tales of Love*
(Columbia University Press, 1987).

Editors' introduction

THERE IS NO OTHER individual essay of Kristeva's that is as frequently
reprinted and widely cited as 'Stabat Mater'. It at once brings together her
postulations on the relation between language and subjectivity, as well as her
historic and theological reflections on the role of the Virgin Mary in the Catholic
tradition, and provides a moving account of her personal experiences with
maternity. Again, more than any other of Kristeva's writings, this piece is
difficult to categorise. It is neither an academic essay, since the learned voice of
the scholar is frequently interrupted by a stream-of-consciousness personal
narrative, nor is it strictly autobiography, since the diary-like passages do not
dominate the text, but bubble up through the fissures and gaps of the scholarly
writing. The ambiguity of genre is certainly intentional, as is the identity
(scholarly/personal) of the speaking voice, since 'Stabat Mater' functions well,
not only as an investigation of the bond that exists between mother and child
(and between a new mother and her own mother), but also as a representation of
Kristeva's theoretical understanding of language operation.

The two distinct speaking voices of 'Stabat Mater' – though one could argue
there are more than two – are physically separated on the page, with the
personal reflections written in a dense, imagistic prose in a column of bold font
placed to the left of the academic writing. At first, these bold columns infre-
quently interrupt the motion of the linear argument being developed by Kristeva

in the right-hand text, but as the essay progresses the bold text comes to take equal space on the page, so that there are two competing columns. Then, at an indefinite point in the writing, the two separated voices mingle and it is no longer clear that the bold text is for personal reflection alone, since it, too, is suffused with theoretical strands of argument and historic considerations.

Early readers of 'Stabat Mater' were quick to note that the two columns could represent Kristeva's bi-polar operative modes of language: the (masculine) symbolic and the (feminine, maternal) semiotic. The symbolic, for Kristeva, is that aspect of language that enables logic, linearity and univocal meaning; it is the referential and communicative facet of language – its denotative properties. The semiotic, on the other hand, is the rhythmic part of any language use, its playful, poetic or illogical element – its connotative properties. However, in an interview on 'Stabat Mater', Kristeva has made it plain that it would be a mistake to read the two columns so simplistically, since no language usage can be fully semiotic or symbolic. That is, all language operation functions through a dialogue or interplay between these two poles of logic. For Kristeva, this exchange between the semiotic–symbolic in language operation is what gives depth and richness to a finely crafted text. It is manifested in a doubling, or otherness, that is implicit in the linguistic contract (in that any statement always means more than it says). This doubling of the text further represents the 'split-subject' of the reader, who, like the language she uses, is never wholly symbolic (that is, unified and complete in her identity), but is always also double, or other: a subject of competing and dissonant bodily drives and desires, a subject, in Kristeva's terms, perpetually 'in-process'.

The duelling columns of 'Stabat Mater' thus represent Kristeva's theory of language and subjectivity, yet the consistent focus on maternity throughout highlights the physical doubling of a woman's body during pregnancy that allows her to be, quite literally, both one and other. The expectant mother represents Kristeva's split-subject *extraordinaire*. Yet, Kristeva notes, it is precisely this experience of alterity during pregnancy that the dominant culture has attempted to efface with its idealisation, and she goes so far as to call it in places a 'fetishization', of the Blessed Virgin Mary. The dominant forms of Catholic theology have employed the divine motherhood of Mary – her own immaculate conception, as well as her perpetual virginity, and later, her bodily assumption into heaven – in order to erase the bodily traces of actual birth, and the necessary mortality linked with bodily origins. This refusal of the body, Kristeva believes, is an attempt by the masculine, symbolic order (represented, here, by Christian theology) to cancel the maternal, semiotic debt to which we all owe our origins. The power of motherhood is thus brought under the domain of the patriarchy.

Of course, no such effacement is wholly possible, as Kristeva traces, citing extensively the work of Marina Warner, some of the cathartic aspects of the cult of the Virgin for her followers. However, Kristeva no longer believes the Marion cult is efficacious for contemporary women; something more is needed. 'Stabat Mater' bristles with criticism at (liberal American) feminism which, Kristeva believes, has devalued or ignored the important role of motherhood in cultural production precisely at a time when women need to value it the most. She calls for a new ethics, 'herethics' (a heretical ethics), based on the maternal experience of division and doubling, where the feminine (semiotic) will not be sacrificed to the masculine (symbolic) order; where there will be a recognition, accommodation and love for the other, as a mother loves her child, and where the actual experiences of motherhood will not be romanticised, as with the Blessed Virgin, but valued on their own terms.

The paradox: mother or primary narcissism

If it is not possible to say of a *woman* what she *is* (without running the risk of abolishing her difference), would it perhaps be different concerning the *mother*, since that is the only function of the 'other sex' to which we can definitely attribute existence? And yet, there too, we are caught in a paradox. First, we live in a civilization where the *consecrated* (religious or secular) representation of femininity is absorbed by motherhood. If, however, one looks at it more closely, this motherhood is the *fantasy* that is nurtured by the adult, man or woman, of a lost territory; what is more, it involves less an idealized archaic mother than the idealization of the *relationship* that binds us to her, one that cannot be localized—an idealization of primary narcissism. Now, when feminism demands a new representation of femininity, it seems to identify motherhood with that idealized misconception and, because it rejects the image and its misuse, feminism circumvents the real experience that fantasy overshadows. The result?—a negation or rejection of motherhood by some avant-garde feminist groups. Or else an acceptance—conscious or not—of its traditional representations by the great mass of people, women and men.

FLASH—instant of time or of dream without time; inordinately swollen atoms of a bond, a vision, a shiver, a yet formless, unnamable embryo. Epiphanies. Photos of what is not yet visible and that language necessarily skims over

Christianity is doubtless the most refined symbolic construct in which femininity, to the extent that it transpires through it—and it does so incessantly—is focused on *Maternality*.[1] Let us call 'maternal' the ambivalent

from afar, allusively. Words that are always too distant, too abstract for this underground swarming of seconds, folding in unimaginable spaces. Writing them down is an ordeal of discourse, like love. What is loving, for a woman, the same thing as writing. Laugh. Impossible. Flash on the unnamable, weavings of abstractions to be torn. Let a body venture at last out of its shelter, take a chance with meaning under a veil of words. WORD FLESH. From one to the other, eternally, broken up visions, metaphors of the invisible.

principle that is bound to the species, on the one hand, and on the other stems from an identity catastrophe that causes the Name to topple over into the unnamable that one imagines as femininity, nonlanguage, or body. Thus Christ, the Son of man, when all is said and done, is 'human' only through his mother—as if Christly or Christian humanism could only be a maternalism (this is, besides, what some secularizing trends within its orbit do not cease claiming in their esotericism). And yet, the humanity of the Virgin mother is not always obvious, and we shall see how, in her being cleared of sin, for instance, Mary distinguishes herself from mankind. But at the same time the most intense revelation of God, which occurs in mysticism, is given only to a person who assumes himself as 'maternal.' Augustine, Bernard of Clairvaux, Meister Eckhart, to mention but a few, played the part of the Father's virgin spouses, or even, like Bernard, received drops of virginal milk directly on their lips. Freedom with respect to the maternal territory then becomes the pedestal upon which love of God is erected. As a consequence, mystics, those 'happy Schrebers' (Sollers) throw a bizarre light on the psychotic sore of modernity: it appears as the incapability of contemporary codes to tame the maternal, that is, primary narcissism. Uncommon and 'literary,' their present-day counterparts are always somewhat oriental, if not tragical—Henry Miller, who says he is pregnant; Artaud, who sees himself as 'his daughters' or 'his mother' . . . It is the orthodox constituent of Christianity, through John Chrysostom's golden mouth, among others, that sanctioned the transitional function of the Maternal by calling the Virgin a 'bond,' a 'medium,' or an 'interval,' thus opening the door to more or less heretical identifications with the Holy Ghost.

This resorption of femininity within the Maternal is specific to many civilizations, but Christianity, in its own fashion, brings it to its peak. Could it be that such a reduction represents no more than a masculine appropriation of the Maternal, which, in line with our hypothesis, is only a fantasy masking primary narcissism? Or else, might one detect in it, in other respects, the workings of enigmatic sublimation? These are perhaps the workings of masculine sublimation, a sublimation just the same, if it be true that for Freud picturing Da Vinci, and even for Da Vinci himself, the taming of that economy (of the Maternal or of primary narcissism) is a requirement for artistic, literary, or painterly accomplishment?

Within that perspective, however, there are two questions, among others, that remain unanswered. What is there, in the portrayal of the Maternal in general and particularly in its Christian, virginal, one, that reduces social anguish and gratifies a male being; what is there that also satisfies a woman so that a commonality of the sexes is set up, beyond and in spite of their glaring incompatibility and permanent warfare? Moreover, is there something in that Maternal notion that ignores what a woman might say or want—as a result, when women speak out today it is in matters of conception and motherhood that their annoyance is basically centered. Beyond social and political demands, this takes the well-known 'discontents' of our civilization to a level where Freud would not follow—the discontents of the species.

A triumph of the unconscious in monotheism

It would seem that the 'virgin' attribute for Mary is a translation error, the translator having substituted for the Semitic term that indicates the sociolegal status of a young unmarried woman the Greek word *parthenos*, which on the other hand specifies a physiological and psychological condition: virginity. One might read into this the Indo-European fascination (which Dumezil analyzed)[2] with the virgin daughter as guardian of paternal power; one might also detect an ambivalent conspiracy, through excessive spiritualization, of the mother-goddess and the underlying matriarchy with which Greek culture and Jewish monotheism kept struggling. The fact remains that western Christianity has organized that 'translation error,' projected its own fantasies into it, and produced one of the most powerful imaginary constructs known in the history of civilizations.

The story of the virginal cult in Christianity amounts in fact to the imposition of pagan-rooted beliefs in, and often against, dogmas of the official Church. It is true that the Gospels already posit Mary's existence. But they suggest only very discreetly the immaculate conception of Christ's mother, they say nothing concerning Mary's own background and speak of her only seldom at the side of her son or during crucifixion. Thus Matthew 1:20 ('. . . the angel of the Lord appeared to him in a dream and said, "Joseph, son of David, do not be afraid to take Mary home as your wife, because she has conceived what is in her by the Holy Spirit"'), and Luke 1:34 ('Mary said to the angel, "But how can this come about since I do not know man?"') open a door, a narrow opening for all that, but one that would soon widen thanks to apocryphal additions, on impregnations without sexuality; according to this notion a woman, preserved from masculine intervention, conceives alone with a 'third party,' a nonperson, the Spirit. In the rare instances when the Mother of Jesus appears in the Gospels, she is informed that filial relationship rests not with the flesh but with the name or, in other words, that any possible matrilinearism is to be repudiated and the symbolic link alone is to last. We thus have Luke 2:48–49 ('. . . his mother said to him, "My child, why have you done this to us? See how worried your father and I have been, looking for you." "Why were you looking for me?" he replied. "Did you not know that I must be busy with my father's affairs?"'), and also John 2:3–5 ('. . . the mother of Jesus said to him, "They have no wine." Jesus said, 'Woman, why turn to me?[3] My hour has not come yet."') and 19:26–27 ('Seeing his mother and the disciple he loved standing near her, Jesus said to his mother, "Woman, this is your son." Then to the disciple he said, "This is your mother." And from that moment the disciple made a place for her in his home.')

Starting from this programmatic material, rather skimpy nevertheless, a compelling imaginary construct proliferated in essentially three directions. In the first place, there was the matter of drawing a parallel between Mother and Son by expanding the theme of the immaculate conception, inventing a biography of Mary similar to that of Jesus, and, by depriving her of sin to deprive her of death. Mary leaves by way of Dormition or Assumption. Next, she needed letters patent of nobility, a power that, even though exercised in the beyond, is nonetheless political, since Mary was to be proclaimed queen, given the attributes and paraphernalia of royalty and, in parallel fashion, declared Mother of the divine institution on earth, the Church. Finally, the relationship with Mary and from Mary was to be revealed as the prototype of a love relationship and followed two fundamental aspects of western love: courtly love and child love, thus fitting the entire range that goes from sublimation to asceticism and masochism.

Neither sex nor death

Mary's life, devised on the model of the life of Jesus, seems to be the fruit of apocryphal literature. The story of her own miraculous conception, called 'immaculate conception,' by Ann and Joachim, after a long, barren marriage, together with her biography as a pious maiden, show up in apocryphal sources as early as the end of the first century. Their entirety may be found in the *Secret Book of James* and also in one of the pseudoepigrapha, the Gospel according to the Hebrews (which inspired Giotto's frescoes, for instance). Those 'facts' were quoted by Clement of Alexandria and Origen but not officially accepted; even though the Eastern Church tolerated them readily, they were translated into Latin only in the sixteenth century. Yet the West was not long before glorifying the life of Mary on its own but always under orthodox guidance. The first Latin poem, 'Maria,' on the birth of Mary was written by the nun Hrotswith von Gandersheim (who died before 1002), a playwright and poet.

Fourth-century asceticism, developed by the Fathers of the Church, was grafted on that apocryphal shoot in order to bring out and rationalize the immaculate conception postulate. The demonstration was based on a simple logical relation: the intertwining of sexuality and death. Since they are mutually implicated with each other, one cannot avoid the one without fleeing the other. This asceticism, applicable to both sexes, was vigorously expressed by John Chrysostom (*On Virginity*: 'For where there is death there is also sexual copulation, and where there is no death there is no sexual copulation either'); even though he was attacked by Augustine and Aquinas, he nonetheless fueled Christian doctrine. Thus, Augustine condemned 'concupiscence' (*epithumia*) and posited that Mary's virginity is in fact only a logical precondition of Christ's chastity. The Orthodox Church, heir no doubt to a matriarchy that was more intense in eastern European societies, emphasized Mary's virginity more boldly. Mary was contrasted with Eve, life with death (Jerome, *Letter 22*, 'Death came through Eve but life through Mary'; Irenaeus, 'Through Mary the snake becomes a dove and we are freed from the chains of death'). People even got involved in torturous arguments in order to demonstrate that Mary remained a virgin after childbirth (thus the second Constantinople council, in 381, under Arianistic influence, emphasized the Virgin's role in comparison to official dogma and asserted Mary's perpetual virginity; the 451 council called her *Aeiparthenos*—ever virgin). Once this was established, Mary, instead of being referred to as Mother of man or Mother of Christ, would be proclaimed Mother of God: *Theotokos*. Nestorius, patriarch of Constantinople, refused to go along; Nestorianism, however, for all practical purposes died with the patriarch's own death in 451, and the path that would lead to Mary's deification was then clear.

Head reclining, nape finally relaxed, skin, blood, nerves warmed up, luminous flow: stream of hair made of ebony, of nectar, smooth darkness through her fingers, gleaming honey under the wings of bees, sparkling strands burning bright . . . silk, mercury, ductile copper: frozen light warmed under fingers. Mane of beast— squirrel, horse, and the happiness of a faceless head, Narcissuslike touching without eyes, sight dissolving in muscles, hair, deep, smooth, peaceful colors. Mamma: anamnesis.

Taut eardrum, tearing sound out of muted silence. Wind among grasses, a seagull's faraway call, echoes of waves, auto horns, voices, or nothing? Or his own tears, my newborn, spasm of syncopated void. I no longer hear anything, but the eardrum keeps transmitting this resonant vertigo to my skull, the hair. My body is no longer mine, it doubles up, suffers, bleeds, catches cold, puts its teeth in, slobbers, coughs, is covered with pimples, and it laughs. And yet, when its own joy, my child's, returns, its smile washes only my eyes. But the pain, its pain—it comes from inside, never remains apart, other, it

Very soon, within the complex relationship between Christ and his Mother where relations of God to mankind, man to woman, son to mother, etc., are hatched, the problematics of *time* similar to that of cause loomed up. If Mary preceded Christ and he originated in her if only from the standpoint of his humanity, should not the conception of Mary herself have been immaculate? For, if that were not the case, how could a being conceived in sin and harboring it in herself produce a God? Some apocryphal writers had not hesitated, without too much caution, to suggest such an absence of sin in Mary's conception, but the Fathers of the Church were more careful. Bernard of Clairvaux is reluctant to extol the conception of Mary by Anne, and thus he tries to check the homologation of Mary with Christ. But it fell upon Duns Scotus to change the hesitation over the promotion of a mother goddess within Christianity into a logical problem, thus saving them both, the Great Mother as well as logic. He viewed Mary's birth as a *praeredemptio*, as a matter of congruency: if it be true that Christ alone saves us through his redemption on the cross, the Virgin who bore him can but be pre-

inflames me at once, without a second's respite. As if that was what I had given birth to and, not willing to part from me, insisted on coming back, dwelled in me permanently. One does not give birth in pain, one gives birth to pain: the child represents it and henceforth it settles in, it is continuous. Obviously you may close your eyes, cover up your ears, teach courses, run errands, tidy up the house, think about objects, subjects. But a mother is always branded by pain, she yields to it. 'And a sword will pierce your own soul too . . .'

Dream without glow, without sound, dream of brawn. Dark twisting, pain in the back, the arms, the thighs—pincers turned into fibers, infernos bursting veins, stones breaking bones: grinders of volumes, expanses, spaces, lines, points. All those words, now, ever visible things to register the roar of a silence that hurts all over. As if a geometry ghost could suffer when collapsing in a noiseless tumult . . . Yet the eye picked up nothing, the ear remained deaf. But everything swarmed, and crumbled, and twisted, and broke—the grinding continued . . . Then, slowly, a shad-

served from sin in 'recursive' fashion, from the time of her own conception up to that redemption.

For or against, with dogma or logical shrewdness, the battle around the Virgin intensified between Jesuits and Dominicans, but the Counter-Reformation, as is well known, finally ended the resistance: henceforth, Catholics venerated Mary in herself. The Society of Jesus succeeded in completing a process of popular pressure distilled by patristic asceticism, and in reducing, with neither explicit hostility nor brutal rejection, the share of the Maternal (in the sense given above) useful to a certain balance between the two sexes. Curiously and necessarily, when that balance began to be seriously threatened in the nineteenth century, the Catholic Church—more dialectical and subtle here than the Protestants who were already spawning the first suffragettes—raised the Immaculate Conception to dogma status in 1854. It is often suggested that the blossoming of feminism in Protestant countries is due, among other things, to the greater initiative allowed women on the social and ritual plane. One might wonder if, in addition, such a flower-

owy shape gathered, became detached, darkened, stood out: seen from what must be the true place of my head, it was the right side of my pelvis. Just bony, sleek, yellow, misshapen, a piece of my body jutting out unnaturally, asymmetrically, but slit: severed scaly surface, revealing under this disproportionate pointed limb the fibers of a marrow . . . Frozen placenta, live limb of a skeleton, monstrous graft of life on myself, a living dead. Life . . . death . . . undecidable. During delivery it went to the left with the afterbirth . . . My removed marrow, which nevertheless acts as a graft, which wounds but increases me. Paradox: deprivation and benefit of childbirth. But calm finally hovers over pain, over the terror of this dried branch that comes back to life, cut off, wounded, deprived of its sparkling bark. The calm of another life, the life of that other who wends his way while I remain henceforth like a framework. Still life. There is him, however, his own flesh, which was mine yesterday. Death, then, how could I yield to it?

ing is not the result of a *lack* in the Protestant religious structure with respect to the Maternal, which, on the contrary, was elaborated within Catholicism with a refinement to which the Jesuits gave the final touch, and which still makes Catholicism very difficult to analyze.

The fulfillment, under the name of Mary, of a totality made of woman and God is finally accomplished through the avoidance of death. The Virgin Mary experiences a fate more radiant than her son's: she undergoes no calvary, she has no tomb, she doesn't die and hence has no need to rise from the dead. Mary doesn't die but, as if to echo oriental beliefs, Taoists' among others, according to which human bodies pass from one place to another in an eternal flow that constitutes a carbon copy of the maternal receptacle—she is transported.

Her transition is more passive in the Eastern Church: it is a Dormition (*Koimesis*) during which, according to a number of iconographic representations, Mary can be seen changed into a little girl in the arms of her son who henceforth becomes her father; she thus reverses her role as Mother into a Daughter's role for the greater pleasure of those who enjoy Freud's 'Theme of the Three Caskets.'

Indeed, *mother* of her son and his *daughter* as well, Mary is also, and besides, his *wife*: she therefore actualizes the threefold metamorphosis of a woman in the tightest parenthood structure. From 1135 on, transposing the Song of Songs, Bernard of Clairvaux glorifies Mary in her role of beloved and wife. But Catherine of Alexandria (said to have been martyred in 307) already pictured herself as receiving the wedding ring from Christ, with the Virgin's help, while Catherine of Siena (1347–80) goes through a mystical wedding with him. Is it the impact of Mary's function as Christ's beloved and wife that is responsible for the blossoming out of the Marian cult in the West after Bernard and thanks to the Cistercians? 'Vergine Madre, figlia del tuo Figlio,' Dante exclaims, thus probably best condensing the gathering of the three feminine functions (daughter–wife–mother) within a totality where they vanish as specific corporealities while retaining their psychological functions. Their bond makes up the basis of unchanging and timeless spirituality; 'the set time limit of an eternal design,' [Termine fisso d'eterno consiglio], as Dante materfully points out in his Divine Comedy.

The transition is more active in the West, with Mary rising body and soul toward the other world in an Assumption. That feast, honored in Byzantium as early as the fourth century, reaches Gaul in the seventh under the influence of the Eastern Church; but the earliest Western visions of the Virgin's assumption, women's visions (particularly that of Elizabeth von Schönau who died in 1164) date only from the twelfth century. For the Vatican, the Assumption became dogma only in 1950. What death anguish was it intended to soothe after the conclusion of the deadliest of wars?

Image of power

On the side of 'power,' Maria Regina appears in imagery as early as the sixth century in the church of Santa Maria Antiqua in Rome. Interestingly enough, it is she, woman and mother, who is called upon to represent supreme earthly power. Christ is king but neither he nor his father are pictured wearing crowns, diadems, costly paraphernalia, and other external signs of abundant material goods. That opulent infringement to Christian idealism is centered on the Virgin Mother. Later, when she assumed the title of Our Lady, this would also be an analogy to the earthly power of the noble feudal lady of medieval courts. Mary's function as guardian of power, later checked when the Church became wary of it, nevertheless persisted in popular and pictorial representation, witness Piero della Francesca's impressive painting, Madonna della Misericordia, which was disavowed by Catholic authorities at the time. And yet, not only did the papacy revere more and more the Christly mother as the Vatican's power over cities and municipalities was strengthened, it also openly identified its own institution with the Virgin: Mary was officially proclaimed Queen by Pius XII in 1954 and *Mater Ecclesiae* in 1964.

Eia mater, fons amoris!

Fundamental aspects of Western love finally converged on Mary. In a first step, it indeed appears that the Marian cult homologizing Mary with Jesus and carrying asceticism to the extreme was opposed to courtly love for the noble lady, which, while representing social transgression, was not at all a physical or moral sin. And yet, at the very dawn of a 'courtliness' that was still very carnal, Mary and the Lady shared one common trait: they are the focal point of men's desires and aspirations. Moreover, because they were unique and thus excluded all other women, both the Lady and the Virgin embodied an absolute authority the more attractive as it appeared removed from paternal sternness. This feminine power must have been experienced as denied power, more pleasant to seize because it was both archaic and secondary, a kind of substitute for effective power in the family and the city but no less authoritarian, the underhand double of explicit phallic power. As early as the thirteenth century, thanks to the implantation of ascetic Christianity and especially, as early as 1328, to the promulgation of Salic laws, which excluded daughters from the inheritance and thus made the loved one very vulnerable and colored one's love for her with all the hues of the impossible, the Marian and courtly streams came together. Around the time of Blanche of Castile (who died in 1252), the Virgin explicitly became the focus of courtly love, thus gathering the attributes of the desired woman and of the holy mother in a totality as accomplished as it was inaccessible. Enough to make any woman suffer, any man dream. One finds indeed in a *Miracle de Notre Dame* the story of a young man who abandons his fiancee for the Virgin: the latter came to him in a dream and reproached him for having left her for an 'earthly woman.'

Nevertheless, besides that ideal totality that no individual woman could possibly embody, the Virgin also became the **Scent of milk, dewed greenery, acid and clear, recall of wind, air, seaweed (as if a body lived without waste): it slides under the skin, does not remain in the** fulcrum of the humanization of the West in general and of love in particular. It is again about the thirteenth century, with Francis of Assisi, that this tendency takes shape with

mouth or nose but fondles the veins, detaches skin from bones, inflates me like an ozone balloon, and I hover with feet firmly planted on the ground in order to carry him, sure, stable, ineradicable, while he dances in my neck, flutters with my hair, seeks a smooth shoulder on the right, on the left, slips on the breast, swingles, silver vivid blossom of my belly, and finally flies away on my navel in his dream carried by my hands. My son.

Nights of wakefulness, scattered sleep, sweetness of the child, warm mercury in my arms, cajolery, affection, defenseless body, his or mine, sheltered, protected. A wave swells again, when he goes to sleep, under my skin—tummy, thighs, legs: sleep of the muscles, not of the brain, sleep of the flesh. The wakeful tongue quietly remembers another withdrawal, mine: a blossoming heaviness in the middle of the bed, of a hollow, of the sea . . . Recovered childhood, dreamed peace restored, in sparks, flash of cells, instants of laughter, smiles in the blackness of dreams, at night, opaque joy that roots me in her bed, my mother's, and projects him, a son, a butterfly soaking up dew

the representation of Mary as poor, modest, and humble— madonna of humility at the same time as a devoted, fond mother. The famous nativity of Piero della Francesca in London, in which Simone de Beauvoir too hastily saw a feminine defeat because the mother kneeled before her barely born son, in fact consolidates the new cult of humanistic sensitivity. It replaces the high spirituality that assimilated the Virgin to Christ with an earthly conception of a wholly human mother. As a source for the most popularized pious images, such maternal humility comes closer to 'lived' feminine experience than the earlier representations did. Beyond this, however, it is true that it integrates a certain feminine masochism but also displays its counterpart in gratification and jouissance. The truth of it is that the lowered head of the mother before her son is accompanied by the immeasurable pride of the one who knows she is also his wife and daughter. She knows she is destined to that eternity (of the spirit or of the species), of which every mother is unconsciously aware, and with regard to which maternal devotion or even sacrifice is but an insignificant price to pay. A price that is borne all

from her hand, there, nearby, in the night. Alone: she, I, and he.

He returns from the depths of the nose, the vocal chords, the lungs, the ears, pierces their smothering stopping sickness swab, and awakens in his eyes. Gentleness of the sleeping face, contours of pinkish jade— forehead, eyebrows, nostrils, cheeks, parted features of the mouth, delicate, hard, pointed chin. Without fold or shadow, neither being nor unborn, neither present nor absent, but real, real inaccessible innocence, engaging weight and seraphic lightness. A child?—An angel, a glow on an Italian painting, impassive, peaceful dream— dragnet of Mediterranean fishermen. And then, the mother-of-pearl bead awakens: quicksilver. Shiver of the eyelashes, imperceptible twitch of the eyebrows, quivering skin, anxious reflections, seeking, knowing, casting their knowledge aside in the face of my non-knowledge: fleeting irony of childhood gentleness that awakens to meaning, surpasses it, goes past it, causes me to soar in music, in dance. Impossible refinement, subtle rape of inherited genes: before what has been learned comes to pelt him, harden

the more easily since, contrasted with the love that binds a mother to her son, all other 'human relationships' burst like blatant shams. The Franciscan representation of the Mother conveys many essential aspects of maternal psychology, thus leading up to an influx of common people to the churches and also a tremendous increase in the Marian cult—witness the building of many churches dedicated to her ('Notre Dame'). Such a humanization of Christianity through the cult of the mother also led to an interest in the humanity of the father-man: the celebration of 'family life' showed Joseph to advantage as early as the fifteenth century.

What body?

We are entitled only to the ear of the virginal body, the tears, and the breast. With the female sexual organ changed into an innocent shell, holder of sound, there arises a possible tendency to eroticize hearing, voice, or even understanding. By the same token, however, sexuality is brought down to the level of innuendo. Feminine sexual experience is thus rooted in the universality of sound, since wit is distributed *equally*

him, ripen him. Hard, mischievous gentleness of the first ailment overcome, innocent wisdom of the first ordeal undergone, yet hopeful blame on account of the suffering I put you through, by calling for you, desiring, creating . . . Gentleness, wisdom, blame: your face is already human, sickness has caused you to join our species, you speak without words but your throat no longer gurgles—it harkens with me to the silence of your born meaning that draws my tears toward a smile.

The lover gone, forgetfulness comes, but the pleasure of the sexes remains, and there is nothing lacking. No representation, sensation, or recall. Inferno of vice. Later, forgetfulness returns but this time as a fall—leaden—grey, dull, opaque. Forgetfulness: blinding, smothering foam, but on the quiet. Like the fog that devours the park, wolfs down the branches, erases the green, rusty ground, and mists up my eyes.

Absence, inferno, forgetfulness. Rhythm of our loves.

A hunger remains, in place of the heart. A spasm that spreads, runs through the blood vessels to the tips of the breasts, to the tips of the

among all men, all women. A woman will only have the choice to live her life either *hyperabstractly* ('immediately universal,' Hegel said) in order thus to earn divine grace and homologation with symbolic order; or merely *different*, other, fallen ('immediately particular,' Hegel said). But she will not be able to accede to the complexity of being divided, of heterogeneity, of the catastrophic-fold-of-'being' ('never singular,' Hegel said).

Under a full, blue gown, the maternal, virginal body allowed only the breast to show, while the face, with the stiffness of Byzantine icons gradually softened, was covered with tears. Milk and tears became the privileged signs of the *Mater Dolorosa* who invaded the West beginning with the eleventh century, reaching the peak of its influx in the fourteenth. But it never ceased to fill the Marian visions of those, men or women (often children), who were racked by the anguish of a maternal frustration. Even though orality—threshold of infantile regression—is displayed in the area of the breast, while the spasm at the slipping away of eroticism is translated into tears, this should not conceal what milk and tears have in common:

fingers. It throbs, pierces the void, erases it, and gradually settles in. My heart: a tremendous pounding wound. A thirst.

Anguished, guilty. Freud's *Vaterkomplex* on the Acropolis? The impossibility of being without repeated legitimation (without books, man, family). Impossibility—depressing possibility—of 'transgression.'

Either repression in which *I* hands the Other what I want from others.

Or this squalling of the void, open wound in my heart, which allows me to be only in purgatory.

I yearn for the Law. And since it is not made for me alone, I venture to desire outside the law. Then, narcissism thus awakened—the narcissism that wants to be sex—roams, astonished. In sensual rapture I am distraught. Nothing reassures, for only the law sets anything down. Who calls such a suffering jouissance? It is the pleasure of the damned.

they are the metaphors of nonspeech, of a 'semiotics' that linguistic communication does not account for. The Mother and her attributes, evoking sorrowful humanity, thus become representatives of a 'return of the repressed' in monotheism. They reestablish what is nonverbal and show up as the receptacle of a signifying disposition that is closer to so-called primary processes. Without them the complexity of the Holy Ghost would have been mutilated. On the other hand, as they return by way of the Virgin Mother, they find their outlet in the arts—painting and music—of which the Virgin necessarily becomes both patron saint and privileged object.

The function of this 'Virginal Maternal' may thus be seen taking shape in the Western symbolic economy. Starting with the high Christly sublimation for which it yearns and occasionally exceeds, and extending to the extralinguistic regions of the unnamable, the Virgin Mother occupied the tremendous territory on this and that side of the parenthesis of language. She adds to the Christian trinity and to the Word that delineates their coherence the heterogeneity they salvage.

The ordering of the maternal libido reached its apotheosis when centered in the theme of death. The *Mater Dolorosa* knows no masculine body save that of her dead son, and her only pathos (which contrasts with the somewhat vacant, gentle serenity of the nursing Madonnas) is her shedding tears over a corpse. Since resurrection there is, and, as Mother of God, she must know this, nothing justifies Mary's outburst of pain at the foot of the cross, unless it be the desire to experience within her own body the death of a human being, which her feminine fate of being the source of life spares her. Could it be that the love, as puzzling as it is ancient, of mourners for corpses relates to the same longing of a woman whom nothing fulfills—the longing to experience the wholly masculine pain of a man who expires at every moment on account of jouissance due to obsession with his own death? And yet, Marian pain is in no way connected with tragic outburst: joy and even a kind of triumph follow upon tears, as if the conviction that death does not exist were an irrational but unshakable maternal certainty, on which the principle of resurrection had to rest. The brilliant illustration of the wrenching between desire for the masculine corpse and negation of death, a wrenching whose paranoid logic cannot be overlooked, is masterfully presented by the famous *Stabat Mater*. It is likely that all beliefs in resurrections are rooted in mythologies marked by the strong

Belief in the mother is rooted in fear, fascinated with a weakness—the weakness of language. If language is powerless to locate myself for and state myself to the other, I assume—I want to believe—that there is someone who makes up for that weakness. Someone, of either sex, *before* the id speaks, before language, who might make me be by means of borders, separations, vertigos. In asserting that 'in the beginning was the Word,' Christians must have found such a postulate sufficiently hard to believe and, for whatever it was worth, they added its compensation, its permanent lining: the maternal receptacle, purified as it might be by the virginal fantasy. Archaic maternal love would be an incorporation of my suffering that is unfail-

dominance of a mother goddess. Christianity, it is true, finds its calling in the displacement of that bio-maternal determinism through the postulate that immortality is mainly that of the name of the Father. But it does not succeed in imposing *its* symbolic revolution without relying on the feminine representation of an immortal biology. Mary defying death is the theme that has been conveyed to us by the numerous variations of the *Stabat Mater*, which, in the text attributed to Jacopone da Todi, enthralls us today through the music of Palestrina, Pergolesi, Haydn, and Rossini.

Let us listen to the baroque style of the young Pergolesi (1710–36), who was dying of tuberculosis when he wrote his immortal *Stabat Mater*. His musical inventiveness,

ing, unlike what often happens with the lacunary network of signs. In that sense, any belief, anguished by definition, is upheld by the fascinated fear of language's impotence. Every God, even including the God of the Word, relies on a mother Goddess. Christianity is perhaps also the last of the religions to have displayed in broad daylight the bipolar structure of belief: on the one hand, the difficult experience of the Word—a passion; on the other, the reassuring wrapping in the proverbial mirage of the mother—a love. For that reason, it seems to me that there is only one way to go through the religion of the Word, or its counterpart, the more or less discreet cult of the Mother; it is the 'artists'' way, those who make up for the vertigo of language weakness with the oversaturation of sign systems. By this token, all art is a kind of counter reformation, an accepted baroqueness. For is it not true that if the Jesuits finally did persuade the official Church to accept the cult of the Virgin, following the puritanical wave of the Reformation, that dogma was in fact no more than a pretext, and its efficacy lay elsewhere. It did

which, through Haydn, later reverberated in the work of Mozart, probably constitutes his one and only claim to immortality. But when this cry burst forth, referring to Mary facing her son's death, *'Eia Mater, fons amoris!'* ('Hail mother, source of love!')— was it merely a remnant of the period? Man overcomes the unthinkable of death by postulating maternal love in its place—in the place and stead of death and thought. This love, of which divine love is merely a not always convincing derivation, psychologically is perhaps a recall, on the near side of early identifications, of the primal shelter that insured the survival of the newborn. Such a love is in fact, logically speaking, a surge of anguish at the very moment when the identity of thought and living body collapses. The possibilities of communication having been swept away, only the subtle gamut of sound, touch, and visual traces, older than language and newly worked out, are preserved as an ultimate shield against death. It is only 'normal' for a maternal representation to set itself up at the place of this subdued anguish called love. No one escapes it. Except perhaps the saint, the mystic, or the writer who, through the power of

not become the opposite of the cult of the mother but its inversion through expenditure in the wealth of signs that constitutes the baroque. The latter renders belief in the Mother useless by overwhelming the symbolic weakness where she takes refuge, withdrawn from history, with an overabundance of discourse.

The immeasurable, unconfinable maternal body.

First there is the separation, previous to pregnancy, but which pregnancy brings to light and imposes without remedy.

On the one hand—the pelvis: center of gravity, unchanging ground, solid pedestal, heaviness and weight to which the thighs adhere, with no promise of agility on that score. On the other—the torso, arms, neck, head, face, calves, feet: unbounded liveliness, rhythm and mask, which furiously attempt to compensate for the immutability of the central tree. We live on that border, crossroads beings, crucified beings. A woman is neither nomadic nor a male body that considers itself earthly only in erotic passion. A mother is a continuous separation, a division of the language, nevertheless succeeds in doing no better than to take apart the fiction of the mother as mainstay of love, and to identify with love itself and what he is in fact—*a fire of tongues*, an exit from representation. Might not modern art then be, for the few who are attached to it, the implementation of that maternal love—a veil over death, in death's very site and with full knowledge of the facts? A sublimated celebration of incest . . .

Alone of her sex

Freud collected, among other objects of art and archeology, countless statuettes representing mother goddesses. And yet his interest in them comes to light only in discreet fashion in his work. It shows up when Freud examines artistic creation and homosexuality in connection with Leonardo da Vinci and deciphers there the ascendancy of an archaic mother, seen therefore from the standpoint of her effects on man and particularly on this strange function of his sometimes to change languages. Moreover, when Freud analyzes the advent and transformations of monotheism, he emphasizes that

very flesh. And consequently a division of language—and it has always been so.

Then there is this other abyss that opens up between the body and what had been its inside: there is the abyss between the mother and the child. What connection is there between myself, or even more unassumingly between my body and this internal graft and fold, which, once the umbilical cord has been severed, is an inaccessible other? My body and . . . him. No connection. Nothing to do with it. And this, as early as the first gestures, cries, steps, long before *its* personality has become my opponent. The child, whether *he* or *she*, is irremediably an other. To say that there are no sexual relationships constitutes a skimpy assertion when confronting the flash that bedazzles me when I confront the abyss between what was mine and is henceforth but irreparably alien. Trying to think through that abyss: staggering vertigo. No identity holds up. A mother's identity is maintained only through the well-known closure of consciousness within the indolence of habit, when a woman protects herself from the borderline that severs her body and expatriates

Christianity comes closer to pagan myths by integrating, through and against Judaic rigor, a preconscious acknowledgment of a maternal feminine. And yet, among the patients analyzed by Freud, one seeks in vain for mothers and their problems. One might be led to think that motherhood was a solution to neurosis and, by its very nature, ruled out psychoanalysis as a possible other solution. Or might psychoanalysis, at this point, make way for religion? In simplified fashion, the only thing Freud tells us concerning motherhood is that the desire for a child is a transformation of either penis envy or anal drive, and this allows her to discover the neurotic equation child-penis-feces. We are thus enlightened concerning an essential aspect of male phantasmatics with respect to childbirth, and female phantasmatics as well, to the extent that it embraces, in large part and in its hysterical labyrinths, the male one. The fact remains, as far as the complexities and pitfalls of maternal experience are involved, that Freud offers only a massive *nothing*, which, for those who might care to analyze it, is punctuated with this or that remark on the part of Freud's mother, proving to him in the

it from her child. Lucidity, on the contrary, would restore her as cut in half, alien to its other—and a ground favorable to delirium. But also and for that very reason, motherhood destines us to a demented jouissance that is answered, by chance, by the nursling's laughter in the sunny waters of the ocean. What connection is there between it and myself? No connection, except for that overflowing laughter where one senses the collapse of some ringing, subtle, fluid identity or other, softly buoyed by the waves.

Concerning that stage of my childhood, scented, warm, and soft to the touch, I have only a spatial memory. No time at all. Fragrance of honey, roundness of forms, silk and velvet under my fingers, on my cheeks. Mummy. Almost no sight—a shadow that darkens, soaks me up, or vanishes amid flashes. Almost no voice in her placid presence. Except, perhaps, and more belatedly, the echo of quarrels: her exasperation, her being fed up, her hatred. Never straightforward, always held back, as if, although the unmanageable child deserved it, the daughter could not accept the mother's hatred—it was not

kitchen that his own body is anything but immortal and will crumble away like dough; or the sour photograph of Marthe Freud, the wife, a whole mute story . . . There thus remained for his followers an entire continent to explore, a black one indeed, where Jung was the first to rush in, getting all his esoteric fingers burnt, but not without calling attention to some sore points of the imagination with regard to motherhood, points that are still resisting analytical rationality.[4]

There might doubtless be a way to approach the dark area that motherhood constitutes for a woman; one needs to listen, more carefully than ever, to what mothers are saying today, through their economic difficulties and, beyond the guilt that a too existentialist feminism handed down, through their discomforts, insomnias, joys, angers, desires, pains, and pleasures . . . One might, in similar fashion, try better to understand the incredible construct of the Maternal that the West elaborated by means of the Virgin, and of which I have just mentioned a few episodes in a never-ending history.

What is it then in this maternal representation that, alone of her sex, goes against both of the two sexes,[5] and

meant for her. A hatred without recipient or rather whose recipient was no 'I' and which, perturbed by such a lack of recipience, was toned down into irony or collapsed into remorse before reaching its destination. With others, this maternal aversion may be worked up to a spasm that is held like a delayed orgasm. Women doubtless reproduce among themselves the strange gamut of forgotten body relationships with their mothers. Complicity in the unspoken, connivance of the inexpressible, of a wink, a tone of voice, a gesture, a tinge, a scent. We are in it, set free of our identification papers and names, on an ocean of preciseness, a computerization of the unnamable. No communication between individuals but connections between atoms, molecules, wisps of words, droplets of sentences. The community of women is a community of dolphins. Conversely, when the other woman posits herself as such, that is, as singular and inevitably in opposition, 'I' am startled, so much that 'I' no longer know what is going on. There are then two paths left open to the rejection that bespeaks the recognition of the other woman as such. Either, not wanting to expe-

was able to attract women's wishes for identification as well as the very precise interposition of those who assumed to keep watch over the symbolic and social order?

Let me suggest, by way of hypothesis, that the virginal maternal is a way (not among the less effective ones) of dealing with feminine paranoia.

—The Virgin assumes her feminine denial of the other sex (of man) but overcomes him by setting up a third person: *I* do not conceive with *you* but with *Him*. The result is an immaculate conception (therefore with neither man nor sex), conception of a God with whose existence a woman has indeed something to do, on condition that she acknowledge being subjected to it.

—The Virgin assumes the paranoid lust for power by changing a woman into a Queen in heaven and a Mother of the earthly institutions (of the Church). But she succeeds in stifling that megalomania by putting it on its knees before the child-god.

—The Virgin obstructs the desire for murder or devouring by means of a strong oral cathexis (the breast), valorization of pain (the sob), and incitement to replace the sexed body with the ear of understanding.

rience her, I ignore her and, 'alone of my sex,' I turn my back on her in friendly fashion. It is a hatred that, lacking a recipient worthy enough of its power, changes to unconcerned complacency. Or else, outraged by her own stubbornness, by that other's belief that she is singular, I unrelentingly let go at her claim to address me and find respite only in the eternal return of power strokes, bursts of hatred— blind and dull but obstinate. I do not see her as herself but beyond her I aim at the claim to singularity, the unacceptable ambition to be something other than a child or a fold in the plasma that constitutes us, an echo of the cosmos that unifies us. What an inconceivable ambition it is to aspire to singularity, it is not natural, hence it is inhuman; the mania smitten with Oneness ('There is only One woman') can only impugn it by condemning it as 'masculine' . . . Within this strange feminine see-saw that makes 'me' swing from the unnamable community of women over to the war of individual singularities, it is unsettling to say 'I.' The languages of the great formerly matriarchal civilizations must avoid, do avoid, personal pronouns: they

—The Virgin assumes the paranoid fantasy of being excluded from time and death through the very flattering representation of Dormition or Assumption.

—The Virgin especially agrees with the repudiation of the other woman (which doubtless amounts basically to a repudiation of the woman's mother) by suggesting the image of A woman as Unique: alone among women, alone among mothers, alone among humans since she is without sin. But the acknowledgment of a longing for uniqueness is immediately checked by the postulate according to which uniqueness is attained only through an exacerbated masochism: a concrete woman, worthy of the feminine ideal embodied by the Virgin as an inaccessible goal, could only be a nun, a martyr, or, if she is married, one who leads a life that would remove her from that 'earthly' condition and dedicate her to the highest sublimation alien to her body. A bonus, however: the promised jouissance.

A skillful balance of concessions and constraints involving feminine paranoia, the representation of virgin motherhood appears to crown the efforts of a society to reconcile the social rem-

leave to the context the burden of distinguishing protagonists and take refuge in
tones to recover an under-
water, transverbal commu-
nication between bodies. It is
a music from which so-called
oriental civility tears away
suddenly through violence,
murder, blood baths. A
woman's discourse, would
that be it? Did not Christianity attempt, among other
things, to freeze that see-
saw? To stop it, tear women
away from its rhythm, settle
them permanently in the
spirit? Too permanently . . .

nants of matrilinearism and
the unconscious needs of primary narcissism on the one
hand, and on the other the re-
quirements of a new society
based on exchange and before
long on increased production,
which require the contribution of the superego and rely
on the symbolic paternal
agency.

While that clever balanced
architecture today appears to
be crumbling, one is led to ask
the following: what are the aspects of the feminine psyche
for which that representation
of motherhood does not pro-
vide a solution or else provides one that is felt as too coercive by
twentieth-century women?

The unspoken doubtless weighs first on the maternal body: as no
signifier can uplift it without leaving a remainder, for the signifier is
always meaning, communication, or structure, whereas a woman as
mother would be, instead, a strange fold that changes culture into nature,
the speaking into biology. Although it concerns every woman's body,
the heterogeneity that cannot be subsumed in the signifier nevertheless
explodes violently with pregnancy (the threshold of culture and nature)
and the child's arrival (which extracts woman out of her oneness and
gives her the possibility—but not the certainty—of reaching out to the
other, the ethical). Those particularities of the maternal body compose
woman into a being of folds, a catastrophe of being that the dialectics of
the trinity and its supplements would be unable to subsume.

Silence weighs heavily nonetheless on the corporeal and psychological
suffering of childbirth and especially the self-sacrifice involved in
becoming anonymous in order to pass on the social norm, which one
might repudiate for one's own sake but within which *one must* include
the child in order to educate it along the chain of generations. A
suffering lined with jubilation—ambivalence of masochism—on account
of which a woman, rather refractory to perversion, in fact allows herself
a coded, fundamental, perverse behavior, ultimate guarantee of society,
without which society will not reproduce and will not maintain a
constancy of standardized household. Feminine perversion does not

reside in the parcelling or the Don Juan-like multiplying of objects of desire; it is at once legalized, if not rendered paranoid, through the agency of masochism: all sexual 'dissoluteness' will be accepted and hence become insignificant, provided a child seals up such outpourings. Feminine perversion [*père-version*] is coiled up in the desire for law as desire for reproduction and continuity, it promotes feminine masochism to the rank of structure stabilizer (against its deviations); by assuring the mother that she may thus enter into an order that is above humans' will it gives her her reward of pleasure. Such coded perversion, such close combat between maternal masochism and the law have been utilized by totalitarian powers of all times to bring women to their side, and, of course, they succeed easily. And yet, it is not enough to 'declaim against' the reactionary role of mothers in the service of 'male dominating power.' One would need to examine to what extent that role corresponds to the biosymbolic latencies of motherhood and, on that basis, to try to understand, since the myth of the Virgin does not subsume them, or no longer does, how their surge lays women open to the most fearsome manipulations, not to mention blinding, or pure and simple rejection by progressive activists who refuse to take a close look.

Among things left out of the virginal myth there is the war between mother and daughter, a war masterfully but too quickly settled by promoting Mary as universal and particular, but never singular—as 'alone of her sex.' The relation to the other woman has presented our culture, in massive fashion during the past century, with the necessity to reformulate its representations of love and hatred—inherited from Plato's *Symposium*, the troubadours, or Our Lady. On that level, too, motherhood opens out a vista: a woman seldom (although not necessarily) experiences her passion (love and hatred) for another woman without having taken her own mother's place—without having herself become a mother, and especially without slowly learning to differentiate between same beings—as being face to face with her daughter forces her to do.

Finally, repudiation of the other sex (the masculine) no longer seems possible under the aegis of the third person, hypostatized in the child as go-between: 'neither me, nor you, but him, the child, the third person, the nonperson, God, which I still am in the final analysis . . .' Since there is repudiation, and if the feminine being that struggles within it is to remain there, it henceforth calls for, not the deification of the third party, but countercathexes in strong values, in strong *equivalents of power.* Feminine psychosis today is sustained and absorbed through passion for politics, science, art . . . The variant that accompanies motherhood might be analyzed perhaps more readily than the others from the standpoint of the rejection of the other sex

The love of God and for God resides in a gap: the broken space made explicit by sin on the one side, the beyond on the other. Discontinuity, lack, and arbitrariness: topography of the sign, of the symbolic relation that posits my otherness as impossible. Love, here, is only for the impossible.

For a mother, on the other hand, strangely so, the other as arbitrary (the child) is taken for granted. As far as she is concerned—impossible, that is just the way it is: it is reduced to the implacable. The other is inevitable, she seems to say, turn it into a God if you wish, it is nevertheless natural, for such an other has come out of myself, which is yet not myself but a flow of unending germinations, an eternal cosmos. The other goes much without saying and without my saying that, at the limit, it does not exist for itself. The 'just the same' of motherly peace of mind, more persistent than philosophical doubt, gnaws, on account of its basic disbelief, at the symbolic's allmightiness. It bypasses perverse negation ('I know, but just the same') and constitutes the basis of the social bond in its generality, in the

that it comprises. To allow what? Surely not some understanding or other on the part of 'sexual partners' within the pre-established harmony of primal androgyny. Rather, to lead to an acknowledgment of what is irreducible, of the irreconcilable interest of both sexes in asserting their differences, in the quest of each one—and of women, after all—for an appropriate fulfillment.

These, then, are a few questions among others concerning a motherhood that today remains, after the Virgin, without a discourse. They suggest, all in all, the need of an ethics for this 'second' sex, which, as one asserts it, is reawakening.

Nothing, however, suggests that a feminine ethics is possible, and Spinoza excluded women from his (along with children and the insane). Now, if a contemporary ethics is no longer seen as being the same as morality; if ethics amounts to not avoiding the embarrassing and inevitable problematics of the law but giving it flesh, language, and jouissance—in that case its reformulation demands the contribution of women. Of women who harbor the desire

sense of 'resembling others and eventually the species.' Such an attitude is frightening when one imagines that it can crush everything the other (the child) has that is specifically irreducible: rooted in that disposition of motherly love, besides, we find the leaden strap it can become, smothering any different individuality. But it is there, too, that the speaking being finds a refuge when his/her symbolic shell cracks and a crest emerges where speech causes biology to show through: I am thinking of the time of illness, of sexual-intellectual-physical passion of death . . .

to reproduce (to have stability). Of women who are available so that our speaking species, which knows it is mortal, might withstand death. Of mothers. For an heretical ethics separated from morality, an *herethics*, is perhaps no more than that which in life makes bonds, thoughts, and therefore the thought of death, bearable: herethics is undeath [*a-mort*], love . . . *Eia mater, fons amoris* . . . So let us again listen to the *Stabat Mater*, and the music, all the music . . . it swallows up the goddesses and removes their necessity.

(1976)

Notes

1 Between the lines of this section one should be able to detect the presence of Marina Warner, *Alone of All Her Sex: The Myth and Cult of the Virgin Mary* (New York: Knopf, 1976) and Ilse Barande, *Le Maternel singulier* (Paris: Aubier-Montaigne, 1977), which underlay my reflections.

2 George Dumezil, *La Religion romaine archaïque* (Paris: Payot, 1974).

3 [The French version quoted by Kristeva ('Woman, what is there in common between you and me?') is even stronger than the King James translation, 'Woman, what have I to do with thee?' – Trans.]

4 Jung thus noted the 'hierogamous' relationship between Mary and Christ as well as the overprotection given the Virgin with respect to original sin, which places her on the margin of mankind; finally, he insisted very much on the Vatican's adoption of the Assumption as dogma, seeing it as one of the considerable merits of Catholicism as opposed to Protestantism. C. G. Jung, *Answer to Job* (Princeton: Princeton University Press, 1969).

5 As Caelius Sedulius wrote, 'She . . . had no peer / Either in our first mother or in all women / Who were to come. But alone of all her sex She pleased the Lord' ('Paschalis Carminis,' Book II, lines 68ff. of *Opera Omnia* [Vienna, 1885]). Epigraph to Marina Warner, *Alone of All Her Sex*.

Chapter 11

Psychoanalysis – A Counterdepressant
and
Holbein's Dead Christ

■ [Abridged] These excerpts were originally published in *Soleil noir, dépression et mélancolie* (Gallimard, 1987), translated as *Black Sun: Depression and Melancholia* by Leon S. Roudiez (Columbia University Press, 1989).

Editors' introduction

IN *BLACK SUN* KRISTEVA undertakes a genealogy of melancholia by investigating its manifestations in different cultures and from various historical time periods, as well as its expression in a range of art forms. Kristeva takes as her point of departure Freud's essay, 'Mourning and Melancholia', and outlines the parallel symptoms of these two different conditions: a complete lethargy overtakes the individual, psychomotor ability is rapidly reduced, then replaced by an insurmountable physiological fatigue and psychic exhaustion; the individual rejects the activity of the world outside and may refuse food, company and suffer from extreme insomnia. But while both the mourner and the melancholic share a process of bereavement, the mourner has a conscious understanding of her loss (the death of a loved one, for example) while the melancholic is left bewildered by the *cause* of her condition and does not consciously comprehend why she suffers from these symptoms of loss.

Kristeva adds to Freud's list of symptoms for the melancholic and finds that the melancholic is marked foremost by a complete *atheism*. For Kristeva this is not just someone who has been stripped of religious conviction, but a kind of *semiotic atheism*, a condition where all faith and values are undone, all signs emptied of their significance, when the promise for meaning of *any kind* has been revoked. Kristeva terms this phenomena 'asymbolia': the inability for symbols, such as language, to provide meaning to an individual. Kristeva's analysis of melancholia, then, is primarily as a *linguistic* disorder.

Conversely, Kristeva's atheistic melancholic is also a kind of *mystic*. For while she rejects linguistic meaning, she immerses herself in a longing for an archaic or unknown Other (the divine or supernatural). This sublime Other (sublime, because it is other-worldly) promises the melancholic absolute meaning, something that language can never offer. But the distance between the sublime Other and the melancholic is insurmountable since the Other only suggests itself, but never makes itself present.

Kristeva's understanding of melancholia has undeniable theological resonance, yet her psychoanalytic musings on the melancholic subject has a this-worldly base. For Kristeva, the sublime Other for which the melancholic longs is none other than the pre-Oedipal, 'archaic' mother. Melancholia consists of a wistful looking back towards the prelinguistic state, to the unity that existed between mother and child before any separation or subject formation took place. Kristeva's melancholy person mourns for 'la Chose' ('the Thing'), the unsignifiable mother–child bond, both a place and a preobject that cannot be articulated, but that the melancholic endeavours to (re)inhabit. Of course, such a symbiosis with the archaic mother is no longer possible, so while the melancholic turns away from the Oedipalisation process (identification with the law of the Father) that grants language meaning, and focuses her energies on that which came before (the pre-Oedipal mother) she can neither attain nor name the longing to which she is drawn.

Though 'la Chose' is not recoverable, nor signifiable as such, Kristeva posits that it can nevertheless be *reclaimed* in artistic expression through the poetic resonance of language or the contours and colours of an image. Such artistic play makes possible the complex multiplicity of meaning and connotation in a single work or even a single sign. Thus traces of the archaic Other can be found in the very excess of language (or art) itself. Kristeva believes that participation in this 'imaginary' realm transforms the defining symptom of the melancholic (asymbolia), and the painful, physical affects that the melancholic bears, back to the realm of signification once again. Thus, by naming her suffering in artistic practice, the melancholic returns *meaning* to it, while the melancholic's longing for the archaic Other is not eradicated, but becomes a foundation for the linguistic transaction.

In 'Holbein's Dead Christ' Kristeva examines the dynamics at work in the expression of melancholia in artistic practice ('sublimation') contained in Holbein's painting of the 'Dead Christ' and in specific practices of Christianity generally. It is because of essays such as this that it is not surprising to find critics mistakenly declaring Kristeva a devout Christian. Christ offers for Kristeva the perfect example of a subject ruptured from and longing for the (archaic) maternal – that painful separation that, Kristeva says, 'necessarily structures our individuation'. And Christianity, along with aesthetic creation, becomes a means to mourn the lost mother via an imaginary identification with the paternal pole in the operations of signification.

Psychoanalysis – a counterdepressant

Melancholia – somber lining of amatory passion

A sad voluptuousness, a despondent intoxication make up the humdrum back-drop against which our ideals and euphorias often stand out, unless they be that fleeting clear-mindedness shredding the amorous hypnosis that joins two persons together. Conscious of our being doomed to lose our loves, we grieve perhaps even more when we glimpse in our lover the shadow of a long lost former loved one. Depression is the hidden face of Narcissus, the face that is to bear him away into death, but of which he is unaware while he admires himself in a mirage. Talking about depression will again lead us into marshy land of the Narcissus myth.[1] This time, however, we shall not encounter the bright and fragile amatory idealization; on the contrary, we shall see the shadow cast on the fragile self, hardly dissociated from the other, precisely by the *loss* of that essential other. The shadow of despair.

Rather than seek the meaning of despair (it is either obvious or metaphysical), let us acknowledge that there is meaning only in despair. The child king becomes irredeemably sad before uttering his first words; this is because he has been irrevocably, desperately separated from the mother, a loss that causes him to try to find her again, along with other objects of love, first in the imagination, then in words. Semiology, concerned as it is with the zero degree of symbolism, is unavoidably led to ponder over not only the amatory state but its corollary as well, melancholia; at the same time it observes that if there is no writing other than the amorous, there is no imagination that is not, overtly or secretly, melancholy. [. . .]

Melancholia/depression

I shall call *melancholia* the institutional symptomatology of inhibition and asymbolia that becomes established now and then or chronically in a person, alternating more often than not with the so-called manic phase of exaltation. When the two phenomena, despondency and exhilaration, are of lesser intensity and frequency, it is then possible to speak of neurotic depression. While acknowledging the difference between melancholia and depression, Freudian theory detects every-where the same *impossible mourning for the maternal object*. Question: impossible on account of what paternal weakness? Or what biological frailty? Melancholia – we again encounter the generic term after having demarcated psychotic and neurotic symptomatologies – admits of the fearsome privilege of situating the analyst's question at the intersection of the biological and the symbolical. Parallel series? Consecutive sequences? A dangerous crossing that needs to be clarified, another relationship that needs to be thought up? [. . .]

The depressive person: full of hatred or wounded, mourned 'object' and mourned 'thing'

According to classic psychoanalytic theory (Abraham, Freud, and Melanie Klein),[2] depression, like mourning, conceals an aggressiveness toward the lost object, thus revealing the ambivalence of the depressed person with respect to the object of mourning. 'I love that object,' is what that person seems to say about the lost object, 'but even more so I hate it; because I love it, and in order not to lose it, I imbed it in myself; but because I hate it, that other within myself is a bad self, I am bad, I am non-existent, I shall kill myself.' The complaint against oneself would therefore be a complaint against another, and putting oneself to death but a tragic disguise for massacring an other. Such logic presupposes, as one can imagine, a stern superego and a whole complex dialectic of idealization and devalorization of self and other, the aggregate of these activities being based on the mechanism of *identification*. For my identification with the loved–hated other, through incorporation–introjection–projection, leads me to imbed in myself its sublime component, which becomes my necessary, tyrannical judge, as well as its subject component, which demeans me and of which I desire to rid myself. Consequently, the analysis of depression involves bringing to the fore the real-ization that the complaint against oneself is a hatred for the other, which is without doubt the substratum of an unsuspected sexual desire. [. . .]

Thing and object

The depressed narcissist mourns not an Object but the Thing.[3] Let me posit the 'Thing' as the real that does not lend itself to signification, the center of attrac-tion and repulsion, seat of the sexuality from which the object of desire will become separated.

Of this Nerval provides a dazzling metaphor that suggests an insistence without presence, a light without representation: the Thing is an imagined sun, bright and black at the same time. 'It is a well-known fact that one never sees the sun in a dream, although one is often aware of some far brighter light.'[4]

Ever since that archaic attachment the depressed person has the impression of having been deprived of an unnameable, supreme good, of something unrepresent-able, that perhaps only devouring might represent, or an *invocation* might point out, but no word could signify. Consequently, for such a person, no erotic object could replace the irreplaceable perception of a place or preobject confining the libido or severing the bonds of desire. Knowingly disinherited of the Thing, the depressed person wanders in pursuit of continuously disappointing adventures and loves; or else retreats, disconsolate and aphasic, alone with the unnamed Thing. The 'primary identification' with the 'father in individual prehistory'[5] would be the means, the link that might enable one to become reconciled with the loss of the Thing. Primary identification initiates a compensation for the Thing and at the same time secures the subject to another dimension, that of imaginary adherence, reminding one of the bond of faith, which is just what disintegrates in the depressed person. [. . .] How can one approach the place I have referred to? Sublimation is an attempt to do so: through melody, rhythm, semantic polyvalency, the so-called poetic form, which decomposes and recomposes signs, is the sole 'container' seemingly able to secure an uncertain but adequate hold over the Thing. [. . .]

Literary creation is that adventure of the body and signs that bears witness to the affect – to sadness as imprint of separation and beginning of the symbol's sway; to joy as imprint of the triumph that settles me in the universe of artifice and symbol, which I try to harmonize in the best possible way with my experience of reality. But that testimony is produced by literary creation in material that is totally different from what constitutes mood. It transposes affect into rhythms, signs, forms. The 'semiotic' and the 'symbolic'[6] become the communicable imprints of an affective reality, perceptible to the reader (I like this book because it conveys sadness, anguish, or joy) and yet dominated, set aside, vanquished. [. . .]

Holbein's dead Christ

'Some may lose their faith'

In 1522 (the underlying coat bears the date 1521) Hans Holbein the Younger (1497–1543) painted a disturbing picture, *The Body of the Dead Christ in the Tomb*, which may be seen at the Basel museum and apparently made a tremendous impression on Dostoyevsky. Prince Myshkin attempted to speak of it, but to no avail, at the very outset of *The Idiot*; only through a new polyphonic twist of the plot did he see a reproduction of it at Rogozhin's house and, 'struck by a sudden thought,' he exclaimed: '[looking] At that picture! Why, some people may *lose their faith* by looking at that picture!'[7] [. . .]

The man of sorrows

Holbein's painting represents a corpse stretched out by itself on a slab covered with a cloth that is scarcely draped.[8] Life size, the painted corpse is seen from the side, its head slightly turned toward the viewer, the hair spread out on the sheet. The right arm is in full view, resting alongside the emaciated, tortured body, and the hand protrudes slightly from the slab. The rounded chest suggests a triangle within the very low, elongated rectangle of the recess that constitutes the painting's frame. The chest bears the bloody mark of a spear, and the hand shows the stigmata of the crucifixion, which stiffen the outstretched middle finger. Imprints of nails mark Christ's feet. The martyr's face bears the expression of a hopeless grief; the empty stare, the sharp-lined profile, the dull blue-green complexion are those of a man who is truly dead, of Christ forsaken by the Father ('My God, my God, why have you deserted me?') and without the promise of Resurrection.

The unadorned representation of human death, the well-nigh anatomical stripping of the corpse convey to viewers an unbearable anguish before the death of God, here blended with our own, since there is not the slightest suggestion of transcendency. What is more, Hans Holbein has given up all architectural or compositional fancy. The tombstone weighs down on the upper portion of the painting, which is merely twelve inches high, and intensifies the feeling of permanent death: this corpse shall never rise again.[9] The very pall, limited to a minimum of folds, emphasizes, through that economy of motion, the feeling of stiffness and stone-felt cold.

The viewer's gaze penetrates this closed-in coffin from below and, following the painting from left to right, stops at the stone set against the corpse's feet, sloping at a wide angle toward the spectators. [. . .]

A composition in loneliness

Italian iconography embellishes, or at least ennobles, Christ's face during the Passion but especially surrounds it with figures that are immersed in grief as well as in the certainty of the Resurrection, as if to suggest the attitude we should ourselves adopt facing the Passion. Holbein, on the contrary, leaves the corpse strangely alone. It is perhaps that isolation – *an act of composition* – that endows the painting with its major melancholy burden, more so than delineation and coloring. To be sure, Christ's suffering is expressed through three components inherent in lines and colors: the head bent backwards, the contortion of the right hand bearing the stigmata, the position of the feet – the whole being bonded by means of a dark palette of grays, greens, and browns. Nevertheless, such realism, harrowing on account of its very parsimony, is emphasized to the utmost through the painting's composition and location: a body stretched out alone, situated above the viewers, and separated from them.

Cut off from us by its base but without any prospect toward heaven, for the ceiling in the recess comes down low, Holbein's *Dead Christ* is inaccessible, distant, but without a beyond. It is a way of looking at mankind from afar, even in death – just as Erasmus saw folly from a distance. It is a vision that opens out not on glory but on endurance. Another, a new morality resides in this painting.

Christ's dereliction is here at its worst: forsaken by the Father, he is apart from all of us. Unless Holbein, whose mind, pungent as it was, does not appear to have lead [sic] him across the threshold of atheism, wanted to include us, humans, foreigners, spectators that we are, forthrightly in this crucial moment of Christ's life. With no intermediary, suggestion, or indoctrination, whether pictorial or theological, other than our ability to imagine death, we are led to collapse in the horror of the caesura constituted by death or to dream of an invisible beyond. Does Holbein forsake us, as Christ, for an instant, had imagined himself forsaken? Or does he, on the contrary, invite us to change the Christly tomb into a living tomb, to participate in the painted death and thus include it in our own life, in order to live with it and make it live? For if the living body, in opposition to the rigid corpse, is a dancing body, doesn't our life, through identification with death, become a 'danse macabre,' in keeping with Holbein's other well-known depiction?

This enclosed recess, this well-isolated coffin simultaneously rejects us and invites us. Indeed, the corpse fills the entire field of the painting, without any labored reference to the Passion. Our gaze follows the slightest physical detail, it is, as it were, nailed, crucified, and is riveted to the hand placed at the center of the composition. Should it attempt to flee it quickly stops, locked in at the distressed face or the feet propped against the black stone. [. . .]

An expenditure of colors and laid-out forms

It is not my point to maintain that Holbein was afflicted with melancholia or that he painted melancholy people. More profoundly, it would seem, on the basis of his oeuvre (including his themes and painterly technique), that a *melancholy moment* (an actual or imaginary loss of meaning, an actual or imaginary despair, an actual or imaginary razing of symbolic values, including the value of life) summoned up his aesthetic activity, which overcame the melancholy latency while keeping its trace. [. . .]

[. . .] The economy of depression is supported by an omnipotent object, a monopolizing Thing rather than the focus of metonymical desire, which 'might account for' the tendency to protect oneself from it through, *among other means*, a splurge of sensations, satisfactions, passions, one as elated as it is aggressive, as intoxicating as it is indifferent. It will be noted, nevertheless, that the common feature of those outlays is a *detachment* – getting rid of it, going elsewhere, abroad, toward others . . . The possibility of unfolding primary processes, spontaneously and under control, artfully, appears, however, as the most efficacious way of overcoming the latent loss. In other words, the controlled and mastered 'expenditure' of colors, sounds, and words is imperative for the artist-subject, as an essential recourse, similar to 'Bohemian life,' 'criminality,' or 'dissoluteness' alternating with 'miserliness,' which one observes in the behavior of such skylarking artists. Hence, very much like personal behavior, artistic *style* imposes itself as a means of countervailing the loss of other and of meaning: a means more powerful than any other because more autonomous (no matter who his patron is, isn't the artist master of his work?) but, in fact and fundamentally, analogous with or complementary to behavior, for it fills the same psychic need to confront separation, emptiness, death. Isn't the artist's life considered, by himself to start with, to be a work of art?

The death of Christ

A depressive moment: everything is dying, God is dying, I am dying.

But how is it possible for God to die? Let us briefly return to the evangelical meaning of Christ's death. Theological, hermetic, and doctrinal accounts of the 'mystery of redemption' are numerous, complex, and contradictory. While the analyst cannot accept them, he or she might try, by examining them, to discover the meaning of the text as it unfolds within his or her hearing. [. . .]

Hiatus and identification

The break, brief as it might have been, in the bond linking Christ to his Father and to life introduces into the mythical representation of the Subject a fundamental and psychically necessary discontinuity. Such a caesura, which some have called a 'hiatus,'[10] provides an image, at the same time as a narrative, for many separations that build up the psychic life of individuals. It provides image and narrative for some psychic cataclysms that more or less frequently threaten the assumed balance of individuals. Thus, psychoanalysis identifies and relates as an indispensable condition for autonomy a series of splittings (Hegel spoke of a 'work of the negative'); birth, weaning, separation, frustration, castration. Real, imaginary, or symbolic, those processes necessarily structure our individuation. Their nonexecution or repudiation leads to psychotic confusion; their dramatization is, on the contrary, a source of exorbitant and destructive anguish. Because Christianity set that rupture at the very heart of the absolute subject – Christ; because it represented it as a Passion that was the solidary lining of his Resurrection, his glory, and his eternity, it brought to consciousness the essential dramas that are internal to the becoming of each and every subject. It thus endows itself with a tremendous cathartic power.

In addition to displaying a dramatic diachrony, the death of Christ offers imaginary support to the nonrepresentable catastrophic anguish distinctive of melancholy persons. It is well known that the so-called 'depressive' stage is essential to the child's access to the realm of symbols and linguistic signs. Such a depression – parting sadness as the necessary condition for the representation of any absent thing – reverts to and accompanies our symbolic activities unless exaltation, its opposite, reappropriates them. A suspension of meaning, a darkness without hope, a recession of perspective including that of life, then reawaken within the memory the recollection of traumatic partings and thrust us into a state of withdrawal. 'Father, why have you deserted me?' Moreover, serious depression or paroxismal clinical melancholia represents a true hell for modern individuals, convinced as they are that they must and can realize all their desires of objects and values. The Christly dereliction presents that hell with an imaginary elaboration; it provides the subject with an echo of its unbearable moments when meaning was lost, when the meaning of life was lost.

The postulate according to which Christ died 'for all of us' appears often in the texts.[11] *Hyper, peri, anti*: the words mean not only 'because of us' but 'in favor of us,' 'in our stead.'[12] They go back to the 'Songs of the Servant of Yahweh' (in the Book of the Consolation of Israel, a collection of prophecies included in the Book of Isaiah) and even earlier to the Hebraic notion of *ga'al*: 'to free by purchasing back goods and people that have become alien property.' Thus, *redemption* (repurchase, liberation) implies a substitution between the Savior and the faithful, which opened the way for many interpretations. One of these is a compelling one in the analyst's literal reading: the one that suggests an imaginary *identification*. Identification does not mean delegating sins or shifting their burden to the person of the Messiah. On the contrary, it calls for a total implication of the subjects in Christ's suffering, in the hiatus he experiences, and of course in his hope of salvation. On the basis of that identification, one that is admittedly too anthropological and psychological from the point of view of a strict theology, man is nevertheless provided with a powerful symbolic device that allows him to experience death and resurrection even in his physical body, thanks to the strength of imaginary identification – and of its actual effects – with the absolute Subject (Christ).

A true initiation is thus elaborated, at the very heart of Christian thought, which takes up again the deep intrapsychic meaning of initiatory rites that were anterior or alien to its domain, and gives them new meaning. Here as elsewhere, *death* – that of the old body making room for the new, death to oneself for the sake of glory, death of the old man for the sake of the spiritual body – lies at the center of the experience. But, if there be a Christian initiation, it belongs first and entirely within the imaginary realm. While opening up the entire gamut of complete identifications (real and symbolic), it allows for no ritualistic ordeal other than the words and signs of the Eucharist. From that standpoint, the paroxysmal and realistic manifestations of asceticism and 'dolor' are indeed extreme positions. Beyond and above that, the implicitness of love and consequently of reconciliation and forgiveness completely transforms the scope of Christian initiation by giving it an aura of glory and unwavering hope for those who believe. Christian faith appears then as an antidote to hiatus and depression, along with hiatus and depression and starting from them.

Could it be superego voluntarism that maintains the image of an oblatory Father, or is it the commemoration of an archaic paternal figure arisen from the paradise of primary identifications? The forgiveness inherent in Redemption condenses *death and resurrection* and presents itself as one of the most interesting and innovative instances of trinitary logic. The key to the nexus seems to be primary identification: the oral and already symbolic oblatory gift exchanged between Father and Son.

For individual reasons, or else on account of the historical crushing of political or metaphysical authority, which is our social fatherhood, the dynamics of primary identification at the foundation of idealization can run into difficulty – it can appear as deprived of significance, illusory, false. The only thing then surviving is the meaning of the deeper workings represented by the cross: that of caesura, discontinuity, depression.

Did Holbein become the painter of such a Christian thought, stripped of its antidepressive carrier wave, and amounting to identification with a rewarding beyond? He leads us, at any rate, to the ultimate edge of belief, to the threshold of nonmeaning. The *form* (of art) alone gives back serenity to the waning of forgiveness, while love and salvation take refuge to the execution of the work. Redemption would simply be the discipline of a rigorous technique.

Notes

1   See my *Tales of Love* (New York: Columbia University Press, 1987).

2   See Karl Abraham, 'Préliminaires à l'investigation et au traitement psychanalytique de la folie maniaco-depressive et des états voisins' (1912), in *Œuvres complètes* (Paris: Payot, 1965), I: 99–113; Sigmund Freud, 'Mourning and Melancholia' (1917), in *The Standard Edition of the Complete Psychological Works of Sigmund Freud* (hereafter *SE*), 24 vols., James Strachey, tr. and ed. (London: Hogarth 1953–74), 14: 237–58; Melanie Klein, 'A Contribution to the Psychogenesis of Manic-Depressive States' and 'Mourning and its Relation to Manic-Depressive States' in *Contributions to Psychoanalysis, 1921–1945* (London: Hogarth Press, 1948), pp. 282–338. Klein's 'A Contribution' is reprinted in Peter Buckley, ed., *Essential Papers on Object Relations* (New York: New York University Press, 1986).

3   Having noted that, from the very dawn of Greek philosophy, holding on to the *thing* is bound up with the utterance of a statement and the assertion of its truth, Heidegger nevertheless throws open the matter of the 'historied' aspect of the *thing*: 'The question of the thing again comes into motion from its beginning' (*What is a Thing?* trans. W. B. Barton, Jr. and Vera Deutsch [Chicago: Henry Regnery, 1967], p. 48). Without going into the history of that conception of the thing but opening it up in the between that extends from the thing to man, Heidegger notes, through a reading of

Kant, 'that this *between* as an anticipation (*Vorgriff*) reaches beyond the thing and similarly back behind us' (*ibid.*, p. 243).

Through the opening created by Heidegger's question, but also following upon Freud's shaking up rational certainties, I shall speak of the *Thing* as being the 'something' that, seen by the already constituted subject looking back, appears as the unspecified, the unseparated, the elusive, even in its determination of actual sexual matter. I shall restrict the term *Object* to the space–time constant that is verified by a statement uttered by a subject in control of that statement.

4   Gérard de Nerval, *Aurelia*, in *Selected Writings*, trans. Geoffrey Wagner (Ann Arbor: University of Michigan Press, 1957), p. 130.

5   See Sigmund Freud, *The Ego and the Id*, SE 19:31.

6   See my *Revolution in Poetic Language*, trans. Margaret Waller (New York: Columbia University Press, 1984), chapter 1, secs. 2 and 5. [. . .]

7   Fyodor Dostoyevsky, *The Idiot*, trans. David Magarshack (New York: Viking Penguin, 1955), p. 236. Emphasis mine [Kristeva's].

8   'Incorporated within the present frame above the painting and running its full length is an inscription, with Angels with Instruments of the Passion, JESVS NAZARENVS REX IVDAEORUM, executed with the brush on paper, almost certainly contemporaneously with the painting. An attribution to Holbein himself, while not certain, is not to be ruled out, even though the Angels recall the work of his recently deceased brother, Ambrosius' (John Rowlands, *Holbein* [Boston: David R. Godine, 1985], p. 127).

9   The relation of height to width is 1:7, but if the plate affixed to the lower margin of the picture is included the relation becomes 1:9.

10 See Urs von Balthasar, *La Gloire et la croix*, 3:2, 'La Nouvelle Alliance' (Paris: Aubier, 1975).

11 See Romans 5:8, 'Christ died for us while we were still sinners'; and also, 'God did not spare his own Son, but gave him up to benefit us all' (Romans 8:32), and 'follow Christ by loving as he loved you, giving himself up in our place *as a fragrant offering and a sacrifice to God*' (Ephesians 5:2); similarly, see Mark 10:45, Matthew 20:28 and 26:28, Mark 14:24, Luke 22:19, and I Peter 2:21–25.

12 See Dufour in *Mort pour nos péchés*, (Brussels: Facultés Universitaires Saint-Louis, 1979), pp.11–45.

Chapter 12

The Chosen People and the Choice of Foreignness

■ This essay, reprinted here in full, was first published in *Étrangers à nous-mêmes* (Fayard, 1988), in English as *Strangers to Ourselves*, translated by Leon S. Roudiez (Columbia University Press, 1991).

Editors' introduction

THE THEME OF ESTRANGEMENT has infused Kristeva's work from the beginning; she is, herself, a stranger ('l'étrangère'), as Roland Barthes has often said of her, both as a woman and as a Bulgarian, in the male-dominated world of French philosophy. Kristeva's writings are concerned with foreignness on a social, cultural and political level but, more importantly, on an individual and psychological plane. For Kristeva, the inner, unconscious wounds of the individual must first be understood before it is possible to establish effective measures for addressing estrangement on a social level. As she has stated in an interview, 'The other is in me. It is my unconscious. And instead of searching for a scapegoat in the foreigner, I must try to tame the demons that are in me' (Kristeva 1996a: 41).

Kristeva invokes individual alterity first in her writing style. With creative flair, Kristeva has employed 'foreignness' as a trope throughout her disparate writings: metaphorically, through narrative doubling in her novels (the döppelganger); linguistically, through poetic word-play in her theoretical works; but also through genre-bending, and fluid discipline boundaries in those works that do not sit comfortably in either category. In Kristeva's writings the word is made strange through a resistance of traditional methods of philosophising that privilege denotative language, univocal meaning and linear logic. Kristeva gives voice to poetic forces in language that break it open and proliferate meanings that defy simple identity categories. This poetic practice displaces and fragments the subject of reading and writing, beckoning to her unconscious dynamic; estrangement is thus played out in Kristeva's writings by a subject who slips between identity positions she can never call home. Foreignness, then, is not so much about a physical place or location, but rather, it is a 'psychic space', the unconscious alterity (difference) at the base of identity itself. This has remained constant throughout more than thirty years of Kristeva's theoretical work, which places unconscious difference at the heart of subject-ivity and language operation, a structuration which makes of any individual a stranger in a strange land.

What is unique to *Strangers to Ourselves* is Kristeva's examination of group identity in relation to difference represented by a physical stranger (a foreigner, refugee or immigrant). Here Kristeva provides an etymological account of a common derogatory word for foreigner: barbarian. The Greek 'barbaros' contains the root expression, 'bara-bara' – a derogatory onomatopoeia of the foreigner's accent which produces unintelligible mumbling to the ear of the native speaker. 'Barbaros', Kristeva notes, was typically used by Greeks to denote foreigners from Asia Minor, but soon became applicable to anyone who was non-Greek. The word developed to indicate someone 'eccentric' or 'inferior'; similarly, current usage of 'barbaric' or 'barbarian' today conveys 'moral inferiority', someone who exceeds the boundaries of civilised behaviour, someone savage, primitive, uncultured.

Kristeva demonstrates that such terms denoting foreignness and foreigners can only be established through a negative logic that distinguishes alterity (difference) from that which can be embraced by the 'same'; that is, those allied characteristics which constitute the identity of any group. But at the same time, and by nature of the logic of negation, group identity, be it political, national-istic, ethnic or religious, defines itself through the foreigner. Groups can achieve a homogenous identity only in contrast to someone or something else, and thus, are dependent upon the outsider for their very formation. As such, the foreigner comes to represent that which must be either assimilated or shunned, marginalised, punished or even murdered in order to protect the homogeneity upon which the group has been established. Yet this expelled other is, by the same token, the hidden lining of any identity. The stranger is the base of any group, and thus exposes the tenuous identification upon which the group is established. The foreigner perpetually troubles the self-perception of the group, making it aware of its inherent gaps and breaks, insinuating its inevitable fracturing.

In her most recent writings, Kristeva has addressed the question of alterity and the place of the Other in a variety of biblical texts. In the essay that follows, Kristeva examines the figure of Ruth in the Hebrew text *The Book of Ruth* as an example of foreignness, particularly feminine alterity, at the base of Jewish identity. Ruth the Moabite represents the forbidden foreigner for the Semitic tribes, yet she nevertheless founds the royal House of David, so important to Jewish identity. Ruth thus provides an abundance of foreign femininity at the base of masculine sovereignty. It is not incidental that it is a woman's body that introduces alterity to the biblical patriarchal line, according to Kristeva, since

woman is the irrecuperable foreigner, the quintessential stranger, in any patriarchal society.

Foreigner or convert

The covenant with God turned the Jewish people into a chosen people (especially
after Jacob and the flight from Egypt) and, if it established the basis of a sacred
nationalism, it nonetheless harbors in its very essence an inherent inscription of
foreignness. There are numerous sections of the Bible that affirm the choice of
the Jewish people to the exclusion of others: 'I will establish my Covenant
between myself and you,' Yahweh said to Abraham, 'and your descendants after
you, generation after generation, a Covenant in perpetuity, to be your God
and the God of your descendants after you.'[1] Those who are opposed to such
a covenant or are not a party to it shall be forcefully rejected: 'Thus speaks
Yahweh Sabaoth: "I will repay what Amalek did to Israel when they opposed
them on the road by which they came out of Egypt. Now, go and strike down
Amalek; put him under the ban with all that he possesses. Do not spare him, but
kill man and woman, babe and suckling, ox and sheep, camel and donkey"';[2]
'In particular: we will not give our daughters to the natives of the land nor take
their daughters for our sons';[3] 'No bastard[4] is to be admitted to the assembly
of Yahweh. No Ammonite or Moabite is to be admitted to the assembly of
Yahweh, not even their descendants to the tenth generation may be admitted to
the assembly of Yahweh, and this is for all time; because they did not come to
meet you with bread and water when you were on your way out of Egypt,
and because they hired Balaam son of Beor from Pethor in Aram of the Two
Rivers to curse you. But Yahweh your God refused to listen to Balaam, and
Yahweh your God turned the curse into a blessing for you, because Yahweh your
God loved you. Never, as long as you live, shall you seek their welfare or their
prosperity.'

Other kinds of foreigners, however, are accepted: 'You are not to regard the
Edomite as detestable, for he is your brother; nor the Egyptian, because you
were a stranger in his land. The third generation of children born to these may
be admitted to the assembly of Yahweh.'[5]

Exclusive as it may be, and while basing that exclusiveness on the moral
misdeed of those who are despised, the Jewish people's covenant with its God is
an outgrowth not of favoritism but of choice founded on ordeal; this implies that,
constantly threatened, the covenant is always to be conquered and its object
remains the continuous improvement of the chosen. According to one tradition:
'Why did the Holy One (let Him be blessed!) choose Israel? Because all the other

people repudiated the Torah and refused to accept it, while Israel accepted and chose the Holy One (let Him be blessed!) and his Torah.'[6]

Furthermore, a biblical universalism comes to light, which allows the possible dignity of humankind in its entirety to emerge, and the foreigner himself might chance to be God's unwonted although inevitable unveiler. In the eyes of rabbis, the Torah would eventually be destined for all mankind.[7] Thus 'Moses expounds the Torah in sixty-six languages';[8] 'You must keep my laws and my customs. Whoever complies with them shall find life in them.'[9] One may conclude that *whoever* obeys the Torah, even a pagan, is equal to the high priest. 'And *is* this the manner of man, Lord Yahweh?'[10] This is interpreted to mean that it is not the manner of priests, Levites, or Israel but of all men.[11]

Since all men were made in the image of God,[12] the precept, 'You must love your neighbor as yourself,'[13] applies not only to the immediate neighbor, one of the same family or the same people, but to 'man, the beloved';[14] 'Just as it has been said, with reference to the man of Israel, you must love your neighbor as yourself, the same expression is used with reference to the foreigner.'[15]

There are several texts that stress even more clearly the respect due to foreigners as such: 'You must not molest the stranger or oppress him, for you lived as strangers in the land of Egypt.'[16] A pagan can claim the same rights as the Jew if he espouses monotheism. The Torah ceaselessly dwells on the duties of Jews toward foreigners, and it may be noted that no other commandment (circumcision, dietary taboos, prohibition against lying and stealing) is repeated as often. The Talmud goes further: 'If a convert comes to learn the Torah do not say to him, the mouth that has eaten impure animals, worms, and reptiles, would like to learn the Torah that has been given to us by God.'[17]Furthermore, the fact of having been 'strangers in the land of Egypt' is not interpreted as a sufficient reason assuring the kindness of Jews toward foreigners: is it not true that the bitterness accumulated in the exile's soul might express itself through the persecution of another exile. God alone watches over all foreigners, and the remainder of the stay in Egypt induces greater humility into the 'chosen people' who might thus view themselves as having once been part of an inferior group. Justice rather than mercy seems to rise from that verse. One will recall another passage with similar meaning; 'If a stranger lives with you in your land, do not molest him. You must count him as one of your own countrymen and love him as yourself – for you were once strangers yourselves in Egypt.'[18] 'Love the stranger then, for you were strangers in the land of Egypt.'[19] Abraham himself is considered as the first 'convert':[20] commentators emphasize that he has left his country behind, his fatherland and his father's house, and all the other peoples of the world, in order to proceed toward the land that God has shown him, as does the convert who has chosen Israel.[21]

The universalism of the prophets, from Amos to Jeremiah, asserts even more strongly the idea that all mankind is respectable in its intrinsic dignity – and this even before Greek philosophy and Stoic cosmopolitanism. The poor, widows and widowers, orphans, servants, foreigners are greeted with equal justice: 'If ever I have infringed the rights of slave/ or maidservant in legal actions against me – / what shall I do when God stands up? / What shall I say when he holds his assize? / They, no less than I, were created in the womb / by the one same God who shaped us all within our mothers. / . . . No stranger ever had to sleep outside, / my door was always open to the traveler.'[22]

The Hebrew term *ger*, meaning 'stranger,' is not without posing problems. Literally, it signifies 'the one who has come to live with' or 'resident,' and it includes the idea of 'convert.' This very word, in the Bible as well as the Talmud or Midrash, is translated either by 'proselyte' or by 'stranger.' Two sub-sets are generated from the same notion: on the one hand, *gertochav*, resident foreigner, on the other hand, just *ger*, which refers to conversion-naturalization. The *ger-tochav* maintains his identity as a foreigner but, whether or not he resides in Israel, he obeys Mosaic laws; these are moral laws that are indispensable to society; they endow one, in the spirit of Judaism, with a spiritual dignity equal to that of the Jew himself. Thus the *ger* is a foreigner who belongs to the Jewish nation-religion. Many rabbis of the Talmudic period, among whom one counts the famous Rabbi Arciba (second century, revolt against Rome), were converts.[23]

Some Talmudic or Midrashic texts, however, do not conceal their rejection or mistrust of converts. R. Helbo says, 'Proselytes are as deplorable [for Israel] as a plague.'[24] Such statements merely represent individual opinions, with the majority on the contrary identifying with the spirit of hospitality. Without proselytism, Jewish religion appears to candidates for conversion as highly demanding, but it subsequently offers its welcome to those who have accepted the ordeal of the covenant. Thus, all candidates for conversion are given solemn warnings concerning punishments following breaches of precepts, but they are also told about the rewards. 'Nevertheless, he must not be excessively deterred';[25] likewise, 'In the presence of a proselyte, even after ten generations, do not insult an Aramean.'[26]

Such demands, where the integration of the foreigner is concerned, which may disturb the modern ideal of tolerance and seem excessive, are still not fundamentally different from those imposed upon foreigners by other religious or moral doctrines (Stoicism, Christianity); the latter, although they claim to be universal, accept into their midst only those who adopt the *same* universality. It will be noted, moreover, that in the spirit of Judaism, the complete integration of the foreigner in the Jewish community is the counterpart of the idea of the 'chosen people': I have been 'chosen,' but the privilege of being chosen is nevertheless 'accessible to any individual, at any given moment'; hence a 'hybrid conception of choice that includes heredity *and* the free joining of any individual or collective consciousness.' Witness this extract from the Talmudic treatise, Pessahim 876: 'Eleazar also said: "God, blessed be His name, has exiled Israel from among the nations solely with the aim that proselytes might join Him." [27]

Exemplary in that respect, the story of Ruth the Moabite shows that unity can be achieved only if an exterior, an 'outside of,' is joined to the 'same'.

Ruth the Moabite

'In the days of the Judges famine came to the land.' The Talmud characterizes that period of ordeals when 'the Judges ruled' as a chaotic moment in Jewish history. Lacking a king,[28] everyone followed his own idea, no leader being able to obtain the people's allegiance. In fact, during the three centuries that separate the arrival of Israel in the promised land and the time of Ruth, the Law was degraded, forgotten. If Judge Ivtzan is the same person as Boaz[29] – something not explicited in the Bible – his marriage to Ruth occurred in the year 2792 (968 B.C.).

On two separate occasions the theme of foreignness is inscribed in this story. First, a venerable man called Elimelech left his country, the land of Judah, instead of helping it in times of distress, and dared to settle in the land of Moab – a foreign kingdom and, what was worse, banned from the covenant for, as we have seen, its people did not assist the Jews when they fled from Egypt.[30] This exile amounts to treason and will be punished: Elimelech died and so did, later on, his two sons, Mahlon and Chilion, leaving no heirs. Their mother Naomi survived along with the two daughters-in-law Orpah and . . . Ruth. The divine sentence coming down on such a betrayal-exile is obvious and harsh, but it is not lacking in ambiguity, as the continuation of the story shows; not only was Ruth saved but she became the matriarch of Jewish royalty, the ancestor of David's line. And who was Ruth?

A princess of Moab, she never would have married a Jew had Elimelech not emigrated. The reprehensible immigration is thus inverted into a necessary condition for the accomplishment of Ruth's destiny. According to one inter-pretation of the Law, only male Moabites were banned from the covenant and not the women, but that interpretation remained unknown until the time Ruth came back to Judea after her husband's death.[31] This means that for Boaz and his compatriots Ruth was first a foreigner. Was she already a convert? According to some, the Moabite princesses would not have become converts in order to marry the two Jewish brothers, Mahlon and Chilion, immigrants in their land – and this amounts to an additional sin for the latter ('They neither converted them nor ritually immersed them').[32] Moreover, had her daughters-in-law been converted, Naomi would not have had the right to send them back to their idolatrous country, as she did. According to others, the conversion really took place, for the two brothers were powerful men and could perfectly well impose their religion on the two young foreign sisters, princesses though they might have been. If that had not been the case, the text would not refer to Naomi as their 'mother-in-law,' nor would it speak of Ruth's submission to Levitic marriage rules.[33]

At any rate, Orpah alone, 'she who turns her head' (*oreph*, 'nape'), returned home (and, generations later, Goliath, the descendant of Orpah, was bested by David, the descendant of Ruth), while Ruth insists on accompanying her mother-in-law back to Bethlehem. Her words certainly show a devotion to Yahweh, but even more so a loyalty – that one might call passionate – between the two women: 'Do not press me to leave you and to turn back from your company, for / "wherever you go I will go / wherever you live I will live. / Your people shall be my people, / and your God, my God. / Wherever you die, I will die / and there I will be buried. / May Yahweh do this thing to me / and more also, / if even death should come between us!"' (Ruth 1:16–17).

Having no Hebrew roots, the name of Ruth has been the object of many pseudo-etymological interpretations that attempt a symbolic reappropriation of her story. One has thus supposed that *rut* comes from the root *rao*, 'to see,' 'take into consideration' – the words of her mother-in-law (Ruth Rabba 2, 9); or from 'saturate' – because she was the ancestor of David who showered God with hymns and prayers until he was saturated (Berchat 7b); it has also been said that the letters forming *Ruth* signify from the esoteric point of view *(Rut – Tor)* the dove ready to be sacrificed before the altar, like Ruth entering the divine Covenant (Zohar Chadash); or that the numerical value of the name is 606, and this coincides with the Torah, which contains 606 commandments in addition to the seven commandments given to Noah, which also concern non-Jews; finally, if the letter *H* represents God, Ruth is related to it and, by means of literal play and permutation, one obtains *Ruth = Thorah*.

Henceforth, Naomi's duty – her name according to the Midrash signifies 'agreeable,' 'pleasing,' 'for her deeds were pleasing and sweet' – was to find Ruth a 'redeemer' who must be, according to the levirate rules, the closest relative of the dead husband, for whom he is substituted when the widow has no children. The first in line was Tov, Elimelech's brother and Mahlon's uncle. The second was Mahlon's cousin, Boaz. In those days, Jews considered it a moral obligation to give offsprings to the widow, even if not, as the law strictly demands, through the agency of the dead man's brother.

The initial meeting between the couple, Boaz and Ruth, which was not lacking in innocent wile and seductiveness, is branded by a strange destiny, guided – one must remember – by the desire of the attractive Naomi: 'So she [Ruth] set out and went to glean in the fields after the reapers. And it chanced that she came to that part of the fields which belonged to Boaz of Elimelech's clan' (Ruth 2:3). One should note, along with Rabbi S. R. Hirsch[34] that the Jewish idea of 'what happens' is foreign to the idea of 'chance' and refers to those moments in life that man does not control but they control him – moments of the divine message. Boaz, then eighty years old, was perfectly warned by his servant that Ruth was a Moabite, but he accepts her in his field, under his protection, and, while calling her 'my daughter,' lets her do the work of an ordinary gleaner,[35] perhaps so as better to observe her and put her to the test. '["]Listen, my daughter, and understand this. You are not to glean in any other field, do not leave here but stay with my servants. Keep your eyes on whatever part of the field they are reaping and follow behind. I have ordered my servants not to molest you . . . ["] Then she fell on her face, bowing to the ground. And she said to him, "How have I so earned your favor that you take notice of me, even though I am a foreigner?" ' (Ruth 2:8–10). Boaz seemed to imply that the law authorizing union with Moabite women had just been recognized and that Ruth, who therefore must not have known it, deserves more spiritual credit for leaving her own land in order to come to the Jewish people.[36] He therefore already suggested that her reward would be *perfect*: 'May Yahweh reward you for what you have done! May perfect recompense be made to you by Yahweh, the God of Israel, to whom you have come, to find shelter beneath his wings' (Ruth 2:12). One cannot help emphasizing, as several commentators have done, that Ruth's merit will be more sound than that of Abraham, and therefore worthy of a *perfect* reward. Could this be because Abraham left his father's house in answer to a call from God, while Ruth the foreigner did it on her own initiative?[37]

What followed in the narrative continues to reveal the charm of the Moabite's discreet but firm independence. Always obedient to her mother-in-law, Ruth becomes the representative of her desire. Thus, following Naomi's advice, she washed, anointed herself, hid beneath her cloak, and lay at Boaz's feet. Captivated for the second time, the old man (whose ordeal, in this instance, has often been considered harder than that of Joseph with Potiphar's wife) dwells not on the foreigner's obvious physical charm but on her 'piety' or 'benevolence, mercy, kindness' (*hesed*): first, she obeyed her mother-in-law, then she selected an old man – 'For this last act of kindness of yours is greater than the first, since you have not gone after young men, poor or rich. Have no fear then, my daughter, I will do whatever you ask, for the people of Bethlehem all know your worth' (Ruth 3:10–11).

Boaz nevertheless wishes to accomplish the law of the levirate and give Ruth to Tov, the closest relative. When the latter declines to do so (it would have deprived him of his own name and of his inheritance as well, to the benefit of the dead man's heirs), Boaz asks the people of Yahweh to be his witnesses, and then he marries Ruth: 'So Boaz took Ruth and she became his wife. And when they came together, Yahweh made her conceive and she bore a son' (Ruth 4:13). This was not a wedding according to the true levirate rules: Boaz 'took' Ruth and had the wedding sanctioned, a ceremony that was not required since, according to the levirate, the widow is normally meant for the closest relative. According to tradition, Boaz died the very night of the wedding's consummation, while Ruth immediately conceived and took her place in Jewish history. If her name received no further mention, Ruth nevertheless enjoyed an exceptional longevity, since she was to have her descendant, Solomon, rise to the throne.[38] Her child, whose birth was favored by Naomi's desire and the affection she showed Ruth and Boaz, became part of Jewish lineage from the moment of his birth. As for Naomi, she was recognized as that child's mother — we would say a symbolic one: 'And the women said to Naomi, "Blessed by Yahweh who has not left the dead man without next of kin this day to perpetuate his name in Israel"' (Ruth 4:14). Ruth's conversion inscribes the child's name in the history of the Jewish people and portends an illustrious destiny for him. It was Naomi, however, who took the child to her bosom and raised him; the Talmud makes quite clear that Ruth bore him and Naomi raised him (Sanhedrin 19b). 'And the women of the neighborhood gave him a name. "A son has been born for Naomi," they said; and they named him Obed' (Ruth 4:17). Obed is the one who 'serves' God: he served as go-between for two peoples and two mothers so as to insert himself in the symbolic lineage of Boaz and Naomi. His descendants would be a line of kings: 'This was the father of David's father, Jesse' (Ruth 4:17). There follows the whole of David's paternal line, which goes back to Pharez, son of Judah, but nevertheless omits the embarrassing story of Judah and Tamar, mentioned in 4:12 (instead of marrying her young brother-in-law after her husband's death, Tamar conceived Pharez with her father-in-law, Judah).

Besides, this insertion of foreignness at the very root of Jewish royalty is somewhat disturbing: 'For how long are they to speak to me wrathfully, saying: is he not of unworthy lineage? Is he not a descendant of Ruth the Moabite?' David beseeches, addressing himself to God.[39]

Nevertheless, the place of foreignness is not exceptional in that chosen lineage. Saved from Sodom's destruction, Lot and his daughters, who believe themselves to be the only survivors on earth, produce two sons through their incestuous relationships, Ammon and Moab. Ruth the Moabite is thus a descendant of that fruit of incest. The transgression committed by Judah and Tamar has also been alluded to. After the time of Ruth, Naamah the Ammonite became the wife of King Solomon.

Foreignness and incest were thus at the foundation of David's sovereignty. The biblical narrative suggests that being chosen is paid and deserved by the possibility of transgressing strict obedience and taking the risk of deviation — provided the latter is subordinated to a global design. It also assumes a conception of sovereignty based on the rejected, the unworthy, the outlaw. According to tradition, the letter *dalet* signifies 'poor': *David* is twice poor, and his ancestor Ruth the foreigner is there to remind those unable to read that the divine revelation often requires a lapse, the acceptance of radical otherness, the recognition of a foreignness that one might have tended at the very first to consider the most degraded. This was not an encouragement to deviate or proselytize but an invitation to consider the fertility of the other. Such indeed is the role of Ruth – the outsider, the foreigner, the excluded. Nonetheless, if the one 'outside-the-covenant' accepts the moral rules of the covenant, the latter finds therein its mainspring, its vital momentum, its sovereignty. Perhaps damaged, worried at any rate, that sovereignty opens up – through the foreignness that founds it – to the dynamics of a constant, inquisitive, and hospitable questioning, eager for the other and for the self as other.

The faithful devour the foreigner, assimilate him and integrate him under the protection of their religion's moral code, which both integrator and integrated support. Covered by such religious ideals, devouring fantasies are not expressed and the guilt they might give rise to is avoided. Even more so, under the protection of the moral ideals that are characteristic of religion, the assimilated foreigner works on the faithful himself from the inside but as a 'double' – calling for an identification with the 'base,' the 'excess,' and the 'outlaw,' which is continuously presented to the believer and stimulates the dynamics of his perfection. If David is *also* Ruth, if the sovereign is *also* a Moabite, peace of mind will then never be his lot, but a constant quest for welcoming and going beyond the other in oneself.

Notes

1   Genesis 17:7. [Unless otherwise indicated, I have used the text of the Jerusalem Bible – LSR]

2   I Samuel 15:2–3. One should remember that Amalek attacked the people of Israel on its rear guard at the time of the flight from Egypt; his descendants, Agag and Haman, were also noted for their hostility toward Israel, going so far as to consider issuing a decree of total annihilation.

3   Nehemiah 10:31.

4   The word *mamzer* is translated by 'half-breed' [in French, *métèque*, a word also having a colloquial, derogatory connotation – LSR]; it originally referred to the (Jewish) son of an (adulterous) union.

5   Deuteronomy 23:3–9.

6   Commentary on Numbers 14:10.

7   See A. Cohen, *Le Talmud* (Paris: Payot, 1970), p. 108.

8   Commentary on Genesis 49:2.

9   Leviticus 18:5.

10 II Samuel 7:19. [This follows the King James' version, which is closer to the French translation quoted by JK – LSR].

11 Likewise, Isaiah 26:2 and Psalms 118–20; 33:1; 125:4; etc.

12 Genesis 9:6.

13   Leviticus 19:18.

14   Avot 3:18.

15   See Leviticus 19:34, according to Torat Conahim, *Kedoshim*, 19.

16   Exodus 22:21.

17   Baba Mezia 58b.

18   Leviticus 19:33–34.

19   Deuteronomy 10:19. The quotations and commentaries in this paragraph are from the translation of Elie Munk, *La Voix de la Thora: Commentaire du Pentateuque* (Paris: Fondation S. & D. Levy, 1972).

20   Genesis 12:1.

21   Thanks are due [to] Betty Rojtman, professor at the Hebrew University of Jerusalem, for her valuable suggestions and her commentaries on this chapter.

22   Job 31:13–15 and 32.

23   There is also the word *nochri*, which denotes the foreigner or 'other' (in the sense of English 'alien') and refers to the apostate (Exodus Rabbah 19:4).

24   Yebamoth 47b.

25   A. Cohen, *Le Talmud*, pp. 110–111.

26   Sanhedrin 94a; 'Aramean' is the generic term used to refer to non-Jews.

27   B. Rotjman, personal letter.

28   Judges 17:6; 18:1; 21:25.

29   Baba Batra 91a.

30   Deuteronomy 23:3–9.

31   *The Book of Ruth*, a new translation with a commentary anthologized from talmudic, midrashic, and rabbinic sources, by Rabbi Meir Zlotavitz and Rabbi Nosson Scherman (New York: Mesorah Publications, 1976), p. xlvi.

32   Rabbi Meir in the Midrash, Ruth Rabba 1:4.

33   According to Zohar Chadash, in *The Book of Ruth*, p. xlix.

34   *The Book of Ruth*, p. 88.

35   It was forbidden to retrace one's steps to glean forgotten ears, for the latter were meant for the poor (Leviticus 19:9 and 13:22); likewise, it was forbidden to reap the corner of the field set aside for the poor.

36   *The Book of Ruth*, p. 95.

37   *Ibid.*, p. 96. [I have maintained the word 'perfect,' a literal rendering of *parfaite*, the one used in the French translation even though the Jerusalem Bible reads 'rich' and the King James' version reads 'full,' for the meanings are close enough; otherwise, the argument would make little sense – LSR.]

38   Baba Batra 91b, see *The Book of Ruth*, p. 131.

39   Ruth Rabba 8:1, *The Book of Ruth*, p. 134.

Chapter 13

Reading the Bible

■   This essay, printed here in full, first appeared as 'Lire la Bible' in
Esprit (September 1982), reprinted in *Les Nouvelles Maladies de l'âme*
(Fayard, 1993). It was translated into English by Ross Guberman in
New Maladies of the Soul (Columbia University Press, 1995).

Editors' introduction

NEW MALADIES OF THE SOUL, the loosely thematic collection of
essays from which this piece originates, is Kristeva's lamentation for the
moral and spiritual crisis of the modern Western subject, who, in her view, and
based on sessions with her psychoanalytic patients, is no longer capable of
sustaining or expressing a rich inner life. In *New Maladies*, Kristeva rails
against the immediacy and proliferation of media and consumer images that
provide us with only superficial forms of representation, and inadequately
replace the complex symbolic and aesthetic representations previously enjoyed
in art, theology and literature. The consequence, Kristeva claims, is that
individuals no longer have a language or a vocabulary to speak their most inner
conflicts, longings, joys and loves. The 'new malady' of which Kristeva speaks
is the resulting separation between somatic drives and desires, and ethical
considerations. She worries that 'modern man is losing his soul' (1995: 7).
The Western individual, Kristeva believes, is characterised by a moral vacuity
and is stunted by the lack of a vocabulary for inner reflection. She turns to
psychoanalysis, but equally to theology and literature, for a solution to this
modern malaise.

In many ways, *New Maladies* can be read as much as a celebration of those
cultural moments which highlight interior and psychic reflection as a lamentation for their demise. So it is not surprising to find Kristeva touting side by side
sacred and profane cultural treasures that are dedicated to an examination of
the inner, some would say 'spiritual', life: the work of Freud, Hélène Deutsche,
Da Vinci, Joyce, and the books of the Bible are all placed within the same field
of hallowed representation by Kristeva.

In 'Reading the Bible', Kristeva extols its 'sacred value', not as a theologian with a faith-investment, but as a psychoanalyst, in so far as the Bible provides a space for expressing the (psychic) crises of the subject. Too, Kristeva suggests a semiotic analysis of the Bible to unravel its particular system of signification, but more importantly, to investigate the process of signification itself, that is, of interpretation itself in all of its manifold alterity and indefinite possibility. It is this rich interpretive ground that Kristeva wishes to emphasise and harness for her analytic purposes.

Each of Kristeva's major themes, already seen elsewhere in this volume, are revisited and brought together in this final piece. In a further examination of Leviticus she finds evidence for her theory of maternal *abjection*, and a firm recognition of *sexual difference* inscribed in Levitical prohibitions. Her understanding of separation and language acquisition as *pre-Oedipal* is reinforced by this reading. She highlights the relation between a subject's separation (from the mother) and the paternal function (*imaginary father*), a relation which is accommodated by a stern and strict Jewish God who nevertheless invites his subjects to earn his love. And she argues that the Hebrew scriptures in particular highlight the subject as a being who is constituted and understood only in relation to the Other.

In the final section, she again contrasts the imaginary constructs of biblical belief to psychoanalytic practice and finds that while both engage in important and cathartic modes of providing psychic meaning and interpretation, psychoanalysis reveals the processes behind its myth-making, and concedes that these are 'necessary fictions' for living a full and healthy psychic life.

In an interview conducted shortly after the publication of *New Maladies*, Kristeva stated, 'Perhaps we are approaching the ideal of a superman who would be satisfied with a pill and a television screen' (Kristeva 1996a: 86). In *New Maladies* she puts the pill bottle away, turns off the screen, and invites her patients to 'read the Bible one more time'. It is no wonder that critics have accused her of a religious orthodoxy in place of a reasoned psychoanalytic theory. But from the beginning of this reflective piece on the richness of biblical narratives, Kristeva makes clear that she is first and foremost a linguist and psychoanalyst, and that her interest in the Bible comes from an absorption with the imagination – in its various guises, including the sacred – and its capacity for making meaningful the lives of her patients.

Two approaches to the sacred

The idea of reading the Bible as we might read Marx's *Das Kapital* or Lautréamont's *Chants de Maldoror*, unraveling its contents as if it were one text among many, is without doubt an approach born out of structuralism and semiology. Although such an approach may seem reductive or even outrageous, we must not forget that any interpretation of a religious text or occurrence assumes that it can be made into an object of analysis, even if it means admitting that it conceals something that cannot be analyzed. Of course, we may question this interpretive obsession that tries so desperately to make the Holy Text say what it does not know it is saying, and I shall return to what I believe to be the motivation behind this eternal return to divinity, a return that may be glorious or profane.

When the 'human sciences' – which rely upon a rationality that seeks to reveal the universal logic embedded in a myth, a hieratic text, or a poem – turn to the Bible, they are forced to limit themselves to the logic or rhetoric of the text. At first they disregard its sacred powers, although they hope that their positive and neutral analysis will guide them toward the mechanism – if not the enigma – of what is seen as 'holy' and of what appears to function as such. Perhaps the Bible lends itself to semiological analysis more easily than do other forms of writing. Indeed, by paving the way for interpretations, the Talmudic and cabalistic traditions are always inviting us to make yet another one . . .

What is more, the Book dominates the Judaic religious experience. It overshadows and ultimately governs the ritual, which enables it to bypass the ritual in favor of the letter, or of its interpretive values and a Single yet Infinite Meaning that supports human desire in the face of God. Are reading and interpreting the Bible perhaps the dominant ritual, the very eruption of the Judaic ritual and sacrament into language and logic?

This paradigm of biblical interpretation has resulted in studies inspired by various schools of thought, but that are unified by their common goal of specifying the profound logic that has generated the sacred value of the biblical text. Let us take the example of Mary Douglas' functionalism. While working independently from specialists in religious studies like Jacob Neusner,[1] Douglas has shown that the Levitical food taboos obey the universal law of exclusion, which states that the impure is that which falls outside a symbolic order. The Bible's obsession with purity seems then to be a cornerstone of the sacred. Nevertheless, it is merely a semantic variant of the need for separation, which constitutes an identity or a group as such, contrasts nature with culture, and is glorified in all the purification rituals that have forged the immense catharsis of society and culture.[2]

J. Soler has proposed a reading of the Levitical abominations that is more 'semiological' in approach. He has unearthed the way in which a taxonomy that bases itself on the separation and exclusion of food combinations has been transformed into a narrative and a ritual.[3] This taxonomy, which is initially dominated by the dichotomy between life and death, also corresponds to the God/Man dyad and provides a schematic version of the commandment 'Thou shall not kill.' In the end, the code of Levitical abominations becomes a veritable code of differences that seeks to eliminate ambiguity. In this sense, one might think of the food taboos that pertain to fish, birds, and insects, which are respectively associated to one of the three elements (water, sky, earth): any food product that mixes and blends these elements is considered impure. According to this interpretation, the Levitical taboos would suggest that the fundamental confusion is incest – an inference that can be drawn from the well-known precept, 'You shall not boil a kid in its mother's milk' (Exod. 23:19; Deut. 14:21).

Using a different approach, Evan Zuesse has delved into the hypostatized value of this exclusionary figure. He has noted that the Bible comprises a metonymic logic of taboos (which rely on displacement) that could be contrasted with the metaphorical nature of the sacrifice (which relies on deletion and substitution). This has led him to suggest that the Bible marks out the end of sacrificial religion and replaces it with a system of rules, prohibitions, and moral codes.[4]

That is all I shall say about these recent studies, which have helped clarify the inner workings of biblical thought in a way that can be distinguished from the historical or philological approach to religions, especially Judaism. I believe that the conclusions they have drawn are essential to any understanding of the Bible. These studies can be characterized, however, by an important omission: no attention is paid to the linguistic subject of the biblical utterance, nor by way of consequence, to its addressee. *Who is speaking in the Bible? For whom?*

This question is especially relevant for our purposes because it seems to suggest a subject who is not at all neutral and indifferent like the subject described by modern theories of interpretation, but who maintains a specific relationship of *crisis*, *trial*, or *process* with his God. If it is true that all texts considered 'sacred' refer to borderline states of subjectivity, we have reason to reflect upon these states, especially since the biblical narrator is familiar with them. Such a reading would tend to focus on the intra- or infrasubjective dynamics of the sacred text. Yet even if these dynamics are manifested in the figure of the text itself, interpreting them would require that we recognize a *new space*, that of the speaking subject, who henceforth ceases to be an impenetrable point that guarantees the universality of logical operations, and who opens himself instead to analyzable spaces. If I am alluding to Freudian theory here, it is because Freud's theory is capable of using the results of the biblical analyses I have mentioned and of transporting them into subjective space. Were an interpretation to internalize these discoveries as devices proper to certain states of the subject of enunciation, it could go beyond a simply descriptive framework and account for the impact that the Bible has on its addressees.

To return to the characteristic figures of biblical food taboos, I have come to realize that the object excluded by these rules, whatever form it may take in biblical narrative, is ultimately the mother. I cannot review the logical process that has led me to this position, but I shall take the liberty of referring you to my *Powers of Horror*.[5] Let me simply state that it is not enough to study the logical processes of exclusion that underlie the institution of these taboos, for attention must also be paid to the semantic and pragmatic value of the excluded object. We notice, among other things, that separating oneself from the mother, rejecting her, and 'abjecting' her; as well as using this negation to resume contact with her, to define oneself according to her, and to 'rebuild' her, constitutes an essential movement in the biblical text's struggles against the maternal cults of previous and current forms of paganism.

Now, the analyst is another person who sees such abjection as necessary for the advent of the subject as a speaking being. Studies on early childhood and on language acquisition have shown that the rejection of the mother causes her to be the originary object of need, desire, or speech. Yet she is also an ambiguous object who is, in fact, an *ab-ject* – a magnet of fascination and repulsion – before (in both the logical and chronological sense) she can be established as an object. This suggests an immersion in that which is not 'one's own,' as well as a dramatic distortion of the narcissistic dyad.

What is more, phobic and psychotic symptoms, which act out uncertainties about the limits of the subject (myself versus other people, inside versus outside), internalize this sort of aggressive fascination with the mother. In the discourse of adults, the mother becomes a locus of horror and adoration. She is ready for the entire procession of part-objects of *disgust* and *anality* that mobilize themselves to support the fragile whole of an ego in crisis.

Therefore, it could be said that a biblical text (the Book of Leviticus), which delineates the precise limits of abjection (from skin to food, sex, and moral codes), has developed a true archeology of the advent of the subject. Indeed, this Book recounts the subject's delicate and painful detachment – moment by moment, layer by layer, step by step – as well as his journey from narcissistic fusion to an autonomy that is never really 'his own,' never 'clean,' never complete, and never securely guaranteed in the Other.

I am suggesting, then, an interpretation that compares the Book of Leviticus to the preoedipal dynamic of the subject's separation. My interpretation is rooted in the fragile status of subjectivity, and it thus serves to explain, at least to some extent, the cathartic value of the biblical text. The Book of Leviticus speaks to me by locating me at the point where I lose my 'clean self.' It takes back what I dislike and acknowledges my bodily discomfort, the ups and downs of my sexuality, and the compromises or harsh demands of my public life. It shapes the very borders of my defeats, *for it has probed into the ambivalent desire for the other*, for the mother as the first other, *which is at the base, that is, on the other side of that which makes me into a speaking being* (a separating, dividing, joining being). The Bible is a text that thrusts its words into my losses. By enabling me to speak about my disappointments, though, it lets me stand in full awareness of them.

This awareness is unconscious – so be it. Nevertheless, it causes me, as a reader of the Bible, to resemble someone who lives on the fringe, on the lines of demarcation within which my security and fragility are separated and merged. Perhaps that is where we might discover what is known as the sacred value of the text: a place that gives meaning to these crises of subjectivity, during which meaning, disturbed as it is by the object–abject of desire, eludes me and 'I' run the risk of falling into the indifference of a narcissistic, lethal fusion.

Across the ages, sacred literature may never have done anything but use various forms of sacrifice to enunciate *murder* as a condition of Meaning. At the same time, this literature has emphasized the breathtaking threat that *fusion libido* inflicts upon meaning, which it can carry, destroy, or kill. The message of the biblical abominations, however, is particular and unique: you must be separated from your mother so that you do not kill anyone. Meaning is what guarantees desire and thus preserves the desire for death. You will displace your hatred into thought; you will devise a logic that defends you from murder and madness, a logic whose arbitrary nature shall be your coronation. The Bible offers the best description of this transformation of sacrifice into language, this displacement of murder into a system of meanings. In this way, this *system*, which counterbalances *murder*, becomes the place where all our crises can be exploded and assimilated. In my view, the fulcrum of this biblical process can be located in its particular conception of the *maternal*: the maternal is a promised land if you are willing to leave it, an object of desire if you are willing to renounce and forbid it; the maternal is delight as well as murder, an inescapable 'abject' whose awareness haunts you, or which may very well be the constitutive double of your own awareness. 'For your hands are defiled with blood/and your fingers with iniquity' (Isa. 59:3).

Love that cannot be represented

The Bible draws attention to the love that the Jewish people have for their God, and it demands or denounces this love when it is found to be insufficient. On the other hand, ancient texts have much less to say about God's love for Israel. Only two references to this love can be found:

> And David comforted his wife, Bathsheba, and went in unto her,
> and lay with her; and she bore a son, and he called his name
> Solomon; and the LORD loved him.
> And he sent by the hand of Nathan the prophet; and he called
> his name Jedidiah, because of the LORD.
>
> (2 Sam. 12:24–25).

The queen of Sheba affirms that the Lord loves Israel: *Blessed be the LORD thy God, which delighted in thee. (I Kings 10:9).*

Christian agape was to turn the situation around and posit that Love falls from the heavens even before we know it as such. The love that the biblical God has for His people is expressed in another way. As direct as it may be, it demands neither worthiness nor justification, for it is interspersed with preferences and choices that immediately establish the loved one as a Subject. Ancient biblical texts do not make a great deal of this love, and when they do intimate it exists, they imply that it cannot be represented. For instance, note that Nathan is the one who says, though without any words, that Solomon is beloved. What is more, the name of Jedidiah the child ('Jedidah' meaning loved by God) does not reappear in the narrative. As for the second passage, a foreign woman is the one who refers to God's love, and she speaks in riddles.

This brings us to the central problem of the biblical God: He cannot be seen, named, or represented. That these traits are particularly applicable to His *love*, as is shown by the passages I have cited, may give the analyst some insight into the infinitely complex question of the Bible's *prohibition of representation*.

When analysts listen to evocations of narcissistic wounds, or better yet, when they listen to subjects who are constituted by a narcissistic wound, they become aware of a ghostly yet secure presence of the father before they become aware of any oedipal hold on the father's love or on love for him. This archaic mirage of the paternal function, which is placed against the background of primary narcissism as the ultimate guarantee of identity, could very well be considered to be an imaginary Father. Although his actual existence may be hallucinatory, he appears to edify the keystone of the capacity to sublimate, especially through art. Freud characterized this particular Father, who is necessary for the Ego-Ideal, as a support for 'primary identification.' He referred to him as the 'Father in personal prehistory' (*Vater der persönlichen Vorzeit*). Freud postulated that apprehension of this father is 'direct and immediate' (*direkte und unmittelbare*), and emphasized that he internalizes both parents and both genders. The immediacy of this absolute, which the young child of a Mother–Father in personal prehistory brings back to a mysterious and direct grasp, guarantees his ability to idealize.

This sheds some scandalous light on the theological or antitheological orientation of philosophy. We know, indeed, that philosophers from Hegel to Heidegger have tried to ascertain the meaning of Being by interpreting the absolute presence of Parousia. We are obliged to note that this two-sided and double-gendered figure of kinship, which is what creates the symbolic, limits the extent to which analysis may search for that which is not simply narcissistic in origin. This, however, does not guarantee symbolic autonomy (or the separation between subject and object that it presumes).

As the zero-degree of symbol formation, this imaginary Father, who is most likely the father desired by the mother (her own father?), is thus the focal point of the processes that lead not to the appearance of the object (along this path, we have found the *abject* and a separative obsession), but to the *position of subjectivity*, that is, a being for and by the Other. The early onset of this moment, as well as its mediation by the mother's desire, causes the subject to believe that this moment is resistant to representation, despite the array of signifiers brought about by the oedipal complex. Those who believe in the God of the Bible do not doubt His love. God – who is impossible to represent, fleeting, and always there though invisible – eludes me and invites me to let go of my narcissism, to venture forth, to inflict suffering and persecution upon myself in order to earn His love. Does He not force these roots into that ineradicable, archaic, and deeply felt conviction that occupies and protects those who accept Him? That is, the conviction that a preoedipal father exists, a *Vater der persönlichen Vorzeit*, an imaginary father?

Is psychoanalysis a 'Jewish science?'

Interpreting the meaning of the sacred text as an elaboration of psychic conflicts that border on psychosis assumes, as I have made clear, that the psychoanalyst is attentive and even vulnerable to the biblical text. Why is it that ever since Freud, analytic attention has invariably focused on the sacred, and more specifically on the biblical sacred?

One might answer that such an orientation stems from the interpretive posture itself. I am made to use silence or speech to listen to and to interpret a discourse that no longer has any meaning for its subject, and that is consequently experienced as painful. I am struck, however, by the fact that analysands are privy to a meaning that is 'already there,' even if this meaning takes the form of the most dramatic explosions of subjective identity or of linguistic coherence. Does this stem from the conviction that there is an imaginary father? Whose father is it?

In like manner, the interpretive construction made by the analyst, who assimilates this speech through transference or counter-transference, also presents itself as a barrier to possible meaning (when I communicate an interpretation) or to a meaning that is arbitrary, if not eccentric (when I resort to silence). This interpretive construction, which can be as portentous as my own desire will allow, is nevertheless my only way – *the* only way? – to guide the analysand's speech from being completely eclipsed toward a state of relative autonomy. Interpretive constructions do not deny that crises occur, but they save us from getting trapped in them or reveling in them. I am proposing, then, an imaginary construction that can serve as an indefinite and infinite truth. As opposed to a positivist interpretation, which would delimit reality by giving itself the last word – the strongest word – analytic interpretation, as an imaginary discourse that serves as truth, makes no attempt to hide its status as fiction, as a *text*.

As a sacred text? This hypothesis, which we should not be too quick to reject, will attract the attention of rationalists on all sides, for a psychoanalyst would be unthinkable, it would seem, at the Collège de France. Nevertheless, we can easily understand that the text of analytic interpretation defuses all beliefs: a psychoanalyst appears suspicious; he is banished from churches and temples. Why?

By normalizing and understanding desire, psychoanalysis does not repudiate it, as commonly believed. It is true that analysis shapes and molds desire, but only as the wings of the Paragon of Faith, as the *subjection of desire to a fascinating object*, perhaps an unnameable one. The analyst remains fully aware that this object drapes itself in the attire of the mother Goddess, who extols our fantasies of origins and our desire for interpretation. Consequently, analyists [sic] are obliged to distance themselves from Faith in the Goddess of Reason as well as from religious Faith.

Hence, analysts find that the Bible offers a particular narration that suggests a treatment for the very symptoms that they are called on to interpret. Yet, this close relationship with biblical narration opens up the possibility of choice. Faced with the hypostatized Meaning of the Other, analysts maintain their interpretation by negating the intriguing power wielded by this Other, Father, or Law.

The analyst is not unaware that interpretive desire, which is abrasive and frustrating for the fantasy of the other, is tied to the fantasy of returning to the mother. It is true that under the demands of monotheism, such an attitude reveals the obsession with the pagan mother who has shaped it. Nevertheless, psychoanalysts can only avoid the trap of an archetypal Jungianism by admitting that their own sadomasochistic jubilation – which stems from approaching the source of that which is said – masks a certain hold on the unnameable Object (by way of the Law of the father as well as the fascination with the mother). What is more, analysts, as providers of meaning, should eventually saw off the branch, as well as the limb they are sitting on, for the driving force behind faith is the fantasy of returning to the mother, from whom biblical faith specifically distances us. The ensuing ambiguity causes Judaism, when it is completely internalized, to be the least religious of religions.

By laying bare the splendors of the Virgin Mary, Christianity, after having relied on a neo-testamentary discretion toward this subject, has unintentionally revealed what lies behind faith. In contrast to Freud, it could be maintained that the presence of the Virgin throughout Christianity is less a return to paganism than an acknowledgment of the hidden side of the sacred mechanism (of any sacred mechanism), which draws us into its soothing and grinding motion in order to leave us with a single path to salvation: having faith in the Father.

Psychoanalysis does not fall short of this, but goes even further: it is 'post-Catholic' by X-raying *meaning* as a *fantasy*, and then going on to take various phantasmatic functions to be an original fantasy in the form of an adoration of the object–*abject of maternal love* and a cause of eternal return. Finally, it is 'post-Catholic' in that it includes *its own process* within this same course of eternal return. Through this three-way loop, the experience of psycho-analysis results in a sort of combustion.

Let us say, then, that everything ends up as fire – the fire of Heraclitus, the fire of the burning bush, the fire that burned Isaiah's tongue, or the fire that bedazzled heads with Pentecostal tongues. The truth of the matter is that I envisage the fate of meaning during an analytic session in a similar fashion – as a meaning that is multifaceted, indefinable, set ablaze, yet One Meaning that exerts its influence everywhere. We can admit that this meaning requires the analyst to cling to the Bible's rigor, logic, and love, so that this fire might *be* and not die down right away. All the same, it must not blind us into thinking that this fire is the only thing that exists, for it need only state the truth at one point or another.

Neither biblical, rationalistic, religious, nor positivist, the place of the analyst is always elsewhere and deceptive, notable for the attention it gives to emptiness. This ambiguous position generates an ethics of construction if not of healing, and it bases itself not on hope but on the fire of tongues. This is enough to irritate believers, which amounts to almost everyone, in spite of what we might think. As Freud said, analysis 'exasperates' human beings; it forces them to contradict themselves.

Nevertheless, the central focus (as well as the stumbling block) of this avoidance-through-profusion that constitutes the serene delicacy of the never-attained end of analysis is analogous to the logic of the Bible. Denying the extent of its impact, which means cleansing the Father in order to decipher the Mother or to decipher a walled-up desire, can easily leads [sic] to an anti-Semitism in good faith. In a clinical sense, this anti-Semitism may portray a patient caught in the maternal bosom of fantasy, hope, and dependence. The un-being of a chosen yet excluded being is extremely difficult to assimilate.

On the other hand, one could delight in a strict, 'mathematical' reading of the biblical text, a reading that avoids all ambiguities, especially the pagan aspect coiled up beside the maternal body, which borders, as I have said, on the logical desire that serves as a foundation for monotheism. This sort of 'scientific' reading would encourage us to make analytic practice into a preferred space for hysteria (in men as well as women), a space targeted by what Lacan would call a paranoid 'lovehate' for the Other. Have we not seen a great deal of this recently in the various schools of thought and their schisms?

What might be done about this?

We should read the Bible one more time. To interpret it, of course, but also to let it carve out a space for our own fantasies and interpretive delirium.

Notes

1   Jacob Neusner, *The Idea of Purity in Ancient Judaism* (Leiden: E. J. Brill, 1973).

2   See Mary Douglas, *Purity and Danger: An Analysis of Concepts of Pollution and Taboo* (London: Routledge and Kegan Paul, 1978).

3   J. Soler, 'Sémiotique de la nourriture dans la Bible,' *Annales* (July–August 1973): 93.

4   E. M. Zuesse, 'Taboo and the Divine Order,' *Journal of the American Academy of Religion* 42, no. 3 (1974): 482–501.

5   Julia Kristeva, *Powers of Horror: Essay on Abjection*, Leon S. Roudiez, tr. (New York: Columbia University Press, 1982).

PART THREE

Catherine Clément

CATHERINE CLÉMENT IS A RESPECTED and internationally known French thinker who has written on many diverse and often provocative topics. Her works have been translated into English, as well as Greek, Dutch, Portuguese, Spanish, Italian, Japanese, Chinese, Korean, Lithuanian, Finnish and Turkish. Although she has studied and taught philosophy, she has chosen not to be identified as a theorist or a philosopher of a rationalist orientation. This does not mean that she is hostile to philosophy as a whole. She cites Spinoza, Pascal, Kierkegaard, Nietzsche and Bergson as philosophers she admires. She also acknowledges Jacques Lacan (Clément 1983 [1981]), Claude Lévi-Strauss (Clément 1970) and Vladimir Jankélévitch (Clément 1978) as strong influences.[1] Clément's preference has been to write novels, for example *La Sultane* (1981), *La Senora* (1992); other more formal investigative studies and essays, for example *Gandhi ou l'athlète de la liberté* (1996c [1989]); and creative exploration, for example *Syncope* (1994 [1990]). These books and essays communicate both her intellectual heritage and the formative experiences of her life. In recent years, she has not lived permanently in France but has served as a French ambassador to India (1987–91), Austria (1991–6) and Senegal (1996–9). These appointments, however, have not impeded her from continually investigating the human condition and the limits of human reason. This is not because she wishes to promote irrationality, but because she is, in a true sense, a lover of wisdom. What becomes clear is that Clément is passionately concerned about the authoritarian way in which both philosophy and organised religions have promoted themselves by imposing their own respective legalistic principles. These artificial categories do not recognise the depth and variety of emotional and corporeal modes of experiencing what she terms 'the sacred'. For Clément, the sacred is not necessarily connected to religion.

Clément would recognise herself, however, as a secular Jew. Yet, even though she proclaims herself an atheist, Clément is particularly fascinated by what is often termed (from a philosophical or traditional religious perspective) as heretical or marginalised behaviour.

Clément is also a romantic at heart, and she appreciates what she experienced during the avant-garde atmosphere of the 1970s. 'It had everything: radicalism, excess, and the necessary annoyances that any serious avant-garde provokes' (1994: 19). In this sense, Clément is a romantic revolutionary, but she is also a romantic in the context of being enchanted by love stories such as in her books *Edwina and Nehru* (1996a [1993]) and *Martin et Hannah* (1998b),[2] as well as their enactment, that is, opera, *Opera, Or, The Undoing of Women* (1988 [1979]). Nonetheless, Clément is explicit in expressing her dismay at the dire fate of most female figures in opera.

Perhaps such romantic tendencies could have influenced Clément when she joined the Communist Party in 1968. Clément has not yet written directly on the subject of her political affiliation, but in a thinly disguised autobiographical novel, *La Putain du diable* (1996d), the female protagonist declares that the act of joining the Communist Party was done in outrage, not at the student rebellion of May 1968, which she initially supported, but at certain students who encouraged the burning of books. The novel's protagonist, perhaps of a Jewish heritage, draws a comparison with a similar burning of books in Nuremberg in 1936. In retrospect, the protagonist affirms that, despite her political *naïveté* when she joined the Party – because intellectually she could not find another suitable refuge – she does not regret her fifteen years of membership. This is because it seemed at the time that the Party affirmed the value of knowledge and 'le Livre',[3] and was prepared to protect it.[4]

During the 1970s and early 1980s, Clément began to work as an editor, contributor and reviewer in several prominent leftist journals,[5] as well as director of cultural affairs for *Le Matin de Paris*. She also attended the famous seminars of Lacan,[6] and it was at this time that Clément began to write in-depth critical and appreciative studies. Among these were both *The Lives and Legends of Jacques Lacan* (1983 [1981]) and *The Weary Sons of Freud* (1987b [1978]). In the latter, Clément is highly critical of psychoanalysts who imitate the style of Lacan, using witty sayings, cryptic references and allusions to abstruse constructs, without having the depth and breadth of knowledge that informed Lacan. Clément's reprimand is based on the following observation: 'If [only] psychoanalysis . . . lived up to what it does. That is, healing; that is, changing our life; that is, giving us the individual and thus the collective means to live better' (1987b: 30). By the time that she published this work, Clément had also tired of what she terms 'the blindness of intellectuals', both of a Marxist or psychoanalytic variety (1987b: 25). Nevertheless, Clément states that she is indebted to both psychoanalysis and Marxism for providing her with tools that she treasures – self-analysis and self-criticism respectively (1987b: 24).

It was as a Marxist that feminist scholars in North America first became aware of Catherine Clément. An article entitled 'Enclave Esclave' appeared in *L'Arc* in 1975. Translated into English as 'Enslaved Enclave', it appeared in *New French Feminisms: An Anthology* (Marks and de Courtivron 1980: 130–6). The article itself was a response to a panel presentation on 'Women and Sexuality' that was part of a larger symposium named 'A Week of Marxist Thought'. In her presentation, Clément had suggested that the condition of women could be more profitably addressed from a Marxist position of class analysis, rather than by regarding the women's movement as a struggle simply between the sexes. This was not well received. In her published article, as a rejoinder to the critics of her conference presentation, Clément vindicates her viewpoint by saying: '"We women are all hysterics": if to be a hysteric is, as I think it is, to suffer in one's body from something that does not come from the body but from elsewhere . . .' (1980: 134).[7] Clément does not believe that women of themselves, as long as they react emotionally, will be strong enough to change the structures of society. The struggle is a political one – women need to undertake the political analysis of their situation, rather than react negatively to those – such as herself – who are trying to help them acquire the needed theoretical knowledge.

In her next English publication, Clément shifted somewhat from an exclusively Marxist approach. A collaboration with Hélène Cixous produced *The Newly Born Woman* (1986 [1975]). This book took some time to be translated into English, but once it arrived it received remarkable attention. In this, in her essay 'The Guilty One', Clément's theme is the exile of women from society. Close to the beginning of her essay, Clément observes: 'Somewhere every culture has an imaginary zone for what it excludes' (1986: 6). This refers to the fact that societies do not allow everybody to participate equally in their cultural organisation – which Lacan would refer to as the 'Symbolic order'. Instead, certain people are designated by names that signal their pariah status: mad men and women, heretics, ecstatics, sorceresses/witches, and hysterics who are acting out the repressed fears of their particular culture. It is in this way that Clément refers to them as figures of the 'Imaginary', because, as representatives of the unconscious mode of a society, they haunt and threaten the stability of the Symbolic order. But this does not suffice to change society.

This societal change cannot happen because, for Clément, women cannot be conscious of, let alone vocalise and act constructively upon, their frustrations at the 'feminine' role. She describes the comparison she discerns between the sorceress and the hysteric accordingly: 'When Freud and Breuer give an account of the therapeutic techniques that they use to treat hysteria, they describe a struggle, like the massive one organised by the European inquisitors to fight demons' (1986: 14). Both are attempts to contain or 'normalise' these women. It would seem that as long as there are inquisitors/psychoanalysts, there will be witches/hysterics caught in a bind that ensures repetition – unless there is a 'cure'. But the cure is only a readjustment to the society that was initially responsible for the problem. This is why Clément is ambivalent about the efficacy of such women rebels, as they cannot bring about a significant political or social change. Here Clément demonstrates that she has moved beyond offering only a Marxist solution, by suggesting that women themselves should begin to analyse and consciously introduce new images and expressions into the Imaginary domain. In this way they can begin to undermine the Symbolic order.

None of Clément's work thus far could be labelled as explicitly feminist, and she does not use that term. What is evident, however, is a concern for the status of women. This is also manifest in her next work *Syncope: The Philosophy of Rapture* (1994 [1990]). Clément's writing is unfettered, exploratory, often enlivened by colloquialisms. She has not left behind her former interests, particularly in the excluded and the exploited, but she now places them in a wider panorama of ideas, all concerned with the notion of syncope. 'Syncope' itself is generally regarded as a musical term that connotes an accentuated weak beat, or a reversal of anticipated accents. For Clément, this movement signifies a moment of disruption, even dispossession. Clément expands this unexpected break in continuity to refer, not only to the effects of music, poetry and dancing (including the whirling dervishes of Turkey), but also to tremors and seizures of all types, including the *coup de foudre* of falling in love, mystical experience, and to the various bodily effluents that can accompany certain of these extreme states.

In *Syncope*, Clément also introduces a number of themes that reflect her experiences in India. She is particularly intrigued by the way that, in the East, a philosophy of rapture is an acceptable element of these cultures. And with her romantic disposition, Clément is fascinated by such traditions that do not seek to contain, by words, by laws, or by other cultural restraints, this access to ecstasy (or *jouissance*). Clément also voices her displeasure at Western philosophy, where there is no recognition or sympathetic acknowledgement of such experiences which cannot be codified according to its rational qualifications.

Yet what interests Clément most in her examination of syncope is the immoderate nature of the exercises that seekers of this experience endure. Here the influence of Georges Bataille, with his own ascetic yet atheistic practices, is obvious (1994: 13). Though Clément cites the extravagances of certain Western women mystics (1994: 205), she draws many of her illustrations from the Eastern religions. As two particular examples, Clément focuses on the Hindu renunciant and on the Buddhist Tantric adept (who can be either a man or a woman). The Hindu renunciant, who irrevocably breaks social and familial ties, is, for Clément, a syncopal figure. This is because, freed of all social constraints, a renunciant wanders indigent and dependent on others for food. Clément appreciates the passivity of this approach, which involves an attitude of non-attachment, of not desiring a specific outcome to any activity. It remains a search for the sacred, but the aim is achieved by the discipline of meditation and yoga to clear the mind of all external and internal impediments. It is in following such procedures that one loses one's mind, or as Clément phrases it: 'Human jouissance [which she associates with syncope] requires that one lose one's head' (1994: 15).

In this work, Clément does not concentrate specifically on women as having a special connection with syncope, but, besides women mystics, she also discusses the Hindu image of the Mother goddess and other goddesses of Hindu mythology. Yet while Clément is aware that there are very few wantonly amorous women, let alone autonomous ones, in this mythology, she does not broach the subject of the actual role of many Indian women today with regard to dowry deaths, female infanticide and abortion of female foetuses. Such a realistic study would be in stark contrast to Clément's romantic tendencies, which are more attuned to grand gestures of abandonment and emotional intensity. In this sense, she seems to have left behind her Marxist concerns with changing the world in favour of an emphasis on the opportunities for personal transformation provided by syncope.

Clément's interest in religion is evident in her next publication translated into English, a novel entitled *Theo's Odyssey* (1999 [1997]). Orchestrated as a tour of world religions, the book focuses on Theo, a boy suffering from a rare blood disease that may kill him, who is guided by his aunt to various sacred sites and holy people. In these excursions, he meets with learned and compassionate experts from their respective traditions and learns to appreciate their wisdom. Yet always in the background, there are ecstatics of many different types, among them Anchorites, healers, mediums, Sufis, yogis, Zen monks, and *orishas* (African spirits). They all contribute to the patchwork of the world of different religions. Thus, while Clément herself is no devotee, her gentle and generous treatment here indicates her respect for, though not assent to, religions.

Le Féminin et le sacré (1998a, as yet not translated into English) is an exchange of letters with Julia Kristeva. It is written in a conversational mode – the correspondence was by e-mail and fax – where both Clément and Kristeva explore some of their favourite themes. It is Kristeva herself, however, who suggested the topic for their conversation – *le féminin* and *le sacré*. The people and subjects discussed are wide-ranging – virtually all the major religions, many philosophers ranging from Plato to Deleuze, sainthood, mystics and psychoanalysis. In their investigations, 'the feminine' is not necessarily equated with women, though two of the principal questions informing their inquiries are: 'Is there a sacred that is specifically feminine?' and 'Do women have an affinity for the sacred?' These questions (and most others posed) are not necessarily answered – but explored and amplified. Indeed, the aim is not to find a definitive response, but to leave the mode of discussion open-ended, without closure. This sets the tone for their dialogue, where Clément and Kristeva speak from often divergent positions, and clearly disagree on several issues.

There are two crucial points, however, where Clément and Kristeva are in agreement. One is that they are both atheists and that the sacred they seek has little, if anything, to do with traditional religion or divinity. The second is that, in speaking from experience, they regard the mother–child relationship as sacred. There are other dimensions of the sacred mentioned – music, the miracle of human life, the imagination. Yet, for Clément, the sacred tends to be associated with flamboyance, excess, reversals, even pollution. Thus Clément's sacred indicates a place of dissent, dissociation, and transvaluation of cultural norms. To be involved in behaviour that seeks to achieve such results is, for Clément, to 'passer à l'envers' (1998a: 215).

Kristeva, in comparison, does not accept the notion of the sacred as either something superior (for example, an ultimate point of reference), or inferior (for example, pollution). She prefers to locate the sacred, particularly as it relates to women – though men are not excluded – as a state of transition which involves the intersection with, and personal negotiation of, powerful cultural codes affecting both mind and body. This task must be undertaken if the passage from unreflective obedience to cultural rules and restrictions, and from forms of dependence on others to personal responsibility and lovingness is to be achieved. From a psychoanalytic perspective, Clément would not dispute this, but her own background, travels and experiences lead her in another direction to what she regards as sacred – 'la mystique du sens' – a transgression of the normal forms of experience.

Notes

1   Clément worked as the equivalent of lecturer and a researcher for Jankélévitch from 1969 to 1973.

2   The first novel is an interpretation of the relationship of Edwina, wife of Lord Mountbatten, the last Viceroy of India, and Pandit Nehru, the first Prime Minister. The second is an interpretation of the relationship of Hannah Arendt and Martin Heidegger.

3   The burning of books has always been associated with intolerance, anti-intellectualism, and fanaticism of one sort or another. 'Le Livre' encompasses everything Clément believes in: learning, culture and tolerance.

4   The heroine states: 'Je resolus de me fixer une limite, une seule: si ce parti
     commetait deux actes de racisme consecutifs, alors je me ferais exclue'
     (1996d: 218).
5   Journals included *L'Arc, La Nouvelle Critique, Tel quel* and *Libération*.
6   See Elisabeth Roudinesco, *Lacan & Co.* (1990).
7   Clément elaborates other examples of women's dependency. This situation
     prevents women from expressing their longing for autonomy or fulfilment
     except in thwarted, ineffective ways.

Chapter 14

Sorceress and Hysteric

■   [Abridged] This extract first appeared in *La Jeune Née* (Union Générale D'Éditions, 1975) with the English edition as *The Newly Born Woman*, co-authored with Hélène Cixous, translated by Betsy Wing (University of Minnesota Press, 1986).

Editors' introduction

CATHERINE CLÉMENT HAS STATED that in every culture there is a repressed mode of the imaginary – that is, images and memories that have been excluded from an official or 'conscious' version of history. For Clément, whose intention is to encourage the 'return of the repressed' elements of Western culture, it is women who, deprived of autonomy, nevertheless seek to express that which remains traditionally unspoken through forms of irregular behaviour. Clément is fascinated by the marginal figures of society, particularly the marginal roles taken on by women throughout history. In the first extract, Clément surveys several images of women who have haunted Western consciousness: the seductress, the sorceress and the hysteric – all the objects of a dominantly masculine culture's tendency to classify women as innately aberrant, if not dangerous, from social, particularly sexual, norms. For Clément, women thus become the focus of the projections of men, and their bodies all too often bear the manifestations of the repressed fears and anger directed at them.

In her attempt to expose the formation of such defamatory images, Clément explores the work of several male writers, including Flaubert and Michelet. Clément observes that though these particular men are more sympathetic (even 'feminine') in their treatment of women, there still needs to be a re-reading of history by women themselves. Clément searches for traces of those women – sorceresses, hysterics – who could provide alternative versions of their censored lives. Her conclusions, however, are not reassuring. Historically, she finds that these women are in an ambiguous situation for, while their lives may seem to be disruptive of the social order, such rebellious women often end up executed or, minimally, re-absorbed into the silent fold of family and history. As a result, women's social situation remains unchanged. The myths surrounding these women also remain constant, and so, for Clément, it is imperative for women to rework the myths for themselves, so that women's voices can be heard and their influence can begin to change the unconscious male fantasies that have marked them.

Clément is very much aware that she is not endorsing a rewriting of social or economic history, but a type of history that draws on myths and images – the imaginary aspect of a culture. In undertaking this project, Clément provides an example of a way women can begin to explore and express a form of truth that is theirs alone.

A woman in tears is leaning on an old man's shoulder. She is dressed in crimson and bears signs of violence and of love: 'She has bite marks on her face, bruises along her arms; her disheveled hair catches in the rips in her ragged clothes; her eyes seem insensitive to light.' She stays silent and listless like this for a long time, 'then she awakens, and utters marvelous things.' She speaks deliriously of an emerald-colored region, with only one tree standing; she speaks of a Greek or Trojan vessel carrying her off by sea. She became a prostitute for the Greek sailors, and here she is now, found by the old man, just as the tempted Saint Anthony dreams her. 'She was the Trojans' Helen whose memory the poet Stesichorus damned. She was Lucretia, the patrician raped by kings. She was Delilah who cut Samson's hair . . . Innocent as Christ, who died for men, she has consecrated herself to women.' These are the words of Simon Magus, performing as Ennoia's showman. Ennoia, Sigheh, Barbelô, Prounikos: woman. 'For Jehovah's impotence,' he adds, 'is shown by Adam's transgression, and the old law, which is opposed to the order of things, must be shaken.'

A woman marches on the city, dresses herself in green, and though she has been a wretched peasant, becomes almost sovereign on the strength of accumulated gold. 'Never had she been more beautiful. In the black pupil and the yellow white flickered a light no one dared to face, a volcano's sulfurous jet.' Then suddenly they are hounding her, cutting her green dress off at the small of her back, the dogs are biting her, and she finds herself again at bay, before the door of her house. 'She was spread out there, like the poor screech owl they nail to farmhouse doors, and their blows rained down all over her.' Now she finds herself in the heart of the forest. It has become her kingdom; she has become like the animals, 'like a wild boar with his acorns' – now her nourishment as well. She lives in the entrance to a caveman's hole. The crows keep her company. People come from all over to consult her, in secret. She is forbidden, menaced by the stake or by the *in-pace*. But she ensures the survival of the pagan forces of desire. 'She has a woman's *craving*. Craving for what? For Everything of course, for the Great Universal Everything . . . To this immense, deep desire, vast as a sea, she succumbs, she sleeps . . . She slept, she dreamed . . . The beautiful dream! And how can it be told? That the marvelous monster of universal life was swallowed up inside her; that from now on life, death, everything was held within her entrails, and at the price of such painful labor, she had conceived Nature.'

A woman is stretched out on a leather couch; she is suffering. Her eyes blink, she looks down, she wrinkles her brows, her nose; she wrinkles everything. She speaks badly, stutters, hiccups. From time to time, she makes a strange clucking with her tongue like the final sound of a mating grouse. 'Fingers crooked and clenched, she makes a motion with her arm as if to push me away, crying out in an anguished voice. "Don't move! Don't say anything! Don't touch me!" "Ah," another time she shudders in terror, "Suppose I found such an animal in my bed. Just imagine opening the box, there is a dead rat in it, a rat pinned down!"'

She has horrible dreams in which everything turns into serpents; a monster with a vulture's head bites her all over. Men whom she doesn't know attack her; they stand at the foot of her bed. She is afraid – of everything; she hurts everywhere – numb, paralyzed, cramped, twisted, warped. When Freud comes to take care of her, to try to force out these wild beasts that terrify her, she screams, 'I am dying of fear. Ah! I can hardly tell you, I hate myself.' And she goes on screaming, 'I am a woman of the past century.'

These three figures of women have three men as their authors. Ennoia, whom Flaubert presents in *The Temptation of St. Anthony*, is a woman suffering in subjection to an old showman who exhibits wild bears and Ennoia herself. The sorceress, as Michelet describes her, is woman finding her autonomy in the satanic dependency of a 'counter-culture,' a cultural backlash. Emmy von N . . . , 40 years old, from Livonia, is painfully exposed to Freud's eyes. Under hypnosis she spits out the toads and earthworms that she feels have tunneled their way in to inhabit her. Three women suffering for women. One who Hellenistic myth says sacrificed herself for women, as Christ did for men. One who consecrated herself to the Devil for want of something better, to succor other women menaced by the Church's oppression. Finally, one who was able to repeat in the register of symptoms all the history written in feminine mythologies and who suffered from the reminiscences of the other two – the hysteric. It is true, it is certain, that these three *men* have traits of their own that pertain to femininity. Flaubert, a hysteric himself, the prey of crises that threatened his sanity, identifies himself with Mme. Bovary, but not in the way literary tradition would have it: he identifies in 'sexual identity' by wearing a woman's skin.

Michelet, who declares himself 'Son of Woman,' surrounds femininity with a reverse idolatry. Freud, who applies psychoanalysis to and against hysteria (hence against femininity), traverses it with ears open but eyes shut. Nevertheless, these men are filters that are less impervious than others to the myths that women, with no cultural function in the transmission of knowledge, could not themselves elaborate until recently. One must go through the audience of writers, psychiatrists, and judges to reconstitute the mythical stage on which women played their ambiguous role. The last figure, the hysteric, resumes and assumes the memories of the others: that was Michelet's hypothesis in *The Sorceress*; it was Freud's in *Studies on Hysteria.* Both thought that the repressed past survives in woman; woman, more than anyone else, is dedicated to reminiscence. The sorceress, who in the end is able to dream Nature and therefore conceive it, incarnates the reinscription of the traces of paganism that triumphant Christianity repressed. The hysteric, whose body is transformed into a theater for forgotten scenes, relives the past, bearing witness to a lost childhood that survives in suffering.

This feminine role, the role of sorceress, of hysteric, is ambiguous, anti-establishment, and conservative at the same time. Antiestablishment because the symptoms – the attacks – revolt and shake up the public, the group, the men, the others to whom they are exhibited. The sorceress heals, against the Church's canon; she performs abortions, favors nonconjugal love, converts the unlivable space of a stifling Christianity. The hysteric unties familiar bonds, introduces disorder into the well-regulated unfolding of everyday life, gives rise to magic in ostensible reason. These roles are *conservative* because every sorceress ends up being destroyed, and nothing is registered of her but mythical traces. Every hysteric ends up inuring others to her symptoms, and the family closes around her again, whether she is curable or incurable. This ambiguity is expressed in an escape that marks the histories of sorceress and hysteric with the suspense of ellipses. The end of the sorceress, as Michelet tells it, is not the stake, it is being carried off on a black horse 'which from his eyes, from his nostrils spurted fire. She mounted him in a leap . . . As she left she laughed, the most awful burst of laughter, and disappeared like an arrow . . . One would like to know, but one will not know, what has become of the wretched woman.' Emmy von N . . . , like Dora, like other hysterics, disappears little by little from the Freudian horizon. News becomes scarce. Does she find another doctor? We don't know what has become of the wretched woman. One might say that because they touched the roots of a certain symbolic structure, these women are so threatened that they have to disappear. We almost forget that there were thousands of sorceresses burned throughout Europe – real disappearance, sanctioned by real death – for which the ecclesiastical power was legally responsible.

She is innocent, mad, full of badly remembered memories, guilty of unknown wrongs; she is the seductress, the heiress of all generic Eves. Both sorceress and hysteric, in their way, mark the end of a type — how far a split can go. It is the demoniac figure that comes to its end with the sorceress — the end sanctioned by the group in death by fire. The 'matrix' alienation, that which fixes the guilt of reproduction on the ill female organs, comes to term with the hysteric. What comes undone in both cases is woman's causality; she/it shifts, changes names at the same time the history of mentalities makes cultural norms evolve. But even if the split shifts, it does not disappear. Somewhere every culture has an imaginary zone for what it excludes, and it is that zone we must try to remember *today*.

This is history that is not over. How could it be? The myth transmits itself making changes in accordance with historical and cultural evolution. It varies, it changes feathers, but it only dies with the people who express it and whose contradictions it serves to resolve. If women begin to want their turn at telling this history, if they take the relay from men by putting myths into words (since that is how historical and cultural evolution will take place), even if it means rereading the most 'feminine' of them (Flaubert, Michelet), it will necessarily be from other points of view. It will be a history read differently, at once the same in the Real and an other in the Imaginary. These narratives, these myths, these fantasies, these fragments of evidence, these tail ends of history do not compose a *true* history. To be that, it would have to pass through all the registers of the social structure, through its economic evolution, through analysis of the contradictions that have made and are making its history. This is not my object. Instead, it is a history, taken from what is lost within us of oral tradition, of legends and myths — a history arranged the way tale-telling women tell it. And from the standpoint of conveying the mythic models that powerfully structure the Imaginary (masculine and feminine, complex and varied), this history will be true. On the level of fantasy, it will be fantastically true: It is still acting on us. In telling it, in developing it, even in plotting it, I seek to undo it, to overturn it, to reveal it, to *expose* it. [. . .]

Chapter 15

The Child, the Savage

■ [Abridged] This extract first appeared in *La Jeune Née* (Union Générale D'Éditions, 1975) with the English edition as *The Newly Born Woman*, co-authored with Hélène Cixous, translated by Betsy Wing (University of Minnesota Press, 1986).

Editors' introduction

C LÉMENT EMPLOYS THE WORK of Freud and Lévi-Strauss in this second extract from *The Newly Born Woman* in order to examine women's roles in celebratory feasts, particularly those of tribal societies. Although women participate in these celebrations, they do not play an active role; thus, for Clément, these rituals demonstrate the ways in which women have been prohibited from an expression of their own desires. Women serve instead, in a variety of ways, as signs or symbolic indicators of particular values in a system that is dominated by male projections and valuations – a system which also functions to control the proper sphere of activity for women's bodies. In contrast, Clément examines a ritual of excess, inversion and instinctual gratification – the witches' sabbat, where women play a dominant role in the proceedings.

According to Lévi-Strauss, women represent 'the place of origins' and their generative capacity constitutes a basic element of the rites surrounding tribal feasting. For Clément, however, this is an ambiguous, even dubious honour for women because while, on the one hand, women are connected with originary creation, on the other, women and women's bodies are associated in particular with all that is unruly and primitive, and in need of (male) regulation and control. In addition, Lévi-Strauss also establishes the tribal feast as a site of 'exchange' with women functioning as the primary objects of both material and linguistic circulation. Thus, as Clément, following Lévi-Strauss, writes: 'At the heart of the primitive or savage feast, words and women are exchanged' – leaving women no intrinsic value of their own.

In contrast, the witches' sabbat (of medieval times) is a distinct celebration of reversals, where all that is held sacred to the dominant culture is overturned.

Where there was prohibition, there is now indulgence. The witch presides over this 'uncivilised' ritual, which features behaviour seen as 'unnatural' according to the tradition of natural law that governs moral conduct in Christian culture. Yet, ironically, such a ritual is all too natural in its expression of instinctual drives and thus comparable to a childhood indulgence of desires, with the instinctual gratifications and inversions of accepted behaviour described in Freud's theory of childhood promiscuity (that is, polymorphous perversity). Clément notes, however, that this ritualised break with civilisation does not lead to any specific change in the situation of women in society. At the end of the sabbat, the witch alone maintains an identity free from 'civilised' controls, while all the other participants return to 'normal existence'. Thus, the witch remains an outcast, though a potent and dangerous one, which is the reason for her violent suppression by the authorities.

What Clément argues in this excerpt, and in 'Sorceress and Hysteric' (see Chapter 14), is that a façade of 'culture' has functioned to keep women under control, especially through religious and other symbolic structures. Nonetheless, these structures can be challenged and subverted, if not totally removed. For Clément, it is possible that, in time, the primal energy of the 'untamed woman' will be honoured instead of demonised. The sorceress, together with the hysteric, need no longer be regarded as 'primitive' or 'savage'. Clément's emphasis is a positive one, urging that the possibility now exists for women to use their strengths and creative energies to transform the world anew. Perhaps then the last outrageous laugh of the sorceress need not be a cackle of farewell, but an affirmation of the potentiality that women, with their new awareness of the workings of the unconscious – particularly its myths and images – can now exultantly express.

[. . .] *Living with one another*: this state, which Lévi-Strauss finds in amazonian daydreams and in myths, corresponds to the state described by Rousseau in his musings on the origin of inequality. It is the youth of the world. One meets another at the well, finding there the water necessary for the life of the body, the language necessary for the life of the heart, and the woman necessary for the life of the group. The place of origins, the feast, is also the place of exchange. Madman, child, and woman have the word there. Especially, they have the mastery that they do not have in ordinary reality. In this archaic structure, Lévi-Strauss finds the two axes of exchange that make men's cultural law: the exchange of words, the exchange of women. The exchange of words (language; the exchange of women (exogamy. Their development, however, is not the same: language perfects itself to the detriment of the information that it carries and progressively separates itself from the wealth of the original meaning. It 'entropies,' having been destined to inevitable degeneration, to an apocalypse of language. We have exchanged so many words that we will end up unable to speak: 'words have been able to become everybody's thing.' The exchange of women, on the other hand, has kept its original value, for women are both sign and value, sign and producer of sign. We know this perfectly well: it happens that women talk, that they step out of their function as sign. This fact still safeguards culture even in this wonderful scientific version of the great Christian myth: woman is in a primitive state; she is the incarnation of origin. 'In men's matrimonial dialogue, woman is not just what is being talked about; because, even if women in general represent a certain category of signs, destined for a certain type of communication, each woman keeps a particular value, which comes from her talent before and after the marriage in holding her part in a duet.' It is true that it is not yet a question of autonomous language. There is no doubt that woman might speak by herself, from herself; at least she is recognized as a producer of signs, whereas the other function allotted to her, like the linguistic function, strictly concerns the exchange between the groups. Duet, song, representation of a relationship as spectacle: exchange object and theatrical object; object of theater, woman in the initial exchange. Still, it has to be seen that all the wealth of this exchange preserves within woman the intrinsic value of origin. Ultimately one might even think, as we know, that the woman must remain in childhood, in the original primitive state, to rescue human exchange from an imminent catastrophe owing to the progressive and inescapable entropy of language. Words have been able to circulate too much, to lose their information, to strip themselves of their sense. At least let women stay as they were in the beginning, talking little but causing men's talk – stay as guardians, because of their mystery, of all language. Lévi-Strauss calls what they are thus able to retain 'affective wealth,' 'fervor,' 'mystery,' 'which at the origin doubtlessly permeated the whole world of human communications.' Later, in *Mythologies*, he will rediscover in Amerindian mythic patterns that 'women's periods, their uncontrolled flow, too close to nature and therefore threatening,' are the *stabilizing* element through which runs the split between nature and culture: simultaneously the rule and the unruly (*règle/règles*). A natural and dangerous order, always open to the possibility of lasting, turning into a cataclysm; hence, perceived by culture, by men who take on its value, as disorder. That is why women, who are still savages, still close to childhood, need good manners – conventions that keep them under control. They have to be *taught how to live*. 'If women are particularly in need of education, it is because they are periodic creatures. Because of it they are constantly threatened – as is the entire world by their being so – by two possibilities which we have just mentioned; either that the rhythm of their periods slow down and immobilize the course of events; or else that it speed up and throw the world into chaos. Because the mind can as easily imagine that women cease to give birth and have periods or that they bleed endlessly and give birth on any plot of grass' (*Mythologiques, l'Origine des manières de table*).[1] Two rhythms oppose each other. The rhythm of feminine periodicity, which the myths know – if not on the grounds of real knowledge, with the unconscious knowledge of primitive logic – guarantees the reproduction of the species. The other rhythm, that of the periodicity of culture, imposed by men on nature, a necessary material transformation, is a rhythm that both follows seasons, plants, animals, and women and restrains them. Affective relations, therefore, must keep a certain backwardness which is attributed to women; the necessary archaism and backwardness determine the climate of passion and of paradise. At the heart of the primitive or savage feast, words and women are 'exchanged' without speech – on the verge of what will later truly be language – on the verge of exchange as well. Culture, breaking its origins in paradise, introduces the exchange of women, of goods, or of words, which begin to circulate at the expense of that larval exchange, silent and precious, of the primitive matrix, the original womb. 'But the hot and moving climate in which began to bloom the symbolic thought and social life which constitute its collective form, still warms our dreams with its mirage. Right up to our own times, humanity has dreamed of grasping and fixing that fugitive moment in which it was permissible to believe one might be clever with with [sic] law of exchange – win without losing, enjoy undivided rights.' When all is said and done, to keep women, one must keep them in a primitive, wild state. It is hard to know whether Lévi-Strauss, as an interpreter, is projecting or faithfully transcribing the myths, but through him the truth of the original pattern asserts itself. No longer to exchange, that is, no longer to exchange women, to live without women, is outside history: *without history*.

So the right and wrong sides of social life play together; at halftime there is a celebration. On the right side: exchange, dividing up, gain, profit, but also the diminishing of fervor, the loss of communication. On the wrong side, nothing is exchanged anymore according to the mythological versions. And in their conflicts, *jouissance*, fusion, and community take place, both on this side of the community and beyond it. The origin is the reverse side of the present. This genesis of a disgraceful inversion is what Freud describes in the myth of origin; *Totem and Taboo, Moses and Monotheism, Civilization and Its Discontents* take the route of the feast. The cannibal feast, the totem meal. And the feast comes through mourning: from mourning to joy, just as the devil shows his presence during exorcism by a radiant face. 'This mourning is followed,' writes Freud, 'by the most boisterous and joyful celebration, with unleashing of all instincts and acceptance of all gratifications. And here we easily catch sight of the nature of the feast. It is not because, ordered to be in a joyful mood, men commit excesses; the excess is part of the very nature of the celebration; the joyful mood is produced by the permission given to do what is forbidden in normal times.' Celebration follows mourning and the father's murder; but the murder is due to the mother's making capital of women, that is to say, it is due to an *absence of exchange*. The sons kill the father – the man who has all the women – and weep for him. But in a memorial gesture where the repressed reappears, where the father lives again in the totem animal, where the parricidal act is again committed, the festival occurs as a repetition of the *absence of exchange*. The cannibal feast dismembers man's body; it is a paradise that celebrates the origin of the distance between man and woman, the origin of regulation of their relations, and it nullifies this distance in the moment of mourning mixed with joy. In the Freudian version of the story, incest takes root on that spot and, at the same time, the institution of generation occurs – the institution of the infinite succession of fathers and sons exchanging daughters. In the celebration, this exchange disappears: 'The desire for mother or sister,' Lévi-Strauss comments, 'the father's murder and son's repentance, doubtlessly do not correspond to any fact or collection of facts that occupy a given place in history. But, perhaps, in a symbolic form they translate a dream that is both ancient and lasting . . . The symbolic satisfactions, in which, according to Freud, the grief over incest is vented, do not constitute commemoration of an event. They are something else, and more than that: the permanent expression of a desire for disorder or rather for counterorder.'

Unless, perhaps, it might be a more roundabout way of finding an ancient order, one no longer valid, though the essential order in its time. Prohibition of incest is present-day law; it is what is currently forbidden ('currently' here must be understood in the context of mythic narrative, the level to which I always confine myself). But Michelet finds a more convincing explanation. At the time of medieval sorcery, incest has such a broad definition that it includes almost all the members of the same village; to take a wife one must actually leave one's hometown and go search outside the regions that this harsh ecclesiastical law would include. Cousins, even in the sixth degree, pals since baptism, kin throughout childhood: just to love in the village is to commit forbidden incest. So on the occasion of the sabbat, the participants commit incest. They rediscover there the objects of their childhood love; there, in this obvious wild state, they rediscover their true order, the order of their first attachments, with neighbors and cousins. 'Incest is the serf's universal condition, a condition perfectly manifested in the sabbat which is their only freedom, their true life, in which they show what they are,' writes Michelet. Paradoxically, or on the contrary – logically, this reverse side is the truth: 'At the sabbat natural attractions bloomed. The young man rediscovered there the one he knew and loved already, the girl whose "little husband" he was called when he was ten. You can be sure he preferred her and scarcely remembered the impediments of church law . . . A strong conspiracy and faithful mutual agreement which kept love tightly bound up within the family, excluded the stranger.' The sabbat, hence, is endogamous love; a repeat of the childish past, it is also anticipation of the future family, restricted and bourgeois, which will succeed the system of extended kinship. The predominant figure chosen by the sorceress is the young cousin and the surrounding women always feel the seductiveness of this ambiguous character, an always pregnant choice. Myths and narratives are good demonstrations of how these endogamous choices that break out on the sabbat are thwarted throughout ordinary existence. Isolde, on her wuthering heights and at Kareol, will achieve the one solution: death. Only there do children raised together rejoin one another. Yet the sabbat is the time and place in which these reunions will happen without obstruction.

This is finally what the sabbat, the witches' celebration, is. Michelet describes it as the apotheosis of woman. 'Woman at the witches' sabbat is all-fulfilling. She is priest and altar and she is the host with which all the people take communion. Basically, is she not God?' Later he goes so far as to insinuate that there, and only there, were sexual practices strictly heterosexual. 'The disgusting fraternity of Templars was unnecessary and unknown; at the Sabbat woman was all.' All: object and subject of this 'communion of revolt,' the Black Mass, which for all its reversal is very much a mass, a gathering, a festival. Of course there was violence; of course one can contrast the free, poetic, revolutionary celebration described by Michelet and depicted by Goya's old witches who greedily feast on children. Both parts of the myth are equally true. Apparently unnatural – 'antinature' – yet deeply bound to nature, which Christianity had repressed. Unnatural: the witches' sabbat is the one place where the sexual act does not result in reproduction. Witches employ effective contraceptive methods (ice water, Michelet seems to suggest), so that the woman-serf 'only ventured to attend the night festival on this express and repeated assurance: "No woman ever came back pregnant."' Opposing nature, the witch midwife comforts and soothes women who are victims of constant childbirth. *The Witches' Hammer* says a little more. 'No one is more harmful to the catholic faith than midwives,' for they alone can kidnap children at birth and consecrate them to demons. Hence, all midwives are potentially witches. Because they help to complete a natural act, they go over to the side of antinature: 'certain witches, going against natural human instincts and even against the nature of all animals, with the sole exception of the she-wolf, habitually dismember and eat children.' Here we have Goya and the cannibal women. The midwife who kidnaps a child and who is invested with the power of passage is dangerous for coming too close, in latent indeterminate meaning, to nature; she will have imputed to her all the death wishes against the child, or more radically, the imminent, fatal significance with which every birth is contaminated. She will pay for terrors yet to come, for the death of the parents of which the child is the sign. Yet, she is the good mother, in the upside-down world of the night; she annuls sexual exchange, renders it ineffective. She mothers the woman, nurses her. Beyond that, as Michelet observes, looms the figure of a sterile woman – sterile in function, but with a sterility that is both saintly and false: the Virgin, 'the Woman who is extolled is not the fertile mother adorned with her children. It is the Virgin and Beatrice, who dies young and childless.' And it is Isolde as well, a sorceress who switches love-potions and invites Tristan to the love-sabbat where she will lead him to his death; Isolde who tends wounds but cannot cure Tristan's, Isolde who loves the night and dies of love, consumed by Wagner on the romantic pyre where the Liebestod replaces the justice of the Inquisition. In romantic myth, woman is situated at the fissure where norms hang in balance, where values overturn, where medieval exclusion reverses itself and becomes saintliness.

The sabbat is over. It began between heaven and earth, on a knoll, on a heath all lit up for the great feast of the people; the sabbat is over, with its Mass and universal revelry, one luminous scene in which children play a part and another dark scene wrapped in haze to which only adults have access. There was a special dance, a round, the witches' round: 'They turned back to back, hands behind and without seeing each other; but often their backs touched. Bit by bit no one knew who he was himself nor whom he had beside him.' A mingling, a mixing of bodies, spatial confusion, disorientation: the body turns upside down, as in the hysteric's fantasy of the head-vagina. A body upside down like the rest of the festival. At the end of the sabbat, only the sorceress remains; Satan has disappeared, everyone has gone home. 'But *she*, she who made Satan, who made everything – good and evil, who smiled on so many things, on love, sacrifices, crimes . . . ! what becomes of her? There she is, alone on the empty heath . . .' And that is when she takes off – laughing.

Note

1   Claude Lévi-Strauss, *L'Origine des manières de table, Mythologiques 3* (Plon); *The Origin of Table Manners* (Harper and Row, 1979) [eds].

Chapter 16

Where Am I?

■   [Abridged] This extract originally appears as part of the
introductory chapter to *La Syncope: Philosophie du ravissement*
(Éditions Grasset & Fasquelle, 1990). Its English translation
appears in *Syncope: The Philosophy of Rapture*, translated by
Sally O'Driscoll and Deirdre M. Mahoney (University of Minnesota
Press, 1994).

Editors' introduction

S YNCOPE – A VARIATION IN rhythmic patterns; a suspension in time,
space and consciousness; a break with regularity, expectation and control –
is the elliptical moment that Catherine Clément explores in her book of the same
name. For Clément, the Western philosophic tradition, with its strong emphasis
on rationality and conscious analysis and systematisation, has largely ignored
the concept of syncope. When it has been given consideration, syncope is most
often aligned with the 'irrational' realm, with both its physical moments of
abandonment (as in bodily tremors and seizures), and its mental aberrations
(as in hysteria and possession). In attempting to annunciate a 'philosophy of
rapture', Clément implicitly advocates giving voice to the repressed elements of
Western thought and culture.

Clément's own time in India, where she believes this phenomenon of excess
finds its natural expression in that country's cultural and religious practices, has
had a strong influence on her work. At the same time, she also acknowledges
that there have been certain instances of this behaviour in the Western tradition
of mysticism, particularly in its manifestations by women.

In this extract, Clément discusses specific aspects of syncope, paying particular attention to how women have often been identified with its divergent
expressions. In addition, she also examines the extravagances of love at first
sight and the creativity of artists, poets and musicians, especially those of the
Romantic and emotional disposition. For Clément, the challenge is not simply to
reawaken rapture by a new consideration of these practices, but also to query

why, in both Western philosophy and religion, the joy and creativity entailed in syncope has been largely regulated or forbidden.

Suddenly, time falters.

First, the head spins, overcome with a slight vertigo. It is nothing; but then the spinning goes wild, the ears start to ring, the earth gives way and disappears, one sinks back, goes away . . . *Where* does one go?

The subject, says the doctor, is inert, pale, without consciousness. Sensitivity is obliterated. There is no respiration, no pulse can be felt . . . after a necessarily short time, the pulse reappears, as does the respiration; the skin regains color; the sick person regains consciousness. Otherwise, the ending is fatal; syncope leads to death.[1]

Syncope: an absence of the self. A 'cerebral eclipse,' so similar to death that it is also called 'apparent death'; it resembles its model so closely that there is a risk of never recovering from it. The romantic and clinical scenario has usually, in our society, been allotted to woman: it is she who sinks down, dress spreading out like a flower, fainting, before a public that hurries forward; arms reach out, carry the unresisting body . . . People slap her, make her sniff salts. When she comes to, her first words will be, 'Where am I?' And because she has come to, 'come back,' no one thinks to ask where she has been. The real question would be, rather, 'Where was I?' But no, when one returns from syncope it is the real world that suddenly looks strange. [. . .]

The mythologies of love at first sight are often radical and explicit. The young Selene, beloved by Zeus, wanted to see him in all his majesty while she was already carrying the king of the gods' child. Finally, Zeus agreed to reveal himself; but his light was so bright that it burned Selene right down to the bone. Only the fetus was not consumed, and the god sewed it up into his own thigh so that it could go to term. Thus was born Dionysus, the god of syncope, son of a mortal woman and a bolt of love. In the universe of the gods, the bolt of love really is a thunderbolt. The God of the Jews and Christians does not escape this terrifying power; when he reveals himself to Moses, it is in the middle of a storm, amid thunder and lightning, on top of a mountain. When he wants to conquer Paul of Tarsus, he overcomes him, blinds him, and cripples him grievously. The gaze is often fragile; no one looks directly at the sun without burning their eyes; how could one look death in the face? That is a characteristic of the gods: to look directly at them is to expose oneself to the thunderbolt. The desire for the impossible confrontation persists in human love at first sight: if they can look at one another, even if it entails being charred at the same moment, then they have both become gods. [. . .]

An abrupt suspension of time, syncope contradicts time's natural progress. Through syncope the motives of desire are swallowed up: passivity, love, the other, God, emptiness, and destruction are there – all mixed up, in the heart of a confusion that one could say was planned. This jerky tremor suppresses the subject's consciousness. But it is also what sets music, dance, and poetry working. This suppression moves us; this passivity is productive. That is the paradox that must be explained. Why is the last beat of musical syncope a 'salvation,' as Rousseau said? What is the point of this little leftover piece of the beat?

It would be too easy to interpret syncope as a lapse, a failed act; in short, it would be premature to put it in the huge cupboard of products of the unconscious. At best, that would be so true that it would not risk being false.

It would be easy to collect all the accidents of thought, language, and deed in Freud's work, and to include syncope with them as a psychosomatic phenomenon, with hysterical origins, rehearsing a forever unknowable primal scene. It would be easy to find in Jacques Lacan's work a series of signifiers covering up emptiness, lack, internal twisting, and to treat syncope as a punctuation mark in life. Neither of these two interpretations would be wrong; I do not exclude meeting Freud, even less encountering Lacan, but that is not enough – or rather, it is no longer enough for me. [. . .]

But how should we begin this venture? In the world that we call modern, the rituals that regulate it have disappeared; others appear, which we hurry to nurture. And though we tolerate the ecstasy of rock and roll, we fight against drug use and we do not deal very well with the depressive *raptus*. The voyage begins with this violent desire for night: depression is the current end-point of a long genealogy of syncopes, which we once knew how to manage. Now, they seem overwhelming.

The history of our classical philosophy, as it is now taught, shows this: Western thought has been busy filling this hole in life. For a long time, it has worked desperately to include syncope in the ranks of unfortunate accidents, sources of disorder, unhealthy disturbances, private and public fanaticisms. It is not until the dawning of Romanticism that this surprise, in all its liveliness, finally finds the position that it had occupied elsewhere, although not in philosophy. When it arrives in thought, it does so with a vengeance, but in poetic forms, with Friedrich Hölderlin, Søren Kierkegaard, Friedrich Nietzsche, like youth finally cured. That is how it acquired its rights in the philosophical world at the moment when it passed, medically, into the realm of madness.

But we stay on the sidelines – Bataille more than anyone else, with an extraordinary stubbornness, and words held in suspense. For how could one succeed in describing the inside of ravished time?

In the East, the abyss where the fan beats like a wing, this chasm where the West has so often got lost, one can succeed in this description. The detour through India makes us discover a philosophical science of syncope, the consummate art of its practice, a comprehensive consideration of its secret powers. By starting in the East, we can then return and rediscover the enclaves into which the art of this dissension has slipped, through the meshes of a tightly drawn net.

There is still one thing, however, that the West has not dared touch, except in those countries where tyranny has temporarily taken over. That is creativity; there are artists whose work reproduces the scenario of syncope: a surprise, a delay of life, a violent anticipation, and a slow return to what one calls the 'self.'

There will be a scandal, for syncope is a warning; it demands attention. It is true that by intruding, it cheerfully breaks the laws of the world. And if it simulates death, it does so the better to fool it.

Joyfully, between laughing and crying, between ecstasy and agony. Joyfully, between the pleasure of orgasm and the happy sadness that follows. Joyfully, playing with our most deeply held beliefs, which, in the space of rapture, no longer exist.

Note

1   Selection from 'La Syncope,' doctoral dissertation for the medical degree, written by Oswald Hermabessière (Libraire Lac, 1931).

Chapter 17

Jouissances: Between the Angel and the Placenta

■ [Abridged] This excerpt comes from the final chapter of *La Syncope: Philosophie du ravissement* (Éditions Grasset & Fasquelle, 1990). Its English translation appears in *Syncope: The Philosophy of Rapture*, translated by Sally O'Driscoll and Deirdre M. Mahoney (University of Minnesota Press, 1994).

Editors' introduction

IN THIS EXTRACT, Catherine Clément explores the phenomenon of *jouissance* as syncope. The ecstasy of *jouissance* is not necessarily restricted to orgasm, but includes the multiple forms of rapture that the sensuous and sexually responsive body can experience. Thus, it is not simply lovers, but Tantric adepts and mystics who participate in this sacred, though not necessarily religious, state.

With reference to the West, specifically women mystics, Clément examines Romain Rolland's postulate of the 'oceanic feeling'. Citing Joan of Arc, Clément describes this mystic's direct communication and commitment with God, rather than obedience to religious institutions. Institutional emphasis on obedience and conformity is why religion in the traditional sense is not, in Clément's view, the locus of mysticism. In contrast, the oceanic feeling is an instance of mystical syncope – a personal exaltation that does not depend on official sanction.

These ecstasies are not simply states that are reached by regular observances and meditation. There can be violence and macabre practices involved. Blood and secretions abound, penitential mortifications are inflicted on the body. Syncope is thus not innocent pleasure. Its preparatory stages are not without agony – self-inflicted or otherwise. As such, this form of ecstatic agony of syncope has not been encouraged by authorities. It marks the preserve of those generally regarded as eccentrics, as mad, or as outcasts of society.

Syncope is also connected to bodily exhalations and to exaggerated intakes and holdings of breath. In fact, syncope is situated at the point of their interaction – the moment when an expected continuity fails. The rhythms of ordinary life cease – life and death no longer demarcate the only limits of the life span. This instance of a break with ordinary consciousness is the moment of syncope.

In the concluding section of the chapter, which is not included in this extract though featured in its title, Clément muses on the aftermath of syncope. She believes that an image of the soul is born, but she does not elaborate on this. She alludes to the birth of a child – and the remainder of the afterbirth. And it is in this connection that she develops her associations of the placenta and the angel as exemplars of syncope's effects.

For Clément, there is no certain outcome. The placenta, regarded as waste, is usually disposed of. Yet Clément also appreciates that ingesting the placenta, as well as other taboo substances, or indulging in excessive behaviours, can be seen as a way of 'making love to God'. Both the angel and the Beast are also part of this next phase and neither entity is necessarily benign. The Beast represents the possibility of an unfortunate outcome – images of torture, of wolf-men, of not returning to the body, prevail. The angel, on the other hand, is not always an agent of light. Angels have been responsible for some dubious undertakings. However, if the angel refrains from sex, and thus, for Clément, goes against nature, it can figure as the being who brings redemption. Thus, for Clément, syncope is multifaceted and equivocal in its results. A rapture out of time does not always promise a positive transformation with re-entry into ordinary time and space.

To speak of love is a jouissance in itself. But to speak of jouissance itself is another matter.

The 'little death,' as it is known in the West, brings to mind images of weakness. The languor experienced at the moment of climax causes us to 'fall' with weakness; we 'lose' consciousness. Popular slang has found an even better expression: to have an orgasm is known as 'to get one's rocks off,'[1] for a man, that is. This is a way of reconnecting with the fallacious and mythical feminine weakness whose nature we saw when the bacchantes tore the fawns apart with their bare hands. No matter, orgasm does bring on a temporary languor, an instantaneous mellowing, a softening of which the diminution of the penis is but a sign.

A noticeable weakness, perhaps, but a sacred one. A prodigious rallying point for the proponents of a new genre.

There was a king named Pandu, meaning 'pale'; his mother had in fact gone pale when she first saw the abominable ugliness of the child presented to her as continuer of the royal race. King Pandu had two wives, and he was happy. Alas, one day he went hunting for antelope, and with a well-aimed arrow in a double blow, he shot through a pair of coupling animals.

Unfortunately for King Pandu, one antelope was not actually an antelope but a yogi sage who had spring fever and who had decided to transform himself into an animal. Accomplished yogis have these powers, and are able to return to nature as an animal in heat without breaking their vows of chastity. The dying yogi, pulling out the deadly arrow, addressed the anxious king. I curse you, he said, because you killed a couple in the moment of weakness that all of nature respects. I curse you: you will not be able to couple with a woman without dying at the same instant. Having said these words, the yogi left his body and died. At first King Pandu was worried: Would he have no offspring? And after negotiating this delicate point with several surrogate procreators, all of whom were gods assembled for the occasion, and after several children were born to him by proxy, he could no longer resist. The same springtime that had inspired the yogi seduced him as well; disregarding the objections of the more beautiful of his wives, he made love to her and died immediately, in rapture. His young woman chose to be burned with him on the funeral pyre.[2]

The only difficult point in this episode of the *Mahabharata* lies in the question of engendering; once this matter was solved, the man-king calmly let himself go, because it is preferable to die while making love than to live without jouissance. The yogi coupling with his beautiful antelope had shown him nature's true path.

But the essence of this natural weakness remains, in the strictest sense, ineffable. The Tantric philosopher allows himself a privileged role: he suspends the male orgasm by attuning it to the cry of the Other. This suspension is neither animal nor human; it reaches a superhuman level where the Tantric practitioner reaches ecstasy, therefore the universe, therefore the other side of nature. The Tantric practitioner has nothing to say about the jouissance of the Other.

Lacan calmly affirmed, rather prudently taking as witnesses those he saw in his audience who 'appeared to be men,' that a woman knows nothing about her own jouissance. She experiences it and is aware of experiencing it, but that is all. In order to escape from feminine muteness on the subject of jouissance, Lacan calls on the mystics for assistance. Because generations of psychiatrists at the end of the nineteenth century wanted to define mystical jouissance as 'matters of sperm,' Lacan reverses the position: it is not psychiatry that is capable of explaining human jouissance but the mystics. But at the densest point their language remains mute as well: like the woman who experiences an orgasm but cannot explain it, the mystic feels and describes a jouissance of which he knows nothing.[3]

In the West as in the East, when male or female mystics speak of this, they all describe the same ocean. A flood; a torrent of waves; a delicious immersion; a feeling of drowning; arriving in a liquid that rolls, shakes, exhausts, and draws one up. Romain Rolland invented the image of the 'oceanic feeling,' and tried to confront Freud, who couldn't do anything with it; he was unable to find the slightest hint of this kind of feeling in himself.[4] Freud was willing to admit that the oceanic feeling is often apparent when, for example, despite all evidence, a lover is so impassioned that he declares himself to be 'one' with the Other; Freud grudgingly accepted the definition of the oceanic feeling as the 'restoration of a narcissism without bounds,' but did not concede the point about religion. The origin of religion is an infantile position of abandonment proclaiming misery. This was a total misunderstanding: Rolland was not speaking of religion but of mystical syncope.

But they were both right: Freud to maintain that oceanic feeling had nothing to do with religion; Rolland to affirm its existence and particularity.

Freud had a valid point; the mystic in the process of dissolving himself inside what he calls his god wastes no time but takes the most direct route. This creates a short circuit: what should be done is to 'skip' the steps marked out by religion. Joan of Arc, when brought before the Church tribunal, persisted in giving an obstinate answer: yes, she would agree to recognize the 'militant' Church, but 'I serve my Lord first,' or 'God is served first.' This is the superb stubbornness of a young girl in direct contact with God or his royal incarnation, and rejecting 'militancy.' Another short circuit: the mystic is of necessity a dissident, cut off from the established circuits. And the dissident must also participate in mysticism, because in order to have direct access to any emotion, whether libertarian, nationalistic, or erotic, the shortest route must be taken, which springs from 'boundless narcissism.' To project the voice or image of divinity outside the self, or to project a passion for liberty outside the self, is a thought process that presupposes a radical breaking-through of the limits of the self. From this apparent weakness narcissism will later find the power of protest and restoration. But oceanic *in and of itself*?

Romain Rolland had experienced the oceanic feeling[5] as an adolescent, thanks to music, especially that of Beethoven.[6] Having become a historian and writer as an adult, he heard about a person who had described uninhibited mystical jouissance better than anyone else: Ramakrishna, a poor illiterate Brahman from Bengal. Ramakrishna was an amazing ecstatic who allowed himself the luxury of having access to all available gods, those of Hinduism, Islam, and Christianity, to such an extent that Rolland, in the biography he wrote of Ramakrishna, called him the 'gods-man.' It is from this small, frail man with a large mouth and distorted gaze that Rolland borrowed the notion of oceanic feeling.

This small man had become tired of waiting for ecstasy, so exhausted from this long, fruitless quest; one day in the temple of Kali, the goddess to whom he was devoted, he saw the large sword of the sanctuary. He swiftly made for the weapon; enough of this life!

And lo! the whole scene, doors, windows, the temple itself vanished . . . It seemed as if nothing existed any more. Instead I saw an ocean of the Spirit, boundless, dazzling. In whatever direction I turned, great luminous waves were rising. They bore down on me with a loud roar, as if to swallow me up. In an instant they were upon me. They broke over me, they engulfed me. I was suffocated. I lost consciousness and I fell.[7]

A classic description, often quoted, and which develops the theme of the ocean that is latent in all Indian texts. This ocean is like the famous statue of St. Theresa's ecstasy: 'All you have to do is go to Rome to look at Bernini's statue to see that there is no doubt, she is orgasmic [*elle jouit*],' said Lacan.[8] The same evidence can be applied to the ocean that swallows up the mystic.

Karoline von Günderrode, whom we encountered at the edge of the abyss of Asia shortly before it swallowed her up whole in a voluntary death, magnificently describes the effects of jouissance as an ocean that had nothing to do with god and everything to do with herself:

Suddenly my heart contracted and was numbed by fog. Soon it vanished: it seemed to me that I was no longer myself, while remaining myself more than ever and if my consciousness had crossed the borders, it was different and larger, nonetheless I felt myself to be within it. I was free from the narrow borders of my self; and ceasing to be an isolated drop, I was returned to the 'all' that I possessed in my turn; I thought the 'all,' I felt the 'all': I was a wave in the ocean, a ray in the sunlight, I was gravity with the stars; everywhere I felt myself and in myself I enjoyed [*jouir*] everything.[9]

If the oceanic feeling is well adapted to the core of syncope – this ecstasy – it is because only there is the horizon found, and the infinite movement of waves rolling in and pulling away; there is the sexual drive of the universe. [. . .]

In 1886, Ramakrishna died; religious books in India, as usual, do not speak of his 'death' but rather of his 'Great Ecstasy.' Ten years later, an unknown Parisian female transient was hospitalized at the La Salpêtrière Hospital and lovingly cared for by Pierre Janet, who made her the tragic heroine of his most important book: *De l'angoisse à l'extase* (From anguish to ecstasy). Madeleine, who identified herself to the police as 'the Goat,'[10] was in fact the emissary of mystical dementia. The therapist was soon able to discover simple orgasms amid the joys of his patient.

'I have,' she told him, 'large sweet patches on my lips and on my stomach that throb with truly divine tremors . . . My whole body trembles when God softly places his burning hands on my body and caresses me all over, it is indescribable, and it seems like the jouissance that I feel makes me faint. I feel as if I am being lifted into the air, it seems as if my body is being carried by a thick rope between my legs, and that this rope is pressing on my genitals, pushing them inside. It begins to affect my bladder; a seal is placed on the opening but this difficulty in urinating is not an agony but rather a sensual delight . . . I very often feel the sweetest tremors both on the inside as well as the outside of my body which are so unusual that I cannot describe them.'[11]

Pierre Janet's commentary is no more self-conscious than that of his patient: 'Let us note here that the appearance of this jouissance is not surprising in the least. When we realize that jouissance exists in all the senses, in all parts of the body, it would be unusual if it were absent from the organs that produce it most easily.'[12] Pierre Janet couldn't have said it better, nor could Madeleine.

The passionate curiosity of essayists, novelists, and philosophers about these testimonies resembles that of children. This is the reality of Hic Rhodus, hic saltus. This is jouissance, *even without the sexual act*. Here is jouissance: falling, rolling, trembling inside. [. . .]

It is actually hard work to put oneself in a state of weakness. In order to do so, mystics have no shortage of methods: crosses, crucifixions, stigmata, bones that are broken or that become paralyzed, ulcers that flourish and that become wormy, even leprosy. One scarcely knows who to choose as emblem: Lydwina of Schiedam, Catherine Emmerich, Angela of Foligno, all of whose bodies became blistered, putrefied, bloodied flesh . . . Such is the extensive register of female saints in the West, celebrated by adoring writers who were often infuriated[13] and who appeared to be in need of orgasms. The corporeal landscape of ecstatics in India, even if it does not feature as many purulent secretions, is also affected by terrible sufferings. But they are not of the same kind.

Take blood, for example. In the bodies of Western ecstatics, it flows from the palms, the soles of the feet, from the heart and from the part of the chest where Christ was struck with a lance. Sometimes, it forms a little bloody cross, as on Catherine Emmerich's chest. Blood springs forth spontaneously, always in the places where Christ's body was wounded. In the Indian practice of ecstasy, respiratory techniques, always excessively congestive, cause the blood to give a flushed cast to the skin all over the body, so much so that one should be able to recognize a yogi by his reddish, 'burned' complexion. Ramakrishna made a point of verifying the skin tone of a person who claimed to be an ecstatic, checking to see if his chest was the right color: whether like burned bread, crayfish red, or, the sign of supreme talent, golden and radiant, the skin retains forever the fire of ecstasy. Sometimes, but not often, blood trickles through the pores. But never does it favor a particular part of the body. In the West, ecstatic martyrs have Christ's blood springing forth from their bodies; in India, ecstatics voluntarily become 'burned.'

Where blood does not flow, there are trembling, convulsions, a metal band squeezing the head, a stiffening of the extremities and bodies in revolt. Janet's Madeleine experienced autonomous flight; Saint Theresa of Avila accepted the sensation of levitation without refusing sexual pulsation. The body leaves wetness behind, dries out and bursts into flames, becomes light, and even winged. Saint Theresa of Avila invented the appropriate expression: 'violent transport.' [. . .]

To travel – or 'trip' – is key for mystics, shamans, witches, and users of drugs. To travel, the pure fantasy of lovers; if the princess is far away, it is necessary to rescue her from across the seas and return her soul to her before even laying eyes on her. To travel out of the body: rubbing an ointment on one's skin, as sorcerers do; holding one's breath; whirling to the sound of a chorus of drums; using alcohol, drugs, or experiencing love at first sight. To extract from psychological teguments for which no language has a name, something that is neither living or dead, neither body or soul, a bird, they say, no doubt. Leaving the body is not only a practice of Indian ecstatics or European saints; customary in shamanism, a ritual in witchcraft, it is the currency of drug addicts' imaginations – who indeed pay a high price for the experience.

Something leaves the body. There is no jouissance without this departure, without the falling away of an unnameable fragment, undefinable as an object. The geography of jouissance is that of the orifices through which the object can escape; each time, the spasm may pulsate there, a cause of all or part of the oceanic tremors. Feces and urine, anus and urethra, principal locations of mystical debasement – of which Ramakrishna is not the sole practitioner – are the closest places to actual genitalia. Purulence, pus, mucus, and spittle are also subject to saintly devotion: so much so that it is clear that the shudder of disgust, sublimated and overcome, can generate the opposite response. The milk flowing from the nipples turns against the fawns that the bacchantes were breast-feeding; in a painting by Ludovico Gimignani we observe Catherine of Siena kneeling at Jesus' side, offering him her breast to suckle, which will provide either milk or blood, it's one and the same.[14] Vapor, breath, voice, cry, chant . . . the buccal cavity is one of the richest in jouissance; and fairy tales describing princesses who had toads, serpents, or indeed pearls drop from their mouths were inventing nothing. It is through the mouth that breath escapes; it is from there that sighs are exhaled, including the final one – that is where one expires. Tears stream from the slits in the eyelids, an essential rippling; at the end of the adventure comes supreme fulfillment.

The ways in are less fortunate; but they open wide to the doors of ecstasy. It is while breathing in that one's breath can be held, causing the blood rush, encumbering one's vision by filling it with flaming points and luminous circles. Taking in breath forces a rhythm, breaking the breathing cycle into two halves: suddenly, time gets stuck. From this door so suddenly shut, from which breath cannot escape, gushes the beginning of ecstasy. But if it is not air filling the body's pipeline, it is wine. Wine is like suffocation: it swells up one's insides, puts pressure on the joints, weakens the rivets. William James put it admirably:

> Sobriety diminishes, discriminates, and says *no*, drunkenness expands, writes, and says *yes*. It is in fact – the great exciter of the *Yes* function in man. It brings its votary from the chill periphery of things to the radiant core. It makes him for the moment one with truth. Not through mere perversity do men run after it. To the poor and the unlettered it stands in the place of symphony concerts and of literature.[15]

The 'time of wine'[16] is also that of all ecstasy: by saying 'yes,' it annuls the bipolarity between yes and no, refuses all contradiction, positions itself on a single side of reality: in a single bound. Whether Christ is represented as a mother proffering a bloody nipple to suckle, or if he is represented as the 'Jesus of the Taverns' who lets the wine of the Wedding at Cana flow into the poor, dilapidated cavity of the human body, he is always the one pouring; the body's bottle does not matter, nor does the nature of the liquid, as long as there is intoxication and as, breathing in God, one becomes one with Him by absorbing Him whole. The mouth becomes enormous, and swallows Him up. Intoxication is like the unconscious as defined by Freud: it ignores contradiction.

What could be more logical? Syncope occurs at the moment when the alternating movement of entering and exiting becomes jammed. The Tantric practitioner, who simultaneously suspends the in-and-out motion of the sex act and of breathing, seeks to grasp the precise moment when 'it' can stop. 'It,' the pulse of life, nourishment swallowed and excreted, breath inhaled and exhaled, life given and taken away, or the ebb and flow of the precious tides that sweep in but eventually cease to surge toward the horizon. Syncope defends its territory by forbidding the ebb-and-flow: 'Stay, O moment, thou art fair,' it says to the instant as it goes by.[17] *Remain*. From then on, the words 'life' and 'death' indeed lose their meaning, and we can cry out, like Saint Theresa: 'I'm dying of not dying.'

Notes

1   I thank Jean-Jacques Brochler for teaching me this slang expression: the French, *s'envoyer à dame*, literally means 'to send oneself to a lady'; the English is not so exclusively male.

2   See *Le Mahabharata*, selections translated into French from the Sanskrit by Jean-Michel Péterfalvi (Paris: Flammarion, 1987), vol. 1, pp. 91–92 ff. 'At

a time so pleasant for all creatures,' complains the antelope, which is the sage Kimdana in disguise, 'at such a perfect time, what wise man would kill an animal that was coupling in the forest?' In the shortened version, which is so well written by Jean-Claude Carrière, the antelopes have become gazelles, and it is quite possible that the complaining antelope is a woman. But here we feel the influence on Carrière of the myth of Tiresias, who is the only man, according to Greek mythology, to know that women experience more pleasure than men (*Le Mahabharata*, trans. Jean-Claude Carrière [Paris: Belfond, 1989]).

3   Lacan, *Encore 1972–73* (Paris: Seuil, 1975).

4   See the close of chapter 16 [of original book – eds].

5   Beginning in 1887, when he was a student at the École Normale Supérieure, Romain Rolland worked on what he called his *credo*: 'I feel, therefore it is.' See especially pp. 107–8 in *Le Cloître de la rue d'Ulm* (The cloister in the rue d'Ulm) (Paris: Cahiers Romain Rolland, Albin Michel, 1952). Ibid., p. 352, *Credo quia verum*. Romain Rolland was twenty-two years old.

6   About Beethoven's music, the same stress as in Bataille, regarding the Leonora Overture. 'A feeling of divine intoxication invaded me which I could neither have described nor can describe in a straightforward way, which I have attempted to follow by evoking the suspended nature – and which brings me to tears – of the depth of being . . .' (Georges Bataille, *Inner Experience*, tr. L. Boldt (Albany, NY: SUNY Press, 1988), p. 69.

7   In Romain Rolland, *Life of Ramakrishna*, trans. E. F. Malcolm-Smith (Calcutta: Advaita Ashrama, 1965), p. 33.

8   Lacan, *Encore*, p. 70.

9   Marcel Brion, *L'Allemagne romantique: Le voyage initiatique* (Paris: Albin Michel, 1976), pp. 12–13. Also see Georges Bataille, in *Inner Experience*, concerning a phrase from Nietzsche, 'Be this ocean: there will be one' (Fragment 80–81). Bataille writes: 'The so simple commandment: "Be that ocean," linked to the *extreme limit*, at the same time makes of a man a multitude, a desert. It is an expression which resumes and makes precise the sense of a community' (p. 27). Bataille understands the link between ecstasy, the ecstatic's loss of identity, and the founding of a utopian community – even if it is in the desert.

10 [Trans.: the French *bouc émissaire* means 'scapegoat'; the words are separated here as 'goat' and 'emissary,' but the connotation still resonates in French.]

11 Pierre Janet, *De l'angoisse à l'extase*: Travaux du Laboratoire de Psychologie de la Salpêtrière (Paris: Librairie Félix Alcan, 1926), vol. 1, pp. 109–10.

12 Ibid., p. 110.

13 I am thinking of Joris-Karl Huysmans's unbelievable hysteria, when he attacked Jews and Freemasons in *Sainte Lydwine de Schiedam* (recently republished by Maren Sell, with an excellent preface by Alain Vircondelet). Huysmans went so far as to regret that it was no longer possible, in order to fan Christianity's dying embers and to eradicate the Jews, to use 'a few well-sulfured shirts and some nicely dried logs'; the interruption of these practices proves, he wrote, 'the loose morals of our time.' In a more subdued vein, there is the lovely book by Jean-Noël Vuarnet, *Extases féminines* (Female ecstasies) (Paris: Arthaud, 1980); a loving admirer, without furor.

14 See the reproduction of this painting in Vuarnet's *Extases féminines*.

15 William James, *The Varieties of Religious Experience* (Cambridge, Mass.: Harvard University Press, 1985), p. 307.

16 As Gérard Depardieu's enchanting expression goes.

17 This is the wager in the game between Faust and Mephistopheles: in order to win the soul of the scientist, the devil must give him the desire to pronounce these words. Faust will only say them at the end of the second *Faust*, looking over the polders in Holland, for which he was the engineer and overseer.

PART FOUR

Hélène Cixous

SINCE THE PUBLICATION OF her first book in 1967, Hélène Cixous has consistently ignored the boundaries that typically define the disciplines of literature, literary criticism, psychoanalysis, philosophy and feminist theory, and has created a body of work that defies classification in any one field or genre. While most of the texts she has published are novels, plays or critical studies of other authors, she is perhaps best known, at least within the Anglo-American academy, for her theoretical feminist writings, especially *The Newly Born Woman* (1986b [1975]), written with Catherine Clément, and 'The Laugh of the Medusa' (1976 [1975]). Even these texts, however, eschew formal academic language in favour of a richly allusive, literary style that is enhanced by many autobiographical references. Indeed, one quality that Cixous maintains through-out her publications is the desire to give voice to otherness, as her writing subverts generic and disciplinary categories in order to allow the Other to speak through the words of her texts. In this way her own texts embody her most well-known concept – *écriture féminine* – a mode of writing undertaken from a feminine subject position that is capable of overturning what she sees as a masculine fear of otherness, and that further enables new forms of relationship between the subject and the Other.

Cixous's abiding interest in and passion for the Other stems largely from her experience of growing up in French-colonial Algeria. Her status within that environment was that of a minority, in part because her mother was Austro-German and Cixous grew up speaking German in her family's home, and in part because of her Sephardic Jewish family background. As is clear from much of Cixous's writing, this minority status contributed to her sense of being an outsider, a sense that is reinforced by her femaleness; indeed, the 'Jewoman' appears often in her texts, and always as a figure of alienation from the dominant group or discourse. Cixous's experience of alienation persisted even after she moved to France in 1956, at the beginning of the Algerian War, and began the study of English and American literature at the Faculté des Lettres of the University of Bordeaux; it has continued throughout her prolific publishing career to shape her perspective.

In 1967, as she was nearing completion of her doctoral dissertation at the Sorbonne (which would appear in 1968 as *L'Exil de James Joyce ou l'art du remplacement*, translated in 1972 as *The Exile of James Joyce*), Cixous published her first work of fiction, a collection of short stories titled *Le Prénom de Dieu*. Cixous's continuing interest in the process of naming is already apparent in the title of this collection (which translates as *The First Name of God*), as is her fascination with divinity. These stories emphasise the process of coming to autonomy, of discovering a full and independent selfhood. Dream narratives abound, and several of the stories are rich in religious imagery. For example, the title of '*Le Veau de plâtre*' ('The Plaster Calf') invokes the golden calf of biblical idolatry, while '*La Baleine de Jonas*' ('Jonas's Whale') clearly refers to the story of Jonah, but also to the legend of Saint George and the dragon. Introducing a theme that will reappear throughout Cixous's writings, this latter story explores the relation of women to the absolute, raising questions about spirituality and sexual difference that are central to Cixous's project.

In 1968, Cixous was put in charge of establishing the experimental Université de Paris VIII à Vincennes, which was envisioned as an alternative educational institution that would be inspired by the anti-hierarchical politics of the May 1968 riots. This university, which has had to fight for its continued existence in the face of governmental indifference and budget-cutting, has nevertheless made a name for itself because of its outstanding faculty. Cixous has remained at Paris VIII since its founding, as professor of English literature; beginning with the publication in 1968 of her dissertation on Joyce, she has pursued a career in academic publishing that, at least in the anglophone world, has drawn more attention than her literary writings.

However, it was the publication in 1969 of Cixous's first 'novel' that propelled her into the public eye, at least in France. Awarded the prestigious Prix Médicis, *Dedans* (translated in 1986 as *Inside*) can only loosely be classified as a novel, because it ignores conventions of narrative to such an extent that it seems to lack plot, characters and chronology. Rather, it explores, by way of an extended meditation on language and sexual difference, Cixous's experience of the death of her beloved father when she was a child – an experience that Cixous has written about extensively, exploiting the opportunity it presents her to assert the power of writing to overcome death by giving form to love. Within this text, Cixous expresses her notion that there exist two distinct modes of relating to life – the feminine and the masculine – and that the feminine is characterised by its mobility, its openness and receptivity, its creation of difference-in-itself, while the masculine is marked by its stasis, its opposition to otherness. For Cixous, as for psychoanalyst Jacques Lacan, the death of the father marks the initiation of the subject into language – but, in *Dedans*, the subject is feminine, and the language into which she is initiated by her father's death embodies a feminine relation to life, in that it opens her up to difference rather than foreclosing its possibility. It is the language, in other words, of *écriture féminine*. Furthermore, since God is invoked in the opening lines of this 'story' – 'It is said that love is as strong as death. But death is as strong as love and I am inside. And life is stronger than death, and I am inside. But God is stronger than life and death' (1986a: 5) – it is apparent that Cixous is also linking her own father with the Father-God; thus it is implicitly the death of God-the-Father that releases the daughter into the feminine economy of language that Cixous privileges.

During the late 1960s and early 1970s, Cixous produced several experimental works of fiction – the novels *The Third Body* (1999), *Les Commencements* and *Neutre*, along with the poetic novella *Un vrai jardin*[1] – that were influenced by both Lacan and the deconstructionism of Jacques Derrida. She continued her attempts to hone the language of *écriture féminine*, hoping both to subvert the linguistic and political conventions of the day and to give voice to the repressed feminine and its capacity for openness to the Other. Here her emphasis is on the body and on embodied desire; she also explores the importance of birth, and the written text itself continues to emerge as an essential instrument in the writer's search to give birth to herself, to her own body and its others. An additional Cixousian theme that appears in *Neutre* is the view that both women and men enact both feminine and masculine modes of relating to life, and are thus, properly speaking, neither masculine nor feminine but rather neuter; this view underlies Cixous's willingness, especially apparent in her later critical studies, to look for examples of *écriture féminine* in the writings of such male writers as Maurice Blanchot, Heinrich Kleist and Franz Kafka, among others.

In 1974, Cixous published *Prénoms de personne*, an early theoretical text that remains untranslated into English. In this collection of essays on such figures as Freud, Kleist and Joyce, Cixous explicitly takes up the theme of women's oppression, arguing that the frequent literary association of women with death in fact reveals the workings of a limited (masculine) economy, which Cixous sees as founded on the death drive, as well as on the desire to constrain feminine otherness. Drawing on the writings of philosopher Georges Bataille, Cixous proposes a (feminine) economy of the gift in which endless expenditure of the self is privileged over the (masculine) morbid fear of the Other that closes off the self in a solitary prison of its own making.

The concern for the oppression of women that motivates *Prénoms de personne* continues to be evident in Cixous's activities and writings of the mid-1970s. In the same year that *Prénoms* was published, Cixous founded the Centre de Recherches en Études Féminines at the Université de Paris VIII à Vincennes; a year later, she published her highly influential essay 'Le Rire de la Méduse', which was translated in 1976, in the journal Signs, as 'The Laugh of the Medusa'. In this essay, Cixous takes up Freud's theory of castration, in order to argue against the psychoanalytic emphasis on the phallus as the privileged signifier of the social symbolic system. In contrast to the erect phallus, paradigmatic of the drive for identity and for unified meaning, Cixous asserts the joyous capacity of laughter to shatter meaning and to open meaning up to (feminine) multiplicity.

Cixous explores these themes at greater length in 'Sorties', her primary contribution to the seminal La Jeune née (co-authored with Catherine Clément; published in English, in 1986b, as The Newly Born Woman). This essay, which clearly articulates Cixous's understanding of the importance of writing and its relationship to the feminine, asserts the power of writing to open up a passage between the self and others, and especially between the self and the others within the self. According to Cixous, it is in its affinity for establishing relations within the irreducibly multiple self that writing is the proper domain of woman, whose selfhood is always already multiple and relational. Cixous also returns in this essay to her notion of the two economies of exchange – the masculine, based on a quid pro quo designed to enhance the status of the subject, and the feminine, characterised by its infinite capacity for giving without thought of return.

It is in Cixous's later writings (primarily those published from the late 1970s through the 1990s), and in the selections from her seminars that have been published only in English, that religious themes emerge most clearly. Indeed, one of the clearest expressions of Cixous's interest in divinity appears in her essay 'Coming to Writing', originally published in 1977 as 'La Venue à l'écriture'. In this essay, which is long and straightforwardly autobiographical, Cixous returns to the figure of the 'Jewoman' to explore the complexities of her relationship to writing. She notes that although for her the desire to write has always carried the same force as God's call to the prophets, as 'Jewoman' she is not authorised to write. Nevertheless, she finds in her childhood intimacy with God, whom she identifies here with both her father and her mother, a source of the strength she needs to overcome the prohibitions that seek to silence her. God becomes her link to writing, by way of the language of the unconscious, and writing in turn – as that which overcomes time and death – emerges as a figuration for divinity itself.

A decade later, in an essay that was first published in English as 'Extreme Fidelity' in a collection of seminar presentations titled Writing Differences (1988),[2] Cixous offers a feminist reading of the Genesis story of Eve and the apple, observing that the significance of the story lies in its expression of the tension between desire and prohibition. Although Eve 'knows' that to eat the apple will result in death, this threat can have no meaning in a paradise that pre-exists death. It is thus inevitable that Eve will eat the forbidden fruit; however, for Cixous, hearkening back to themes developed in her earlier writings, this is the triumph of the feminine economy – that Eve will allow herself the pleasure that accompanies taking the fruit into herself (that is, establishing a relationship with the otherness of the apple), precisely *because* it means her death, the loss of herself.

In 'The School of Dreams', a lecture given in 1990 and originally published in English in *Three Steps on the Ladder of Writing* (1993), Cixous takes up another biblical narrative – the story of Jacob's ladder – in order to develop parallels between the process of writing and the ladder that Jacob traversed in his dream encounter with the angels. Her reading/(re)writing of the Genesis story allows for an intertextuality that lets Cixous herself participate in the creation of sacred text, thus collapsing the opposition between sacred and mundane.

In 'Grace and Innocence: Heinrich Kleist' (originally published in English as a chapter in *Readings: The Poetics of Blanchot, Joyce, Kafka, Kleist, Lispector, and Tsvetayeva* (1991d)), Cixous returns to the Garden of Eden, and explores the notion that there are two kinds of innocence: the false innocence of Eve in Eden, before she has taken the risk of knowledge and guilt, and the innocence that interests Cixous, the second innocence that can only be attained after paradise has been lost. Also in this chapter, Cixous argues that grace must be given not by God but by humanity itself, and that grace is defined in the moment of its being given and received, rather than in the possession of it, which Cixous sees as impossible. As with all of Cixous's work, this meditation on grace and innocence is motivated by the desire to enter into and to enact in writing a relationship with otherness. In other words, the problem with the innocence that precedes knowledge, for Cixous, is that it remains closed off to the possibility of contact with the Other. Similarly, the attempt to possess grace is misguided because it represents the desire to appropriate the otherness of the Other for oneself, thus precluding real relationship.

Perhaps the most striking statement of Cixous's fascination with the theological, however, appeared in 1986 in an essay titled 'Le Dernier Tableau ou le portrait de Dieu', translated as 'The Last Painting or the Portrait of God', in *'Coming to Writing' and Other Essays* (1991b). Here Cixous writes poetically of her hope for the impossible, of her desire to write the impossible into existence. 'When I am done', she sings, 'all I will have done will have been to attempt a portrait of God. Of the God. Of what escapes us and makes us wonder. Of what we do not know but feel. Of what makes us live. I mean our own divinity, awkward, twisted, throbbing, our own mystery – we who are lords of this earth and do not know it . . .' (1991b: 129). Writing thus emerges in this text as the practice by which we create or establish contact with 'our own divinity'. That this can only happen, for Cixous, when we learn how to write the body, when the feminine is no longer the repressed of Western culture but finds its way to expression – these conditions are contained, for her, in the notion that through writing one can 'attempt a portrait of God'.

Notes

1   See Cixous, Hélène (1970) *Les Commencements*, Paris: Grasset; (1971) *Un vrai jardin*, Paris: L'Herne; and (1972) *Neutre*, Paris: B. Grasset.
2   A revised version of this essay was published as 'The Author in Truth', in *'Coming to Writing' and Other Essays* (1991b); excerpts from this later version are included in this reader.

Chapter 18

Sorties

■ [Abridged] This extract appears in French as 'Sorties' in *La Jeune née* (Union Générale d'Éditions, 1975). The English translation was published in *The Newly Born Woman*, translated by Betsy Wing (University of Minnesota Press, 1986).

Editors' introduction

RELIGIOUS THEMES ARE NOT a particular focus of this selection. However, Cixous does introduce several motifs that take on a more explicitly religious or spiritual significance in her later writings. These motifs include: writing as a feminine practice of self-discovery and self-overcoming, the two economies of the gift, and the place of woman under the Law of the Father.

This essay gives a clear articulation of Cixous's understanding of the importance of writing and its relationship to the feminine. As she asserts here, writing necessitates the admission that an 'other' exists, even within the self, and that the 'self' is actually plural and fluid. In her view, writing effects a passage, or many passages, among the unknown and always-changing others who, together, are misconstrued in the post-Enlightenment philosophical tradition as a single unified (and implicitly masculine) self. Cixous notes that this encounter with the others within oneself is unsettling, even threatening, to a fixed selfhood. For this reason, she argues, writing is the natural domain of woman, whose selfhood is defined under patriarchy in terms of its ability to give endlessly, to empty itself out for the sake of others.

In this context, Cixous also touches on her notion that there are two economies of giving, the masculine and the feminine. In her view, it is impossible to give without expectation of return; however, the kind of return one expects when one gives is significant. Within the masculine economy, a gift is always a transaction meant to guarantee an increase in the masculinity of the giver – more power, more authority, more money, more status. That is, the gift is seen as an investment. Within the feminine economy of the gift, on the other hand, the gift circulates endlessly, never returning to the giver in the form of a recovery of expenses. While the giver does gain something from giving, the gain is found in the pleasure of the giving itself, rather than in any enhancement of status or power. It is for this reason, then, that Cixous associates writing with the feminine economy of the gift; writing, like giving in the feminine mode, entails an endless outpouring of oneself, a willingness to give up the comforts of the illusion of being selfsame – a single and unitary self. Note, however, that Cixous also cautions here against the tendency of feminine giving to leave itself open to exploitation by the masculine.

In the last section of this excerpt, which is entitled 'The Dawn of Phallocentrism', Cixous explores the relationship of woman to the Law of the Father. Responding to passages from Freud, Joyce and Kafka, she begins by considering the notion that fatherhood represents an abstraction that has no verifiable basis in sensory perception. She goes on to explore the resonance between the place of woman within patriarchy and the place of the Jews in relation to their father-God, suggesting that in both cases the Law of the Father – rendered here as 'L– –' in order to make clear its symmetry with the 'G– –' of the Hebrews – is a fiction passing itself off as truth. However, as is the case with the phallus, with which it is also associated (especially in Lacanian theory) the illusory nature of God/the Law does not rob it of the power to oppress. Thus, for Cixous, to be a 'Jewoman' is to be doubly excluded from the metaphysical dream of presence, and this is a theme to which she returns again in later writings.

[. . .] I will say: today, writing is woman's. That is not a provocation, it means that woman admits there is an other. In her becoming-woman, she has not erased the bisexuality latent in the girl as in the boy. Femininity and bisexuality go together, in a combination that varies according to the individual, spreading the intensity of its force differently and (depending on the moments of their history) privileging one component or another. It is much harder for man to let the other come through him. Writing is the passageway, the entrance, the exit, the dwelling place of the other in me – the other that I am and am not, that I don't know how to be, but that I feel passing, that makes me live – that tears me apart, disturbs me, changes me, who? – a feminine one, a masculine one, some? – several, some unknown, which is indeed what gives me the desire to know and from which all life soars. This peopling gives neither rest nor security, always disturbs the relationship to 'reality,' produces an uncertainty that gets in the way of the subject's socialization. It is distressing, it wears you out; and for men this permeability, this nonexclusion is a threat, something intolerable.

In the past, when carried to a rather spectacular degree, it was called 'posses-sion.' Being possessed is not desirable for a masculine Imaginary, which would interpret it as passivity – a dangerous feminine position. It is true that a certain receptivity is 'feminine.' One can, of course, as History has always done, exploit feminine reception through alienation. A woman, by her opening up, is open to being 'possessed,' which is to say, dispossessed of herself.

But I am speaking here of femininity as keeping alive the other that is confided to her, that visits her, that she can love as other. The loving to be other, another, without its necessarily going the rout of abasing what is same, herself. >

As for passivity, in excess, it is partly bound up with death. But there is a nonclosure that is not submission but confidence and comprehension; that is not an opportunity for destruction but for wonderful expansion.

Through the same opening that is her danger, she comes out of herself to go to the other, a traveler in unexplored places; she does not refuse, she approaches, not to do away with the space between, but to see it, to experience what she is not, what she is, what she can be.

Writing is working; being worked; questioning (in) the between (letting oneself be questioned) of the same *and of* other without which nothing lives; undoing death's work by willing the togetherness of one-another, infinitely charged with a ceaseless exchange of one with another – not knowing one another and beginning again only from what is most distant, from self, from other, from the other within. A course that multiplies transformations by the thousands.

And that is not done without danger, without pain, without loss – of moments of self, of consciousness, of persons one has been, goes beyond, leaves. It doesn't happen without expense – of sense, time, direction.

But is that specifically feminine? It is men who have inscribed, described, theorized the paradoxical logic of an economy without reserve. This is not contradictory; it brings us back to asking about their femininity. Rare are the men able to venture onto the brink where writing, freed from law, unencumbered by moderation, exceeds phallic authority, and where the subjectivity inscribing its effects become feminine.

Where does difference come through in writing? If there is difference it is in the manner of spending, of valorizing the appropriated, of thinking what is not-the-same. In general, it is in the manner of thinking any 'return,' the relationship of capitalization, if this word 'return' (*rapport*) is understood in its sense of 'revenue.'

Today, still, the masculine return to the Selfsame is narrower and more restricted than femininity's. It all happens as if man were more directly threatened in his being by the nonselfsame than woman. Ordinarily, this is exactly the cultural product described by psychoanalysis: someone who still has something to lose. And in the development of desire, of exchange, he is the en-grossing party: loss and expense are stuck in the commercial deal that always turns the gift into a gift-that-takes. The gift brings in a return. Loss, at the end of a curved line, is turned into its opposite and comes back to him as profit.

But does woman escape this law of return? Can one speak of another spending? Really, there is no 'free' gift. You never give something for nothing. But all the difference lies in the why and how of the gift, in the values that the gesture of giving affirms, causes to circulate; in the type of profit the giver draws from the gift and the use to which he or she puts it. Why, how, is there this difference?

When one gives, what does one give oneself?

What does he want in return – the traditional man? And she? At first what *he* wants, whether on the level of cultural or personal exchanges, whether it is a question of capital or of affectivity (or of love, of *jouissance*) – is that he gain more masculinity: plus-value of virility, authority, power, money, or pleasure, all of which reenforce his phallocentric narcissism at the same time. Moreover, that is what society is made for – how it is made; and men can hardly get out of it. An unenviable fate they've made for themselves. A man is always proving something; he has to 'show off,' show up the others. Masculine profit is almost always mixed up with a success that is socially defined.

How does she give? What are her dealings with saving or squandering, reserve, life, death? She too gives *for*. She too, with open hands, gives herself – pleasure, happiness, increased value, enhanced self-image. But she doesn't try to 'recover her expenses.' She is able not to return to herself, never settling down, pouring out, going everywhere to the other. She does not flee extremes; she is not the being-of-the-end (the goal), but she is how-far-being-reaches.

If there is a self proper to woman, paradoxically it is her capacity to depropriate herself without self-interest: endless body, without 'end,' without principal 'parts'; if she is a whole, it is a whole made up of parts that are wholes, not simple, partial objects but varied entirety, moving and boundless change, a cosmos where eros never stops traveling, vast astral space. She doesn't revolve around a sun that is more star than the stars.

That doesn't mean that she is undifferentiated magma; it means that she doesn't create a monarchy of her body or her desire. Let masculine sexuality gravitate around the penis, engendering this centralized body (political anatomy) under the party dictatorship. Woman does not perform on herself this regionalization that profits the couple head-sex, that only inscribes itself within frontiers. Her libido is cosmic, just as her unconscious is worldwide: her writing also can only go on and on, without ever inscribing or distinguishing contours, daring these dizzying passages in other, fleeting and passionate dwellings within him, within the hims and hers whom she inhabits just long enough to watch them, as close as possible to the unconscious from the moment they arise; to love them, as close as possible to instinctual drives, and then, further, all filled with these brief identifying hugs and kisses, she goes and goes on infinitely. She alone dares and wants to know from within where she, the one excluded, has never ceased to hear what-comes-before-language reverberating. She lets the other tongue of a thousand tongues speak – the tongue, sound without barrier or death. She refuses life nothing. Her tongue doesn't hold back but holds forth, doesn't keep in but keeps on enabling. Where the wonder of being several and turmoil is expressed, she does not protect herself against these unknown feminines; she surprises herself at seeing, being, pleasuring in her gift of changeability. I am spacious singing Flesh: onto which is grafted no one knows which I – which masculine or feminine, more or less human but above all living, because changing I. [. . .]

The dawn of phallocentrism

Freud:

> Under the influence of external conditions – which we need not follow up here and which in part are also not sufficiently known – it happened that the matriarchal structure of society was replaced by a patriarchal one. This naturally brought with it a revolution in the existing state of the law. An echo of this revolution can still be heard, I think, in the *Oresteia* of Aeschylus. This turning from the mother to the father, however, signifies above all a victory of spirituality over the senses – that is to say, a step forward in culture, since maternity is proved by the senses whereas paternity is a surmise based on a deduction and a premiss. This declaration in favour of the thought-process, thereby raising it above sense perception, has proved to be a step with serious consequences.
>
> (*Moses and Monotheism*, p. 145–146) [Freud, Sigmund, trans. Katherine Jones, New York: Vintage Books.]

Joyce:

> Fatherhood, in the sense of conscious begetting, is unknown to man. It is a mystical estate, an apostolic succession, from only begetter to only begotten. On that mystery and not on the madonna which the cunning Italian intellect flung to the mob of Europe the church is founded and refounded irremovably because founded, like the world, macro- and microcosm, upon the void. Upon uncertitude, upon

unlikelihood. *Amor matris*, subjective and objective genitive, may be
the only true thing in life.

>   (*Ulysses*, p. 204–205) [Joyce, James,
>   New York: Random House, 1946.]

What is a father? 'Fatherhood is a legal fiction,' said Joyce. Paternity, which
is a fiction, is fiction passing itself off as truth. Paternity is the lack of being which
is called God. Men's cleverness was in passing themselves off as fathers and
'repatriating' women's fruits as their own. A naming trick. Magic of absence.
God is men's secret.

> Among the precepts of Mosaic religion is one that has more signific-
> ance than is at first obvious. It is the prohibition against making an
> image of God, which means the compulsion to worship an invisible
> God. I surmise that in this point Moses surpassed the Aton religion
> in strictness. Perhaps he meant to be consistent; his God was to have
> neither a name nor a countenance. The prohibition was, perhaps,
> a fresh precaution against magic malpractices. If this prohibition was
> accepted, however, it was bound to exercise a profound influence.
> For it signified subordinating sense perception to an abstract idea;
> it was a triumph of spirituality over the senses; more precisely, an
> instinctual renunciation accompanied by its psychologically necessary
> consequences.
>
>   (*Moses and Monotheism*, p. 144)

Jewoman:

And in the same story, as Kafka told it,[1] the man from the country, the one-
who-doesn't-know-but-believes, comes before the law. A doorkeeper stands
before the law. And the gullible man asks to go into the law. But even though
the door opens, one doesn't go in. Maybe later. Nothing keeps the poor fellow
from entering. Except everything: the doorkeeper, the way he looks, his black
beard, the door, the fact of its being open; the fact that nothing keeps him from
entering the law, except what the law is; except that it is what it is. And waiting.

> In the first years he curses his evil fate aloud; later, as he grows
> old, he only mutters to himself. He grows childish, and since in his
> prolonged watch he has learned to know even the fleas in the
> doorkeeper's fur collar, he begs the very fleas to help him and to
> persuade the doorkeeper to change his mind. Finally his eyes grow
> dim and he does not know whether the world is really darkening
> around him or whether his eyes are only deceiving him. But in the
> darkness he can now perceive a radiance that streams immortally
> from the door of the Law. Now his life is drawing to a close. Before

he dies, all that he has experienced during the whole time . . . condenses into one question, which he has never yet put to the doorkeeper. He beckons the doorkeeper, since he can no longer raise his stiffening body. The doorkeeper has to bend far down to hear him, for the difference in size between them has increased very much to the man's disadvantage. 'What do you want to know now?' asks the doorkeeper, 'you are insatiable.' 'Everyone strives to attain the Law,' answers the man, 'how does it come about, then, that in all these years no one has come seeking admittance but me?' The doorkeeper perceives . . . that his hearing is failing, so he bellows in his ear: 'No one but you could gain admittance through this door, since this door was intended only for you. Now I am going to shut it.'

(pp. 63–65)

And no one is there now to learn what the man devoted his whole life just to begin to think, no one to reap the discovery that could come about only at the price of a whole life, at the moment of death. There is never anyone there when what has never been not-open or open closes, the door, the threshold of the law. What law? The law where? who? whose?

But the Real has very clearly crystallized in the relationship of forces between the petitioner 'outside-the-law' and the doorkeeper, the first in a series of representatives of the L– –, the cop, the first level of a power with a thousand laws. 'Outside' law? What is inside law? Is there an 'inside' to law? A place? A country maybe? A city, a kingdom? As long as he lived, that is what he believed.

Was he ever outside in relation to the desired inside that is reserved for every man – that place, that L– –, which he believed was his good, his right, his 'accessible' object. *Into* which he would enter and which he was going to enjoy.

So it is the L– – that will have served as 'life' for him, will have assigned him his place before the L– –, permanently. Immobilized, shriveled. And no one will have been there to learn from the dying man, from the dead man, what he began to think maybe at the last second: that the law isn't within, it has no place, it has no place other than the gullible man's body that comes to rot in front of the door, which has always been in the L– –, and the L– – has only existed to the extent that it appears before what he doesn't see it is behind, around, before, *inside him* that it is nothing without him, that its apparently absolute power is inexhaustible, because like Moses's God, it doesn't exist; it is invisible; it doesn't have a place to take place; it doesn't have anything. It 'is' hence it is only if he makes it; it is nothing more than the tremendous power of the invisible.

Exploited by thousands of its representatives – supposed-to-represent-it, who draw their dissuasive, repressive power, their calm and absolute violence from this nothing that is out of sight.

You will not pass. You will not see me. A woman is before the door of the law. And the bearded watchman – his beard so pointed, so threatening – warns her not to go through. Not to go, not to enjoy. And by looking toward, and looking in, and feeling herself looked at without knowing where the L– –'s look is coming from, she gets it to come, she believes she sees a glimmer radiating, which is the little flame that the constant flow of her gaze keeps burning in emptiness, in nothing. But from always being looked at without seeing, she pales, she shrinks, she grows old, she is diminished, sees no more, lives no more. That is called 'internalizing.' She is full of nothing that she imagines and that she pines for. Sublimation? Yes, but negative, turning the power – whose source she is without knowing it – back against herself. Her powerlessness, her paralysis, her feebleness? They are the measure of her power, her desire, her resistance, her blind confidence in their L– –. Suppose she 'entered?' Why not have taken this step? Not even the first step? Does she fear the other doors? Or does she have forbodings? Or is it the choice between two mockeries of life inscribing themselves in the nothingness that she embodies and that rivets her in the visible, on the lowest level, in relation to her nearest interlocutor: fleas in the doorkeeper's coat, a flea herself.

⟨Or maybe there is an L– – and it is the petrifying result of not-knowing reinforced by power that produces it.⟩

And they told her there was a place she had better not go. And this place is guarded by men. And a law emanates from this place with *her* body for its locus. They told her that inside her law was black, growing darker and darker. And a doorkeeper preached prudence to her, because beyond it was even worse.

And she doesn't enter her body; she is not going to confirm the worst, it is not even properly hers. She puts it in the hands of the doorkeeper.

So, the resounding blow of this same trick echoes between Jew and woman. In the tabernacle it is metamorphosed as a box full of nothing that no one would miss. The trick of the 'omnipotent.' The voice saying 'I-am-who-I-say-I-am.' My name is 'the-one-who-is-where-you-aren't.' What is a father? The one taken for father. The one recognized as the true one. 'Truth,' the essence of fatherhood, its force as law. The 'chosen' father. [. . .]

Note

1   *Vor Dem Gesetz* [*Before the Law*], in Kafka's *Parables and Paradoxes* (Schocken, 1975), is also the key to the end of *The Trial*, in which the riddle is revealed in an 'interminable' explication. The necessity for K.'s death is inscribed within it.

Chapter 19

The Author in Truth

■ [Abridged] This extract originally appeared in French as part of 'L'Auteur en vérité', in *L'Heure de Clarice Lispector* (Des Femmes, 1989), and in English in *'Coming to Writing' and Other Essays*, edited by Deborah Jenson, translated by Sarah Cornell *et al.* (Harvard University Press, 1991). An earlier version of this text was translated into English by Ann Liddle and Susan Sellers, and appears as 'Extreme Fidelity' in *Writing Differences: Readings from the Seminar of Hélène Cixous*, edited by Susan Sellers (Open University Press, 1988).

Editors' introduction

IN THE ORIGINAL FRENCH text of this excerpt, Cixous plays at length with the homophony between *scène* (scene) and *cène* (meal): the primitive scene is also the primitive meal, and 'the scene of the *cène*' is what concerns Cixous here. In other words, this discussion of the Genesis myth of Eve and the apple is haunted throughout by the 'primitive scene' of psychoanalytic theory – the moment when the child witnesses her parents in the sex act. This is so because, for Cixous, the significance of the biblical story lies in its expression of the tension between desire and prohibition, pleasure and law. The apple, paradigmatic object of desire, is also the paradigmatic 'thou shalt not', and it is no accident that it is for Eve, the first woman, that the primal struggle between the forces of desire and of the law unfolds.

In the first section of this excerpt, Cixous alludes to one of her most frequent themes, the existence of masculine and feminine economies, or modes of interpersonal exchange – of energy, goods and so on. According to Cixous, the masculine economy is characterised by a single-minded concern with increasing the phallic power of the masculine subject, while the feminine economy is marked by the pleasure to be found in an unrestricted opening up of oneself to another, without fear of the loss of self entailed therein. Cixous's implication, here, is that the biblical story of original (and originary) temptation makes sense only within a feminine economy. That is, only Eve, as primordial feminine, could open herself to the otherness of the apple, and to the pleasure of eating its juicy flesh, without concern for what she would lose as a result.

In the second section, Cixous elaborates on the tensions manifest in the story. She notes that although the apple is forbidden on pain of death, this prohibition can have no meaning in the edenic world where no death yet exists. Furthermore, the apple is irresistible: it promises unimaginable knowledge and power to she who would taste it, would take it into herself. I-as-desire is present to Eve – she can see the fruit, gleaming before her – while the apple-as-law is absent, existing only in unknowable abstraction. It seems inevitable, then, that Eve will 'succumb', that she will say yes to the possibility of experiencing interiority (of the apple, of herself in the apple). For Cixous, the feminine pleasure that arises from eating the apple, even *because* it means death (that is, loss of self), is characteristic of the feminine economy alluded to in the first section.

The primitive meal[1]

For the sake of convenience, I have often spoken of 'libidinal economies.' In order to try to distinguish the vital functions, I say that they exist; but they are not decisively distinguished in reality. In real life traits are effaced, blended together. I have fun trying to suspend these economies at their most visible and most readable moment: at the moment of what I have called *libidinal education*. The material, the origin, of the literature of apprenticeship, the *Bildungsroman* brings together so many texts that relate the development of the individual, her history, the story of her soul, the story of her discovery of the world, of its pleasures and its prohibitions, its pleasures and its laws, always on the trail of the first story of all human stories, the story of *Eve and the Apple*. World literature abounds in texts of libidinal education because every writer, every artist, is brought at one moment or another to work on the genesis of his or her own artistic being, this strangeness of destiny. The *Bildungsroman* is the supreme text, written as one turns back to revisit the place where one gambles to win or lose life. The stakes are simple. A mere question of the apple: Does one eat it or not? Will one enter into contact or not with the intimate inside of the fruit?

The book begins with a primitive S-cene. Scene of the meal in which desire and prohibition coexist, opposing currents. Will I take pleasure, the hero asks himself, will I go so far as to take this pleasure and give you pleasure? And softly, the text asks itself. Come eat!

The apple, the yes, gleams, is desirable. It reigns with such an innocence that it can't help attracting famished guilt.

Will the delicious Percival of the *Quest for the Holy Grail* enjoy the marvelous meal or not? In these stories, as in childhood, the fate of the *so-called feminine economy* is at stake. I say 'feminine' in connection with Percival, yes, for this economy is not the endowment solely of women. So why 'feminine'? Because of the old story; because in spite of everything, ever since the Bible and ever since bibles, we have been divided up as descendants of Eve and descendants of Adam. The Book wrote this story. The Book wrote that the first person who had to deal with the question of pleasure was a woman, the woman; probably because it really was a 'woman' who, in this always cultural system, underwent this test to which men and women have been subjected ever since. Every entrance to life finds itself *before the Apple*. So I resolve to qualify the relationship to pleasure, the relationship to spending, as 'feminine' and 'masculine' because we are born into language, and because I cannot do otherwise than to find myself preceded by words. They are there. We could change them, we could replace them with synonyms, which would become as closed, as immobile and petrifying, as the words 'masculine' and 'feminine,' and they would lay down the law for us. And so? There is nothing to be done, except to shake them all the time, like apple trees.

'An economy said to be F.,' 'an economy said to be M.' — why distinguish between them? Why keep words that are so entirely treacherous, dreadful, warmongering? This is where all the traps are set. I give myself poetic license; otherwise I would not dare speak. It is the poet's right to say something unusual and then to say: believe it if you want to, but believe weeping; or, as Genet does, to erase it by saying that all truths are false, that only false truths are true, and so on.

The scene of the *cène*

The first fable of our first book puts our relationship to the law at stake. Enter two great puppets: the word of the Law (or the discourse of God) and the Apple. It's a struggle between the Apple and the discourse of God. In this brief scene, everything transpires before a woman. The Story begins with the Apple: at the beginning of everything, there is an apple, and this apple, when spoken of, is spoken of as a fruit-not-to. There is an apple, and straightaway there is the law. This is the first step of libidinal education: one begins by sharing in the experience of the *secret*, because the law is incomprehensible. It emits its radiations from the point of its imperceptibility. God says, 'If you taste the fruit of the tree of knowledge, you will die.' This is what is absolutely incomprehensible to me. For Eve, 'you will die' means nothing, since she is in the paradisiacal state where there is no death. She receives the most hermetic message there is, the absolute discourse. The discourse we will find again in the story of Abraham receiving an order from God, which might also seem incomprehensible (the order to sacrifice his son, the one he loves), and which Abraham obeys absolutely, without question. This is the experience of the secret, the enigma of the apple, of this apple invested with every kind of power. We are told that

knowledge could begin with the mouth, the discovery of the taste of something. Knowledge and taste go together. Yet the mystery of the stroke of the
law is also staged here, absolute, verbal, invisible, negative. A symbolic *coup de
force*. Its power lies in its invisibility, its nonexistence, its force of denial, its
'not.' And facing the law, there is the apple which is, is, is. The struggle between
presence and absence, between an undesirable, unverifiable, indecisive absence,
and a presence which is not only a presence: the apple is visible, is promise, is
appeal – 'Bring me to your lips'; it is full, it has an *inside*. What Eve will discover
in her relationship to concrete reality is the inside of the apple, and this inside
is good. The Fable tells us how the genesis of 'femininity' goes by way of the
mouth, through a certain oral pleasure, and through the nonfear of the inside.

So, in my particular fashion I read: astonishingly, our oldest book of dreams
relates to us, in its cryptic mode, that Eve is not afraid of the inside, neither of
her own nor of the other's. The relationship to the interior, to penetration, to
the touching of the inside, is positive. Obviously Eve is punished for it, but that
is a different matter, the matter of the jealousy of God and society.

God knows what the apple must conceal, in order for death to follow the act
of tasting it!

Unless it could be that the interdiction is symmetrical with the order given to
Abraham, a do-not-do-that, apparently as senseless as the you-will-kill.

Unless it could be that the apple is an insignificant screen for the war between
God and me.

Finally, I take the apple and bite in. Because 'it's stronger than me.'

A given pleasure merits a given death. This is what women think: that desire
carries all. Not the hunger of Esau, but the desire to know with the lips the
strange fruit and the common fruit. At the risk of losing one's life. Being ready
to pay such a price is, he says, exactly what is reprehensible. It is, she says, the
proof of the apple, its vital truth. Feeling pleasure means losing oneself? Losing
oneself is such a joy . . .

This is where the series of 'you-shall-not-enter' begins. It is not insignificant
that in the beginning there is a scene of pleasure taking this form. It is a game and
it is not a game. [. . .]

Note

1   'Cène Primitive': For an elaboration of this term, see Hélène Cixous,
'Reaching the Point of Wheat, or A Portrait of the Artist as a Maturing
Woman,' *New Literary History* 19 (1987–1988): 2. 'I'd like you also to
consider the primitive scene in the way we would write the word *cène* in
French without an *s*; without an *s*, it means "the meal." "The primitive
scene" is also "the primitive meal."' [eds].

Chapter 20

Coming to Writing

■   [Abridged] This extract originally appeared in French as part of 'La Venue à l'écriture', in *La Venue à l'écriture*, co-authored with Madeleine Gagnon and Annie Leclerc (Union Générale d'Éditions, 1977), and was republished in French in *Entre l'écriture* (Des Femmes, 1986). It appears in English in *'Coming to Writing' and Other Essays*, edited by Deborah Jenson, translated by Sarah Cornell *et al.* (Harvard University Press, 1991).

Editors' introduction

THIS SERIES OF EXCERPTS is taken from a long and strikingly autobiographical essay in which Cixous explores her own desire to write, as well as the obstacles she has faced in her writing. Because writing, for Cixous, is invested with religious significance, the essay as a whole is replete with religious themes and allusions, from the opening sentence – 'In the beginning, I adored' (1991b: 1) – to the meditations on writing as a way to cancel the power of death, to the vision of Cixous's 'breast as the Tabernacle [with] lungs like the scrolls of the Torah' (1991b: 52). Cixous also borrows material from familiar fairy tales, including Little Red Riding Hood and Cinderella, in her attempt to articulate the difficulties with which the compulsion to write has confronted her. This mixing of religious and popular images pushes the reader to rethink the proper domains of the sacred and the mundane, and indeed, such a provocation seems to motivate much of Cixous's work.

With the title of the first section of this excerpt, Cixous implicitly invokes Freud's essay 'A Child is Being Beaten', in which Freud suggests that the infantile beating fantasies of several of his (female) analysands offer an imaginary opportunity for those young women to experience sexual pleasure with their fathers. Her playful but critical allusions to Freud's text appear multiple. The first concerns the power of writing to enable Cixous to (re)unite with her dead father, whom she loves deeply; as she notes in the opening pages of this essay (not included in this excerpt), 'I write and you are not dead' (1991b: 4). But for Cixous, writing entails pain as well as pleasure; it is marked by the pain of giving oneself to the point of absolute loss; her invocation of 'A Child is Being Beaten' suggests that this pain expresses itself violently in her very being. And just as Freud acknowledges that the fantasised father who beats the (girl) child need not be the personal father, but may be any father figure, Cixous too envisages that father figure as the Father God who enforces the Christian values of the French culture within which Cixous lives and writes.

In much of this excerpt Cixous echoes a theme that she has developed extensively elsewhere: that as 'Jewoman' she is denied the right to express herself in writing. For Cixous, the irrepressible desire to write carries with it the same force as the compulsion to speak with which God seizes those he has chosen to be his prophets. Yet, although she *must* write in response to this divine call, as a woman, a foreigner and a Jew, she is forbidden to write.

Still, in spite of this prohibition, Cixous has written, and continues to write. Why? Or rather, how? Perhaps the secret lies in the ambivalent intimacy, even the eroticism, of the relationship with God that she enjoyed as a small child, a relationship which she describes in the final passages of this excerpt. The God of her childhood, object of her desire, is figured here as both masculine and feminine, father and mother. But more importantly, this God emerges as her link to writing, because s/he (God) introduced Cixous to the language of the unconscious, where the contradiction between pleasure and pain holds no sway. Books spoke to Cixous as if from a burning bush; reading was a direct link to God. And, finally: 'Reading, I discovered that writing is endless. Everlasting. Eternal' (1991b: 23). Writing, that is, emerges as more than merely religious. Writing, for Cixous, is God.

A girl is being killed[1]

In the beginning, I desired.
'What is it she wants?'
'To live. Just to live. And to hear myself say the name.'
'Horrors! Cut out her tongue!'
'What's wrong with her?'
'She can't keep herself from flying!'[2]
'In that case, we have special cages.'

Who is the Superuncle who hasn't prevented a girl from flying, the flight of the thief, who has not bound her, not bandaged the feet of his little darling, so that they might be exquisitely petite, who hasn't mummified her into prettiness?

How would I have written?

Wouldn't you first have needed the 'right reasons' to write? The reasons, mysterious to me, that give you the 'right' to write? But I didn't know them. I had only the 'wrong' reason; it wasn't a reason, it was a passion, something shameful – and disturbing; one of those violent characteristics with which I was afflicted. I didn't 'want' to write. How could I have 'wanted' to? I hadn't strayed to the point of losing all measure of things. A mouse is not a prophet. I wouldn't have had the cheek to go claim my book from God on Mount Sinai, even if, as a mouse, I had found the energy to scamper up the mountain. No reasons at all. But there was madness. Writing was in the air around me. Always close, intoxicating, invisible, inaccessible. I undergo writing! It came to me abruptly. One day I was tracked down, besieged, taken. It captured me. I was seized. From where? I knew nothing about it. I've never known anything about it. From some bodily region. I don't know where. 'Writing' seized me, gripped me, around the diaphragm, between the stomach and the chest, a blast dilated my lungs and I stopped breathing.

Suddenly I was filled with a turbulence that knocked the wind out of me and inspired me to wild acts. 'Write.' When I say 'writing' seized me, it wasn't a sentence that had managed to seduce me, there was absolutely nothing written, not a letter, not a line. But in the depths of the flesh, the attack. Pushed. Not penetrated. Invested. Set in motion. The attack was imperious: 'Write!' Even though I was only a meager anonymous mouse, I knew vividly the awful jolt that galvanizes the prophet, wakened in mid-life by an order from above. It's a force to make you cross oceans. Me, write? But I wasn't a prophet. An urge shook my body, changed my rhythms, tossed madly in my chest, made time unlivable for me. I was stormy. 'Burst!' 'You may speak!' And besides, whose voice is that? The Urge had the violence of a thunderclap. Who's striking me? Who's attacking me from behind? And in my body the breath of a giant, but no sentences at all. Who's pushing me? Who's invading? Who's changing me into a monster? Into a mouse wanting to swell to the size of a prophet?

A joyful force. Not a god; it doesn't come from above. But from an inconceivable region, deep down inside me but unknown, as if there might exist somewhere in my body (which, from the outside, and from the point of view of a naturalist, is highly elastic, nervous, lively, thin, not without charm, firm muscles, pointed nose always quivering and damp, vibrating paws) another space, limitless; and there, in those zones which inhabit me and which I don't know how to live in, I feel them, I don't live them, they live me, gushing from the wellsprings of my souls, I don't see them but I feel them, it's incomprehensible but that's how it is. There are sources. That's the enigma. One morning, it all explodes. My body experiences, deep down inside, one of its panicky cosmic adventures. I have volcanoes on my lands. But no lava: what wants to flow is breath. And not just any old way. The breath 'wants' a form.[3] 'Write me!' One day it begs me, another day it threatens. 'Are you going to write me or not?' It could have said: 'Paint me.' I tried. But the nature of its fury demanded the form that stops the least, that encloses the least, the body without a frame, without skin, without walls, the flesh that doesn't dry, doesn't stiffen, doesn't clot the wild blood that wants to stream through it forever. 'Let me through, or everything goes!'

What blackmail could have made me give in to this breath? Write? Me? Because it was so strong and furious, I loved and feared this breath. To be lifted up one morning, snatched off the ground, swung in the air. To be taken by surprise. To find in myself the possibility of the unexpected. To fall asleep a mouse and wake up an eagle! What delight! What terror. And I had nothing to do with it, I couldn't help it. And worse, each time the breathing seized me, the same misery was repeated: what began, in spite of myself, in exultation, proceeded, because of myself, in combat, and ended in downfall and desolation. Barely off the ground: 'Hey! What are you doing up there? Is that any place for a mouse? For shame!' Shame overcame me. There is no lack on earth, so there was no lack in my personal spaces, of guardians of the law, their pockets filled with the 'first stone' to hurl at flying mice. As for my internal guardian – whom I didn't call superego at the time – he was more rapid and accurate than all the others: he threw the stone at me before all the other-relatives, masters, prudent contemporaries, compliant and orderly peers – all the noncrazy and antimouse forces – had the chance to let fire. I was the 'fastest gun.' Fortunately! My shame settled the score without scandal. I was 'saved.'

Write? I didn't think of it. I dreamed of it constantly, but with the chagrin and the humility, the resignation and the innocence, of the poor. Writing is God. But it is not your God. Like the Revelation of a cathedral: I was born in a country where culture had returned to nature – had become flesh once again. Ruins that are not ruins, but hymns of luminous memory, Africa sung by the sea night and day. The past wasn't past. Just curled up like the prophet in the bosom of time. At the age of eighteen, I discovered 'culture.' The monument, its splendor, its menace, its *discourse*. 'Admire me. I am the spirit of Christianity. Down on your knees, offspring of the bad race. Transient. I was erected for my followers. Out, little Jewess. Quick, before I baptize you.' 'Glory': what a word! A name for armies or cathedrals or lofty victories; it wasn't a word for Jewoman. Glory, stained-glass windows, flags, domes, constructions, masterpieces – how to avoid recognizing your beauty, keep it from reminding me of my foreignness?

One summer I get thrown out of the cathedral of Cologne. It's true that I had bare arms; or was it a bare head? A priest kicks me out. Naked. I felt naked for being Jewish, Jewish for being naked, naked for being a woman, Jewish for being flesh and joyful! – So I'll take all your books. But the cathedrals I'll leave behind. Their stone is sad and male.

The texts I ate, sucked, suckled, kissed. I am the innumerable child of their masses.

But write? With what right? After all, I read them without any right, without permission, without their knowledge.

The way I might have prayed in a cathedral, sending their God an impostor-message.

Write? I was dying of desire for it, of love, dying to give writing what it had given to me. What ambition! What impossible happiness. To nourish my own mother. Give her, in turn, my milk? Wild imprudence. [. . .]

Write? Taking pleasure as the gods who created the books take pleasure and give pleasure, *endlessly*; their bodies of paper and blood; their letters of flesh and tears; they put an end to the end. The human gods, who don't know what they've done; what their visions, their words, do to us. How could I have not wanted to write? When books took me, transported me, pierced me to the entrails, allowed me to feel their disinterested power; when I felt loved by a text that didn't address itself to me, or to you, but to the other; when I felt pierced through by life itself, which doesn't judge, or choose, which touches without designating; when I was agitated, torn out of myself, by love? When my being was populated, my body traversed and fertilized, how could I have closed myself up in silence? Come to me, I will come to you. When love makes love to you, how can you keep from murmuring, saying its names, giving thanks for its caresses?

You can desire. You can read, adore, be invaded. But writing is not granted to you. Writing is reserved for the chosen. It surely took place in a realm inaccessible to the small, to the humble, to women. In the intimacy of the sacred. Writing spoke to its prophets from a burning bush. But it must have been decided that bushes wouldn't dialogue with women.

Didn't experience prove it? I thought it addressed itself not to ordinary men, however, but only to the righteous, to beings fashioned out of separation, for solitude. It asked everything of them, took everything from them, it was merciless and tender, it dispossessed them entirely of all riches, all bonds, it lightened them, stripped them bare; then it granted them passage: toward the most distant, the nameless, the endless. It gave them leave – this was a right and a necessity. They would never arrive. They would never be found by the limit. It would be with them, in the future, like no one.

Thus, for this elite, the gorgeous journey without horizon, beyond everything, the appalling but intoxicating excursion toward the never-yet-said.

But for you, the tales announce a destiny of restriction and oblivion; the brevity, the lightness of a life that steps out of mother's house only to make three little detours that lead you back dazed to the house of your grandmother, for whom you'll amount to no more than a mouthful. For you, little girl, little jug of milk, little pot of honey, little basket, experience reveals it, history promises you this minute alimentary journey that brings you back quickly indeed to the bed of the jealous Wolf, your ever-insatiable grandmother, as if the law ordained that the mother should be constrained to sacrifice her daughter, to expiate the audacity of having relished the good things in life in the form of her pretty red offspring. Vocation of the swallowed up, voyage of the scybalum.

So for the sons of the Book: research, the desert, inexhaustible space, encouraging, discouraging, the march straight ahead. For the daughters of the housewife: the straying into the forest. Deceived, disappointed, but brimming with curiosity. Instead of the great enigmatic duel with the Sphinx, the dangerous questioning addressed to the body of the Wolf: What is the body for? Myths end up having our hides. Logos opens it great maw, and swallows us whole. [. . .]

His mouth

When I was three years old, God was an elegant and maternal young man, whose head, perhaps ceremonially hatted, soared into the clouds, and whose slim legs were sheathed in impeccably pleated pants. Not an athlete. Rather, a refined man with a vague chest, whose musculature was spiritual.

I lived in the left-hand pocket of his coat. Despite my tender age, I was his Pocket-Woman. As such, I didn't resemble myself, I was my opposite, svelte, fairy-like, petite, red-headed, clothed in a green dress. If I had come upon the idea of seduction, I would have pictured myself up there as seductive. I was, when I was living in the divine pocket, my other. From this position I began to look at the universe. I was happy. No one could reach us. As close as possible to the heart of God, to his middle and his lungs. His light gray suit. Never did I see his hands. I knew that he had a beautiful mouth. The lips of his Word: its pods of flesh with their neatly drawn contours. His mouth detached itself from his face, shone, distinguished itself. Thy mouth is a slice of pomegranate (I corrected the Bible).

Face: I lived it, received it. Primitive figure of a cosmos in which the dominant star, the sun, was the mouth. I didn't think of the eyes. I don't remember ever having seen or imagined the eyes of God. And God didn't flash withering looks: he smiled. He opened up.

And I went in and out of his breast pocket. The body of God was superior. Smile! In I go: mouse.[4]

Later I vaguely made him eyes like mouths. The lids had the engraving of the adored lips. Sometimes the lids fluttered and the eyes took sudden flight.

But the mouth of God advanced slowly, the lips parted and I lost myself in the contemplation of his teeth. Up above, I lived in the humid light of the teeth. His mouth, my hole, my temple; mouse, I go in and out between the teeth of the good lord cat.

My life down below, tumult and rage. As myself, I was a center of passions, fear and trembling, fury and vengeance. No precise form. All I knew of my body was the play of forces, not the play, the firing. Down below it was war. I was war. War and pleasure. Pleasure and despair. Power and feebleness. I watched, I kept vigil, I spied, I never closed my eyes, I saw the incessant work of death. Me: the lamb. Me: the wolf. [. . .]

I adored God my mother. Love me! Don't abandon me! He who abandons me is my mother. My father dies: thus father you are my mother. My mother remains. In me forever the fighting mother, the enemy of death. My father falls. In me, forever, the father is afraid, the mother resists.

Up above, I live in writing. I read to live. I began to read very early: I didn't eat, I read. I always 'knew,' without knowing it, that I nourished myself with texts. Without knowing it. Or without metaphor. There was little room for metaphor in my existence, a very confined space which I frequently nullified. I had two hungers: a good one and a bad one. Or the same one, suffered differently. Being hungry for books was my joy and my torture. I had almost no books. No money, no book. I gnawed through the municipal library in a year. I nibbled, and at the same time I devoured. As with the Hanukkah cakes: little annual treasure of ten cakes with cinnamon and ginger. How to conserve them while consuming them? Torture: desire and calculation. Economy of torment. Through the mouth I learned the cruelty of each decision, one single bite, the irreversible. Keeping and not enjoying. Enjoying and no longer enjoying. Writing is my father, my mother, my endangered nurse.

I was raised on the milk of words. Languages nourished me. I hated to eat what was on a plate. Dirty carrots, nasty soups, the aggression of forks and spoons. 'Open your mouth.' 'No.' I let myself be fed only by voice, by words. A deal was made: I would swallow only if I was given something to hear. Thirst of my ears. Blackmail for delights. While I was eating, incorporating, letting myself be force-fed, my head was enchanted, my thoughts escaped, my body here, my spirit on endless journeys. If I tasted anything, it was the stuff of speech. I remember, from the same period, the last bottle and the first book. I let go of one only for the other. [. . .]

I beat my books: I caressed them. Page after page, O beloved, licked, lacerated. With nail marks all around the printed body. What pain you cause me! I read you, I adore you, I venerate you, I listen to your word, O burning bush, but you consume yourself! You're going to burn out! Stay! Don't abandon me. Blessing of the book: once the cakes were incorporated, I found myself empty, deceived, condemned again. A year to get through! (But a year, I've learned, is too long and is nothing. I learned all the subtleties of time very early, its elasticity in inflexibility, its meanness in compassion, its ability to return.)

The book – I could reread it with the help of memory and forgetting. Could begin again. From another perspective, from another and yet another. Reading, I discovered that writing is endless. Everlasting. Eternal.

Writing or God. God the writing. The writing God. I had only to break in and train my appetites.

Notes

1   '*On tue une fille.*' The title of this passage echoes the title of Freud's essay 'A Child is Being Beaten' [eds].

2   '*Peut pas s'empêcher de voler!*' – '*En ce cas, nous avons des cages extra.*' The verb *voler* means both 'to fly' and 'to steal.' In this scene, a young girl irrepressibly steals – apparently language, in this case – and simultaneously flies (from the scene of the crime, in a flight of words). She is then punished with 'special cages,' meaning not only prison for the thief, but foot-binding to restrain the mobility of the girl who 'flies.' See Nancy Kline's introduction to *The Tongue Snatchers*, by Claudine Herrmann, for a gloss on Cixous's development of this term [eds].

3   '*Le souffle "veut" une forme.*' The word *souffle* means both 'breath' and spirit, as in *le souffle créateur*, 'the breath of God.' It is also used to indicate inspiration, as in *avoir du souffle*, 'to be inspired.' Throughout this passage (and elsewhere in Cixous's work, such as the 1975 fiction *Souffles*), the vocabulary of breathing, or respiration, is aligned with a parallel vocabulary of inspiration [eds].

4   '*Souris! J'entre: souris.*' The images of the narrator as mouse and God as the 'good lord cat' converge here through the homonym *souris*. *Souris* denotes both the noun 'mouse' and the singular imperative of the verb 'to smile': God smiles, and the narrator enters the mousehole of his mouth [eds].

Chapter 21

Grace and Innocence:
Heinrich von Kleist

■ [Abridged] This extract is taken from one of a series of seminars
given by Cixous between 1980 and 1986 at the Centre d'Études
Féminines, Université de Paris VIII. To date it has been published only
in English, in *Readings: The Poetics of Blanchot, Joyce, Kafka, Kleist,
Lispector, and Tsvetayeva,* edited and translated by Verena Andermatt
Conley (University of Minnesota Press, 1991).

Editors' introduction

IN THE CHAPTER FROM which this excerpt was taken, Cixous reads the
texts of German playwright and poet Heinrich von Kleist alongside those
of Clarice Lispector and others in order to discover particular paradigms of
grace and innocence: grace that would be given not by God but by oneself,
and innocence that can be attained only after the innocence of paradise is
irrevocably lost (after one has passed through knowledge and guilt).

In the opening pages of this chapter (not included here), Cixous asks the
question that seems to motivate this study, as it does much of her work: 'Is it
possible to have a relationship with something *truly* other, something so strange
that it remains so?' (1991d: 30). Clearly, such a relationship is not thinkable
within the innocence of paradise, because paradisal innocence is oblivious to
otherness. For Adam and Eve, before the fall, innocence is reducible to an
infantile state of unknowing; there is no acknowledgement of otherness within
Eden, and thus, for Cixous, no meaningful innocence.

In place of this first, false innocence, Cixous wants to articulate an innocence
that is expressed in a paradise that can exist only in contrast to hell, an
innocence that is profoundly linked with guilt as its inescapable other. What is
essential to Cixous's notion of innocence is that it entail the risk of guilt; the
fruit of the tree of knowledge of good and evil must be eaten. Humanity cannot

remain in Eden, but must venture out of paradise and be exposed to the dangers of hell in order to discover true innocence.

Also of interest in this excerpt is Cixous's emphasis on the impossibility of actually possessing grace. To attempt to have grace, to exist in a state of grace, is, for Cixous, to appropriate the otherness of grace and thereby to render it graceless. Grace *is* only in the moment of receiving it, a moment which must be entered into again and again, in a kind of active passivity. One gives oneself grace, but one never *has* grace; to attempt to possess grace is to yield to 'the temptation of being the other' (1991d: 67). That is, it is to eliminate the strangeness of otherness in a movement of understanding that leads away from the mystery of grace and towards the immobility of boredom.

Clearly, though, these meditations on grace and innocence are not compelling in only a theological sense, for Cixous. Rather, she warns, in the context of an 'aside' concerning Knut Hamsun's fascination with Nazism, that 'there is always, even if we are navigating in largely mythical spaces, a political side to our problem' (1991d: 42). This is arguably one of the central wagers of French feminist theory as a whole, as well as for feminism in general; that is, even those realms of human experience that might seem to lie outside of politics have political implications. For Cixous, in the context of this chapter, even theological notions like innocence and grace can serve as opportunities for political intervention. She wants her readers to remember that the false innocence that consists in a romanticism of the natural, or, more generally, in that refusal of knowledge known as denial, is an innocence that humanity cannot afford and must guard against. In other words, we must find our innocence on the other side of knowledge, rather than in its absence, if we are to avoid a re-emergence of Nazism and a repetition of the Holocaust.

[. . .] Grace refers to a world, which can be a superior world, where someone decides not on human but on divine grace. I want us to leave the ground but not so as to forget the reality principle, especially the principle of our quotidian reality. I would like to avoid the trap that consists in constituting innocence as an infantile state, where it becomes synonymous with irresponsibility. One could say that in paradise, the question of responsibility was kept silent or did not exist. But we are no longer in paradise. And since, at the same time, we have to think of paradise in order to be able to work on these complex notions, let us not forget hell. Clarice [Lispector] never forgets that there is no paradise without hell.

Innocence is always linked to risk, since by definition it is outside of a certain type of knowledge. It risks being misunderstood and leads to catastrophes. There is a dangerous innocence and a misleading innocence.

Innocence, with its mark on the side of a first, *primary* knowledge, which is bliss and on which I insisted elsewhere when I worked on the Biblical character of Eve, is something that in ordinary reality can lead to regression, of which one has to be aware.

For example, a writer like Knut Hamsun was fascinated by a primal, archaic libido, close to nature. During World War II, he threw himself into hell while mistaking it for paradise. He started to celebrate Nazism in all of its glory, interpreting it as the ideology of nature and of the primitive form. He did in Norway what Ezra Pound did in Italy. He started from a personal myth of resistance to bad culture and became a racist without noticing it. I insist that there is always, even if we are navigating in largely mythical spaces, a political side to our problem, and it is important never to lose sight of it. [. . .]

I want to work on the temptation of being the other. First, I would like to insist that one can think loss other than in the negative, other than as punishment, in a movement that goes up to the very extinction of loss, to the loss of loss that would be the most human path to grace. With the danger of the fall, I go back into the space of Biblical reference. If there is temptation, it is on the side of having, of being the other. In the world of thought, this is related to understanding. All is happening between understanding and not understanding. To understand is to have, to take, to appropriate the other, and once that is understood, boredom sets in.

Freud gives his libido a viscous consistency, a kind of resisting fluidity. One can imagine a moment when this fluidity becomes crystallized. Some economies do not flow well. They jell and thicken in the sense of marmalade. Usually, a contentment sets in that either suffices or does not. From this contentment, there is a new drive toward a new desire, a new mystery. I insist on the value of movement, of mobility, and of a good viscosity. I also repeat that grace can only be in movement. One never *has* grace, it is always given. Grace is life itself. In other words, it is an incessant need, but even if it is given, like life itself, this does not mean that it will be received. To have received grace does not mean to *have* it, once and for all. Adam and Eve were the only people who 'had' it but without knowing. And they were in Paradise at a time when there was no having. We mortals have the *chance*, the luck of being on the passage of grace. In the 'Marionette Theater,' there was a tiny, very subtle detail that consisted in marking the moment of brushing (*frôlement*) in the puppet's movement. The brushing makes the difference between an innocent innocence that we do not know – like that of Adam and Eve before they were expelled from Paradise – and another, for which we have to look, as Kleist reminds us, at the other end of the world. In Clarice's terms, we would find it after having gone through knowledge so as to arrive at the other end of knowledge, and there again to begin not to know any longer. That is when we arrive at the second innocence that, contrary to the first, does not not know itself. This second innocence is precisely the grace one gives to oneself. I would say, one does without (*on se fait grâce de*) knowledge. To be capable of it, one has to know that one knows. But at the same time, one has to be disenfranchised of knowledge. This can be done in a very delicate movement of detachment. For example, we know something but we do not hold on to it. We all know how much we hold on to what we know or what we think we know. One has to know how not to possess what one knows. I tend to criticize the prejudice for truth, which consists in knowing that one has knowledge and in giving it a mortal, limited, subjective, or even a universal value. To have only the value of knowledge is not to have the value of life, or love. It is only a *moment* in a process of reasoning, a step on a certain methodical path, a moment or a means, something of a useful or necessary passage but limited to a certain usage. It is not an end in itself and is without final value. It can be abandoned, lost, or given up. This kind of lightness in the gesture of appropriation is something that is not cramped, but supple (*délié*). These qualities can be found with what I call the other or the second innocence. To repeat, I am not speaking of an innocence that does not know or of one whose mark is to be constantly threatened by the demon of knowledge. But it is threatened in any case and has to be so. It must run the risk of losing itself; it can never be a state. If it is not constantly threatened, we are not susceptible of either having it all at once, or of losing it. That is what I mean by 'brushing.' In the dance of innocence, there occurs an imperceptible moment of brushing, a risk of interruption. This risk is the mark of the human being, who otherwise would be on the side of the divine. Humans are always at the door of paradise, on the point of losing it and not inside.

I come back to the word 'confidence,' which functions in the same way. Innocent innocence is not of interest to us. The notion applies either to the village idiot or to the newly born child. What can be called innocence, in the course of human life, is the most acute stage of awareness of the possibility of human guilt. One can be innocent only if one is absolutely guilty. At the end of an infinite guilt, one can become innocent.

Grace and innocence have no meaning outside of being in relation. The Biblical Paradise *is* without other. Grace and innocence have no meaning outside of a relation of temptation with their other. We can read such temptations in texts like Kleist's, where it is always a question of linking and unlinking, of binding and unbinding, of attaching and detaching, in love or in friendship. [. . .]

Biblical
Paradise
is without other.

Chapter 22

The School of Dreams

■ [Abridged] 'The School of Dreams' was originally published
in English as a section of *Three Steps on the Ladder of Writing*, edited
and translated by Sarah Cornell and Susan Sellers (Columbia University
Press, 1993). *Three Steps* was a revision of Cixous's 'Wellek Library
Lectures on Critical Theory' given in English in 1990 at the University
of California, Irvine.[1]

Editors' introduction

THE LETTER 'H' OPENS this section, providing for Cixous a pictorial
representation, albeit in miniature, of a runged ladder that extends both
upwards and downwards in physical space. The image of the ladder – embodied
in 'H' – imprints this passage with a visual metaphor of the mobility required
(from the conscious to all that is unconscious) by individuals engaged in the
activity of dreaming, of transgression, of writing – always, for Cixous, of the
sacred.

With an exploratory prosody – one hesitates to call this an essay – Cixous
celebrates the act of writing and its engagement with the unconscious world
of dreams and the sacred, while at the same time making manifest the
creative elements that come together to make writing – and this piece in
particular – possible. 'The School of Dreams' is at once an analysis of the
ancient Hebrew story of Jacob's Ladder (Genesis 28), a personal dream journal
and first-person diary entry, and a psychoanalytic exploration of the themes of
transgression and alienation, but ultimately it functions as a celebration of
the creative process.

Cixous retells the story of Jacob's ladder: after a monumental transgression
(with his Mother's help, Jacob tricks his older brother Esau out of his birthright), Jacob is sent out to a foreign land, lays his head on a rock to rest, and
dreams a strange dream of angels ascending and descending, from the earth, to
and from heaven. For Cixous, the dream of Jacob's ladder acts as a kind
of originary story of the unconscious – 'the first dream of dreams' – appearing

as it does in the Book of Genesis in the Hebrew Bible, and retold in countless rabbinic, theological and literary texts. The dream of Jacob's ladder depicting angelic messengers moving between two regions represents the logic of the dream itself – of dreaming itself – in Cixous's metaphoric exposé.

For Cixous Jacob's ladder conveys the idea of movement, of going forth, from the self, towards something other, something unknown, a traversal of space; but also, the ladder represents a traversal of time, of the abundance of the moment formed by a rich past, and promising unknown and unknowable futures. Writing, as dreaming, is able to give birth – Genesis – to something other, something new and not yet seen, only because it traverses time, via the ladder, in all of its ancient and historic capacity, and because it traverses generations – in all of their moral vicissitudes (good and evil) and with all of the violence of life and death. Writing can only 'generate' when repression is traversed, on the ladder of Jacob's dream, making the generations present to us.

With Midrashic interpretative ingenuity and playfulness, Cixous re-reads a sacred text (Jacob's ladder) as a literary creation from which other writing ventures begin – as intertext – and thus elevates the process of writing itself to the level of the sacred. Writers, as are other artists, are thus, always for Cixous, constant re-writers of the Bible – 'We are those who later on transform, displace, and canonise the Bible, paint and sculpt it another way' – fellow travellers working their way up and down Jacob's ladder.

The school of the dead

H: you see the stylized outline of a ladder. This is the ladder writing climbs; the one that is important to me. Perhaps you were going to tell me this H is an *H*. I mean the letter *H*. After all, in French *H* is a letter rich in significance. Indeed, I write *H*, and I hear *hache* (axe). *H* is pronounced *ash* in French. This is already transporting for whosoever desires to write. In addition to this *hache* – a cutting instrument, an axe to clear new paths – the letter is granted uncommon favors in the French alphabet. If *A* is masculine, as is *B*, *C*, *D*, *E*, etc., only *H* is masculine, neuter, or feminine at will. How could I not be attached to *H*?

In addition, in French, *H* is a letter out of breath. Before it was reduced to silence during the French Empire, it was breathed out, aspirated. And it remembers this, even if we forget. It protects *le héros*, *la hardiesse*, *la harpe*, *l'harmonie*, *le hasard*, *la hauteur*, *l'heure* from any excessive hurt.

I can only tell you these mysteries silently in French. But in English there's breath; let's keep it.

I was saying: this H, this ladder is writing. This is how I figure it: the ladder is neither immobile nor empty. It is animated. It incorporates the movement it arouses and inscribes. My ladder is frequented. I say *my* because of my love for it: it's climbed by those authors I feel a mysterious affinity for; affinities, choices, are always secret. [. . .]

The school of dreams

Dreaming in 1990

My son is no bigger than a grub. This is why we almost forget him, we don't really believe in him, my dream and I. Where does he live? At the moment, between the leaves of a book. This is where he runs the least risk of being lost. Inversely, he risks being squashed, if someone puts something on the book. Otherwise he rests between the leaves without much difficulty. What is the future for such a grub? Not much hope. He'll vegetate. If he stays this size. But then he slowly takes on substance. This is doubtless the result of my efforts: sometimes I take him out, I place him on a bed, or outside, for after all he has a right to the world, and he seems to lean toward life. The danger that someone unaware will crush him remains. Little by little he even gains in intelligence. He begins to think, to be happy, to become a real living being. Obviously, he is very far behind, since he has existed in this form for months. But now he has really decided to catch up. Now I spy him running, having gone downstairs, and climbing on dangerous edges. I am worried because he doesn't know what danger is.

I feel happiness, love for my grub leaving his twilight state. Seeing life 'crystallize' is such a blessing. Suddenly, it's the descent between rough red boulders, in an invisible 'taxi' that turns in circles several times in the circus of boulders, as if there were no way out. But in fact there is one.

Here is the portrait of my first written dream.

I'll return via my ladder to the first dream of dreams, the one everyone knows – except those who are not of Judeo-Christian culture, that is – Jacob's dream. At the beginning of this story, there is the whole matter of Jacob's genealogy. There are the two brothers, Jacob and Esau, and the father Isaac, the son of Abraham. Let's imagine we are the young Jacob. The parental genealogy provides a background. Stemming from Abraham we are constantly in the space where Good and Evil are infinitely tangled. Violent events are strewn through the characters' biographies. Then, as in a novel, we come to the small Isaac we left on the mountain, we progress through the story, and find a completely different Isaac. The Bible, like the dream, always brings us the violent sense of generations. We live bizarrely clinging to the level of our age, often with a vast repression of what has preceded us: we almost always take ourselves for the person we are at the moment we are at in our lives. What we don't know how to do is to think – it's exactly the same as for death – about what is in store for us. We don't know how to think about age; we are afraid of it and we repress it.

Writing has as its horizon this possibility, prompting us to explore all ages. Most poets are saved children: they are people who have kept their childhood alive and absolutely present. But the most difficult thing for human beings to do is to think ahead, to put ourselves in the shoes of those we have not yet been. Hence our difficulty in thinking over what is parked behind the so-called Golden Age barrier. What the Bible does for us is to make us live all along the generation ladder. With the Bible, we climb up and down through generations. The baby we picked up yesterday in the dust is now, in the next chapter, a tottering blindman. The one who is going to dream this well-known dream is the special son of a blind father, a most unusual man. There is ascension, this movement that gives us the feeling that beings mature and grow up. But they are human beings, so they waste away. They are not good: sometimes they are good, sometimes evil. They don't hesitate to act in all kinds of unclassifiable ways, and they are open to everything that, in the chilliness of our imaginations, would plunge a character outside a 'noble' scene. The story of Moses' youth, for example, is astonishing. There is no one more ordinary than Moses; he is a man who experiences all manner of unexpected passions within himself, our Moses who, for centuries, has been the Moses of Michelangelo and not the Moses of the Bible. The Bible's Moses cuts himself while shaving. He is afraid, he is a liar. He does many a thing under the table before being Up There with the other Tables. This is what the oneiric world of the Bible makes apparent to us. The light that bathes the Bible has the same crude and shameless color as the light that reigns over the unconscious. We are those who later on transform, displace, and canonize the Bible, paint and sculpt it another way.

departure

To begin with, Jacob leaves. We always find departure connected to decisive dreams: the bed is pushed aside. The nature of the dream in or from which we dream is important. We may have to leave our bed like a river overflowing its bed. Perhaps leaving the legitimate bed is a condition of the dream. Jacob leaves, after an incident in which he robs his older brother Esau of his birthright, by deceiving old blind Isaac with his mother's help. At which old Isaac sends Jacob away far from this country toward another branch of the family. He places him at a distance and, at the same time, sends him off to live his life as an ordinary man, one who gets married, and so on . . . Night falls, Jacob is abroad.

> Jacob left Beer-sheba, and went toward Haran. And he came to a
> certain place, and stayed there that night, because the sun had set.
> Taking one of the stones of the place, he put it under his head and

lay down in that place to sleep. And he dreamed that there was a
ladder set up on the earth, and the top of it reached to heaven; and
behold, the angels of God were ascending and descending on it![2]

In my own version, inscribed forever in my dream room, I always see the
same thing: the ladder and the angels' movement of ascent and descent. I was
especially delighted by this crowd of *descending* angels.

Let me now return to this. This is actually the portrait of the first dream of
my life: it is figurative, for me it is a ladder with one step. The other steps would
be invented by the people climbing up and down the ladder. You have probably
guessed that it is the figure of Jacob's ladder. I was introduced to dreams by
Jacob's ladder when I was small. This passage comes early in the Bible, in the
book of Genesis. I always felt glad, when I later grew up out of the Garden, that
this dream came early in the Bible, that the Bible started dreaming quickly; I
appropriated this dream. It remained my own version, and I realized much later
when I reread the book and checked and looked for the story, that I had dropped
some of its elements I did not like. I only kept Jacob, the ladder, and the stone
– one element had completely disappeared from my memory: God. Let me read
the passage again:

> Jacob left Beer-sheba, and went toward Haran. And he came to a
> certain place, and stayed there that night, because the sun had set.
> Taking one of the stones of the place, he put it under his head and
> lay down in that place to sleep. And he dreamed that there was a
> ladder set up on the earth, and the top of it reached to heaven; and
> behold, the angels of God were ascending and descending on it![3]

I stopped there. For me it was everything. What I particularly enjoyed was the
fact that the angels went up *and down*. Had I read a version about angels ascending
to Heaven I would not have been interested. What interested me was their
climbing down. But the story continues:

> And behold, the Lord stood above it and said, 'I am the Lord, the
> God of Abraham your father and the God of Isaac; and the land on
> which you lie I will give to you and to your descendants; and your
> descendants shall be like the dust of the earth, and you shall spread
> abroad to the west and to the east and to the north and to the south;
> and by you and your descendants shall all the families of the earth
> bless themselves. Behold, I am with you and will keep you wherever
> you go, and will bring you back to this land; for I will not leave you
> until I have done that of which I have spoken to you.' Then Jacob
> woke from his sleep and said, 'Surely the Lord is in this place; and

I did not know it.' And he was afraid, and said, 'How awesome is this place! This is none other than the house of God, and this is the gate of heaven.'[4]

As I said, I had forgotten God. Rereading I liked the fact that God is in the dream. He is not outside the dream. He is inside the dream.

The Bible continues in such a way that you never really know whether God is inside or outside the dream. He is inside – so you might think that this is where it occurs: that God and Jacob awake afterward from sleep.

As I reread this dream I realized there is a sequel I always eliminate. I always stop my memory at the pure vision of the angels climbing up and down. This is my ladder, this toing and froing of messengers whose journey interests me most when it descends. *The dream scene* was always far more important to me than the scene of revelation. It is the first dream. In order for the ladder that enables us to pass from one place to another to be set up, we have to leave. Moreover, if we follow Jacob's path, it's through a system of permitted transgressions, since Isaac blessed Jacob well in spite of himself; yet this is the way we must go, leaving home behind. Go toward foreign lands, toward the foreigner in ourselves. Traveling in the unconscious, that inner foreign country, foreign home, country of lost countries.

For this, the bed must be pulled aside; we must descend by the ladder hidden under the legal bed and, breaking all ties and rules, with blows of the axe, pass over to the other side.

Thus, in the beginning, it has to do with leaving 'home' by passing through 'the door' in the depths of oneself. [. . .]

Notes

1   The first section of this selection is from the first essay by Cixous, *Three Steps on the Ladder of Writing* (1993), 'The School of the Dead'. The subsequent selections are from the second essay of the same volume, 'The School of Dreams'.

2   *The Holy Bible*, Revised Standard Version (New York: Thomas Nelson and Sons, 1952), p. 21.

3   *Ibid.*

4   *Ibid.*, pp. 13–17.

Chapter 23

Writing Blind

■ [Abridged] An early version of this text first appeared as 'Écrire aveugle' in *TriQuarterly* 97 (1996): 7–20. The English translation by Eric Prenowitz first appeared in *Stigmata: Escaping Texts* (Routledge, 1998).

Editors' introduction

WORD PLAY DICTATES THE direction of this excerpt from *Stigmata*, a volume in which many of the essays cluster around the theme of divinity understood through an aesthetic lens. 'Writing Blind' opens with an irreverent exchange of signifiers for that holiest of signs, 'Dieu' (God). Via phonetic similitude (sound) and semantic contiguity (meaning), Cixous travels from 'le mot Dieu' (the word God) to 'le mot d'yeux' (the word of the eyes) and 'le mot dit eux' (the word says them) in the French and from 'God' to 'dog' in the English, supplanting the absolute sign by a seemingly infinite linguistic web.

Yet while making light of the sign for God ('Dieu') Cixous at the same time makes clear that all writing is a writing of God. The sign 'Dieu' (and its implicit signified) connotes a fullness – a promise of absolute meaning – but without presence; 'God' simply does not deliver. However, the very promise of 'God' (of meaning in its fullest sense) generates a multiplicity of signs – a potentially infinite free play of signifiers. Simultaneously this same 'God' is also able to afford protection from the chaotic meaninglessness that such a linguistic abundance threatens. 'God' makes the creative infinite by naming it, and thus, conversely, giving it a frame and boundary. Cixous can then say, somewhat mischievously – echoing but also refuting the theologian's ontological proof for the existence of God – that writing, as a perpetual exercise in the pursuit of meaning, constitutes itself a 'proof of the existence of gods'.

Cixous is quick to indicate that her faith in 'God' is not antifeminist as many critics would first suppose. Her 'God' is not the patriarch of Bible classes and dusty theological tomes. Instead she reinvents God, alternately naming God in the feminine (she/her) and masculine (he/his), but always keeping the capitalisation of a personal name. God becomes for Cixous the promise of revelation in writing, the unexpected that writing brings forth. God thus forms the future and unknown word(s); writing becomes the absolute act of faith.

In the concluding section of this excerpt there is a seemingly radical shift in the tone and tenor of the discussion from semiotic surfeit in the divine to a portrait of the ridiculous ordinariness of daily life. Cixous images Cleopatra with glasses, Cixous tells of reading the Bible and going without her daily shower. Where is her 'epic decorum'?, she muses wryly. In this final section Cixous makes clear that while language contains within it all the elements of the sacred, waiting to be written and spoken, full of messianic latency, this same sacred writing process is equally mundane, of the body, and absurd: the Grande dame of Literature calling forth the promise of 'Dieu' in each word that follows the other on the page, with tea stains on her loose leaf and jam smudged on the corner of her upturned lips.

The word *God* in French: *le mot Dieu*: *le mot d'yeux*: the word (of the) eyes. Melodious. The name God: *le nom Dieu*.

Whom do I call God, what do I call god? Necessity of the word god. No language can do without a word god. I like the French word god. The word-god: *le mot-dieu*. *Le mot dit eux*: the word says them. *Le mode yeux*. God is *dog* in the English mirror.

This page writes itself without help, it is the proof of the existence of gods.

God is always already *di-eu*, di/vided, aimed at by us, hit, split. Lips open in his absence of face. And he smiles on us. The smile of *Dieu* speaks of the wound that we are to him.

I have never written without *Dieu*. Once I was reproached for it. *Dieu* they said is not a feminist. Because they believed in a pre-existing God. But God is of my making. But god, I say, is the phantom of writing, it is her pretext and her promise. God is the name of all that has not yet been said. Without the word *Dieu* to shelter the infinite multiplicity of all that could be said the world would be reduced to its shell and I to my skin. *Dieu* stands for the names that have never yet been invented. *Dieu* is the synonym. God is not the one of religions, the one that is attached like Samson the donkey to the wheel of religions.

His true name? We will know it on the last day, it's promised.

The force that makes me write, the *always unexpected Messiah* {*Messie toujours inattendu*}, the returning spirit or the spirit of returning – it is you.

Everybody knows that one must not wait expectantly for the Messiah, he can only come to leave, by leaving, from [*il ne peut arriver qu'à partir*].

You have always just left, you come from leaving: *tu viens de partir*. Leaving is the condition for returning. Then an 'I believe-you-will-return' begins. It is always accompanied by a But if . . . ? *Mais si . . . ? But if* you did not return??

It is an I want that does not dare believe it. Not-daring-to-believe is a very delicate form of belief.

The temptation to not believe and belief breathe in the same breath.

I *believe* that you will come and this belief is accompanied by its indissociable double which is (a) *but-if*: a *mais-si*.

Just before you arrive, when I almost hear your footsteps, I am *struck with belief*, even though I *knew* you would come. I did not know. And I begin to tremble.

Knowing is not *believing*. Knowing does not believe. Knowing is without fever and without life.

My thinking self waits for you. And there is another myself who trembles.

I myself, I do not believe in miracles. One must not believe in miracles. If you believe in miracles, then there are none.

I have a cat who took me so much by surprise that she is named miracle.

In my writing night I am subject to the laws of hospitality. I welcome newly arrived terms. And if they want to leave again, I do not hold them.

I have a submission for what arrives, and a submission for what returns. This is why I tremble and fear. I fear that the Messiah will arrive and I fear that the Messiah will not arrive.

If I had known that I would come to (have) a cat or that one day a cat would come to me, I would have said no. I would not have wanted it.

This is how she came. Unwanted. Entirely unexpected. Never desired beforehand.

And I love her. We cannot not love the found child. What we love is the undesired. The arrival of what is desired satisfies but does not fill with enthusiasm. Enthuse says god. The word enthuse(s) . . .

More than everything in the world we love the creature we would never have expected. Never thought of loving.

Me, a cat?

This is a chapter of a book that could be called the imitation of the cat [*la chatte*].

How does a book arrive? Like a barely weaned cat who sticks a small paw-hand out from under the wood-stove. And a few days later it is she who explains humanity to you.

Who would have believed that I could *love* an animal and imitate a she-cat? And now I believe.

I have already learned a lot from her. She brings me closer to the formation of the soul.

I will stop shortly.

The sense of the ridiculous is the first difference between a god and me. The sense of the ridiculous is my modern comic dimension. I burst out laughing in the tension between the two measurements of our own character. Between the giant and the dwarf that we are. When the dwarf puts on a dress that is too big and the giant a shoe that is too small, we stumble. Walking is difficult, uneven. Freudian slip, subconsciously deliberate mistake, lapsus, disjunction, inadequacy – my story is ridiculous as is yours. The smallness of the great character is multiplied by his greatness. Those political men are very ridiculous. Their tongue forks and they claim to command us.

The Fall is ridiculous. But in the Bible one does not laugh. The sense of sin keeps God from laughing. It is coming up against the limit that makes us laugh.

In my Bible, one has the sense of the ridiculous. It is a great liberty. We enjoy it when we do not have the constraint of contrition. So chased from paradise, I go off precipitately and concretely without having had the time to take my shower. Then I spend the whole day looking for a bathroom. In complete contravention of the sense of epic decorum.

And glasses? Can we imagine a literature without glasses today? How did the myopic heroes manage before the walls of Troy?

We cannot imagine Phaedra entering on stage with glasses. And yet? Cleopatra with glasses is an act of violence. I want Phaedra not to be ashamed to wear glasses.

My effort in language and in thematics is to break with interdictions and false modesties. This is why I go so willingly into the house of dreams: I admire them for their aptitude for nondiscrimination. It is in their house that the equal light from before the guilty feeling reigns. Neither pride, nor shame. It is only in dreams that we are strong and generous enough to look God in the face while he bursts out laughing. That creation, really! Those creatures! It takes some doing! And I also laugh to have caught God doing what he has never done elsewhere.

PART FIVE

Monique Wittig

F EMINIST SCHOLARS OF RELIGION, and most feminist scholars
  generally, would not have to read much of the Anglo-feminist literature
produced in the 1980s before coming across a quotation from Monique Wittig's
Les Guérillères (1971 [1969]: 89):

> There was a time when you were not a slave, remember that. You
> walked alone, full of laughter, you bathed bare-bellied. You say you
> have lost all recollection of it, remember . . . You say there are no
> words to describe this time, you say it does not exist. But remember.
> Make an effort to remember. Or, failing that, invent.

This impassioned petition to take pride in an utopian past, even if it has to be
constructed, became the mantra of a goddess-centred feminism that hearkened
back to a 'prehistoric' time (not without controversy) when matrilineal and
matriarchal societies ruled the earth, when women were strong and independent,
and when goddess deities reigned supreme. Wittig certainly had no intention
of becoming the spokeswoman for a decade of new-age scholars of religion, but
as a radical lesbian feminist, she shares with this group the imperative to recover
and celebrate the heritage of women-made culture in order to make possible a
future where women are defined, not by their biology, nor through their relation
to men and masculine cultural activities, but through their individual agency,
and their capacity to love one another as individuals.

Wittig is a novelist, essayist, feminist activist and academic who has made
it her aim from the start of her remarkable writing career to give primacy to
the dynamism of independent female communities, and to articulate, at long
last, the silenced vocabulary of a lesbian love and desire. Wittig achieved almost

overnight literary acclaim in France with the publication of her first novel, *The Opoponax* (1966 [1964]), which was awarded the prestigious Médicis literary prize. *The Opoponax* is written almost entirely with the indefinite French pronoun 'on' ('one'/'you'/'we') and tells the coming of age story of a Catholic schoolgirl, Catherine Legrand. The patterned use of the indefinite pronoun of the narration shifts dramatically to an erotically charged first person prose after the main character expresses desire for another Catholic school girl. Wittig thus establishes an individuated identity for her main character through a love relationship between women, unhampered and unmitigated by male influence. This erotic dynamic between the two girls, which gives their characters shape, depth and definition, is contrasted with the homogenous mass of undefined and androgynous nuns who bow down before their masculine god.

But it was with the publication of her second novel, *Les Guérillères*, that Wittig took the feminist scene by storm. The word 'guérillères' is a feminised neologism that suggests 'guerrilla', that is, fighter, or warrior, as well as 'war' or 'guerrilla warfare' (playing on the homophony between *le guérillero*, *la guerre* and *la guérrilla*), and provides the defining features of the collective Amazonian protagonists who dominate the book's focus. Throughout the narrative, Wittig also employs the seldom heard feminine plural pronoun 'elles' ('they'), using it normatively in place of 'ils' ('they'), the masculine plural that conventionally functions in French as the neuter (non-gendered) term. Wittig thus eradicates the privilege of the masculine subject position ('ils'), while the feminine ('elles') becomes the new universal point of discourse. From the outset, then, Wittig declares war on masculinised language and, in order to prioritise the subject position of women, and relations between women, she destroys the linguistic oppositions between the genders (masculine–feminine) by refusing the masculine form and using exclusively the feminine form. As a woman, she takes possession of the French language, lays siege, and declares it her own, to use in her own image.

Les Guérillères was written in France during the revolutionary period of May 1968 and embodies the radical spirit of this time period. It tells the story of a collective of women who aspire to end patriarchal rule through armed conflict with their male oppressors. Wittig's prose is explicitly violent and anarchic, as the female warriors destroy every hallowed vestige of the masculinised order: religion, law, culture and language. Everything, Wittig suggests, must be eradicated in order for women to enjoy a truly liberated and independent agency. Wittig is a vehement opponent of feminists who wish to declare women, or 'the feminine', as necessarily loving, caring and passive nurturers (based on their biological capacity for motherhood and in opposition to male agency and aggression). Wittig's vision of woman, on the other hand, is as violent warrior who must destroy the current order to re-create the world according to her needs. All (guerrilla) activity in the book is written with verbs in the present tense, further emphasising Wittig's belief in the imperative for political action.

Religion is an important site of political struggle for Wittig. Eve is recast (along with Sappho and other historically and mythically dominant women) as a heroine; she stands alone in the Garden of Eden and attains essential knowledge for womankind with her consumption of the fruit. The foundational myth of Judaism and Christianity is thus revisioned with the deletion of Adam's partici-pation in the order of human knowledge. Wittig also saturates her text with an eclectic presence of goddesses from cultures throughout the ages and across religious traditions. Again, these are not the maternal earth goddesses of a soft, gentle feminism; rather, Wittig celebrates warrior goddesses and omnipotent rulers, and emphasises the long tradition of sun goddesses (in contrast to the earth goddesses of the new-age movement). Similarly, the erotic, sensual and sexual power of women is emphasised, over women's procreative capacity. Wittig radically restructures the identity of all that is 'feminine' by a complete refusal of the masculine pole. She attempts to establish a space in her literary text where women are not defined over against the masculine site of privilege, but on their own, individual terms.

In *The Lesbian Body* (1975 [1973]) and *Lesbian Peoples: Material for a Dictionary* (1979 [1976]), Wittig goes a step further and while still refusing the masculine pole for definition, redefines female subjectivity through lesbian desire. *The Lesbian Body* is an affirmation in erotic and divinised language of the desire and love that one woman has for another. There is an emphasis on the materiality of the physical body, but in an unromanticised form, without metaphor and clichéd (masculine) imagistic descriptions. Instead the female body is lovingly dismembered and reconstituted in literal (and not literary) prose. Wittig herself describes *The Lesbian Body* as a 'total rupture' with traditional literary forms since it is an expression of love between women, by a woman, for women (1992: 87).

Similarly, *Lesbian Peoples* (co-authored with Sande Zeig) celebrates this interrelational erotics and subjective dynamics between women. Strictly speak-ing, *Lesbian Peoples* is a dictionary, and is organised like one, with terms defined in brief in alphabetical order. Wittig thus reclaims one of the most masculinised of literary forms, the 'scientific' canonical tome of language itself. But the words defined in Wittig's dictionary are given lesbian expression. All words are feminised and within the definitions there is recounted a vast history of women and lesbian-made culture. 'Eve and Lilith' are thus described as 'two famous companion lovers who lived in Palestine during the Bronze Age', while the term 'Woman' is rejected: 'This word once applied to beings fallen in an absolute state of servitude. Its meaning was, "one who belongs to another"' (1979: 52, 165). Again, religion becomes a central site of cultural struggle, with powerful Amazonian figures and warrior goddesses making a frequent appearance.

In a series of critical essays, written over a period of a decade (1980–1990) and collected together in *The Straight Mind and Other Essays* (1992), Wittig makes clear the theoretical constructs and political perspectives which frame her prose work. She defines her feminist project over against scholars, such as Cixous, who espouse an *écriture féminine*, and those who theorise sexual difference on the basis of biology. In fact, Wittig refuses completely the categories of masculine and feminine, which, she believes, are a product of patriarchal discourse which makes of men 'the general' or the norm, with 'the feminine' as the only truly gendered position; there is no such thing as a 'feminine essence' in Wittig's understanding. Wittig is antagonistic to psychoanalytic language that, she believes, focuses on biologically based sexual difference in order to disable a material analysis of women's oppression by men, and consequently, hinder political action.

With such a negative view of sexual difference and *écriture féminine*, Wittig is more naturally aligned with egalitarian feminists than with the psychoanalytically driven Psych et Po[1] feminist movement she so often criticises, even having been published regularly in the *Questions féministes* (which was aligned with material feminism in France). But Wittig is not so easily categorised. Her political and activist credentials (and thus, her social and material analyses) are unquestionable; however, like the Psych et Po movement she criticises, Wittig acknowledges the crucial arena of symbolic discourse (language, religion, literature, law) as the imperative site of feminist struggle. She has stated that while there is a need for feminist materialism, there is also, in her view, 'the necessity of going beyond it, through theory' (1992: xvii). It is no surprise, then, to find Wittig's writings, which are simultaneously political, theoretical and aesthetic, rewriting and reclaiming the major cultural (linguistic) productions of a masculinised culture.

Wittig caused a radical schism within the feminist journal collective of egalitarian feminists, *Questions féministes*, and broke with them in 1980, with the publication of 'La pensée straight' (the title essay of *The Straight Mind*). Here, she combines her social analysis with her theoretical ingenuity and goes a step beyond the theorists of sexual difference by establishing heterosexuality and heterosexual discourse (that is, *the very site of sexual difference*) as the dominant structure of oppression for all women. Heterosexuality, she challenges, orders all human relations and grounds our conceptual paradigms. As such, lesbianism, and the establishment of a lesbian culture, is the ultimate form of political resistance. Wittig argues:

> Lesbian is the only concept I know of which is beyond the category of sex (woman and man), because the designated subject (lesbian) is

not a woman, either economically, or politically, or ideologically.
For what makes a woman is a specific social relation to a man, a
relation that we have previously called servitude. (53)

The only female subject with agency, in Wittig's conception, is the lesbian
subject. In this sense, free from male domination and definition, Wittig can
firmly assert: 'Lesbians are not women' (32).

Overall, each of Wittig's works could be understood as part of a larger project
to revision and rewrite male canonical texts, while defining male religious,
mythic and historic movements in lesbian terms. *Across the Acheron* (1987
[1985]) is modelled loosely on Dante's *Divine Comedy* (the French title,
Virgile, non, conveys more clearly the satirical invocation of Dante), and is
written as a great epic quest, not with the goal of individual salvation, as is
Dante's, but in pursuit of the salvation of all women. This is Wittig's first
autobiographically directed prose-text which is set in America, where Wittig
subsequently moved from her home in France. The narrative begins and ends in
paradise, a utopian lesbian space, while hell is described as women's current
suffering and oppression on earth. In this text, sacred and profane categories
are blurred, and Wittig lesbianises standard Christian eschatology in her own
political vision.

Most recently Wittig has taken up a teaching position at the University of
Arizona in the Departments of Women's Studies and French Studies. She
continues to write in a proliferation of forms, with mention of a forthcoming
screenplay, a play and short stories, in a recent interview.[2] Her work, beautifully
crafted and passionately expressed throughout, has endeavoured to create a
space for the linguistic expression of lesbian love, and for the possibility of real
community between women, as true subjects and self-defined agents.

Notes

1   Psych et Po was an organised branch of the feminist movement in post-'68
     France that emphasised psychoanalytically driven theories of sexual dif-
     ference. See the introductory essay, 'French Feminisms and Religion', for
     details.
2   Savigneau, Josyane (1996), 'French Lesbian Writers?', *Yale French
     Studies* 90: 236.

Chapter 24

The Lesbian Body [excerpts]

■   [Abridged] The following extracts originally appeared in *Le Corps lesbien* (Minuit, 1973), in English as *The Lesbian Body*, translated by David Le Vay (Morrow, 1975).

Editors' introduction

WHILE CRITICS HAVE TRADITIONALLY labelled *The Lesbian Body* a 'novel' it could more aptly be described as an extended prose-poem that details a lover's invocations to her beloved. It is written from the perspective of a nameless lover who describes in detailed passages of longing the all-consuming depths of her passion. Wittig quite consciously appropriates religious language, particularly the discourse of Catholic liturgy, and infuses her text with biblical resonance. *The Lesbian Body* is structured and styled on the *Song of Songs* from the Hebrew Bible, wherein a heterosexual love relationship is divinised in its fullest sensual expression. However, whereas the *Song of Songs* establishes the tradition in the West of the love poem between man and woman, and metaphorically, between a male devotee and his masculine God, Wittig metamorphosises this formula for her expression of a divinised love relationship between women.

   Like its biblical counterpart, *The Lesbian Body* presents 'the beloved', as she is named, as a deified figure with awesome powers. She is throughout addressed by multiple and interchangeable titles – my beloved, my accursed adored, she with ten thousand eyes, Astarte, Ishtar, mother goddess – but primarily she is known as she who cannot be named: 'I cry to you, I call to you, you unnameable unnamed, she whose name I may not utter'; this fatal interdiction on naming the deity parallels the tetragrammaton (YHWH) of the Hebrew Bible, where the proper name of the masculine god may never be spoken or written in its full, sacred form. In *The Lesbian Body*, Wittig harnesses the sensual power of the *Song of Songs* and mirrors her beloved on the Hebrew God in order to place the feminine, and the female body in particular, at the centre of religious and sensual love.

   As is common in all of Wittig's texts, her usage of pronouns is atypical and difficult to translate. In the French original the first person pronoun is written as

J/e with its possessives as m/a and m/es. The English translation of 'I' and 'm/y' inadequately expresses the fractured, unfixed and fluid subject position of the speaker of *The Lesbian Body*. Wittig takes similar liberties with gendered nouns in her French original, feminising all people and things, as well as adjectives and adverbs. Previously male gods, Osiris for example, become feminised – Osirisa – and traditionally masculine forms are modelled on feminine verbal structures ('voyeur' becomes 'voyeuse'). Thus Wittig erases all references to masculinity; the celebration of the feminine gender and of the lesbian body is absolute.

Wittig's transformation of language parallels her rewriting of traditional masculine religious structures. Her poem recounts the crucifixion of Christ, but this time it is the female lover who is crucified for her love of the goddess. The lover consumes the body of the beloved in a Eucharistic setting, but again the body is woman's body and the faithful devoted is a woman. The beloved dies and her body is scattered to the earth and resurrected by her lover, like the Egyptian myth of Osiris and Isis, but again the divinised figure has a female body and her lover, a woman; the union of god and devotee is expressed in terms of lesbian love.

The beloved of the poem is a synchronic assemblage of a variety of ancient and 'modern' (Sappho is divinised here) gods and goddesses whose properties are not fixed and whose qualities interchange at will, but whose gender is always feminine. Wittig's goddess figure is not the gentle earth mother of the 'new age' movement, but a horrific, powerful and dangerous deity who pulverises and reconstitutes the subjectivity of the one devoted to her; the lover is perpetually destroyed and resurrected in her love and yearning for the goddess, made one with the divine figuration of the female body in a mystical union and then painfully separated from her once again. The manifold and contradictory characteristics of the goddess figure perhaps most resemble the feminine deity from the Gnostic prayer, 'The Thunder Perfect Mind'; this is stylistically echoed in the sequence where the goddess declares '*I* am she' and what follows is a list of all possible attributes, both beneficent and ferocious in their power.

The Lesbian Body contains a poem within a poem; the main body of the text is periodically interrupted with a lengthy and detailed inventory of female body parts and functions. This anatomical listing jars the rhythm of the main prose with its disassembled subject of love, simultaneously preventing a romanticisation of the female body, as is standard in male poetic texts, and fleshifying the (divine) subject of longing. The goddess is thus made immanent without lacking her full divinity and the erotic pleasures of the female body are made transcendent.

The two poems intertwine to make *The Lesbian Body* nothing less, as the final lines of the poem state, than the literal 'figuration of lesbian love' in all of its earthly and divine forms.

In this dark adored adorned gehenna say your farewells m/y very beautiful one m/y very strong one m/y very indomitable one m/y very learned one m/y very ferocious one m/y very gentle one m/y best beloved to what they, the women, call affection tenderness or gracious abandon. There is not one who is unaware of what takes place here, which has no name as yet, let them seek it if they are determined to do so, let them indulge in a storm of fine rivalries, that which I so utterly disown, while you with siren voice entreat some woman with shining knees to come to your aid. But you know that not one will be able to bear seeing you with eyes turned up lids cut off your yellow smoking intestines spread in the hollow of your hands your tongue spat from your mouth long green strings of your bile flowing over your breasts, not one will be able to bear your low frenetic insistent laughter. The gleam of your teeth your joy your sorrow the hidden life of your viscera your blood your arteries your veins your hollow habitations your organs your nerves their rupture their spurting forth death slow decomposition stench being devoured by worms your open skull, all will be equally unbearable to her.

If some woman should speak your name I feel as if m/y ears were about to fall heavily to the ground, I feel m/y blood warming in m/y arteries, I perceive at a glance the networks it irrigates, a cry fit to make m/e burst issues from the depth of m/y lungs, I repress it with difficulty, suddenly I become the place of the darkest mysteries, m/y skin bristles and becomes covered with stains, I am the pitch that burns the assailants' heads, I am the knife that severs the carotid of the newborn ewe-lambs, I am the bullets of the submachine-guns that perforate the intestines, I am the pincers brought to red heat in the fire that tear the flesh, I am the plaited whip that flagellates the skin, I am the electric current that blasts and convulses the muscles, I am the gag that gags the mouth, I am the bandage that hides the eyes, I am the bonds that tie the hands, I am the mad tormentor galvanized by torture and your cries intoxicate m/e m/y best beloved the more that you restrain them. At this point I invoke your help m/y incomparable Sappho, give m/e by thousands the fingers that allay the wounds, give m/e the lips the tongue the saliva which draw one into the slow sweet poisoned country from which one cannot return.

I discover that your skin can be lifted layer by layer, *I* pull, it lifts off, it coils above your knees, *I* pull starting at the labia, it slides the length of the belly, fine to extreme transparency, *I* pull starting at the loins, the skin uncovers the round muscles and trapezii of the back, it peels off up to the nape of the neck, *I* arrive under your hair, m/y fingers traverse its thickness, *I* touch your skull, *I* grasp it with all m/y fingers, *I* press it, *I* gather the skin over the whole of the cranial vault, *I* tear off the skin brutally beneath the hair, *I* reveal the beauty of the shining bone traversed by blood-vessels, m/y two hands crush the vault and the occiput behind, now m/y fingers bury themselves in the cerebral convolutions, the meninges are traversed by cerebrospinal fluid flowing from all quarters, m/y hands are plunged in the soft hemispheres, *I* seek the medulla and the cerebellum tucked in somewhere underneath, now *I* hold all of you silent immobilized every cry blocked in your throat your last thoughts behind your eyes caught in m/y hands, the daylight is no purer than the depths of m/y heart m/y dearest one.

You gaze at m/e with your ten thousand eyes, you do so and it is *I*, *I* do not stir, m/y feet are completely embedded in the ground, *I* allow m/yself to be reached by your ten thousand glances or if you prefer by the single glances of your ten thousand eyes but it is not the same, such an immense gaze touches m/e everywhere, *I* hesitate to move, if *I* raise m/y arms toward the sun you slant your eyes to adjust to the light, they sparkle but you look at m/e or else if *I* should move into the shade *I* am cold your eyes are not visible there where you follow m/e *I* too am unseen by you, *I* am dumb in this desert devoid of your ten thousand eyes darker than the dark where your eyes would appear to m/e ten-thousand fold black and shining, *I* am alone until the moment when *I* hear a variety of sounds of bells of tintinnabulations, *I* tremble, *I* am giddy, it reverberates within m/e, it makes m/e quiver, it is the music of the eyes *I* say to m/yself, either they clash together gently and with violence or they produce these many sounds by themselves, *I* fling m/yself flat on m/y face in front or behind this side or that, *I* gesticulate wildly to learn that *I* cannot escape the multiplicity of your regard, wherever *I* may be m/y ineffable one you gaze at m/e with your ten thousand eyes.

I shall not utter your adorable name. Such is the interdict you have laid on m/e, so be it. *I* shall recount only how you come to seek m/e in the very depths of hell. You swim across the muddy waters of the river heedless of the semi-living lianas the roots the eyeless snakes. You sing without pause. The female guardians of the dead mollified close their gaping mouths. You obtain their permission to bring m/e back as far as the light of the living on condition that you do not turn round to look at m/e. The march along the underground passages is interminable. *I* can see your broad back one or other of your breasts when your movements show you in profile, *I* see your strong and powerful legs your straight pelvis, *I* see the hair that reaches your shoulders whose chestnut colour *I* find so beautiful to look at that a pain rises in m/y breast. You do not once turn round. The stink of m/y bowels surrounds us at m/y every movement. You seem not to notice it, you walk on steadily calling m/e in a loud voice all the love names you were used to call m/e. From time to time m/y yellow decaying arms from which long worms emerge brush against you, some climb on your back, you shudder, *I* can see your skin bristle right across your shoulders. We traverse the length of the galleries the underground tunnels the crypts the caves the catacombs you singing with victorious voice the joy of m/y recovery. M/y kneecaps appear at m/y knees from which shreds of flesh fall. M/y armpits are musty. M/y breasts are eaten away. *I* have a hole in m/y throat. The smell that escapes from m/e is noisome. You do not stop your nostrils. You do not exclaim with fright when at a given moment m/y putrescent and half-liquid body touches the length of your bare back. Not once do you turn round, not even when *I* begin to howl in despair the tears trickling down m/y gnawed cheeks to beg you to leave m/e in m/y tomb to brutally describe to you m/y decomposition the purulence of m/y eyes m/y nose m/y vulva the caries of m/y teeth the fermentation of m/y vital organs the colour of m/y rotten-ripe muscles. You interrupt m/e, you sing with strident voice your certainty of triumph over m/y death, you do not heed m/y sobs, you drag m/e to the surface of the earth where the sun is visible. Only there at the exit towards the trees and the forest do you turn to face m/e with a bound and it is true that looking into your eyes *I* revive with prodigious speed. [. . .]

THE LESBIAN BODY THE JUICE THE
SPITTLE THE SALIVA THE SNOT
THE SWEAT THE TEARS THE WAX
THE URINE THE FAECES THE
EXCREMENTS THE BLOOD THE

LYMPH THE JELLY THE WATER
THE CHYLE THE CHYME THE
HUMOURS THE SECRETIONS THE
PUS THE DISCHARGES THE SUP-
PURATIONS THE BILE THE JUICES
THE ACIDS THE FLUIDS THE
FLUXES THE FOAM THE SULPHUR
THE UREA THE MILK THE
ALBUMEN THE OXYGEN THE
FLATULENCE THE POUCHES THE
PARIETES THE MEMBRANES THE
PERITONEUM, THE OMENTUM,
THE PLEURA THE VAGINA THE
VEINS THE ARTERIES THE VESSELS
THE NERVES [. . .]

Unnameable one you buzz in m/y ears, the sound spreads with celerity beyond the cochlea, it gains the cerebellum, it strikes the cerebral hemispheres, it insinuates itself the whole length of the scalp so that *I* bristle with horror, it descends the spinal cord, it hammers m/y ribs, it traverses m/y lungs, *I* pant, *I* shudder. *I* tremble. *I* cannot keep m/y mouth closed, *I* cry to you, *I* call to you, you unnameable unnamed, she whose name *I* may not utter she whose unnameable name pronounced by m/e makes the wasps leave their hives, they are on m/e in swarms, they blind m/e, they strike m/e with their bodies as they fall on m/e, they stab m/e with their stings in thousands, they stun m/e with their infernal buzzing, they enter m/y ear-passages, they penetrate m/e, they burst m/y eardrums, they obstruct m/y sinuses, they inject the poison of their stings into m/y tissues, they insert your anger into m/e, cruel unnameable one call off your wasps, *I* beg for mercy, *I* am utterly consumed, long long is the fire, the poison-hoarding white demons have envenomed m/e in your name, now *I* hate you m/y most unnameable one, not once *I* swear to you will *I* utter your name. [. . .]

You are m/y glory of cyprine m/y tawny lilac purple one, you pursue m/e throughout m/y tunnels, your wind bursts in, you blow in m/y ears, you bellow, your cheeks are flushed, you are m/yself you are m/yself (aid m/e Sappho) you are m/yself, *I* die enveloped girdled supported impregnated by your hands infiltrated suave flux infiltrated by the rays of your fingers from labia to throat, m/y ears affected liquefy, *I* fall *I* fall, *I* drag you down in this fall this hissing spiral, speak to m/e accursed adored eddying maelstrom torment of pleasure joy joy tears of joy, *I* drag you down, your arms twined round m/e embrace two bodies lost in the silence of the infinite spheres, what am *I*, can anyone standing at her window say that she sees m/e pass, gentle muzzled suckling-lamb cat *I* spit you out *I* spit you out. [. . .]

THE AREOLAS THE ECCHYMOSES
THE WOUNDS THE FOLDS THE
GRAZES THE WRINKLES THE
BLISTERS THE FISSURES THE
SWELLINGS THE SUNBURN THE
BEAUTY-SPOTS THE BLACKHEADS
THE HAIR FOLLICLES THE WARTS
THE EXCRESCENCES THE PAPULES
THE SEBUM THE PIGMENTATION
THE EPIDERMIS THE DERMIS THE
CUTANEOUS NERVES THE INNER-
VATIONS THE PAPILLAE THE
NERVE NETWORKS THE NERVE-
ROOTS THE BUNDLES THE
BRANCHES THE PLEXUSES THE
MOTOR NERVES THE SENSORY THE
CERVICAL THE PNEUMOGASTRIC
[. . .]

On the hillside the women do round dances in the evening. Often and often *I* look at them without daring to approach. *I* know them all by their names from having studied them in the library books. *I* list their attributes, *I* consider their bearing, *I* am not sorry that their severity should have remain [sic] attached to the books since they are here before m/e so totally devoid of it. M/y heart beats at times when *I* see you among them m/y best beloved m/y unnameable one you whom *I* desire from the bottom of m/y stomach shall never die. *I* watch you holding the hand of Artemis laced in leather over her bare breasts then that of Aphrodite, the black goddess with the flat belly. There is also the triple Persephone, there is sunheaded Ishtar, there is Albina eldest of the Danaïds, there is Epone the great horsewoman, there is Leucippa whose mare runs in the meadow below white and shining, there is dark Isis, there is red Hecate, there are Pomona and Flora holding each other by the hand, there is Andromeda of the fleet foot, there is blonde Cybele, there is Io with the white cow, there are Niobe and Latone intertwined, there is Sappho of the violet breasts, there is Gurinno the swift runner, there is Ceres with the corn in her hair, there is white Leucothea, there is moon-headed Rhamnusis, you all dance, you all beat the ground with the soles of your feet with increasing force. None seems fatigued, while Minerva the daughter of Zeyna blows her flute and Attis beloved of Sappho beats the tom-tom. If amongst all of them you are the only one to perspire it bedecks you m/y unique one, their complaisant fingers touch you, then you shine with many fires, rays leave your body descending to the ground, hammered for the nth time. *I* am troubled to see you at your ease among the women eyes shining loins twisted by spasms your pelvis thrust forward in the rhythm of the dance. Amicably you share the sacred mushroom, each one bites the edge of the cap, no one asks to become bigger or smaller. At a sign from blessed Aphrodite all around you exchange their colours. Leucothea becomes the black one, Demeter the white, Isis the fair one, Io the red, Artemis the green, Sappho the golden, Persephone the violet, the transformations spread from one to the other, the rainbow of the prism passes across their faces while you unchanging in the chestnut colour of your hair you start to cry out while *I* regard you in your great ecstasy though deprived of the sacred mushroom awaiting you in the laurels with their hidden flower and you come near m/e at one moment or another. [. . .]

Be seated firmly on your heels m/y dearest one, let your thighs be of bronze, your knees of red mud of clay, your adorable hands opposed to your vasti externi whether they be gold amethyst liquid mercury, let your breast be green and shining of the same consistence as the underside of the leaves of trees, let your bust be of tempered steel, your shoulders of copper, let your loins be iron, your neck silver, your nape tin, let your cheeks be platinum, let your eyes m/y favoured one be of lead of molten lead and milk, let your vulva be of fiery infusible violent iridium, let your vulva – labia heart clitoris iris crocus – be of odorous refractory osmium, be strong m/y most beautiful one the most

febrile the most flagrant m/y hands breaking on touching you m/y voice seeking
to re-echo your voice. [. . .]

THE ARTERIAL BLOOD THE AORTIC
BLOOD THE VENULES THE
ARTERIOLES THE CAPILLARY VES-
SELS THE AORTA THE CAROTID
THE CEPHALIC THE JUGULAR THE
CORONARY THE OESOPHAGEAL
THE PULMONARY THE FACIAL THE
TEMPORAL THE SUBCLAVIAN THE
MAMMARY THE BRACHIAL THE
MESENTERIC THE RENAL THE LUM-
BAR THE ILIAC THE SACRAL THE
RADIAL THE SAPHENOUS THE
TIBIALS THE VENA CAVA THE
PORTAL VEIN THE PULMONARY
THE COAGULATION THE CLOTTING
THE CONCRETIONS THE CLOTS
THE SOLIDIFICATIONS
[. . .]

The women lead m/e to your scattered fragments, there is an arm, there is a
foot, the neck and head are together, your eyelids are closed, your detached ears
are somewhere, your eyeballs have rolled in the mud, *I* see them side by side,
your fingers have been cut off and thrown to one side, *I* perceive your pelvis,
your bust is elsewhere, several fragments of forearms the thighs and tibiae are
missing. M/y vision blurs at this sight, the women support m/e under the
shoulders, m/y knees give way, m/y cries are stiffled in m/y breast, they ask
m/e where you should be interred in what order to collect your fragments which
makes m/e recoil shrieking, *I* pronounce a ban on the recording of your death so
that the traitress responsible for your being torn to pieces may not be alerted. *I*
announce that you are here alive though cut to pieces, *I* search hastily for your
fragments in the mud, m/y nails scrabble at the small stones and pebbles, *I* find

your nose a part of your vulva your labia your clitoris, *I* find your ears one tibia then the other, *I* assemble you part by part, *I* reconstruct you, *I* put your eyes back in place, *I* appose the separated skin edge to edge, *I* hurriedly produce tears vaginal juice saliva in the requisite amount, *I* smear you with them at all your lacerations, *I* put m/y breath in your mouth, *I* warm your ears your hands your breasts, *I* introduce all m/y air into your lungs, *I* stand erect to sing, far off *I* perceive the island shore and the sun shining on the sea, *I* turn away the goddesses of death squatting on their heels around you, *I* begin a violent dance around your body, m/y heels dig into the ground, *I* arrange your hair on the clumps of grass, *I* Isis the all-powerful *I* decree that you live as in the past Osiris m/y most cherished m/y most enfeebled *I* say that as in the past we shall succeed together in making the little girls who will come after us, then you m/y Osiris m/y most beautiful you smile at m/e undone exhausted. [. . .]

The tears flow fast on your cheeks, m/y hands repair there and are moistened there, the tears fall larger and larger tepid salt against m/y mouth, they cover your neck your shoulders your breasts, *I* scatter them, *I* disperse them over your entire body, the tears continue to flow, your breast heaves with sobs, you begin to hiccup, the saliva falls in great strings from your mouth, *I* hold its elastic substance between m/y fingers, *I* carry it on m/y mouth on m/y forehead on m/y eyes on m/y cheeks, *I* stop breathing, *I* roll you in your own tears, now they make quite a pool around you, incessantly *I* utter words to make you redouble your tears, you weep without stopping, you weep for yourself, you weep for m/e with marvellous force, your entire body is involved, your shoulders heave, now you start you sob you cry out, your tears fall all at once when you straighten your neck, you implore m/e with strident voice but *I* remain utterly ferocious towards you, then you begin to weep harder still, you make yourself drunk and you intoxicate m/e while your water m/y intemperate mistress, m/y most tormented one, descends in runnels across the beach of the island to the sea. [. . .]

You turn m/e inside out, *I* am a glove in your hands, gently firmly inexorably holding m/y throat in your palm, *I* struggle, *I* am frantic, *I* enjoy fear, you count the veins and the arteries, you retract them to one side, you reach the vital organs, you breathe into m/y lungs through m/y mouth, *I* stifle, you hold the long tubes of the viscera, you unfold them, you uncoil them, you slide them round your neck, slopping you let them go, you cry out, you say delightful stink, you rave, you seek the green fluid of the bile, you plunge your fingers into the stomach, you cry out, you take the heart in your mouth, you lick it for a long time, your tongue playing with the coronary arteries, you take it in your hands, *I* cannot speak, your teeth biting m/y cheeks your lips unscathed at the edge of m/y lips you, your sovereign hair over m/y face, bent over you look, you, your eyes not quitting m/y eyes, covered with liquids acids chewed digested nourishment, you full of juices corroded in an odour of dung and urine crawl up to m/y carotid in order to sever it. Glory. [. . .]

THE CONGEALINGS THE CALCULI
THE STONES THE NODULES THE IN-
DURATIONS THE LAYERS THE
SCALES THE FIBRES THE FIBRILS
THE LIGAMENTS THE TENDONS
THE EXTENSORS THE SUSPENSOR-
IES THE FLEXORS THE ADDUCT-
ORS THE ABDUCTORS THE
SYNERGISTS THE ANTAGONISTS
THE TENSORS THE ROTATORS THE
ACCESSORIES THE RECTI THE
OBLIQUES THE ORBICULARS THE
TRANSVERSE THE SPHINCTERS
THE VISCERAL MUSCLES THE
SMOOTH MUSCLES THE CARDIAC
MUSCLE THE SKELETAL MUSCLES
THE TRAPEZII THE PECTORALS
[. . .]

You are the tallest, Ishtar goddess of goddesses you are the powerful one, blessed be your name over centuries of centuries. You are the possessor of all power, you are strong impassive while you abide in the green in the violet of the heavens while they all await you, head erect you shine in the black nights, you are blinding in the days of summer, desire for you overwhelms m/e once for all together with terror as befits all your adorers, the earth the trees the waters the rivers the torrents the seas the stars of the sky do they not tremble at the mere utterance the mere vibration of your formidable name, Oh that *I* might be dumb or m/y tongue fall out when *I* seek your black shining visage your gilded limbs your vigorous knees, foolish *I* am if *I* complain aloud of the glorious supremely divine Astarte she who has no beginning who has no end she who is, she who cannot have been that which she will not be. Ishtar Astarte m/y beloved eternal one *I* invoke you *I* implore you, *I* thirst for your benevolent tears as much as your rage and your ferocity, not one has prayed to you without your hearing her voice you who have created all woman to be loved by you, m/y adorable one appear once more tonight that *I* may lay m/yself down beside you that m/y hands may touch you that m/y perfumes may please you, *I* shall speak or else not say a word as you wish, *I* shall sing or else stay waiting for your voice to issue from your mouth m/y solestial one m/y celestial one m/y sovereign mistress, blessed be thy name. [. . .]

M/y fingers are spread out nailed down, m/y palms are turned towards the sun, the metacarpals the phalanges are extended. M/y hands are like stars. *I* see at m/y wrists the blue veins, a broad network on the inside of m/y arms. You apply your new procedure to m/e to inoculate the sun, the veins and arteries of m/y wrists artificially dilated. You are obliged to hold m/e on the ground because of the shaking of m/y body. The tips of your fingers are sheathed in supple mirrors. They radiate they catch the heat they irradiate they burn. M/y veins and arteries affected gradually catch fire. A subtle warmth reaches m/y palms m/y arms m/y elbows under m/y armpits. M/y heart ventricles and auricles suddenly begin to explode. Your lips are applied firmly to m/y throat. The heat becomes explosive. Colours violet orange red pervade m/y entire body, m/y eyes are caught in the overthrow the fall of intense colouration, they fall they fall, *I* receive them on m/y belly. M/y ears lips tongue abandon m/e in their turn, they bound here and there on m/y breasts and m/y thighs. You diffuse the sun's fire over m/e, you impose it on m/e without pause, dispersed throughout the circuits of m/y blood it fastens on m/y liver m/y lungs m/y spleen. A smell of burnt flesh rises, now you hold m/e round the waist, the roasting reaches you, a smoke-screen forms before your eyes, the muscles splutter disappearing around our cheeks. At last our blackened skulls clash together, at last boneless with black holes to see you with without hands to touch you *I* am you you are m/e irreversibly m/y best-beloved. [. . .]

I begin with the tips of your fingers, *I* chew the phalanges *I* crunch the metacarpals the carpals, *I* slaver at your wrists, *I* disarticulate the ulnae with great delicacy, *I* exert pressure on the trochlea, *I* tear away the biceps from the humerus, *I* devour it, *I* eat m/y fill of you m/y so delectable one, m/y jaws snap, *I* swallow you, *I* gulp you down. Separated from the acromion both your arms are detached from your shoulders. You sovereign radiant you regard m/e. M/y saliva spreads over your breasts, long fragments of flesh separate from the muscles falling over your neck staining your white throat, carefully *I* take them between m/y teeth, *I* chew them voraciously, then *I* look at you and *I* am overwhelmed with great pity to see you so mutilated deprived of both your arms your bust bloodied. The food you are weighs on m/e within m/y stomach, *I* am suddenly revolted, *I* vomit you up, a great liquid half-digested stinking steaming mass falls on your belly. You become very pale at this point you throw yourself back with a great cry, tears spurt strongly from your eyes splattering m/e, you say it is unbearable to see m/e vomit you up, *I* am overcome by greater pity than ever, *I* begin to eat you again as fast as *I* can m/y so adored one *I* lick the last scraps on your belly, *I* get rid of the traces of blood, *I* absorb you m/y very precious one, *I* retain you within m/e.

I am at the Golgotha you have all abandoned. You sleep among the women a paper tigress, you sleep one arm folded over your head your hair wildly disposed around your face, you resemble one of the Gorgons terrible powerful ruddy in dream. During this period deprived of the aid of your strength *I* lie face to the ground, fear grips m/e and the desire to go on living with you in this garden, not one of you knows anything of m/y anguish, then *I* implore the great goddess m/y mother and *I* say to her mother mother why have you forsaken m/e, she remains silent while you sleep, not a breath of wind stirs m/y hair, *I* cry out in m/y distress mother mother why have you forsaken m/e, someone turns over groaning in her sleep, *I* move crawling toward the top of the garden, *I* leave you m/y dearest, hardly have *I* left the place where you lie than *I* can no longer perceive you in the expanse of sleeping bodies, now *I* shriek fit to burst m/y lungs, not one of you awakens, yet m/y voice issues so powerfully from m/y throat that it injures m/e in passage, *I* do not recognize it, a red mist comes before m/y eyes, a bloody sweat traverses m/y pores, suddenly it covers m/e entirely, m/y very tears dripping in great drops on m/y arms stain them with blood, bloody m/y saliva falling in strings from m/y mouth, red the moon when she appears in the sky red the earth red the night *I* see all red around m/e, *I* cry out in m/y great distress mother mother why have you forsaken m/e, *I* hear nothing but the continued stridulations of the crickets, the low close-packed crowns of the olive-trees do not separate to make way for her coming to m/e bare-footed her black hair and garments visible between the pale leaves, I turn towards you but you are all asleep. [. . .]

THE GAIT THE WRITHING THE
RUNNING THE LEAPS THE BOUNDS
THE RETREATS THE GESTICULA-
TION THE TREMORS THE CON-
VULTIONS THE THROWING THE
BRAWLING THE TUSSLE THE GRIP-
PING THE HAMMERINGS THE
BLOWS THE EMBRACES THE MOVE-
MENTS THE SWIMMING THE
SHOULDERS THE NECK THE
CHEEKS THE ARMPITS THE BEND
OF THE ELBOWS THE ARMS THE
WRISTS THE HANDS THE FISTS THE
KNUCKLES THE ANKLES THE
KNEES THE CLAVICLES THE EYES
[. . .]

I am she who bellows with her three horns, I am the triple one, I am the formidable benevolent infernal one, I am the black the red the white, I am the very great tall powerful one she whose noxious breath has poisoned thousands of generations so be it, I am seated in the highest of the heavens in the starry circle where dwells Sappho of the violet cheeks, as with her the stars' dazzle pales m/y cheeks, I am the sovereign one, I thunder with m/y three voices the clamorous the serene the strident, but I immediately relinquish m/y indubitably hierarchical position at your arrival, I raise you from your kneeling posture, I tear your mouth from m/y knees, possessed by a lively fever I cast m/yself at your feet from which m/y tongue licks the dust, I say blessed art thou among women who art come the first to release m/e from m/y condition glittering maybe but sombre nonetheless because of m/y very great solitude, may you lose the sense of morning and evening of the stupid duality with all that flows therefrom, may you conceive yourself as *I* at last see you over the greatest possible space, may your understanding embrace the complexity of the play of the stars and of the feminine agglomerations, may you yourself in this place strive in a frenzied confrontation whether in the shape of the angel or the shape of the demon, may the music of the spheres envelop your struggle, may you not lose your way in pursuing the stillborn, may the black star crown you finally, giving you to sit at m/y side at the apogee of the figuration of lesbian love m/y most unknown. [. . .]

THE MOUTH THE LIPS THE JAWS
THE EARS THE RIDGES OF THE EYE-
BROWS THE TEMPLES THE NOSE
THE CHEEKS THE CHIN THE FORE-
HEAD THE EYELIDS THE COM-
PLEXION THE ANKLE THE THIGHS
THE HAMS THE CALVES THE HIPS
THE VULVA THE BACK THE CHEST
THE BREASTS THE SHOULDER-
BLADES THE BUTTOCKS THE
ELBOWS THE LEGS THE TOES THE
FEET THE HEELS THE LOINS THE
NAPE THE THROAT THE HEAD THE
INSTEPS THE GROINS THE TONGUE
THE OCCIPUT THE SPINE THE
FLANKS THE NAVEL THE PUBIS
THE LESBIAN BODY.

Bibliography

This book highlights the reception of French feminist writing in Anglo-academic circles. For this reason, only books that have been translated into English, or will soon be translated, have been included in our primary source bibliographies. Further, the bibliographies are organised according to English publication dates; information on the original French editions is included following the English entry.

The bibliography is organised into two main sections; the first includes a lengthy list of publications on the French feminist movement generally. The second section lists the primary and secondary source materials dealing with each of the five writers covered in this book – Cixous, Clément, Irigaray, Kristeva and Wittig. Secondary sources on Kristeva and Irigaray number into the thousands, so only those texts that deal primarily with religious issues are listed here. General secondary sources are listed in the Cixous, Clément and Wittig sections for your information.

This bibliography is by no means exhaustive; see the 'Other bibliographies' section for a listing of further resources.

I French feminism

General

Adkins, Lisa and Leonard, Diana (eds) (1995) *Sex in Question: French Materialist Feminism*, London: Taylor & Francis.

Allen, Jeffner and Young, Iris Marion (eds) (1989) *The Thinking Muse: Feminism and Modern French Philosophy*, Bloomington: Indiana University Press.

Allwood, Gill (1998) *French Feminisms: Gender and Violence in Contemporary Theory*, Bristol, PA: UCL Press.

Anderson, Pamela Sue (1998) *A Feminist Philosophy of Religion*, Oxford: Blackwell.

Armour, Ellen (1991) 'Recent French Feminist Works' (Review Essay), *Religious Studies Review* 17 (July): 205–208.

Barr, Marleen (1987) 'Feminist Fabulation: The Feminist Anglo-American Critical Empire Strikes Back', *Restant: Review for Semiotic Theory* 15, 3: 105–119.

Caron, Anita (ed.) (1991) *Femmes et pouvoir dans l'Église*, Montreal: VLB éditeur.

Delphy, Christine (1995) 'The Invention of French Feminism: An Essential Move', in Lynne Huffer (ed.), *Another Look, Another Woman: Retranslations of French Feminism, Yale French Studies* 87: 190–221.

—— (1996) 'French Feminism: An Imperialist Invention', in Diane Bell and Renate Klein (eds), *Radically Speaking, Feminism Reclaimed*, Victoria, Australia: Spinifex, pp. 383–392.

Duchen, Claire (1986) *Feminism in France: From May '68 to Mitterrand*, London: Routledge, Kegan & Paul.

—— (ed.) (1987) *French Connections: Voices from the Women's Movement in France*, Amherst: University of Massachusetts Press.

Dumais, Monique and Roy, Marie-Andrée (eds) (1989) *Souffles de femmes: Lectures féministes de la religion*, Montreal: Éditions Paulines.

Finel-Honigman, Irene (1981) 'American Misconceptions of French Feminism', *Contemporary French Civilization* 5: 317–325.

Fraser, Nancy and Bartky, Sandra Lee (eds) (1992) *Revaluing French Feminism: Critical Essays on Difference, Agency, and Culture*, Bloomington: Indiana University Press.

Gallop, Jane (1982) *Feminism and Psychoanalysis: The Daughter's Seduction*, London: Macmillan.

—— (1985) *Reading Lacan*, Ithaca: Cornell University Press.

Gaudin, Colette *et al.* (eds) (1981) *Feminist Readings: French Texts/American Contexts*, Special Issue of *Yale French Studies* 62.

Gelpi, Barbara Charlesworth *et al.* (eds) (1981) *French Feminist Theory*. Special Issue of *Signs: Journal of Women in Culture and Society* 7, 1, Chicago: University of Chicago Press.

Grosz, Elizabeth (1989) *Sexual Subversions: Three French Feminists*, Sydney: Allen & Unwin.

Huffer, Lynne (ed.) (1995) *Another Look, Another Woman: Retranslations of French Feminism, Yale French Studies* 87.

Jantzen, Grace (1999) *Becoming Divine: Towards a Feminist Philosophy of Religion*, Bloomington: Indiana University Press.

Jardine, Alice (1981) 'Pre-texts for the Transatlantic Feminist', *Yale French Studies* 62: 220–236.

—— (1988) 'Exploding the Issue: "French" "Women" "Writers" and "The Canon"?', *Yale French Studies* 75: 229–258.

Jardine, Alice and Menke, Anne M. (eds) (1993) *Shifting Scenes: Interviews on Women, Writing, and Politics in Post-68 France*, New York: Columbia University Press.

Jenson, Jane (1990) 'Representations of Difference: The Varieties of French Feminism', *New Left Review* 180: 127–160.

Jouve, Nicole Ward (1990) '"Bliss Was it in that Dawn . . .": Contemporary Women's Writing in France and the Éditions des femmes', in Margaret Atack and Phil Powrie (eds), Manchester: Manchester University Press, pp. 128–140.

Joy, Morny, O'Grady, Kathleen and Poxon, Judith L. (eds) (2002) *French Feminisms and Religion: Critical Perspectives*, London and New York: Routledge.

Lloyd, Caryl L. (1992) 'The Politics of Difference: French Feminism in the Nineties', *Contemporary French Civilization* 16, 2 (Summer–Fall): 174–193.

Marks, Elaine (1978) 'Women and Literature in France', *Signs: Journal of Women in Culture and Society* 3, 4: 832–842.

Marks, Elaine and de Courtivron, Isabelle (eds) (1980) *New French Feminisms: An Anthology*, Amherst: University of Massachusetts Press.

Melman, Deborah (1980) 'Feminist Explorations: Life under Patriarchy' (Review Essay), *Canadian Journal of Political and Social Theory* 4, 2: 64–68.

Minsky, Rosalind (1996) *Psychoanalysis and Gender*, London: Routledge.

Moi, Toril (1985) *Sexual/Textual Politics: Feminist Literary Theory*, London: Methuen.

—— (ed.) (1987) *French Feminist Thought: A Reader*, Oxford: Blackwell.

—— (1988) 'Feminism, Postmodernism, and Style: Recent Feminist Criticism in the United States', *Cultural Critique* (Spring): 3–22.

Moses, Claire (1996) 'Made in America: "French Feminism" in the United States Academic Discourse', *Australian Feminist Studies* 11, 23: 17–31.

Oliver, Kelly (ed.) (2000) *French Feminism Reader*, Lanham, MD: Rowman & Littlefield Publishers.

Richman, Michele (1980), 'Sex and Signs: The Language of French Feminist Criticism', *Language and Style* 13, 4: 62–80.

Schor, Naomi (1995) 'French Feminism is a Universalism', *Differences: A Journal of Feminist Cultural Studies* 7, 1 (Spring): 15–47.

Schor, Naomi and Weed, Elizabeth (eds) (1994) *The Essential Difference*, Bloomington: Indiana University Press.

Sellers, Susan (1992) *Language and Sexual Difference: Feminist Writing in France*, New York: St Martin's Press.

Simonaitis, S., St.Ville, S. M. and Kim, C. W. (1991) 'In Process/On Trial: Reviewing Feminist Theologies and French Feminisms', *Criterion* 30 (Fall): 33–39.

—— (eds) (1993) *Transfigurations: Theology and the French Feminists*, Minneapolis: Augsburg Fortress Press.

Spivak, Gayatri Chakravorty (1981) 'French Feminism in an International Frame', *Yale French Studies* 62: 154–184.

—— (1992) 'French Feminism Revisited: Ethics and Politics', in Judith Butler and Joan W. Scott (eds), *Feminists Theorize the Political*, New York: Routledge, pp. 54–85.

Stanton, Domna C. (1980) 'Language and Revolution: The Franco-American Dis-Connection', in Hester Eisenstein and Alice Jardine (eds), *The Future of Difference*, Boston: G.K. Hall, pp. 73–87.

—— (1986) 'Difference on Trial: A Critique of the Maternal Metaphor in Cixous, Irigaray, and Kristeva', in Nancy K. Miller (ed.), *The Poetics of Gender*, New York: Columbia University Press, pp. 156–179.

Todd, Janet (1988) 'French Theory', in Todd, *Feminist Literary History*, New York: Routledge, pp. 51–68.

Winter, Bronwyn (1997) '(Mis) Representations: What French Feminism Isn't', *Women's Studies International Forum*, 20, 2: 211–224.

Other bibliographies

Gelfand, Elissa A. (1985) *French Feminist Criticism: Women, Language and Literature, An Annotated Bibliography*, New York: Garland.

Nordquist, Joan (1991) *French Feminist Theory: Luce Irigaray and Hélène Cixous, A Bibliography*. Social Theory Bibliographic Series, no. 20, Santa Cruz, CA: Reference and Research Services.

—— (1993) *French Feminist Theory II: Michele Le Dœuff, Monique Wittig, Catherine Clément, A Bibliography*, Santa Cruz, CA: Reference and Research Services.

O'Grady, Kathleen (1997) *Julia Kristeva: A Bibliography of Primary and Secondary Sources in French and English; 1966–1996*, Bowling Green, OH: Philosophy Documentation Center.

II French Feminism and Religion, Primary and Secondary Sources

Hélène Cixous

Primary sources

Cixous, Hélène (1972) *The Exile of James Joyce*, trans. Sally Purcell, New York: D. Lewis. French edition (1968) *L'Exil de James Joyce ou l'art du remplacement*, Paris: B. Grasset.

—— (1976) 'The Laugh of the Medusa', trans. Keith Cohen and Paula Cohen, *Signs: Journal of Women in Culture and Society* 1, 4 (Summer): 875–893.

—— (1979a) *Portrait of Dora*, trans. Anita Barrows, Dallas: Riverrun Press. French edition (1976) *Portrait de Dora*, Paris: Des femmes.

—— (1979b) *Vivre l'orange/To Live the Orange*, Paris: Des femmes.

—— (1985) *Angst*, trans. Jo Levey, New York: Riverrun Press. French edition (1977) *Angst*, Paris: Des femmes.

—— (1986a) *Inside*, trans. Carol Barko, New York: Schocken Books. French edition (1969) *Dedans*, Paris: B. Grasset.

—— (1986b) *The Newly Born Woman*, with Catherine Clément, trans. Betsy Wing, Minneapolis: University of Minnesota Press. French edition (1975) *La Jeune née*, Paris: Union Générale D'Éditions.

—— (1986c) 'The Conquest of the School of Madhubai', trans. Deborah Carpenter, *Women and Performance: A Journal of Feminist Theory* 3, 1: 59–96.

—— (1988) *Writing Differences: Readings from the Seminar of Hélène Cixous*, Susan Sellers (ed.), Buckingham: Open University Press.

—— (1990) *Reading with Clarice Lispector*, trans. Verena Andermatt Conley, Minneapolis: University of Minnesota Press.

—— (1991a) *The Book of Promethea*, trans. Betsy Wing, Lincoln: University of Nebraska Press. French edition (1983) *Le Livre de Promethea*, Paris: Gallimard.

—— (1991b) *'Coming to Writing' and Other Essays*, Deborah Jenson (ed.), trans. Sarah Cornell, Deborah Jenson, Ann Liddle and Susan Sellers, Cambridge, MA: Harvard University Press.

—— (1991c) *The Name of Oedipus*, trans. Christiane Makward and Judith Miller, in *Out of Bounds: Women's Theater in French*, Ann Arbor: University of Michigan Press. French edition (1978) *Nom d'Oedipe*, Paris: Des femmes.

—— (1991d) *Readings: The Poetics of Blanchot, Joyce, Kafka, Kleist, Lispector, and Tsvetayeva*, Verena Andermatt Conley (ed. and trans.), Minneapolis: University of Minnesota Press.

—— (1993) *Three Steps on the Ladder of Writing,* ed. and trans. Sarah Cornell and Susan Sellers, New York: Columbia University Press.

—— (1994a) *The Hélène Cixous Reader,* Susan Sellers (ed. and trans.), London: Routledge.

—— (1994b) *Manna, for the Mandelstams for the Mandelas,* trans. Catherine A. F. MacGillivray, Minneapolis: University of Minnesota Press. French edition (1988) *Manne: aux Mandelstams aux Mandelas,* Paris: Des femmes.

—— (1994c) *The Terrible but Unfinished Story of Norodom Sihanouk, King of Cambodia,* trans. Juliet Flower MacCannell, Judith Pike and Lollie Groth, Lincoln: University of Nebraska Press. French edition (1985) *Histoire terrible mais inachevée de Norodom Sihanouk, roi du Cambodge,* Paris: Théâtre du soleil.

—— (1997) *Rootprints,* with Mireille Calle-Gruber, trans. Eric Prenowitz, London: Routledge. French edition (1994) *Hélène Cixous, photo de racines,* Paris: Des femmes.

—— (1998a) *Firstdays of the Year,* trans. Catherine A. F. MacGillivray, Minneapolis: University of Minnesota Press.

—— (1998b) *Stigmata: Escaping Texts,* trans. Eric Prenowitz, London: Routledge.

Secondary sources

Calle-Gruber, Mireille (ed.) (1996) *On the Feminine,* trans. Catherine McGann, Atlantic Highlands, NJ: Humanities Press. French edition (1992) *Du feminin,* Sainte-Foy, Quebec: Le Griffon D'Argile.

Conley, Verena Andermatt (1992) *Hélène Cixous: Writing the Feminine,* Toronto: University of Toronto Press.

Cremonese, Laura (1997) *Dialectique du masculin et du féminin dans l'œuvre d'Hélène Cixous,* Paris: Didier.

Fisher, Claudine Guégan (1988) *La Cosmogonie d'Hélène Cixous,* Amsterdam: Rodopi.

Jacobus, Lee A. and Barreca, Regina (eds) (1999) *Hélène Cixous: Critical Impressions,* Amsterdam: Gordon and Breach.

Motard-Noar, Martine (1991) *Les Fictions d'Hélène Cixous: une autre langue de femme,* Lexington, KY: French Forum.

O'Grady, Kathleen (1997) 'Guardian of Language: Interview with Hélène Cixous', trans. Eric Prenowitz, *Women's Education des femmes* 12, 4 (Winter): 21–36. Online at 'Voice of the Shuttle': http://www.vos.ucsb.edu/

Penrod, Lynn Kettler (1996) *Hélène Cixous,* New York: Twayne Publishers.

Sellers, Susan (1996) *Hélène Cixous: Authorship, Autobiography and Love,* Oxford: Polity Press.

Shiach, Morag (1991) *Hélène Cixous: A Politics of Writing,* London: Routledge.

Upton, Lee (1993) 'Coming to God: Notes on Dickinson, Bogan, Cixous', *Denver Quarterly* 27, 4 (Spring): 83–94.

Wilcox, Helen (1990) *The Body and the Text: Hélène Cixous*, London: Harvester Wheatsheaf.

Catherine Clément

Primary sources

Clément, Catherine (1970) *Lévi-Strauss ou la structure et le maleur*, Paris: Seghers, rev. edn 1985.

—— (1978) *Au rhapsode, écrit pour Vladimir Jankélévitch*, Paris: Flammarion.

—— (1981) *La Sultane*, Paris: Grasset et Fasquelle.

—— (1983) *The Lives and Legends of Jacques Lacan*, trans. Arthur Goldhammer, New York: Columbia University Press. French edition (1981) *Vies et légendes de Jacques Lacan*, Paris: B. Grasset.

—— (1986) *The Newly Born Woman*, with Hélène Cixous, trans. Betsy Wing, Minneapolis: University of Minnesota Press. French edition (1975) *La Jeune Née*, Paris: Union Générale D'Éditions.

—— (1987a) 'Psychoanalysis is Dead; Long Live Psychoanalysis', *The New Statesman* 114, 2946: 19–21.

—— (1987b) *The Weary Sons of Freud*, trans. Nicole Ball, New York: Verso. French edition (1978) *Les Fils de Freud sont fatigués*, Paris: B. Grasset.

—— (1988) *Opera, Or, The Undoing of Women*, trans. Betsy Wing, Minneapolis: University of Minnesota Press; London: Virago Press. French edition (1979), *L'Opéra, ou la défaite des femmes*, Paris: B. Grasset.

—— (1991) *Growing an Indian Star*, New Delhi: Vikas Publishing House.

—— (1992) *La Senora*, Paris: Calmann-Lévy.

—— (1994) *Syncope: The Philosophy of Rapture*, trans. Sally O'Driscoll and Deirdre M. Mahoney, Minneapolis: University of Minnesota Press. French edition (1990) *La Syncope: Philosophie du ravissement*, Paris: Éditions Grasset & Fasquelle.

—— (1996a) *Edwina and Nehru*, New Delhi: Penguin. French edition (1993) *Pour l'amour de l'Inde*, Paris: Flammarion.

—— (1996b) *Gandhi, Father of a Nation*, trans. Ruth Sharman, London: Thames and Hudson.

—— (1996c) *Gandhi, The Power of Pacifism*, trans. Ruth Sharman, New York: Harry Altman. French edition (1989) *Gandhi ou l'athlète de la liberté*, Paris: Gallimard.

—— (1996d) *La Putain du diable*, Paris: Flammarion.

—— (1998a) *Le Féminin et le sacré*, with Julia Kristeva, Paris: Stock. English translation (in press 2001) Columbia University Press.

—— (1998b) *Martin et Hannah,* Paris: Calmann-Lévy.

—— (1999) *Theo's Odyssey,* trans. Steve Cox and Ros Schwartz, London: HarperCollins; New York: Arcade. French edition (1997) *Le Voyage de Théo,* Paris: Seuil.

Secondary sources

Roudinesco, Elisabeth (1990) *Jacques Lacan & Co.,* Chicago: University of Chicago Press. French edition (1986) *La Bataille de cent ans: Histoire de la psychanalyse en France,* Paris: Seuil.

Luce Irigaray

Primary sources

Irigaray, Luce (1985a) *Speculum of the Other Woman,* trans. Gillian C. Gill, Ithaca: Cornell University Press. French edition (1974) *Speculum de l'autre femme,* Paris: Les Éditions de Minuit.

—— (1985b) *This Sex Which Is Not One,* trans. Catherine Porter, Ithaca: Cornell University Press. French edition (1977) *Ce sexe qui n'en est pas un,* Paris: Les Éditions de Minuit.

—— (1986a) 'The Fecundity of the Caress', in Richard A. Cohen (ed.), *Face to Face with Levinas,* Albany: SUNY Press, pp. 231–256.

—— (1986b) 'Women, the Sacred, and Money', *Paragraph: A Journal of Modern Critical Theory* 8: 6–17.

—— (1989) 'Sorcerer Love: A Reading of Plato's "Symposium: Diotima's Speech"', *Hypatia* 5: 32–44.

—— (1991a) 'Ecce Mulier?', trans. Madeleine Dobie, *Graduate Faculty Philosophy Journal* 15: 144–158.

—— (1991b) 'Equal to Whom?', trans. Robert Mazzola in Naomi Schor and Elizabeth Weed (eds), *The Essential Difference,* Bloomington: Indiana University Press.

—— (1991c) *The Irigaray Reader,* Margaret Whitford (ed.), Cambridge: Basil Blackwell.

—— (1991d) 'Love between Us', trans. Robert Mazzola, in Eduardo Cadava *et al.* (eds), *Who Comes after the Subject?,* New York: Routledge.

—— (1991e) *Marine Lover of Friedrich Nietzsche,* trans. Gillian C. Gill, New York: Columbia University Press. French edition (1980) *Amante marine de Friedrich Nietzsche,* Paris: Les Éditions de Minuit.

—— (1991f) 'Questions to Emmanuel Levinas on the Divinity of Love', trans. Margaret Whitford, in Robert Bernasconi and Simon Critchley (eds), *Re-Reading Levinas,* Bloomington: Indiana University Press.

—— (1992) *Elemental Passions*, trans. Joanne Collie and Judith Still, New York: Routledge. French edition (1982) *Passions élémentaires*, Paris: Les Éditions de Minuit.

—— (1993a) *An Ethics of Sexual Difference*, trans. Carolyn Burke and Gillian C. Gill, Ithaca: Cornell University Press. French edition (1984) *Ethique de la différence sexuelle*, Paris: Les Éditions de Minuit.

—— (1993b) *Je, Tu, Nous: Toward a Culture of Difference*, trans. Alison Martin, New York: Routledge. French edition (1990) *Je, tu, nous*, Paris: Editions Grasset & Fasquelle.

—— (1993c) *Sexes and Genealogies*, trans. Gillian C. Gill, Ithaca: Columbia University Press. French edition (1987) *Sexes et parentés*, Paris: Les Éditions de Minuit.

—— (1994) *Thinking the Difference: For a Peaceful Revolution*, trans. Karin Montin, New York: Routledge. French edition (1989) *Le Temps de la différence: Pour une revolution pacifique*, Paris: Librairie Générale Française.

—— (1995) 'The Question of the Other', *Yale French Studies* 87: 7–19.

—— (1996a) *I Love to You: Sketch of a Possible Felicity in History*, trans. Alison Martin, New York: Routledge. French edition (1992) *J'aime à toi: esquisse d'une felicité dans l'histoire*, Paris: B. Grasset.

—— (ed.) (1996b) *Le Souffle des femmes: Présente des credos au féminin*, Paris: L'Action Catholique Générale Féminin.

—— (1999a) *The Age of the Breath/Die Zeit des Atems/L'epoca del respiro/Le Temps du souffle*, Rüsselsheim, Germany: Christel Göttert Verlag.

—— (1999b) *Entre Orient et Occident: De la singularité à la communauté*, Paris: B. Grasset. English translation forthcoming 2002, Columbia University Press.

—— (1999c) *The Forgetting of Air in Martin Heidegger*, trans. Mary Beth Mader, Austin: University of Texas Press. French edition (1983) *L'Oubli de l'air chez Martin Heidegger*, Paris: Les Éditions de Minuit.

—— (1999d) *To Be Two*, London: Athlone. French edition (1997) *Être deux*, Paris: B. Grasset.

Secondary sources

Armour, Ellen T. (1993) 'Questioning "Woman" in Feminist/Womanist Theology: Irigaray, Ruether and Daly', in S. Simonaitis *et al.*, *Transfigurations*, Minneapolis: Augsburg Fortress Press, pp. 109–142.

—— (1997) 'Questions of Proximity: "Woman's Place" in Derrida and Irigaray', *Hypatia* 12, 1: 63–78.

—— (1998) 'American/French Intersections: The Play of Race/Class/Politics in Irigaray', in L. Langsdorf, S. H. Watson and K. A. Smith (eds),

Reinterpreting the Political: Continental Philosophy and Political Theory,
Selected Studies in Phenomenology and Existential Philosophy, vol. 20,
Albany, NY: SUNY Press.

—— (1999) 'Irigaray: Thinking Difference(s)', in Armour, *Deconstruction,
Feminist Theology, and the Problem of Difference: Subverting the Race/
Gender Divide*, Chicago: University of Chicago Press, pp. 103–135.

Berry, Philippa (1994) 'The Burning Glass: Paradoxes of Feminist Revelation
in Speculum', in C. Burke *et al.* (eds), *Engaging with Irigaray*, New York:
Columbia University Press, pp. 229–246.

Chanter, Tina (1995) *Ethics of Eros: Irigaray's Rewriting of the Philosophers*,
New York: Routledge.

Cheah, Pheng and Grosz, Elizabeth (eds) (1998) *Irigaray and the Political
Future of Sexual Difference*, Special Issue of *Diacritics* 28, 1 (Spring).

Deutscher, Penelope (1994) '"The Only Diabolical Thing About Women . . .":
Luce Irigaray on Divinity', *Hypatia* 9, 4: 88–111.

Grosz, Elizabeth (1993) 'Irigaray and the Divine', in Simonaitis, *Transfigurations*, pp. 199–214.

Hollywood, Amy (1994) 'Beauvoir, Irigaray, and the Mystical', *Hypatia* 9, 4:
158–185.

—— (1998) 'Deconstructing Belief: Irigaray and the Philosophy of Religion',
Journal of Religion 78, 2: 230–245.

—— (1999) 'Divine Woman/Divine Women: The Return of the Sacred in
Bataille, Lacan and Irigaray' in Frank Ambrosio (ed.), *The Questions of
Christian Philosophy*, New York: Fordham University Press.

Jantzen, Grace M. (1997) 'Feminism and Pantheism', *The Monist* 80, 2: 266–
285.

Jones, Serene (1993) 'The God Which Is Not One: Irigaray and Barth on the
Divine', in Simonaitis, *Transfigurations*, pp. 109–142.

Joy, Morny (1998) 'What's Love Got to Do with It?', in Kathleen O'Grady, Ann
L. Gilroy and Janette Gray (eds), *Bodies, Lives, Voices: Gender in
Theology*, Sheffield: Sheffield Academic Press, pp. 231–266.

—— (1999) 'Metaphor and Metamorphosis: Luce Irigaray and an Erotics of
Ethics and Hermeneutics', in Gary Madison and Marty Fairbairn (eds),
The Ethics of Postmodernity, Evanston, IL: NorthWestern Univeristy
Press, pp. 191–213.

—— (2000) 'Love and the Labor of the Negative: Irigaray and Hegel',
in Dorothea Olkowski (ed.), *Resistance, Flight, Creation: Feminist Enact-
ments of French Philosophy*, Ithaca: Cornell University Press, pp. 113–
123.

Oliver, Kelly (1993) 'The Plaint of Ariadne: Luce Irigaray's *Amante Marine de
Friedrich Nietzsche*', in Keith Ansell-Pearson and Howard Caygill (eds),
The Fate of the New Nietzsche, Aldershot, England: Avebury.

Reineke, Martha. J. (1987) 'Lacan, Merleau-Ponty, and Irigaray: Reflections on a Specular Drama', *Auslegung* 14, 1 (Winter): 67–85.

Schor, Naomi (1989) 'This Essentialism Which Is Not One: Coming to Grips with Irigaray', *Differences* 1, 2: 38–58.

Ziarek, Eva Plonowska (1998) 'Toward a Radical Female Imaginary: Temporality and Embodiment in Irigaray's Ethics', *Diacritics* 28, 1: 60–75.

Julia Kristeva

Primary sources

Kristeva, Julia (1970) *Le Texte du roman: approche sémiologique d'une structure discursive transformationelle*, The Hague: Mouton.

—— (1977) *About Chinese Women*, trans. Anita Barrows, New York: Urizen Books. French edition (1974) *Des Chinoises*, Paris: Des femmes.

—— (1980) *Desire in Language: A Semiotic Approach to Literature and Art*, trans. Thomas S. Gora, Alice Jardine and Leon S. Roudiez, with Leon S. Roudiez (ed.), New York: Columbia University Press. French editions (1969) *Sèméiotikè, recherches pour une sémanalyse*, Paris: Seuil; and (1977) *Polylogue*, Paris: Seuil.

—— (1982) *Powers of Horror: An Essay on Abjection*, trans. Leon S. Roudiez, New York: Columbia University Press. French edition (1980) *Pouvoirs de l'horreur: essai sur l'abjection*, Paris: Seuil.

—— (1984) *Revolution in Poetic Language*, (abridged) trans. Margaret Waller, introduction by Leon S. Roudiez, New York: Columbia University Press. French edition (1974) *La Révolution du langage poétique: l'avant-garde à la fin du XIXe siècle. Lautréamont et Mallarmé*, Paris: Seuil.

—— (1986) *The Kristeva Reader*, ed. Toril Moi, New York: Columbia University Press.

—— (1987a) *In the Beginning Was Love: Psychoanalysis and Faith*, trans. Arthur Goldhammer, New York: Columbia University Press. French edition (1985) *Au commencement était l'amour: psychoanalyse et foi*, Paris: Hachette.

—— (1987b) *Tales of Love*, trans. Leon S. Roudiez, New York: Columbia University Press. French edition (1983) *Histoires d'amour*, Paris: Denoël.

—— (1989a) *Black Sun: Depression and Melancholia*, trans. Leon S. Roudiez, New York: Columbia University Press. French edition (1987) *Soleil noir, dépression et mélancolie*, Paris: Gallimard.

—— (1989b) *Language the Unknown: An Initiation into Linguistics*, trans. Anne M. Menke, London: Harvester Wheatsheaf. French edition (1969) *Le Langage, cet inconnu: une initiation à la linguistique*, Paris: Seuil.

—— (1991) *Strangers to Ourselves,* trans. Leon S. Roudiez, New York: Columbia University Press. French edition (1988) *Étrangers à nous-mêmes,* Paris: Librairie Arthème Fayard.

—— (1992) *The Samurai: A Novel,* trans. Barbara Bray, New York: Columbia University Press. French edition (1990) *Les Samouraïs,* Paris: Librairie Arthème Fayard.

—— (1993a) *Nations without Nationalism,* trans. Leon S. Roudiez, New York: Columbia University Press.

—— (1993b) *Proust and the Sense of Time,* trans. Stephen Bann, London: Faber and Faber.

—— (1994) *The Old Man and the Wolves,* trans. Barbara Bray, New York: Columbia University Press. French edition (1991) *Le Vieil Homme et les loups,* Paris: Librairie Arthème Fayard.

—— (1995) *New Maladies of the Soul,* trans. Ross Mitchell Guberman, New York: Columbia University Press. French edition (1993) *Les Nouvelles Maladies de l'âme,* Paris: Librairie Arthème Fayard.

—— (1996a) *Julia Kristeva Interviews,* Ross Mitchell Guberman (ed.), New York: Columbia University Press.

—— (1996b) *Time and Sense: Proust and the Experience of Literature,* trans. Ross Guberman, New York: Columbia University Press. French edition (1994) *Le Temps sensible: Proust et l'expérience littéraire,* Paris: Gallimard.

—— (1997a) *The Portable Kristeva,* Kelly Oliver (ed., contrib.), New York: Columbia University Press.

—— (1997b) *La Révolte intime: Pouvoirs et limites de la psychoanalyse II* (Discours direct), Paris: Librairie Arthème Fayard.

—— (1998a) *Le Féminin et le sacré,* with Catherine Clément, Paris: Stock. Forthcoming English translation (2001) Columbia University Press.

—— (1998b) *Possessions,* trans. Barbara Bray, New York: Columbia University Press. French edition (1996) *Possessions (roman),* Paris: Librairie Arthème Fayard.

—— (1999) *Le Génie féminin: la vie, la folie, les mots: Hannah Arendt,* Paris: Fayard. Forthcoming English translation (2001) Columbia University Press.

—— (2000a) *Crisis of the ~~European~~ Subject,* trans. Susan Fairfield, New York: Other Press.

—— (2000b) *The Sense and Non-Sense of Revolt: The Powers and Limits of Psychoanalysis,* trans. Jeanine Herman, New York: Columbia University Press. French edition (1996) *Sens et non-sens de la révolte: Pouvoirs et limites de la psychoanalyse I* (Discours direct), Paris: Librairie Arthème Fayard.

Secondary sources

Anderson, Pamela Sue (1998) '"Abjection . . . the Most Propitious Place for Communication": Celebrating the Death of the Unitary Subject', in Kathleen O'Grady, Ann L. Gilroy and Janette Gray (eds), *Bodies, Lives, Voices: Gender in Theology*, Sheffield: Sheffield Academic Press, pp. 209–231.

Chopp, Rebecca (1993) 'From Patriarchy into Freedom: A Conversation Between American Feminist Theology and French Feminism', in Simonaitis, *Transfigurations*, pp. 31–49.

Crownfield, David (ed.) (1992) *Body/Text in Julia Kristeva: Religion, Women, and Psychoanalysis*, Albany, NY: SUNY Press.

DiCenso, James (1995) 'New Approaches to Psychoanalysis and Religion', *Studies in Religion* 24, 3: 279–295.

—— (1999) 'Psycho-cultural Inquiry from Freud to Kristeva', in DiCenso, *The Other Freud: Religion, Culture and Psychoanalysis*, London: Routledge, pp. 119–143.

Edelstein, Marylin (1992) 'Metaphor, Meta-Narrative and Mater-Narrative in Kristeva's "Stabat Mater"', in D. Crownfield, *Body/Text in Julia Kristeva*, pp. 27–52.

Fischer, David (1992) 'Kristeva's *Chora* and the Subject of Postmodern Ethics', in D. Crownfield, *Body/Text in Julia Kristeva*, pp. 91–106.

Fletcher, John and Benjamin, Andrew (eds) (1990) *Abjection, Melancholia and Love: The Work of Julia Kristeva*, London: Routledge.

Hollywood, Amy (1993) 'Violence and Subjectivity: *Wuthering Heights*, Julia Kristeva, and Feminist Theology', in Simonaitis, *Transfigurations*, pp. 81–108.

Huntington, Patricia J. (1998) *Ecstatic Subjects, Utopia, and Recognition: Kristeva, Heidegger, Irigaray*, Albany, NY: SUNY Press.

Jonte-Pace, Diane (1992) 'Situating Kristeva Differently: Psychoanalytic Readings of Women and Religion', in D. Crownfield, *Body/Text in Julia Kristeva*, pp. 1–22.

—— (1997) 'Julia Kristeva and the Psychoanalytic Study of Religion: Rethinking Freud's Cultural Texts', in Janet Jacobs and Donald Capps (eds), *Readings in Contemporary Theory*, Boulder, CO: Westview Press, pp. 240–268.

—— (1999) '"Legitimation of Hatred or Inversion into Love": Religion in Kristeva's Re-Reading of Freud', *Research in the Social Scientific Study of Religion* 10: 17–35.

—— (2001) 'Analysts, Critics and Inclusivists: Feminist Voices in the Psychology of Religion', in William Parsons and Diane Jonte-Pace (eds), *Religion and Psychology: Mapping the Terrain*, New York: Routledge, pp. 129–146.

Kaminski, Phyllis H. (1995) 'Kristeva and the Cross: Rereading the Symbol of Redemption', in Mary Ann Hinsdale and Phyllis Kaminski (eds), *Women and Theology*, Maryknoll, NY: Orbis Press, pp. 234–257.

Kavanaugh, Graham (1992) 'Love and the Beginning: Psychoanalysis and Religion', *Contemporary Psychoanalysis* 28, 3: 442–449.

Kearns, Cleo McNelly (1992) 'Art and Religious Discourse in Aquinas and Kristeva', in D. Crownfield, *Body/Text in Julia Kristeva*, pp. 111–124.

—— (1993) 'Kristeva and Feminist Theology', in Simonaitis, *Transfigurations*, pp. 49–80.

Lechte, John (1990) *Julia Kristeva*, London: Routledge.

McCance, Dawne (forthcoming) 'Julia Kristeva and the Ethics of Exile', in Betty Ring (ed.), *Kristeva: A Critical Reader*, London: Scholar Press.

O'Grady, Kathleen (1997) 'The Pun or the Eucharist? Umberto Eco and Julia Kristeva on the Consummate Model for the Metaphoric Process', *Literature and Theology* 11, 1: 93–115.

—— (2002) 'The Tower and the Chalice: Julia Kristeva and the Story of Santa Barbara', *Feminist Theology*, forthcoming.

Oliver, Kelly (1993a) *Ethics, Politics, Difference in Julia Kristeva's Writing*, New York: Routledge.

—— (1993b) *Reading Kristeva: Unraveling the Double-Bind*, Bloomington: Indiana University Press.

Reineke, Martha. J. (1988) 'Life-Sentences: Kristeva and the Limits of Modernity', *Soundings* 71, 4 (Winter): 67–85.

—— (1990) 'This Is My Body: Reflections on Abjection, Anorexia, and Medieval Women Mystics', *Journal of the American Academy of Religion* 58, 2: 245–265.

—— (1992) 'The Mother in Mimesis: Kristeva and Girard on Violence and the Sacred', in D. Crownfield, *Body/Text in Julia Kristeva*, pp. 67–85.

—— (1997) *Sacrificed Lives: Kristeva on Women and Violence*, Bloomington: Indiana University Press.

Richardson, William J. (1992) 'Love and the Beginning: Psychoanalysis and Religion', *Contemporary Psychoanalysis* 28, 3: 423–442.

Smith, Anna (1993) 'Julia Kristeva and the Virgin Mary: "Alone of All Their Sex"?', in Howard McNaughton (ed.), *Remembering Representation*, Christchurch, NZ: University of Canterbury Press, pp. 65–75.

—— (1996) *Julia Kristeva: Readings of Exile and Estrangement*, New York: St Martin's Press.

Smith, Joseph H. (1989) 'On Psychoanalysis and the Question of Nondefensive Religion', in J. H. Smith and Susan A. Handelman (eds), *Psychoanalysis and Religion: Psychiatry and the Humanities*, Volume 11, Baltimore: Johns Hopkins Press, pp. 188–242.

Wyschogrod, Edith (1990) 'Postmodern Ecstatics and Saintliness: Kristeva', in Wyschogrod, *Saints and Postmodernism: Revisioning Moral Philosophy*, Chicago: University of Chicago Press, pp. 243–251.

Monique Wittig

Primary sources

Wittig, Monique (1966) *The Opoponax; A Novel*, trans. Helen Weaver, Plainfield, VT: Daughter Inc. French edition (1964) *L'Opoponax*, Paris: Les Éditions de Minuit.

—— (1971) *Les Guérillères*, trans. David Le Vay, New York: Viking Press. French edition (1969) *Les Guérillères*, Paris: Les Éditions de Minuit.

—— (1975) *The Lesbian Body: Escaping texts*, trans. David Le Vay, New York: Morrow. French edition (1973) *Le Corps lesbien*, Paris: Les Éditions de Minuit.

—— (1979) *Lesbian Peoples: Material for a Dictionary*, with Sande Zeig, New York: Avon. French edition (1976) *Brouillon pour un dictionaire des amantes*, Paris: B. Grasset.

—— (1987) *Across the Acheron*, trans. David Le Vay, Chester Springs, PA: Dufour Editions. French edition (1985) *Virgile, non*, Paris: Les Éditions de Minuit.

—— (1992) *The Straight Mind and Other Essays*, Boston: Beacon Press.

Secondary sources

Crowder, Diane Griffin (1983) 'Amazons and Mothers?: Monique Wittig, Hélène Cixous and Theories of Women's Writing', *Contemporary Literature* 24, 2: 117–144.

Farwell, Marilyn R. (1988) 'Toward a Definition of the Lesbian Literary Imagination', *Signs: Journal of Women in Culture and Society* 14, 1: 100–118.

Higgins, Lynn (1976) 'Nouvelle Nouvelle Autobiographie: Monique Wittig's *Le Corps lesbien*', *Sub-Stance* 14: 160–166.

Ostrovsky, Erika (1991) *A Constant Journey: The Fiction of Monique Wittig*, Carbondale and Edwardsville, IL: Southern Illinois University Press.

Rosenfeld, Marthe (1981) 'The Linguistic Aspect of Sexual Conflict: Monique Wittig's *Le Corps lesbien*', *Mosaic* 17, 2: 235–241.

Shaktini, Namascar (1982) 'Displacing the Phallic Subject: Wittig's Lesbian Writing', *Signs: Journal of Women in Culture and Society* 8, 1: 29–44.

Wenzel, Hélène Vivienne (1981) 'The Text as Body/Politics: An Appreciation of Monique Wittig's Writings in Context', *Feminist Studies* 7, 2: 264–287.

Zimmerman, Bonnie (1985) 'What Has Never Been: An Overview of Lesbian Feminist Criticism', in G. Greene and C. Kahn (eds), *Making a Difference: Feminist Literary Criticism*, New York: Methuen, pp. 177–210.

Index